Mastering Tableau 2019.1
Second Edition

An expert guide to implementing advanced business
intelligence and analytics with Tableau 2019.1

Marleen Meier
David Baldwin

BIRMINGHAM - MUMBAI

Mastering Tableau 2019.1
Second Edition

Commissioning Editor: Sunith Shetty
Acquisition Editor: Yogesh Deokar
Content Development Editor: Nathanya Dias
Technical Editor: Kushal Shingote
Copy Editor: Safis Editing
Project Coordinator: Kirti Pisat
Proofreader: Safis Editing
Indexer: Rekha Nair
Graphics: Jisha Chirayil
Production Coordinator: Deepika Naik

First published: December 2016
Second edition: February 2019

Production reference: 1280219

Published by Packt Publishing Ltd.
Livery Place
35 Livery Street
Birmingham
B3 2PB, UK.

ISBN 978-1-78953-388-0

www.packtpub.com

`mapt.io`

Mapt is an online digital library that gives you full access to over 5,000 books and videos, as well as industry leading tools to help you plan your personal development and advance your career. For more information, please visit our website.

Why subscribe?

- Spend less time learning and more time coding with practical eBooks and Videos from over 4,000 industry professionals

- Improve your learning with Skill Plans built especially for you

- Get a free eBook or video every month

- Mapt is fully searchable

- Copy and paste, print, and bookmark content

Packt.com

Did you know that Packt offers eBook versions of every book published, with PDF and ePub files available? You can upgrade to the eBook version at `www.packt.com` and as a print book customer, you are entitled to a discount on the eBook copy. Get in touch with us at `customercare@packtpub.com` for more details.

At `www.packt.com`, you can also read a collection of free technical articles, sign up for a range of free newsletters, and receive exclusive discounts and offers on Packt books and eBooks.

Contributors

About the authors

Marleen Meier has worked in the field of data science and business intelligence since 2013. Her experience includes Tableau training, proof of concepts, implementations, project management, user interface designs, and quantitative risk management. In 2018, she was a speaker at the Tableau conference, where she showcased a machine learning project. Marleen uses Tableau, combined with other tools and software, to get the best business value for her stakeholders. She is also very active within the Tableau community and recently joined the Dutch Tableau user group as one of their four leaders.

David Baldwin has provided consultancy services in the business intelligence sector for 17 years. His experience includes Tableau training and consulting, developing BI solutions, project management, technical writing, and web and graphic design. His vertical industry experience includes the financial, healthcare, human resource, aerospace, energy, education, government, and entertainment sectors. As a Tableau trainer and consultant, David enjoys serving a variety of clients throughout the USA. Tableau provides David with a platform that collates his broad experience into a skill set that can service a diverse client base.

About the reviewers

Dmitry Anoshin is an expert in analytics area with 10 years of experience. Start using Tableau as primary BI tool in 2011 as a BI consultant in Teradata. He is certified with both Tableau Desktop and Server. He leads probably the biggest Tableau user community with more than 2000 active users. This community has 2-3 Tableau talks every month leading by the top Tableau experts, Tableau Zen Masters, Viz Champions, and so on. In addition, Dmitry previously has written three books with Packt and reviewed more than seven books. Finally, he is an active speaker at Data conferences and helping to adopt Cloud Analytics.

Manideep Bhattacharyya is a Tableau enthusiast and certified professional. He has more than 16 years of industry experience, having graduated with a science degree from a college in Calcutta in 2003. He began his career with IBM, as a Siebel certified professional, working there for seven years. He has contributed to many global multinational projects and later joined an Indian conglomerate. He brought the data visualization concept and implemented Tableau with a large-scale multi-billion row dataset. He also set a new standard for data discovery and visualization for many CxOs and top management professionals.

Dave Dwyer has a BS in Information Systems from RIT (Rochester Institute of Technology), MBA from Drexel University, certified Six Sigma Black Belt and PMP. In his 20+ years as an IT professional, he has worked in a wide range of technical and leadership roles, in companies ranging from startups to Fortune 100 enterprises. A chance introduction to reporting and analytics 10 years ago hooked him and he never left. Dave feels the data science landscape of analytics, visualization, big data, and machine learning will drive more real changes in business over the next 10 years than any other area.

Packt is searching for authors like you

If you're interested in becoming an author for Packt, please visit authors.packtpub.com and apply today. We have worked with thousands of developers and tech professionals, just like you, to help them share their insight with the global tech community. You can make a general application, apply for a specific hot topic that we are recruiting an author for, or submit your own idea.

Table of Contents

Section 2: Section 2: Advanced Calculations, Mapping, Visualizations

Preface

Tableau is one of the leading BI tools used to solve business intelligence and analytics challenges. With this book, you will master the Tableau's features and offerings in various paradigms of business intelligence domain.

This book is an update to our successful Mastering Tableau series with new features, examples, updated code and more. This works as a handy resource to cover all the essential Tableau concepts to help you delve into advanced functionalities. You will learn how to handle and prepare data using Tableau Hyper and Tableau Prep. You will perform complex joins, spatial joins, union, and data blending tasks using various examples. You will learn to perform data densification to display more granular data. Expert level examples to cover advanced calculations, mapping and visual design using various Tableau extensions. Also, this book will cover examples on improving dashboard performance, the know-how of data visualizations, connecting Tableau Server, and more. Later you will cover advanced use cases such as self-service analytics, Time Series Analytics and Geo-Spatial Analytics and learn how to connect Tableau to R, Python, and MATLAB.

By the end of the book, you will master the advanced offerings of Tableau and will be able to tackle common and not-so-common challenges faced in business intelligence domain.

Who this book is for

This book is designed for business analysts, BI professionals and data analysts who want to master Tableau to solve a range of data science and business intelligence problems. The book is ideal if you have a good understanding of Tableau and want to take your skills to the next level.

What this book covers

Chapter 1, *Getting Up to Speed – A Review of the Basics*, covers the basic and essential Tableau concepts to get you started.

Chapter 2, *All About Data – Getting Your Data Ready*, covers an understanding of Tableau data-handling engine, after which we will dive into knowledge-discovery process models, as well as data mining. Last but not least, we will talk about data cleaning.

Chapter 3, *Tableau Prep*, is all about Tableau Prep, the new member of the Tableau Family.

Chapter 4, *All About Data – Joins, Blends, and Data Structures*, is introduced with the big question that Tableau users face on a daily base: Should I blend or should I join my data? Regarding joins, we will spend some words on the join calculations and spatial joins, which are fairly new features in Tableau. Likewise, unions are also covered in this chapter.

Chapter 5, *All About Data – Data Densification, Cubes, and Big Data*, We will discuss data densification and how we can display more granular data than the given granularity of the dataset. Once this is covered, we will move on to cube data and how to deal with it, followed by big data in Tableau.

Chapter 6, *Table Calculations*, introduces the dashboard where the user will learn to create calculated field. The next few pages are dedicated to table calculations in the process flow, and why table calculations are still relevant now that level of detail calculations are available. We will also learn about the Table Calc Assistant.

Chapter 7, *Level of Detail Calculations*, talks about the pain of LODs that every Tableau user has to go through once. This chapter should make it easier to understand how to use LODs in a way that you won't want to live without them anymore. In the second step, we will combine LOD calculations with table calculations, sets, and parameters.

Chapter 8, *Beyond the Basic Chart Types*, introduces some widely-used chart types, along with some special ones, all beyond the Show Me section, with detailed instruction. The new feature of Tableau extensions will be explained too.

Chapter 9, *Mapping*, will cover all aspects of Tableau mapping and extending Tableau Mapping with other technologies.

Chapter 10, *Tableau for Presentations*, shows how the user can use Tableau for presentations. Tableau is typically thought of as a BI and analytics platform; however, it can be, and often is, used as a presentation tool. On the following pages, you will get some insight into tips and tricks with this.

Chapter 11, *Visualization Best Practices and Dashboard Design*, will explore different Tableau visualization techniques and dashboard designs.

Chapter 12, *Advanced Analytics*, will test your knowledge on two use-cases.

Chapter 13, *Improving Performance*, is all about performance on Tableau and various methods about improvement.

Chapter 14, *Interacting with Tableau Server*, covers different offerings of the Tableau Server architecture and functionalities.

Chapter 15, *Programming Tool Integration*, shows how to integrate Tableau with R , Python, and MATLAB.

To get the most out of this book

Basic knowledge of Tableau is required for which you need to sign up for the free 14-days trial version of Tableau latest version of Tableau. Before reading this book, the readers are also expected to have a basic knowledge of R and also know how to use RStudio.

Download the example code files

You can download the example code files for this book from your account at www.packt.com. If you purchased this book elsewhere, you can visit www.packt.com/support and register to have the files emailed directly to you.

You can download the code files by following these steps:

1. Log in or register at www.packt.com.
2. Select the **SUPPORT** tab.
3. Click on **Code Downloads & Errata**.
4. Enter the name of the book in the **Search** box and follow the onscreen instructions.

Once the file is downloaded, please make sure that you unzip or extract the folder using the latest version of:

- WinRAR/7-Zip for Windows
- Zipeg/iZip/UnRarX for Mac
- 7-Zip/PeaZip for Linux

The code bundle for the book is also hosted on GitHub at https://github.com/PacktPublishing/Mastering-Tableau-2019.1-Second-Edition. In case there's an update to the code, it will be updated on the existing GitHub repository.

We also have other code bundles from our rich catalog of books and videos available at https://github.com/PacktPublishing/. Check them out!

Download the color images

We also provide a PDF file that has color images of the screenshots/diagrams used in this book. You can download it here: https://www.packtpub.com/sites/default/files/downloads/9781789533880_ColorImages.pdf

Conventions used

There are a number of text conventions used throughout this book.

CodeInText: Indicates code words in text, database table names, folder names, filenames, file extensions, pathnames, dummy URLs, user input, and Twitter handles. Here is an example: "The sum of [Number of Records] is divided by the sum of [Quantity]."

A block of code is set as follows:

```
SELECT ['Happiness Report$'].[Happiness.Score] AS [Happiness.Score],
  AVG(['Happiness Report$'].[Happiness.Rank]) AS [avg:Happiness.Rank:ok]
FROM [dbo].['Happiness Report$'] ['Happiness Report$']
GROUP BY ['Happiness Report$'].[Happiness.Score]"
```

Bold: Indicates a new term, an important word, or words that you see onscreen. For example, words in menus or dialog boxes appear in the text like this. Here is an example: "Locate **Department** within the **Dimensions** portion of the **Data** pane."

Warnings or important notes appear like this.

Tips and tricks appear like this.

Section 1: Tableau Concepts, Basics

1

Part 1 of this book will cover the general concepts of Tableau that will allow you to start working with Tableau.

The following chapters are in this section:

Getting Up to Speed - A Review of the Basics

1

Tableau is one of the leading tools used to solve **business intelligence (BI)** and analytics challenges. With this book, you will master Tableau's features and offerings in various paradigms of the business intelligence domain. It's an update to the successful *Mastering Tableau* series, which covers essential Tableau concepts, data preparation, and calculations with Tableau. But this book will also include examples on improving dashboard performance, the know-how of data visualizations, and connecting to Tableau Server. This book covers the latest and most exciting features, such as Tableau Prep, the connections with Python and MATLAB, Tableau Extensions, Joins, and Unions, and last but not least, three use cases of powerful Self-Service Analytics, Time Series Analytics, and Geo-Spatial Analytics in order to manifest the learned content. By the End of this book, you'll have mastered the advanced offerings of Tableau and its latest updates, up to Tableau version 2019.1.

Those who are fairly new to Tableau should find this chapter helpful in getting up to speed quickly; however, since this book targets advanced topics, relatively little time is spent considering the basics. For a more thorough consideration of fundamental topics, consider *Learning Tableau Edition 3.0*, written by Joshua Milligan and published by Packt Publishing.

In this chapter, we'll discuss the following topics:

- Creating worksheets and dashboards
- Connecting Tableau to your data
- Connecting to Tableau Server
- Connecting to saved data sources
- Measure Names and Measure Values
- Three essential Tableau concepts
- Exporting data to other devices

Creating worksheets and dashboards

At the heart of Tableau are **worksheets** and **Dashboards**. Worksheets contain individual visualizations and Dashboards contain one or more worksheets. Additionally, worksheets and Dashboards may be combined into **stories** to communicate particular insights to the end user through a presentation environment. Lastly, all worksheets, Dashboards, and stories are organized in **workbooks** that can be accessed with the Tableau desktop, Server, reader or the Tableau mobile app. In this section, we'll survey creating worksheets and Dashboards, with the intention of communicating the basics, but we'll also provide some insight that may prove helpful to more seasoned Tableau users.

Creating worksheets

At the most fundamental level, a visualization in Tableau is created by placing one or more fields on one or more shelves. As an example, note that the visualization created in the following diagram is generated by placing the **Sales** field on the **Text** shelf:

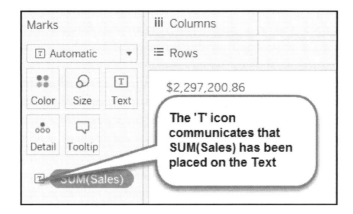

Exercise: fundamentals of visualizations

Let's explore the basics of creating a visualization using an exercise:

1. **Navigate to** `https://public.tableau.com/profile/marleen.meier` to locate and download the workbook associated with this chapter.

2. In the workbook, find the tab labeled **Fundamentals of Visualizations**:

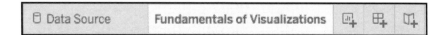

3. Locate **Department** within the **Dimensions** portion of the **Data** pane:

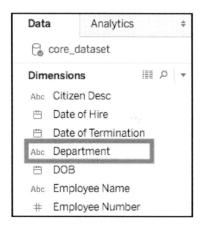

4. Drag **Department** to the **Color** shelf:

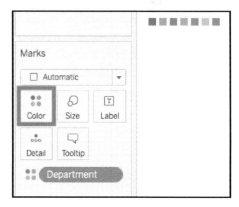

5. Click on the **Color** shelf and then on **Edit Colors** to adjust the colors as desired:

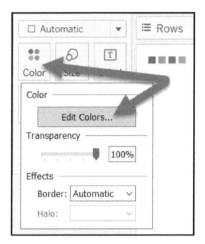

6. Move Department to the **Size, Label/Text, Detail, Columns,** and **Rows** shelves. After placing **Department** on each shelf, click on the shelf itself to access additional options.

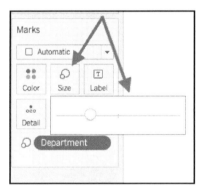

8. Drop other fields on various shelves to continue exploring Tableau's behavior.

As you explore Tableau's behavior by dragging and dropping different fields onto different shelves, you'll notice that Tableau responds with default behaviors. These defaults, however, can be overridden, which we'll explore next.

Beyond the default behavior

In the preceding exercise, *Fundamentals of visualizations*, we can notice that the **Marks** card reads **Automatic**. This means that Tableau is providing the default view. The default view can be easily overridden by choosing a different selection from the drop-down menu:

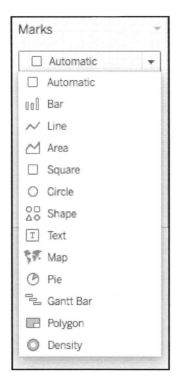

Another type of default behavior can be observed when dragging a field onto a shelf. For example, dragging and dropping a measure onto a shelf will typically result in the **SUM ()** aggregation.

In Windows, you can override this default behavior by right-clicking and dragging a field from the **Data** pane and dropping it onto a shelf. Tableau will respond with a dialog box with possible options.

Here's a screenshot of the popup that will appear:

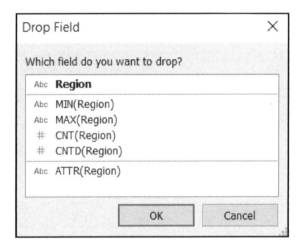

Exercise: overriding defaults

Let's walk through an exercise where we'll override the two default behaviors shown in the preceding screenshot:

1. In the workbook associated with this chapter, navigate to the **Overriding Defaults** worksheet.
2. Right-click and drag **Date of Hire** to the **Columns** shelf.

3. In the resulting dialog box, choose the second instance of **MONTH (Date of Hire)**:

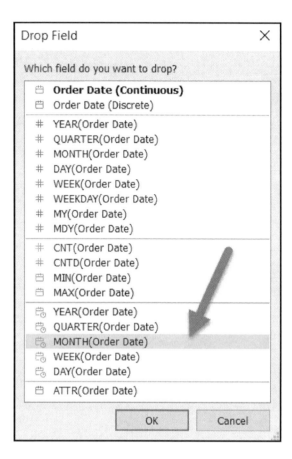

4. Place **Number of Records** on the **Rows** shelf and **Department** on the **Detail** shelf.

5. Click on the **dropdown** in the **Marks** card and select **Area**:

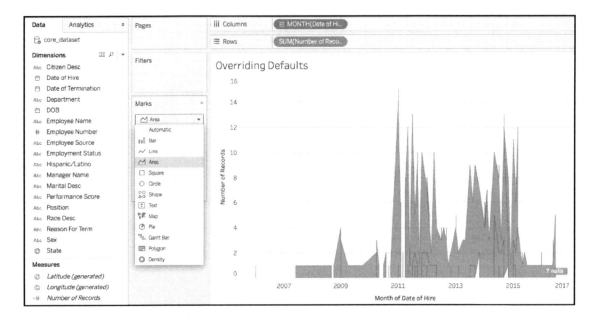

Show Me

Show Me allows the Tableau author to create visualizations at the click of a button. To understand how it works, let's refer to the following screenshot:

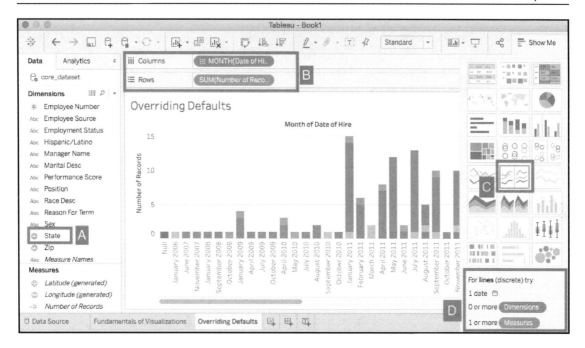

Now let's look at the following aspects that are highlighted in the preceding screenshot:

- **A**: Selected fields in the **Data** pane.
- **B**: Fields deployed in the view, that is, pills.
- **C**: The recommended view.
- **D**: Help text that communicates the requirements for creating the recommended view or any selection choice over which the cursor is placed.

Every icon in **Show Me** that isn't greyed out represents a visualization that can be created simply by clicking on it. For example, in the diagram preceding, the Tableau author may choose to click on the pie chart icon to create a pie chart based on the selected and deployed fields.

Show Me options are highlighted based on two criteria: the selected fields in the **Data** pane and the fields deployed in the view.

Show Me may be effectively used for the following reasons:

- **Efficiency**: The proficient Tableau author already knows how to create the basic visualization types. **Show Me** automates these basic types and thus may be used for quicker production.
- **Inspiration**: Determining an effective way to visualize a dataset can be challenging. **Show Me** can help with this challenge by allowing the Tableau author to quickly consider various options.
- **Education**: An inexperienced Tableau author may access **Show Me** to better understand how various visualizations are created. By reading the help text displayed at the bottom of **Show Me** and observing the results generated by clicking on various options, much can be learned.

These three reasons demonstrate the strong capabilities that **Show Me** provides for worksheet creation, however, be careful not to use it as a crutch. If you click on the various options without understanding how each visualization is created, you're not only shortchanging the educational process, but you may generate results that aren't well-understood, and could thus lead to detrimental business decisions.

Creating dashboards

Although, as stated in the *Creating worksheets and dashboards* section, a Dashboard contains one or more worksheets, and Dashboards are much more than static presentations. They're an essential part of Tableau's interactivity. In this section, we'll populate a Dashboard with worksheets and then deploy actions for interactivity.

Exercise: building a dashboard

The following are the steps for building a Dashboard:

1. In the **Chapter 1** workbook, navigate to the **Building a Dashboard** tab.

2. In the **Dashboard** pane, located on the left side of the screen, double-click on each of the following worksheets (in the order in which they are listed) to add them to the Dashboard pane: **Age/State**, **Pay Rate**, **Tree Map**, **Date of Hire**, and **Date of Termination**:

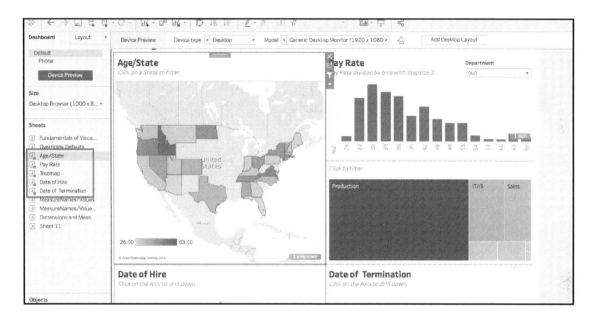

3. In the bottom-right corner of the **Dashboard** pane, click in the blank area to select a container. After clicking in the blank area, you should see a blue border around the filter and the legends. This indicates that the vertical container is selected:

4. Select the vertical container handle and drag it to the left side of the **Customers** worksheet. Note the grey shading, which communicates where the container will be placed:

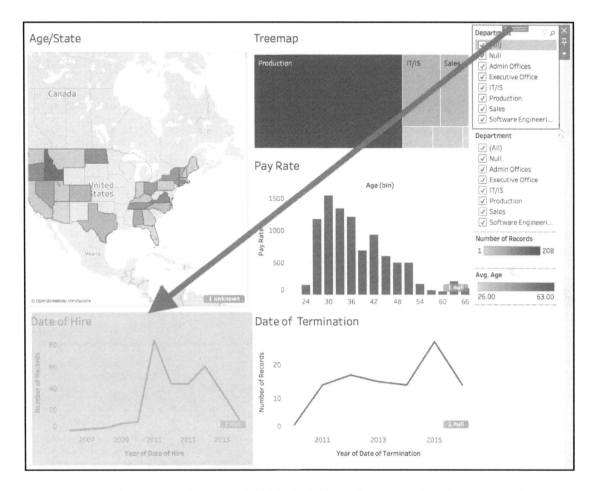

The grey shading provided by Tableau when dragging elements, such as worksheets and containers, onto a Dashboard, helpfully communicates where the element will be placed. Take your time and observe carefully when placing an element on a Dashboard or the results may be unexpected.

5. Format the dashboard as desired. The following tips may prove helpful:

- Adjust the sizes of the elements on the screen by hovering over the edges between each element and then clicking and dragging as desired.
- Note that the **Age legend** and **Department** filter in the following screenshot are floating elements. Make an element floating by right-clicking on the element handle and selecting Floating (see the previous screenshot and note that the handle is located immediately above the word **Region** in the top-right corner).
- Create horizontal and vertical containers by dragging those objects from the bottom portion of the **Dashboard** pane.
- Drag the edges of containers to adjust the size of each worksheet.
- Display the **Dashboard** title through the **Dashboard**, right-click **Show Title**:

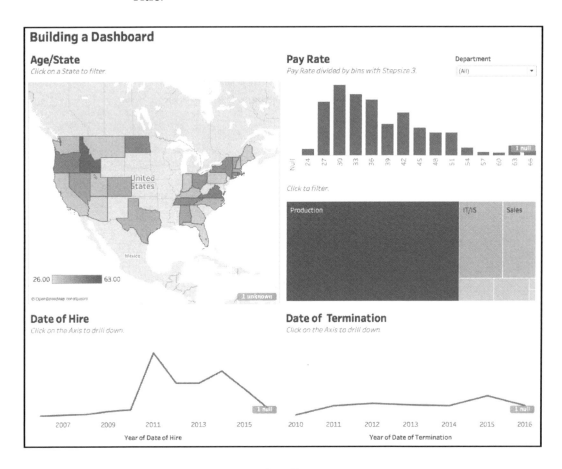

Exercise: adding interactivity to a dashboard

One of the primary benefits of Tableau is the interactivity it provides the end user. Dashboards aren't simply for viewing; they're meant for interaction. In this exercise, we'll add interactivity to the Dashboard that was created in the previous exercise:

1. Starting where the previous exercise ended, click the drop-down menu associated with the **Department** filter and select **Apply to Worksheets**, and then **All Using This Data Source**:

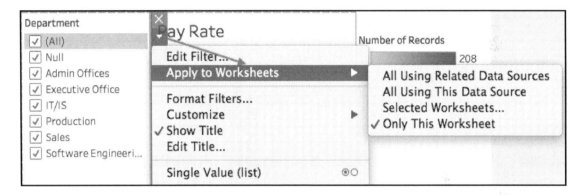

2. To use the map as a filter for the other worksheets on the **Dashboard** pane, click the **Use as Filter** icon located at the top-right corner of the **Age/State** worksheet:

3. Set Pay Rate to **Use as Filter**.
4. Navigate to **Dashboard** > **Actions**.

5. In the dialog box, click **Add Action** > **Filter** and create a filter, as shown:

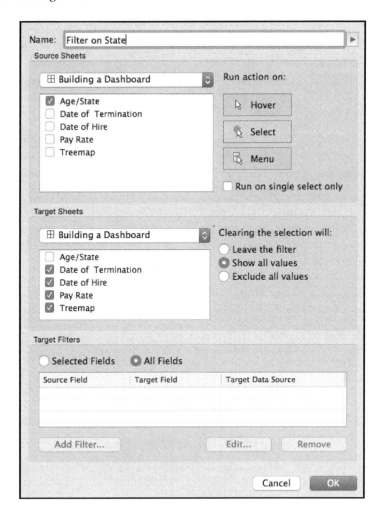

Having completed the preceding dashboard exercise, you should now be able to click on various objects on the dashboard to observe the interactivity. To learn advanced dashboard techniques, be sure to check out `Chapter 11`, *Visualization Best Practices and Dashboard Design*.

Connecting Tableau to your data

At the time of writing, Tableau's data connection menu includes 70 different connection types. And that's somewhat of an understatement since some of those types contain multiple options. For example, the selection choice, Other Files, includes 34 options. Of course, we won't cover the details for every connection type, but we will cover the basics.

Upon opening a new instance of Tableau Desktop, you'll notice a link in the top-left corner of the workspace. Clicking on that link will enable you to connect to the data. Alternatively, you can click on the New Data Source icon on the toolbar:

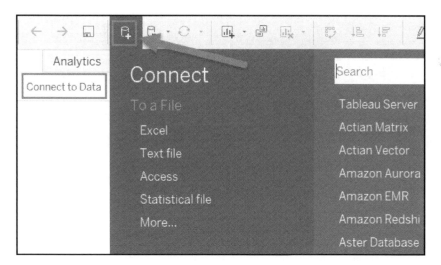

Although in future chapters we'll connect to other data sources, here we'll limit the discussion to connecting to the Microsoft Excel and text files.

Exercise: observing metadata differences

Let's compare the instance of the Superstore data source with a new connection to the same data:

1. In a new instance of Tableau, navigate to **Data | New Data Source | Excel** to connect to the sample—**Superstore** dataset that installs with Tableau desktop (it should be located on your hard drive under **My Tableau Repository | Datasources**).
2. Double-click on the **Orders** sheet.
3. Click on the **Sheet 1** tab.
4. Place **Discount** on the **Text** shelf.
5. Double-click on **Profit** and **Sales**.
6. Compare the results of the new worksheet to that of the worksheet entitled **Observing Metadata Differences** in the **Chapter 1** workbook:
   - **A**: The data source name has been altered in the **Chapter 1** workbook.
   - **B**: In the **Chapter 1** workbook, the default aggregation of **Discount** is **AVG**. In the unaltered instance, the default is **SUM**.
   - **C**: **Product Hierarchy** exists only in the **Chapter 1** workbook.
   - **D**: The format of **Discount**, **Profit**, and **Sales** differs between the two instances.
   - **E**: **Profit Ratio** exists only in the **Chapter 1** workbook:

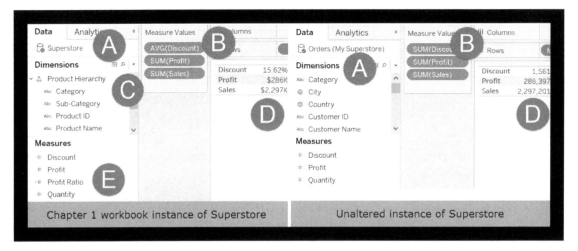

[26]

Connecting to Tableau Server

Connecting to Tableau Server is perhaps the single most important server-connection type to consider, since it's frequently used to provide better performance than may otherwise be possible. Additionally, connecting to Tableau Server enables the author to receive not only data, but information regarding how that data is to be interpreted; for example, whether a given field should be considered a measure or a dimension.

Exercise: connecting to Tableau Server

The following are the steps for connecting to Tableau Server:

1. To complete this exercise, access to an instance of Tableau Server is necessary. If you don't have access to Tableau Server, consider installing a trial version on your local computer.
2. In the workbook associated with this chapter, navigate to the Connecting to Tableau Server worksheet.
3. Right-click on the Superstore data source and select **Publish to Server**.
4. Log in to Tableau Server and follow the prompts to complete the publication of the data source.
5. Open a new instance of Tableau Desktop and select **Data** | **New Data Source** | **Tableau Server** to connect to the data source published in the previous step.
6. Click on **Sheet 1** in the new workbook and observe that the changes made in the **Chapter 1** workbook have been preserved.
7. In the **Data** pane, right-click on **Profit Ratio** and note that it isn't directly editable.

Having completed the preceding two exercises, let's discuss the most germane point, that is, metadata. Metadata is often defined as data about the data. In the preceding case, the data source name, default aggregation, default number formatting, and hierarchy are all examples of Tableau remembering changes made to the metadata. This is important because publishing a data connection allows for consistency across multiple Tableau authors. For example, if your company has a policy regarding the use of decimal points when displaying currency, that policy will be easily adhered to if all Tableau authors start building workbooks by pointing to data sources where all formatting has been predefined.

In *step 7* of this exercise, the fact that the **Profit Ratio** calculated field wasn't directly editable when accessed by connecting to Tableau Server as a data source has important implications. Imagine the problems that would ensue if different Tableau authors defined **Profit Ratio** differently. End users would have no way of understanding what **Profit Ratio** really means. However, by creating a workbook based on a published data source, the issue is alleviated. One version of **Profit Ratio** is defined and it can only be altered by changing the data source. This functionality can greatly assist consistency across the enterprise.

Connecting to saved data sources

Connecting to a saved data source on a local machine is very similar to connecting to a data source published on Tableau Server. Metadata definitions associated with the local data source are preserved just as they are on Tableau Server. Of course, since the data source is local instead of remote, the publication process is different.

Exercise: creating a local data connection

Let's explore the following steps for creating a local data connection using an example:

1. In the workbook associated with this chapter, navigate to the **Local Data Connection** tab.
2. In the **Data** pane, right-click on the **Superstore** data source and select **Add to Saved Data Sources**.
3. Using the resulting dialog box, save the data source as **Superstore** in **My Tableau Repository** | **Datasources**, which is located on your hard drive.
4. Click on the Go to Start icon located in the top-left part of your screen and observe the newly-saved data source:

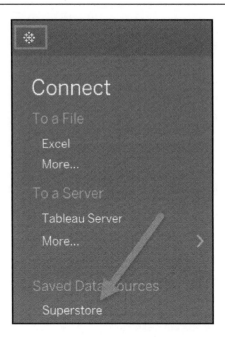

You can save a local data source that points to a published data source on Tableau Server. First, connect to a published data source on Tableau Server. Then right-click on the data source in your workspace and choose **Add to Saved Data Sources**. Now you can connect to Tableau Server directly from your Start page!

Measure Names and Measure Values

I've observed the following scenario frequently, wherein a new Tableau author creates a worksheet and drags a measure to the **Text** shelf. The author does this in order to create another row to display a second measure but doesn't know how. They drag the second measure to various places on the view and gets results that seem entirely unpredictable. The experience is very frustrating for the author since it's so easy to accomplish this in Microsoft Excel! The good news is that it's also easy to accomplish this in Tableau. It just requires a different approach. Let's explore the solution with an exercise.

Measure Names and **Measure Values** are generated fields in Tableau. They don't exist in the underlying data, but they're indispensable for creating many kinds of views. As may be guessed from its placement in the **Data** pane and its name, **Measure Names** is a dimension whose members are made up of the names of each measure in the underlying dataset. **Measure Values** contains the numbers or values of each measure in the dataset. Watch what happens when measure names and measure values are used independently. Then observe how they work elegantly together to create a view.

Exercise: Measure Names and Measure Values

The following are the steps for the exercise:

1. In the workbook associated with this chapter, navigate to the **MeasureNames/Values** worksheet.
2. Drag **Measure Values** to the **Text** shelf and observe the results:

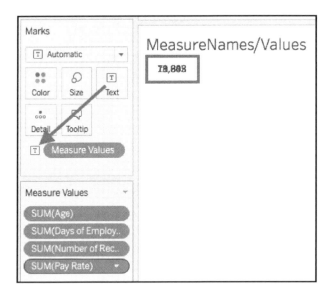

3. Clear the worksheet by clicking on the **Clear Sheet** icon on the toolbar:

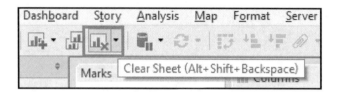

4. Drag **Measure Names** to the **Rows** shelf and observe that the view merely displays **No Measure Value**.

5. Drag **Measure Values** to the **Text** shelf. Note the list of measures and associated values.

Perhaps the interrelationship between **Measure Names** and **Measure Values** is best explained by an analogy. Consider several pairs of socks and a partitioned sock drawer. *Step 2* is the equivalent of throwing the socks into a pile. The results are well, disorganized. *Step 4* is the equivalent of an empty sock drawer with partitions. The partitions are all in place but where are the socks? *Step 5* is a partitioned drawer full of nicely-organized socks. **Measure Names** is like the partitioned sock drawer. **Measure Values** is like the socks. Independent of one another, they aren't of much use. Used together, they can be applied in many different ways.

Exercise: Measure Names and Measure values shortcuts

Tableau provides various shortcuts to quickly create a desired visualization. If you're new to the software, this shortcut behavior may not seem intuitive. But with a little practice and a few pointers, you'll quickly gain an understanding of it. Let's use the following exercise to explore how you can use a shortcut to rapidly deploy **Measure Name**s and **Measure Values**:

1. In the workbook associated with this chapter, navigate to the **MeasureNames/Values ShrtCts** worksheet.

2. Drag **Age** directly on top of the **Pay Rate** number in the view (**Show Me** appears):

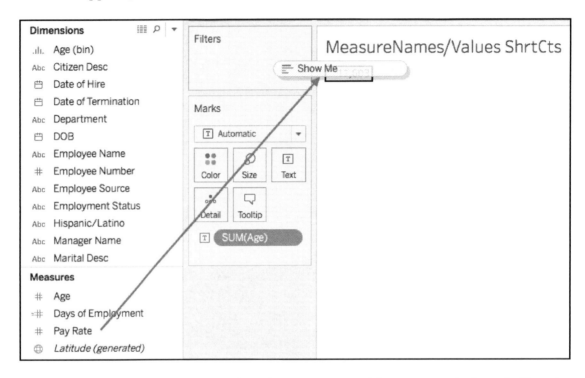

3. Observe the results, including the appearance of the **Measure Values** shelf, and the deployment of **Measure Names** on the **Rows** and **Filters** shelves and **Measure Values** on the **Text** shelf:

Exercise: commentary

Several things happened in step 2 of the *Measure Names and Measure Values shortcuts* exercise. After placing Age on top of the Pay Rate number in the view, Tableau did the following:

1. Deployed **Measure Names** on the **Filters** shelf.
    *   Open the Measure Names filter and observe that only **Age** and **Pay Rate** are selected. This limits the view to display only those two measures.

2. Deployed **Measure Names** on the **Rows** shelf.
   - **Measure Names** is acting like a partitioned container, that is, like the sock drawer in the analogy. Because of the filter, the only rows that display are for **Age** and **Pay Rate**.

3. Displayed the **Measure Values** shelf.
   - The **Measure Values** shelf is somewhat redundant. Although it clearly shows the measures that display in the view, it essentially acts as an easy way to access the filter. You can simply drag measures on and off of the **Measure Values** shelf to adjust the filter and thus display/hide additional **Measure Values**. You can also change the order within the **Measure Values** shelf to change the order of the measures in the view.

4. Deployed **Measure Values** on the **Text** shelf.
   - **Measure Values** is simply defining the numbers that will display for each row; in this case, the numbers associated with **Age** and **Pay Rate**.

If the visualization has an axis, the shortcut to deploy **Measure Names** and **Measure Values** requires the placement of a second measure on top of the axis of an initial measure, as follows:

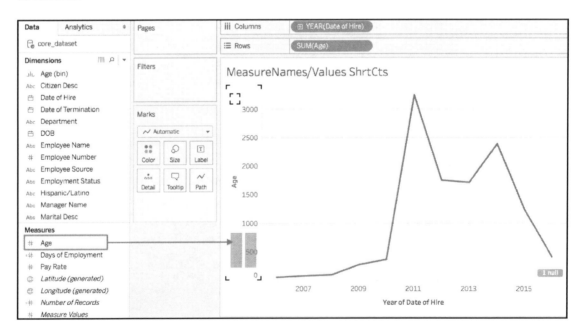

Three essential Tableau concepts

The road to mastering Tableau begins with three essential concepts. We'll discuss each of the following concepts:

- Dimensions and Measures
- Row Level, Aggregate Level, Table Level
- Continuous and Discrete

Dimensions and measures

Tableau categorizes every field from an underlying data source as either a dimension or a measure. A dimension is qualitative or, to use another word, categorical. A measure is quantitative or aggregable. A measure is usually a number but may be an aggregated, non-numeric field, such as **MAX (Date of Hire)**. A dimension is usually a text, Boolean, or date field, but may also be a number, such as **Pay Rate**. Dimensions provide meaning to numbers by slicing those numbers into separate parts/categories. Measures without dimensions are mostly meaningless.

Exercise: dimensions and measures

Let's look at an example to better understand:

1. In the workbook associated with this chapter, navigate to the **Dimensions and Measures** worksheet.
2. Drag **Number of Records** to the **Rows** shelf.

3. Place **Date of Hire** and **Department** on the **Columns** shelf:

The result of *step 2* is mostly meaningless. The **Number of Records** measure is about 302, but without the context supplied by slicing the measure with one or more dimensions, there is really no way to understand what it means. *Step 2* brings meaning. Placing **Date of Hire** and **Department** on the **Columns** shelf provides context, which imparts meaning to the visualization.

Row level, aggregate level, table level

There are three levels of calculations in Tableau: Row, Aggregate, and Table. To understand how these three levels function, it's important to know the Tableau process flow.

We can see the process flow in the following diagram:

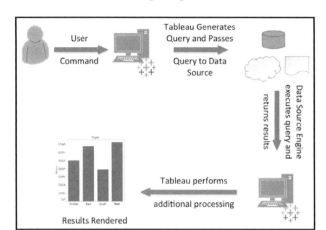

Let's follow the flow to understand where the three levels of calculations take place. We'll do so with an example that considers the **Number of Records** and **Quantity** fields. Assuming we're using SQL, consider the following calculation types, calculated fields, and queries. Note that the SQL is slightly simplified for the sake of this example.

Let's take a deeper look at the three levels of calculations and consider the example in the following table:

Calculation type	Calculated field in Tableau	Query passed to data source
Aggregate level	Sum([Number of Records])/Sum(Quantity)	SELECT SUM([Profit]), SUM(Sales) FROM [Orders]
Table level	WINDOW_AVG(Sum([Number of Records])/Sum(Quantity))	SELECT SUM([Profit]), SUM(Sales) FROM [Orders]

For the Row- and Aggregate-level calculations, the computation is actually completed by the data source engine. Tableau merely displays the results. This, however, isn't the case for the Table-level calculation. Although the query passed to the data source for the Table-level calculation is identical to the query for the Aggregate-level calculation, Tableau performs additional computations on the returned results. Let's explore this further with an exercise using the same calculated fields.

Exercise: row level, aggregate level, table level

Let us look at the following steps and begin our exercise:

1. In the workbook associated with this chapter, navigate to the **Row_Agg_Tbl** worksheet.

2. Select **Analysis** > **Create Calculated Field** to create the following calculated fields. Note that each must be created separately, that is, it isn't possible in this context to create a single calculated field that contains all three calculations:

Name	Calculation
Lev – Row	[Number of Records]/[Quantity]
Lev – Agg	SUM ([Number of Records])/SUM (Quantity)
Lev – Tab	WINDOW_AVG ([Lev – Agg])

3. In the **Data** pane, right-click on the three calculated fields you just created and select **Default Properties** | **Number format**.

4. In the resulting dialog box, select **Percentage** and click **OK**.

5. Place **Order Date** on the **Columns** shelf.

6. Place **Measure Names** on the **Rows** shelf, and **Measure Values** on the **Text** shelf.

7. Exclude all values except for **Lev - Row**, **Lev - Agg**, and **Lev - Tab**:

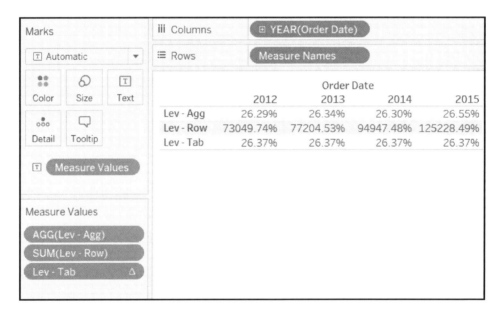

Exercise: commentary

Lev - Agg is an aggregate-level calculation. The computation is completed by the data source engine. The sum of [Number of Records] is divided by the sum of [Quantity]. The results of the calculation are likely useful for the Tableau author.

Lev - Row is a row-level calculation. The computation is completed by the data source engine. [Number of Records] is divided by [Quantity] for each row of the underlying data. The results are then summed across all rows. Of course, in this case, the row-level calculation doesn't provide useful results; however, since a new Tableau author may mistakenly create a row-level calculation when an aggregate-level calculation is what's really needed, the example is included here.

Lev - Tab is a table calculation. Some of the computation is completed by the data source engine, that is, the aggregation. Tableau completes additional computation on the results returned from the data source engine. Specifically, the results of **Lev - Agg** are summed and then divided by the number of members in the dimension. For the preceding example, this is *(26.29% + 26.34% + 26.30% + 26.55%)/4*. Once again, the results in this case aren't particularly helpful but do demonstrate knowledge the budding Tableau author should possess.

Continuous and discrete

Continuous and discrete aren't concepts that are unique to Tableau. Indeed, both can be observed in many arenas. Consider the following example:

The preceding diagram is of two rivers: River-Left and River-Right. Water is flowing in River-Left. River-Right is composed of ice cubes. Could you theoretically sort the ice cubes in River-Right? Yes! Is there any way to sort the water in River-Left? In other words, could you take buckets of water from the bottom of the river, cart those buckets upstream and pour the water back into River-Left and thereby say, I have sorted the water in the river? No. The H_2O in River-Left is in a continuous form, that is, water. The H_2O in River-Right is in a discrete form, that is, ice.

Having considered continuous and discrete examples in nature, let's turn our attention back to Tableau. Continuous and discrete in Tableau can be more clearly understood with the following seven considerations:

- Continuous is green. Discrete is blue:
    - Select any field in the **Data** pane or place any field on a shelf and you'll note that it's either green or blue. Also, the icons associated with fields are either green or blue.
- Continuous is always numeric. Discrete may be a string.
- Continuous and discrete aren't synonymous with dimension and measure:
    - It's common for new Tableau authors to conflate continuous with measure and discrete with dimension. They aren't synonymous. A measure may be either discrete or continuous. Also, a dimension, if it's a number, may be discrete or continuous. To prove this point, right-click on any numeric or date field in Tableau and note that you can convert it:

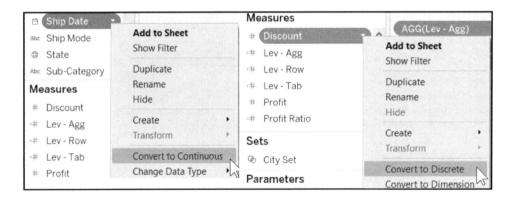

- Discrete values can be sorted. Continuous values can't:
    - Sortable/Not sortable behavior is most easily observed with dates, as shown in the following example:

- Continuous colors are gradients. Discrete colors are distinct.
  - The following example shows **Profit as continuous** and then as discrete. Note the difference in how colors are rendered. The left portion of the screenshot demonstrates that continuous results in gradients, and the right portion demonstrates that discrete results in distinct colors:

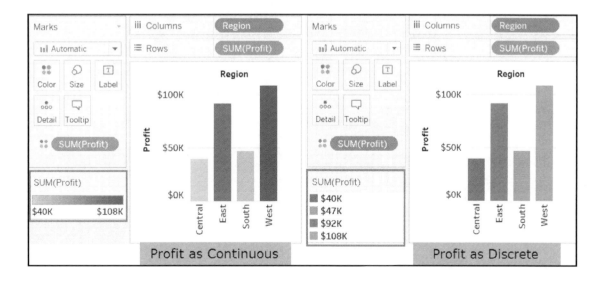

- Continuous pills can be placed to the right of discrete pills, but not to the left.
    - The Tableau author is able to place **Region** to the right of **Year** when **Year** is discrete.
    - The Tableau author is unable to place **Region** to the right of **Year** when **Year** is continuous:

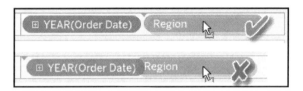

- Continuous creates axes. Discrete creates headers:
    - Note in the left portion of the following screenshot that **Year(Order Date)** is continuous and the **Year of Order Date** axis is selected. Since **Year of Order Date** is an axis, the entire x-plane is selected. In the right portion of the following screenshot, **Year(Order Date)** is discrete and 2012 is selected. Since 2012 is a header only, it's selected and not the entire x-plane:

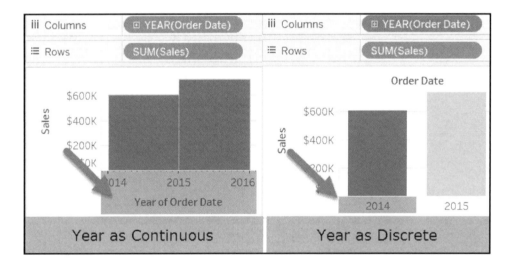

Exporting data to other devices

Once a Dashboard looks as it's expected to, the developer has different choices of sharing the work. An upload to the Tableau Server is the most likely option. The end user might not look at the results on just a laptop; they could use a tablet or cellphone, too.

Exporting data to a mobile phone

While developing a Dashboard, the Tableau Creator has the option to take a look at **Device Designer** or **Device Preview**. You can find it here:

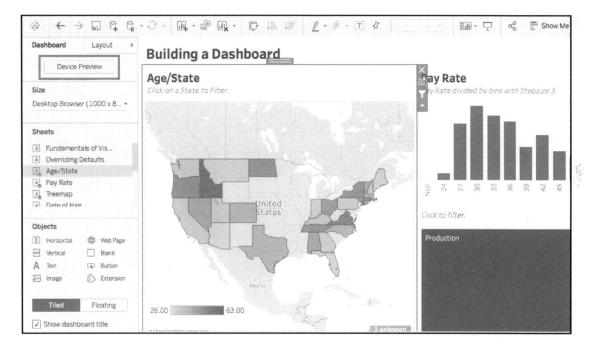

Please be aware that you can only use the sheets that are in the default layout of your Dashboard. Once you're in the **Device Designer** mode, select a **Device type** and you'll get choices of the most common Models:

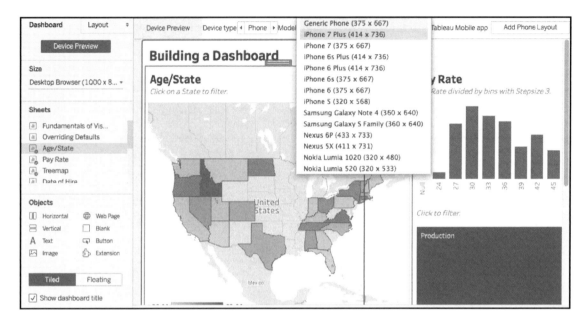

A cellphone is usually designed in portrait orientation. Now move the content in a way that the sheets you want to see on your phone are within the device frame. Satisfied? Then add this layout (top-right corner) to the workbook. It will appear under the **Default** one on the top-left side:

The user can now select the design needed, whenever opening a Workbook from the Tableau Server.

A Tablet Dashboard works exactly the same as the cellphone one. Follow the preceding steps to create it, except you have to choose the Tablet Device Type of course and a Tablet's Dashboard is usually in Landscape orientation.

Summary

In this chapter, we covered the basics of Tableau. We began with some basic terminology, then we looked at the basics of creating worksheets and Dashboards. We focused on default behavior, how to override that behavior, and we considered best practices. Then we reviewed Measure Names and Measure Values.

After that, we explored three essential Tableau concepts: Dimensions and Measures, Row-, Aggregate-, and Table-level, and Continuous and Discrete. Of particular importance is understanding that row- and aggregate-level calculations are computed by the data source engine, while table-level calculations are handled by Tableau. Finally, we saw how to adjust your Dashboard for other devices, such as a cellphone or tablet.

In the next chapter, we'll continue our Tableau exploration by looking at data. We'll explore how to prepare data for Tableau by looking at joins, blends, and data structures, such as data densification, cubes, and big data.

2
All About Data - Getting Your Data Ready

Ever asked yourself whether your data is clean enough to be analyzed? I guess everyone has! That's why the next pages are dedicated to getting your data ready.

The first part of this chapter is theory-oriented and does not include exercises. A careful reading of this information is encouraged, since it provides a foundation for greater insight. The latter portion of the chapter provides various exercises specifically focused on data preparation.

Now let's dive into this fascinating topic, with the goal of enriching our understanding and becoming ever-better data stewards.

In this chapter, we will discuss the following topics:

- Understanding Tableau's data handling engine, hyper
- The Tableau data handling engine
- Hyper takeaways
- Data mining and knowledge discovery process models
- CRISP-DM
- Focus on data preparation
- Surveying data
- Cleaning the data

Understanding Tableau's data handling engine, hyper

Since Tableau Desktop 10.5 is on the market, you must have heard the expression Hyper. You haven't? Well, continue reading!

Tableau's data handling engine is usually not well understood by even advanced developers, because it's not an overt part of day-to-day activities; however, if you want to truly grasp how to ready data for Tableau, this understanding is indispensable. In this section, we will explore Tableau's data handling engine, and how it enables structured yet organic data mining processes in the enterprise. With Tableau 10.5, we can now make use of Hyper, a high-performing database, allowing us to query faster than ever before.

Originally, Hyper was a research project at the University of Munich in 2008. In 2016, Tableau acquired Hyper, which is now the dedicated data engine group of Tableau with its base in Munich and around 30 employees.

As mentioned before, in 10.5, Hyper replaced the earlier data handling engine, first only for extracts. It is still true that live connections are not touched by Hyper, but in the meanwhile, Prep is running on the Hyper engine too, with more use cases to follow.

What makes Hyper so fast? Let's have a look under the hood!

The Tableau data handling engine

The vision of the founders of Hyper was to create a high-performing, next-generation database; one system, one state, no trade-offs, and no delays. And it worked out. Hyper today can serve general database purposes, data ingestion, and analytics at the same time.

If we go back in time, in 1996 1 GB of data cost $45,000. Today, much more than that can be found on every phone, or even on a smartwatch, costing $2. Memory prices have decreased exponentially. The same goes for CPUs; transistor counts increased according to Moore's law, while other features stagnated. Memory is cheap, but processing still needs to be improved.

Moore's Law is the observation made by Intel co-founder Gordon Moore that the number of transistors on a chip doubles every two years while the costs are halved. In 1965, Gordon Moore noticed that the number of transistors per square inch on integrated circuits had doubled every two years since their invention. Investopedia

While experimenting with Hyper, the founders measured that handwritten C code is faster than any existing database engine, so they came up with the idea to transform Tableau Queries into LLVM code and optimize it simultaneously, all behind the scenes, so the Tableau user won't notice it. The translation and optimization comes at a cost; traditional database engines can start executing code immediately. Tableau needs to first translate queries into code, optimize it, then it compiles it to machine code, and then it can be executed. So the big question is, is it still faster? Yes it is! Many tests on Tableau Public and other workbooks have proven so, and this is still not all!

If there is a query estimated to be faster if executed without the compilation to machine code, Tableau has its own VM in which the query will be executed right away. And next to this, Hyper can utilize 99% of CPUs, whereas other paralyzed processes can only utilize 29% of all available CPUs. This is due to the unique and innovative technique of morsel-driven parallelization. If you want to know more about it, I can highly recommend about it the following video: `https://www.youtube.com/watch?v=h2av4CX0k6s`.

Hyper parallelizes three steps of traditional Data Warehouses: **Transactions and Continous Data Ingestion (OLTP)**, **Analytics (OLAP)**, and **Beyond Relational (OBRP)**, making it more efficient and more performant, while in traditional systems those three steps are separated.

To sum up, Hyper is a highly specialized database engine that allows us users to get the best out of our queries, called **VizQL**. Another hidden gem in your Tableau Desktop.

VizQL is generated when a user places a field on a shelf. VizQL is then translated into SQL, MDX, or **Tableau Query Language** (TQL), and passed to the backend data source with a driver. Two aspects of the VizQL module are of primary importance:

- VizQL allows you to change field attributions on the fly
- VizQL enables table calculations

Changing field attribution

Let us look at the World Happiness Report. We create the following worksheet by placing **AVG(Happiness Score)** and **Country** on the **Columns** and **Rows** shelves respectively. **AVG(Happiness Score)** is, of course, treated as a measure in this case.

Let's take a look at it in the following screenshot:

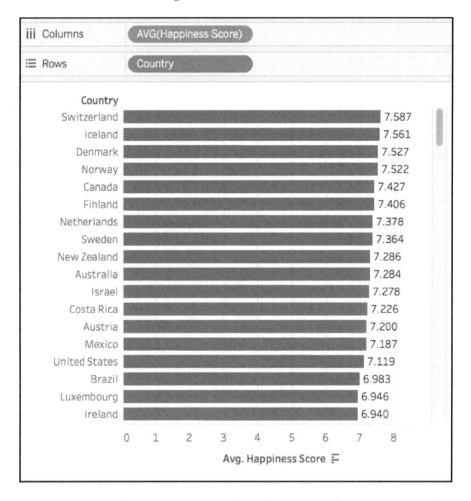

Next, please create a second worksheet to analyze the scores relative to the ranks by using **Happiness Score** and **Happiness Rank**.

In order to accomplish this, the user defines **Happiness Score** as a **Dimension**, as shown in the following screenshot:

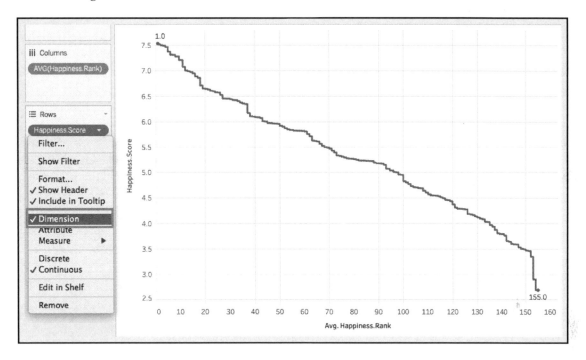

 In order to get the steps, please click on **Path** in the **Marks** field and select the second option, **Step**.

Studying the SQL generated by VizQL to create the preceding visualization is particularly insightful:

```
SELECT ['Happiness Report$'].[Happiness.Score] AS [Happiness.Score],
AVG(['Happiness Report$'].[Happiness.Rank]) AS [avg:Happiness.Rank:ok] FROM
[dbo].['Happiness Report$'] ['Happiness Report$'] GROUP BY ['Happiness
Report$'].[Happiness.Score]"
```

The `Group By` clause clearly communicates that Happiness Score is treated as a dimension. The takeaway is to note that VizQL enables the analyst to change the field usage from measure to dimension without adjusting the source metadata. This on-the-fly ability enables creative exploration of the data that's not possible with other tools, and avoids lengthy exercises attempting to define all possible uses for each field.

You can view the code generated by Tableau that is passed to the data source with the Performance Recorder, which is accessible through **Help**, then **Settings and Performance**, and then **Start Performance Recording**. See Chapter 13, *Improving Performance*, for additional details.

Table calculation

In the following example, note that **Freedom** on the right axis is set to **Quick Table Calculation**, and **Moving Average**. Calculating a **Moving Average** or **Running Total** or other such comparison calculations can be quite challenging to accomplish in a data source. Not only must a data architect consider what comparison calculations to include in the data source, but they must also determine dimensions for which these calculations are relevant.

VizQL greatly simplifies such challenges using table calculations, as seen in the following screenshot:

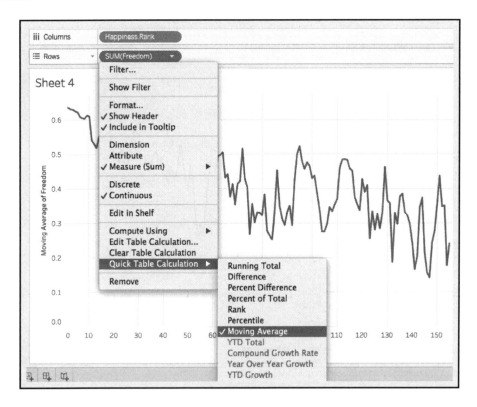

Taking a look at the relevant portion of SQL generated by the preceding worksheet shows that the table calculation is not performed by the datasource. Instead, it is performed in Tableau by the VizQL module.

The following is the SQL query:

```
SELECT SUM([Happiness Report$].[Freedom]) AS [sum:Freedom:ok],
  [Happiness Report$].[Happiness.Rank] AS [Happiness.Rank]
FROM [dbo].[Happiness Report$] [Happiness Report$]
GROUP BY ['Happiness Report$'].[Happiness.Score]
```

To reiterate, nothing in the preceding call to the data source generates the moving average. Only an aggregated total is returned, and Tableau calculates the moving average with VizQL.

Hyper takeaways

This overview of the Tableau data handling engine demonstrates a flexible approach to interfacing with data. Knowledge of the data handling engine is helpful if you want to understand the parameters for Tableau data readiness. Two major takeaways from this section are as follows:

- It is not necessary to explicitly define data types and roles for optimal Tableau usage.
- Comparison calculations such as moving averages and running totals can be addressed by table calculations in Tableau and thus do not need to be calculated in advance.

The knowledge of these two takeaways can reduce data preparation and data modeling efforts, and thus helps us streamline the overall data mining life cycle.

Data mining and knowledge discovery process models

Data modeling, data preparation, database design, data architecture, the question that arises is; how do these and other similar terms fit together? This is no easy question to answer! Terms may be used interchangeably in some contexts and be quite distinct in others. Also, understanding the inter-connectivity of any technical jargon can be challenging.

In the data world, data mining and knowledge discovery process models attempt to consistently define terms and contextually position and define the various data sub-disciplines. Since the early 1990s, various models have been proposed.

 The following list is adapted from *A Survey of Knowledge Discovery and Data Mining Process Models* by Lukasz A. Kurgan and Petr Musilek and published in *The Knowledge Engineering Review* Volume 21 Issue 1, March 2006.

Survey of the process models

In the following table, we can see a comparison of five Process Models:

	Fayyad et al.	KDD	CRISP-DM	Cios et al.	SEMMA
	Developing and Understanding of the Application Domain	Selection	Business understanding	Understanding the data	Sample
	Creating a target dataset Data cleaning and pre-processing	Pre-processing	Data understanding	Understanding the data	Explore
Steps	Data reduction and projection	Transformation	Data preparation	Preparation of the data	Modify
	Choosing the DM task Choosing the DM algorithm	Data mining	Data preparation	Preparation of the data	Modify
	DM	DM	Modeling	DM	Model

	Interpreting mined patterns Consolidating discovered knowledge	Interpretation/ evaluation	Evaluation Deployment	Evaluation of the discovered knowledge Using the discovered knowledge	Assess

Only three of these models are currently in use, namely KDD, CRISP-DM, and SEMMA. Since CRISP-DM is used by four to five times the number of people as the closest competing model (SEMMA), it is the model we will consider in this chapter. For more information,

see `http://www.kdnuggets.com/2014/10/crisp-dm-top-methodology-analytics-data-mi ning-data-science-projects.html`.

The important takeaway is that each of these models grapples with the same problems, particularly, understanding, preparing, modeling, and interpreting data.

CRISP–DM

Cross Industry Standard Process for Data Mining (CRISP-DM) was created between 1996 and 2000 as a result of a consortium including SPSS, Teradata, Daimler AG, NCR Corporation, and OHRA. It divides the process of data mining into six major phases, as shown in the CRISP-DM reference model. This model provides a bird's-eye view of a data mining project life cycle. The sequence of the phases are not rigid; jumping back and forth from phase to phase is allowed and expected. Data mining does not cease upon the completion of a particular project. Instead, it exists as long as the business exists, and should be constantly revisited to answer new questions as they arise.

In the next section, we will consider each of the six phases that comprise CRISP-DM and explore how Tableau can be used effectively throughout the life cycle. We will particularly focus on the data preparation phase, as that is the phase encompassing data cleansing. As Tableau has evolved over the years, more and more data cleansing capabilities have been introduced.

CRISP–DM Phases

The following sections, we will briefly defines each of the six CRISP-DM phases and includes high-level information on how Tableau might be used.

Phase I: business understanding

- This phase determines the business objectives and corresponding data mining goals. It also assesses risks, costs, and contingencies, and culminates in a project plan.
- Tableau is a natural fit for presenting information to enhance business understanding.

Phase II: data understanding

- This phase begins with an initial data collection exercise. The data is then explored to discover the first insights and identify data quality issues.
- Once the data is collected into one or more relational data sources, Tableau can be used to effectively explore the data and enhance data understanding.

Phase III: data preparation

- This phase includes data selection, cleansing, construction, merging, and formatting.
- Tableau can be effectively used to identify the preparation tasks that need to occur; that is, Tableau can be used to quickly identify the data selection, cleansing, merging, and so on, that should be addressed. Additionally, Tableau can sometimes be used to do actual data preparation. We will walk through examples in the next section.

 As Tableau has evolved, functionality has been introduced, such that it enables it to be used to not just identify data preparation tasks, but also to do more and more of the actual data preparation work.

Phase IV: modeling

- In this phase, data modeling methods and techniques are considered and implemented in one or more data sources. It is important to choose an approach that works well with Tableau, for example, as discussed in Chapter 5, *All About Data – Data Densification, Cubes, and Big Data*, Tableau works better with relational data sources than with cubes.
- Tableau has some limited data modeling capabilities, such as pivoting datasets through the data source page.

 Note that this functionality is only available for use with Excel, text files, and Google Sheets.

Phase V: evaluation

- The evaluation phase considers the results, the processes, and determines the next steps.
- Tableau is an excellent fit for considering the results during this phase.

Phase VI: deployment

- This phase should begin with a carefully considered plan to ensure a smooth rollout. The plan should include ongoing monitoring, and maintenance to ensure continued streamlined access to quality data. Although the phase officially ends with a final report and accompanying review, the data mining process, as stated earlier, continues for the life of the business. Therefore, this phase will always lead to the previous five phases.
- Tableau should certainly be considered a part of the deployment phase. Not only is it an excellent vehicle for delivering end user reporting, it can also be used to report on the data mining process itself. For instance, Tableau can be used to report on the performance of the overall data delivery system and thus be an asset for ongoing monitoring and maintenance.

Focus on data preparation

As discussed earlier, Tableau can be effectively used throughout the CRISP-DM phases. Unfortunately, a single chapter is not sufficient to thoroughly explore how Tableau can be used in each phase. Indeed, such a thorough exploration may be worthy of an entire book! Our focus, therefore, will be directed to data preparation, since that phase has historically accounted for up to 60% of the data mining effort. Our goal will be to learn how Tableau can be used to streamline that effort.

Surveying data

Tableau can be a very effective tool for simply surveying data. Sometimes in the survey process you may discover ways to clean the data or populate incomplete data based on existing fields. Sometimes, regretfully, there are simply not enough pieces of the puzzle to put together an entire dataset. In such cases, Tableau can be useful to communicate exactly what the gaps are, and this, in turn, may incentivize the organization to more fully populate the underlying data.

In this exercise, we will explore how to use Tableau to quickly discover the percentage of null values for each field in a dataset. Next, we'll explore how data might be extrapolated from existing fields to fill in the gaps.

Exercise: surveying data

The following are the steps for surveying the data:

1. Navigate to `https://public.tableau.com/profile/marleen.meier` to locate and download the workbook associated with this chapter.

2. Navigate to the worksheet entitled **Surveying & Exploring Data**.

3. Drag **Region** and **Country** to the **Rows** shelf. Observe that in some cases the **Region** field has **Null** values for some countries:

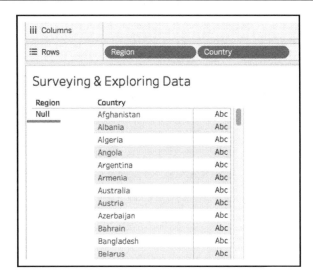

4. Create and show a parameter entitled **Select Field** with the **Data Type** set to **Integer** and a list that contains an entry for each field name in the dataset:

5. In the **Data** pane, right-click on the parameter just created and select **Show Parameter Control**.

6. Create a calculated field entitled % `Populated` and write the following code:

```
SUM([Number of Records]) / TOTAL(SUM([Number of Records]))
```

7. In the **Data** pane, right-click on **% Populated** and select **Default Properties | Number Format**.

8. In the resulting dialog box, choose **Percentage**.

9. Create a calculated field entitled `Null & Populated` and write the following code. Note that the complete case statement is fairly lengthy but is also repetitive.

In cases requiring a lengthy but repetitive calculation, consider using Excel to more quickly and accurately write the code. By using Excel's concatenate function, you may be able to save time and avoid typos.

In the following code block, the code lines represent only a percentage of the total but should be sufficient to enable you to produce the whole:

```
CASE [Select Field]
WHEN 1 THEN IF ISNULL ([Country]) THEN 'Null Values' ELSE
'Populated Values'
END
 WHEN 2 THEN IF ISNULL ([Region]) THEN 'Null Values' ELSE '
Populated Values'
 END
 WHEN 3 THEN IF ISNULL ([Economy (GDP per Capita)]) THEN 'Null
Values' ELSE 'Populated Values'
 END
 WHEN 4 THEN IF ISNULL ([Family]) THEN 'Null Values' ELSE
'Populated Values'
 END
WHEN 5 THEN IF ISNULL ([Freedom]) THEN 'Null Values' ELSE
'Populated Values'
 END
WHEN 6 THEN IF ISNULL ([Happiness Rank]) THEN 'Null Values' ELSE
'Populated Values'
 END
WHEN 7 THEN IF ISNULL ([Happiness Score]) THEN 'Null Values' ELSE
'Populated Values'
 END
WHEN 8 THEN IF ISNULL ([Health (Life Expectancy)]) THEN 'Null
Values' ELSE 'Populated Values'
 END
WHEN 9 THEN IF ISNULL ([Standard Error]) THEN 'Null Values' ELSE
```

```
'Populated Values'
  END
END
```

10. Remove **Region** and **Country** from the **Rows** shelf.

11. Place **Null & Populated** on the **Rows** and **Color** shelves and **% Populated** on the **Columns** and **Label** shelves.

12. Select various choices in the **Select Field** parameter and note that some fields have a high percentage of null values. For example, in the following diagram, **32.98%** of records do not have a value for **Region**:

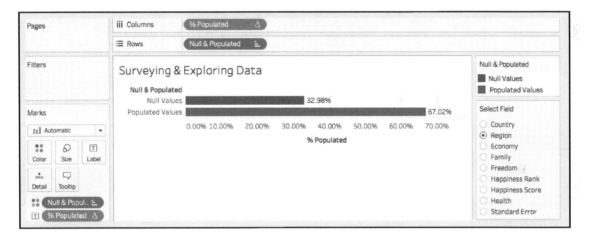

Next up, commentary will be provided for the exercise you've just completed. Before doing so, however, we'll explore how we might cleanse and extrapolate data from existing data using the same dataset.

Exercise: extrapolating data

This exercise will expand on the previous exercise by cleansing existing data and populating some of the missing data from known information. We will assume that we know which country belongs to which region. We'll use that knowledge to fix errors in the **Region** field and also to fill in the gaps using Tableau:

1. Starting where the previous exercise ended, create a calculated field entitled `Region Extrapolated` with the following code block:

```
CASE [Country]
  WHEN 'Afghanistan' THEN 'Southern Asia'
```

```
WHEN 'Albania' THEN 'Central and Eastern Europe'
WHEN 'Algeria' THEN 'Middle East and Northern Africa'
WHEN 'Angola' THEN 'Sub-Saharan Africa'
WHEN 'Argentina' THEN 'Latin America and Caribbean'
WHEN 'Armenia' THEN 'Central and Eastern Europe'
WHEN 'Australia' THEN 'Australia and New Zealand'
WHEN 'Austria' THEN 'Western Europe'
//complete the case statement with the remaining fields in the data
set
END
```

2. Add a **RegionExtrapolated** option to the **Select Field** parameter:

3. Add the following code to the **Null & Populated** calculated field:

```
WHEN 10 THEN IF ISNULL ([Region Extrapolated]) THEN 'Null
Values' ELSE 'Populated Values' END
```

4. Note that the **Region Extrapolated** field is now fully populated:

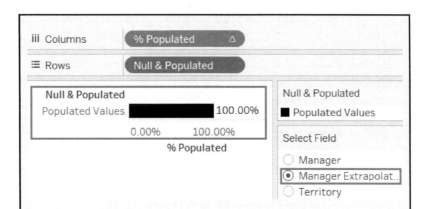

Exercise: commentary

Now let's consider some of the specifics from the previous two exercises, *Surveying data* and *Extrapolating data*. Let us look at the following code block:

```
CASE [% Populated]
  WHEN 1 THEN IF ISNULL ([Manager]) THEN 'Null Values' ELSE
'Populated Values'
  END
  . . .
```

1. Note that the complete case statement is several lines long. The preceding is a representative portion.
2. This case statement is a row-level calculation that considers each field in the dataset and determines which rows are populated and which are not. For example, in the representative line of the preceding code, every row of the field **Manager** field is evaluated for nulls.
3. This code is the equivalent of the quick table calculation **Percent of Total**. In conjunction with the **Null & Populated** calculated field, it allows us to see what percentage of our fields are actually populated with values:

```
SUM([Number of Records]) / TOTAL(SUM([Number of Records]))
```

It's a good idea to get in the habit of writing table calculations from scratch, even if an equivalent quick table calculation is available. This will help you more clearly understand table calculations.

4. This case statement is an example of how you might use one or more fields to extrapolate what another field should be. For example, the **Region** field in the dataset had a large percentage of null values, and even the existing data has errors. Based on our knowledge of the business (which country belongs to which region) we were able to use the **Country** field to achieve 100% population with accurate information:

```
CASE [Country]
WHEN 'Afghanistan' THEN 'Southern Asia'
 ...
END
```

5. Nulls are a part of almost every extensive real dataset. Understanding how many nulls are present in each field can be vital to ensuring that you provide accurate business intelligence. It may be acceptable to tolerate some null values when the final results will not be substantially impacted. Too many nulls invalidate results. Also, as demonstrated here, in some cases one or more fields can be used to extrapolate the values that should be in an underpopulated or erroneously populated field.

The ability to use Tableau to effectively communicate to your data team, what values are missing, which are erroneous, and how possible workarounds can be invaluable to the overall data mining effort.

Cleaning the data

The United States government provides helpful documentation for various bureaucratic processes. For example, the **Department of Health and Human Services (HSS)** provides lists of ICD-9 codes, otherwise known as International Statistical Classification of Diseases and Related Health Problems codes. Unfortunately, these codes are not always in easily-accessible formats. As an example, let's consider an actual HHS document known as R756OTN, https://www.cms.gov/Regulations-and-Guidance/Guidance/Transmittals/downloads/R756OTN.pdf

Exercise: cleaning the data

Please navigate to the Cleaning the Data worksheet in this workbook and execute the following steps:

1. Within the **Data** pane, select the **R756OTN Raw** data source:

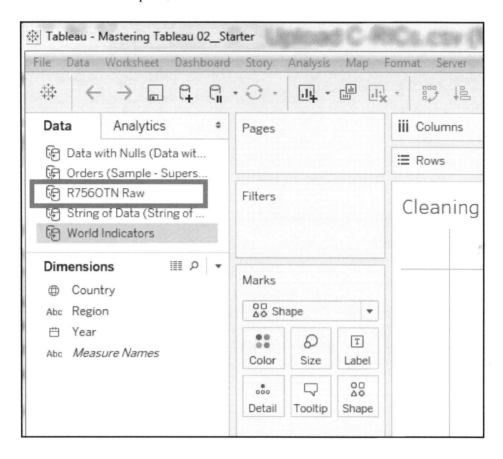

2. Drag **Diagnosis** to the **Rows** shelf and observe the text in the view. Note the junk data that occurs in some rows:

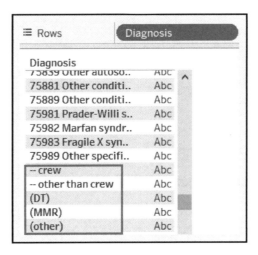

3. Create a calculated field named **DX** with the following code:

```
SPLIT( [Diagnosis], " ", 1 )
```

4. Create a calculated field named **Null Hunting** with the following code:

```
INT(MID([DX],2,1))
```

5. In the **Data** pane, drag **Null Hunting** from **Measures** to **Dimensions**.
6. Drag **DX** and **Null Hunting** to the **Rows** shelf after **Diagnosis**. Observe that **Null** is returned when the second character in the **Diagnosis** field is not numeric:

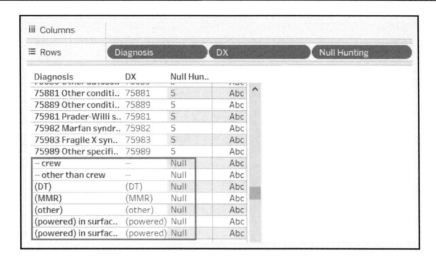

7. Create a calculated field named **Exclude from ICD codes** with the following code:

```
ISNULL([Null Hunting])
```

8. Clear the sheet of all fields and set the **Marks** card to **Shape**.

9. Place **Exclude from ICD Codes** on the **Rows**, **Color**, and **Shape** shelves, and then place **DX** on the **Rows** shelf. Observe the rows labeled as **True**:

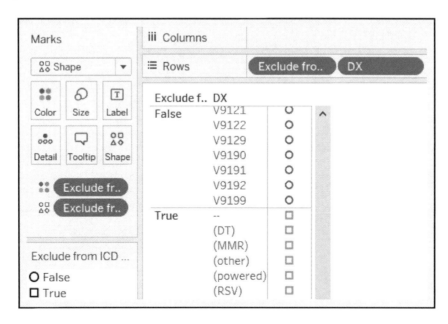

10. In order to exclude the junk data (that is, those rows where **Exclude from ICD Codes** equates to TRUE), place **Exclude from ICD Codes** on the **Filter** shelf and deselect TRUE.

11. Create a calculated field named **Diagnosis Text** with the following code:

```
REPLACE([Diagnosis],[DX] + " ","")
```

12. Place **Diagnosis Text** on the **Rows** shelf after **DX**. Also, remove **Exclude from ICD Codes** from the **Rows** shelf:

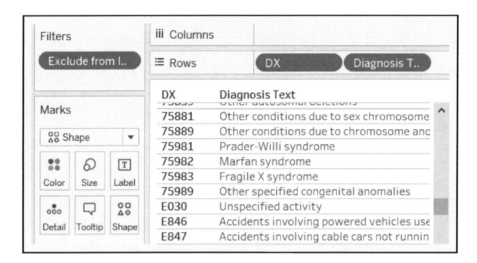

Exercise: commentary

Now that we've completed the exercise, let's take a moment to consider the following code:

```
SPLIT( [Diagnosis], " ", 1 )
```

- The SPLIT function was introduced in Tableau 9.0. As described in the help documentation about the function, the function does the following:

Returns a substring from a string, as determined by the delimiter extracting the characters from the beginning or end of the string.

- To add a point of clarification to the preceding description, to extract characters from the end of the string, the token number (that is, the number at the end of the function) must be negative:

```
INT(MID([DX],2,1))
```

- The use of MID is quite straightforward, and is much the same as the corresponding function in Excel. The use of INT in this case, however, may be confusing. Casting an alpha character with an INT function will result in Tableau returning **Null**. This satisfactorily fulfills our purpose. Since we simply need to discover those rows not starting with an integer by locating the nulls.

- ISNULL is a Boolean function that simply returns TRUE in the case of Null:

```
ISNULL([Null Hunting])
```

- This calculated field uses the ICD-9 codes isolated in DX to remove those same codes from the **Diagnosis** field and thus provides a fairly clean description. Note the phrase *fairly clean*. The rows that were removed were initially associated with longer descriptions that thus included a carriage return. The resulting additional rows are what we removed in this exercise. Therefore, the longer descriptions are truncated in this solution:

```
REPLACE([Diagnosis],[DX] + " ","")
```

The final output for this exercise could be to export the data from Tableau as an additional source data. This data could then be used by Tableau and other tools for future reporting needs. For example, the **DX** field could be useful in data blending.

Does Tableau offer a better approach that might solve for the issue of truncated data associated with the above solution? Yes! Let's turn our attention to the next exercise, where we will consider regular expression functions.

Exercise: extracting data

Although, as shown in the previous Exercise *Cleaning the data*, the SPLIT function can be useful for cleaning data, regular expression functions are far more powerful and represent a broadening of the scope from Tableau's traditional focus on visualization and analytics to also include data cleansing capabilities. Let's look at an example that requires us to deal with some pretty messy data in Tableau. Our objective will be to extract phone numbers.

The following are the steps:

1. If you have not already done so, please open the **Chapter 2** workbook from here: `https://public.tableau.com/profile/marleen.meier`.
2. Select the **Extracting the Data** tab.
3. In the **Data** pane, select the **String of Data** data source and drag the **String of Data** field to the **Rows** shelf. Observe the challenges associated with extracting the phone number:

4. Access the underlying data and copy several rows:

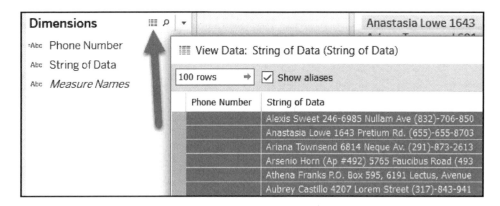

5. Navigate to `http://regexpal.com/` and paste the data into the pane labeled **Test String**; that is, the second pane:

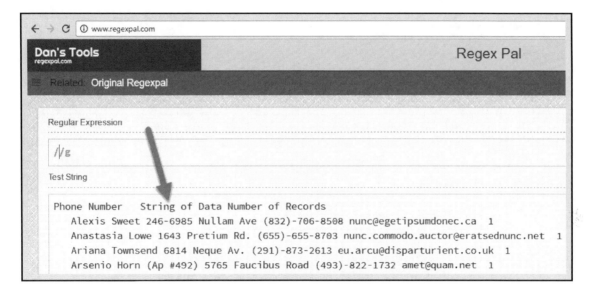

6. In the first pane (the one labeled **Regular Expression**), type the following:

   ```
   \([0-9]{3}\)-[0-9]{3}-[0-9]{4}
   ```

7. Return to Tableau and create a calculated field called **Phone Number** with the following code block:

   ```
   REGEXP_EXTRACT([String of Data],'(\([0-9]{3}\)-[0-9]{3}-
   [0-9]{4})')
   ```

8. Note the regular expression nested in the calculated field.
9. Place **Phone Number** on the **Text** shelf.

   See the result:

Exercise: commentary

Now let's consider some of the specifics in detail from the preceding exercise, *extracting data* in the following code block:

```
REGEXP_EXTRACT([String of Data],'()')
```

- The expression pattern is purposely excluded here as it will be covered in detail later. The `'()'` code acts as a placeholder for the expression pattern.
- The `REGEXP_EXTRACT` function used in this example is described in the help documentation:

  Returns a substring of the given string that matches the capturing group within the regular expression pattern.

- Note that as of this writing, the Tableau documentation does not communicate how to ensure that the pattern input section of the function is properly delimited. For this example, be sure to include `'()'` around the pattern input section to avoid a Null output.
- There are numerous regular expression websites that allow you to enter your own code and help you out, so to speak, by providing immediate feedback based on sample data that you provide. `http://regexpal.com/` is only one of those sites. Search as desired to find one that meets your needs.
- In this context, the \ indicates that the next character should not be treated as special but as literal. For our example, we are literally looking for an open parenthesis:

  ```
  \([0-9]{3}\)-[0-9]{3}-[0-9]{4}
  ```

- `[0-9]` simply declares that we are looking for one or more digital characters. Alternatively, consider `\d` to achieve the same results.
- The `{3}` immediately after `[0-9]` designates that we are looking for three consecutive digits.
- As with the opening parenthesis at the beginning of the pattern, the\ character designates the closing parentheses as a literal.
- The- is a literal that specifically looks for a hyphen.
- The rest of the expression pattern should be decipherable based on the preceding information.

After reviewing this exercise and the accompanying commentary, you may be curious about how to return just the email address. According to http://www.regular-expressions.info/email.html, the regular expression for email addresses adhering to the RFC 5322 standard is as follows:

 Emails do not always adhere to RFC 5322 standards, so additional work may be required to truly clean email address data.

```
(?:[a-z0-9!#$%&'*+/=?^_`{|}~-]+(?:\.[a-z0-9!#$%&'*+/=?^_`{|}~-
]+)*|"(?:[\x01-\x08\x0b\x0c\x0e-\x1f\x21\x23-\x5b\x5d-
\x7f]|\\[\x01-\x09\x0b\x0c\x0e-\x7f])*")@(?:(?:[a-z0-9](?:[a-z0-9-
]*[a-z0-9])?\.)+[a-z0-9](?:[a-z0-9-]*[a-
z0-9])?|\[(?:(?:25[0-5]|2[0-4][0-9]|[01]?[0-9][0-9]?)\.){3}(?:25[0-
5]|2[0-4][0-9]|[01]?[0-9][0-9]?|[a-z0-9-]*[a-z0-9]:(?:[\x01-
\x08\x0b\x0c\x0e-\x1f\x21-\x5a\x53-\x7f]|\\[\x01-\x09\x0b\x0c\x0e-
\x7f])+)\])
```

Although I won't attempt a detailed explanation of this code, you can read all about it at http://www.regular-expressions.info/email.html, which is a great resource for learning more about regular expressions. If you make frequent use of this website for your regular expression code, be sure to leave a donation. I did! Also, YouTube has several helpful regular expression tutorials.

The final output for this exercise should probably be used to enhance existing source data. **Data dumps** such as this example do not belong in data warehouses; however, even important and necessary data can be hidden in such dumps, and Tableau can be effectively used to extract it.

Summary

We began this chapter with a discussion of the Tableau data handling engine. This illustrated the flexibility Tableau provides in working with data. The data handling engine is important to understand in order to ensure that data mining efforts are intelligently focused. Otherwise, effort may be wasted on activities not relevant to Tableau.

Next, we discussed data mining and knowledge discovery process models, with an emphasis on CRISP-DM. The purpose of this discussion was to get an appropriate bird's-eye view of the scope of the entire data mining effort. Tableau authors (and certainly end users) can become so focused on the reporting produced in deployment so as to forget or short-change the other phases, particularly data preparation.

Our last focus in this chapter was on that phase that can be the most time-consuming and labor-intensive, namely data preparation. We considered using Tableau for surveying and also cleansing data. The data cleansing capabilities represented by the regular expression functions are particularly intriguing.

Having completed our first data-centric discussion, we'll continue with Chapter 3, *Tableau Prep*, one of the newer features Tableau has brought to the market. It's a dedicated data pre-processing interface that is able to reduce the amount of time you need for pre-processing even more. We'll take a look at cleaning, merging, filtering, joins, and the other functionality Tableau Prep has to offer.

3
Tableau Prep

At the same time as Hyper, the Tableau Data Engine that we discussed in `Chapter 2`, *All About Data – Getting Your Data Ready*, Tableau Prep was introduced with version 10.5 of Tableau.

What can we use Tableau Prep for? Correct: data preparation. The good news is, Tableau Prep is fully integrated with Tableau Desktop, and starting from version 2019.1, also with Tableau Server. That means you can schedule jobs in Prep to clean your data before you even arrive at the office. Additionally, Tableau Prep is as visual as its big brother, Tableau Desktop, meaning that you can literally see every step of data preparation.

Therefore, let's dive into the **Graphical User Interface (GUI)** and be amazed by another high-end product.

In this chapter, the following topics will be discuss:

- Connecting to data
- The Tableau Prep GUI
- Prepping data
- Exporting data

Connecting to data

When you are familiar with Tableau Desktop, Tableau Prep will be an easy game for you, the handling and interfaces are very similar and connecting to data, if it's a text file, a database or an extract, works all the same! At first sight you might not even notice a difference between the Tableau Prep and the Tableau Desktop GUI, which provides the handy advantage that you can start prepping right away:

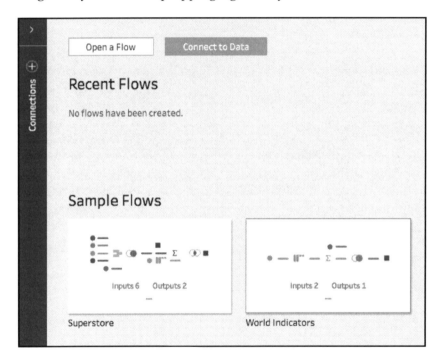

Click on the + in order to open a file. The following screen will appear:

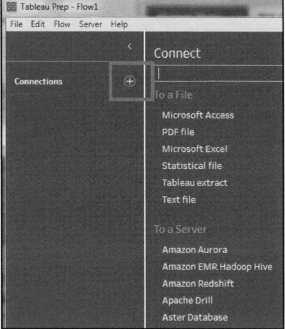

From the preceding screenshot, we can see that you can choose the type of data you want to connect to in the search bar. Just as in Tableau, multiple database are in the repertoire of Tableau Preps too.

Exercise: connecting data to Tableau Prep

For this exercise, we need the following dataset: `https://www.kaggle.com/chicago/chicago-red-light-and-speed-camera-data`. Please download it by clicking on the **DownloadAll** button on the right site of the page. Alternatively, download it from the workbook associated with this chapter on Tableau Public: `https://public.tableau.com/profile/marleen.meier`.

First, we going to start with the `red-light-camera-locations.csv` file. Add it to the empty Prep canvas by making a connection with a text file, followed by the selection of your `.csv` file. You will now see the following:

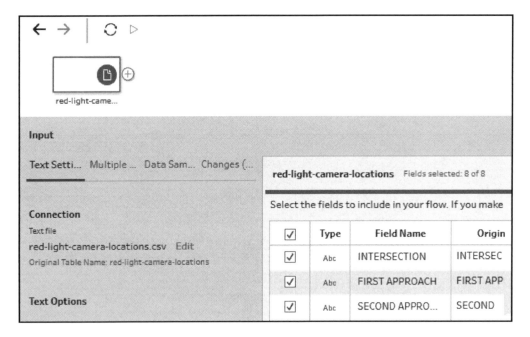

Congratulations—you've just made your first Tableau Prep connection. In the following section, I will describe the GUI in more detail.

The Tableau Prep GUI

User Experience is an import topic, not only when you build a dashboard but also when you use Tableau. One of the biggest selling points is and has always been the ease of using Tableau, the graphical user interface (GUI) is only one of the reasons Tableau is the tool customers love. The Tableau Prep GUI has two important canvases to look at. Right after you connected data to Tableau Prep, the screen will split in three parts, the connection pane, the flow pane and the input pane:

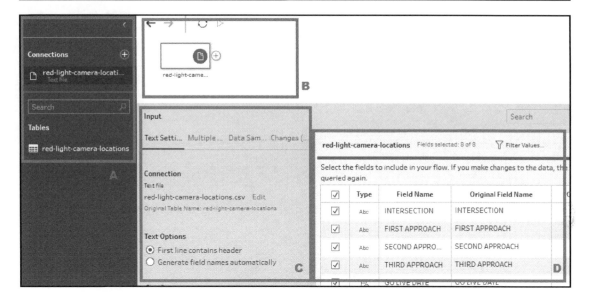

Let's look at what we can see from the preceding screenshot:

- **A**: The connection pane, showing you the input files available on the location selected
- **B**: The flow pane, showing you your current prep flow which always starts with an input step
- **C**: The input pane settings, gives you several options to specify your input
- **D**: The input pane samples, showing the fields you moved to A, including sample values

In the input pane, you can use the wildcard union (multiple fields) function to add multiple files from the same directory. Also, you can limit the sample set that Tableau Prep will print in order to increase performance. In the input pane samples (the section marked with **D)** you can select and deselect the fields you want to import and change their data types. Option are for example: String, Date or Number.

The second GUI is the profile pane. Once you've selected the input data needed, please click on the **+** in the flow pane and select **Add Step**. Now the profile pane will appear:

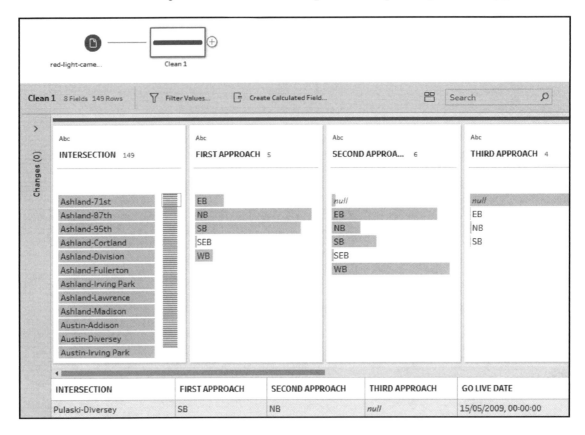

In the preceding screenshot, the profile pane shows every column from the data source in two sections. The upper sections show aggregates. For example, column 5, **GO LIVE DATE**, shows the number of rows per date in a small histogram. The columns can all be sorted by clicking on the sort icon next to the column name and by selecting one item. Let's take, for example, **EB**, in **FIRST APPROACH** (column 2). All related features will be highlighted:

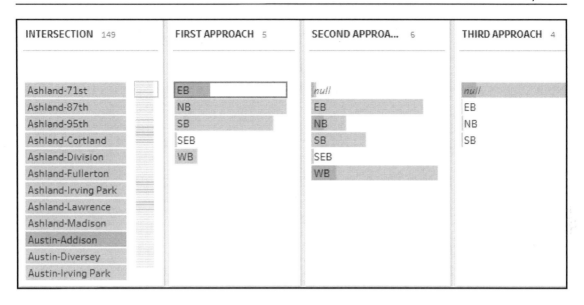

This gives you the chance to get some insights into the data before we even start to clean it up.

In the following screenshot of the lower part of the profile pane, each row is shown as it is in the data source:

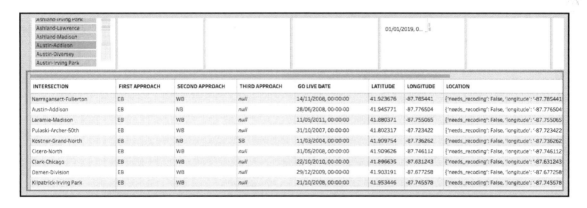

Exercise: getting to know Tableau Prep

Let's start with a practical example.

Next to the `red-light-camera-locations.csv` file, drag the following .csv files onto the flow pane:

- `speed-light-camera-loctions.csv`
- `red-light-camera-violations.csv`
- `speed-light-camera-violations.csv`

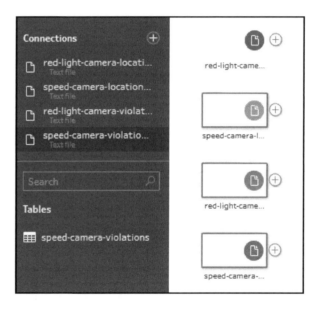

Can you answer the following questions?

- How many year's difference are there between the go-live date of the first red-light and the first speed-light camera?
- On which intersection did the most red-light-camera violations happen?
- On which day did the first speed-light-violation happen for camera CHI040?

Solutions can be found in the workbook associated with this chapter at the following link: https://public.tableau.com/profile/marleen.meier

TIP

All the changes you made to the dataset can be traced back on the left side of the profile pane. But don't forget to add a proper name to each step, this will make it much easier for others to understand what you did, and for yourself, months later.

Here you see, as an example that I used to filter on **CAMERA ID** in order to answer the third question: *On which day did the first speed-light-violation happen for camera CHI040?*

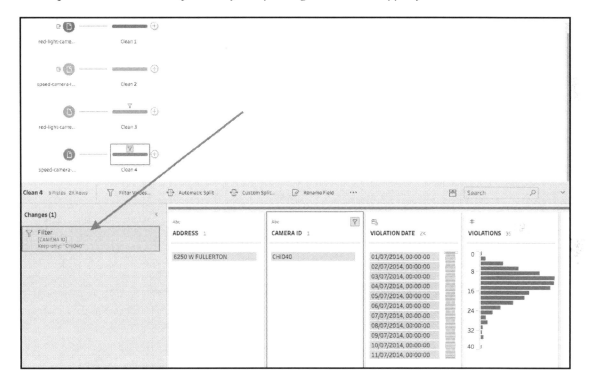

After the first few clicks, it already starts to feel natural, doesn't it? I agree! So, let's continue to the cleaning features of Tableau Prep.

Prepping data

Tableau Prep comes with different prepping steps. We will divide them in four subcategories: cleaning, joins and unions, aggregating, and pivoting.

Cleaning data

The following canvas we have seen before in *The Tableau Prep GUI* section. The user can simply click on + next to the input and select **Add Step**, which will create the cleaning step. During the cleaning step, multiple things can be done, such as filtering and creating a calculated field:

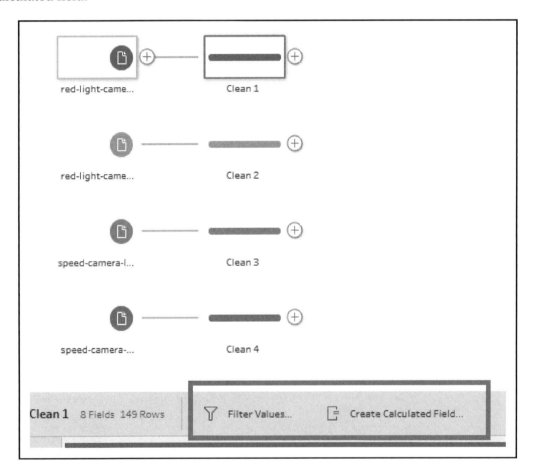

1. Once a value is selected, you have the options to keep it, exclude it, edit it, or replace it with **Null**:

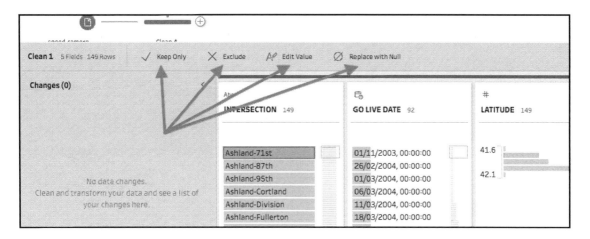

2. Another slightly hidden option is to click on the ellipses (**...**) next to the column header and select **Clean**.

The following is the screenshot:

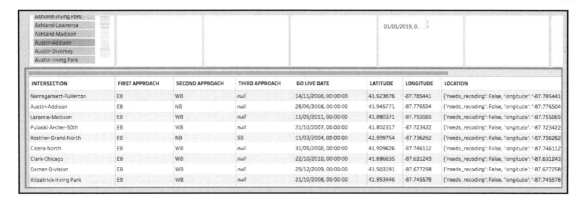

This **clean** functionality is based on the datatype of the column. In the preceding screenshot, the datatype is a string. For other datatypes, it will be greyed out.

Data Type	Cleaning Functionality
String	Make Uppercase
	Make Lowercase
	Remove Letters
	Remove Numbers
	Remove Punctuation
	Trim Spaces
	Remove Extra Spaces
	Remove All Spaces
Date & Time	-
Date	-
Number (Decimal)	-
Number (Whole)	-

The datatype can be changed just above each column header, you will find a symbol on top of the column name which can be changed by clicking on it. Just as in Tableau Desktop.

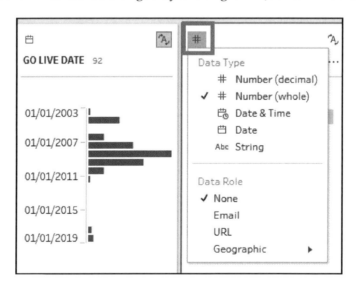

During the cleaning step, fields can be removed even if they were already used in a calculation, unlike in Tableau Desktop.

Exercise: cleaning data

If you haven't done so yet, please download the workbook associated with this chapter from `https://public.tableau.com/profile/marleen.meier` and download the data. Next, connect Tableau Prep with this dataset.

Please execute the following tasks:

- Remove the field **Location** from the red-light-camera-locations and speed-camera-locations dataset using Tableau Prep

Unions and joins

In our example, we look at speed- and red-light camera data. However, we currently have four different datasets, which ideally need to be combined. In order to do this, we will create two unions and a join. Let's start!

Exercise: unions and joins

If you haven't done so yet, please download the workbook associated with this chapter from `https://public.tableau.com/profile/marleen.meier` and use the **view data** button to download the data.

Next, connect Tableau Prep with this dataset.

1. Use a **Union** on the two location and the two violation datasets by dragging them on top of each other:

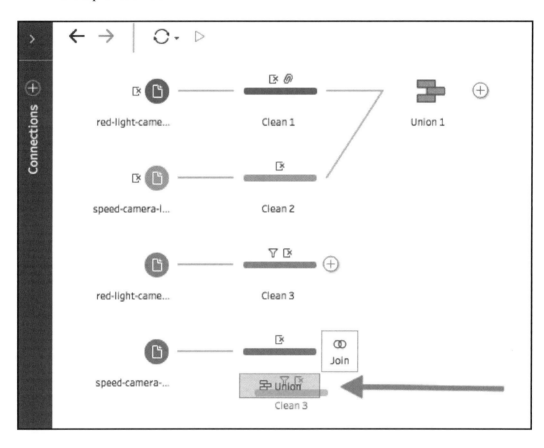

2. Check whether all fields match:

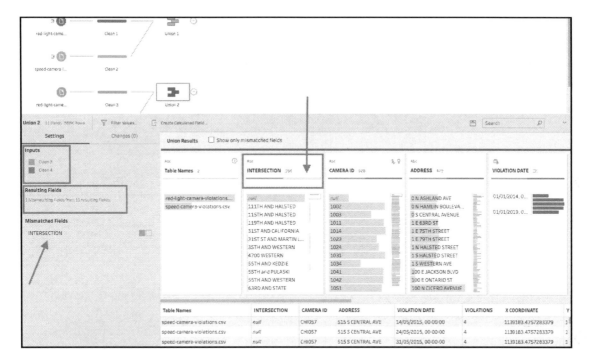

In the preceding screenshot, you can see that on the left, you have information about the union, the inputs, and the associated colors (which are the same in the flow pane), the resulting fields with one mismatch, and finally, the mismatched field. The colors next to it show that green, our red-light-camera-violations intersection field does not exist in red, our `speed-camera-violations.csv`. The same can be seen again in the profile pane.

There might be a situation where you see a mismatch due to different column headers. Let's view this in the following screenshot:

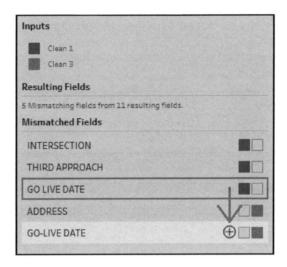

In this example, **GO LIVE DATE** and **GO-LIVE DATE** are not exactly the same. Tableau Prep does recognize similarities and marks it yellow. To union those two fields, you simply select one of the two and click on the + icon that appears.

Now, remove the **null** values from **LATITUDE** and **LONGITUDE**, we need this later for the join.

Tableau created a new column, **Table Names**. Please change the values to *red-light* and *speed*. Do this for both unions.

Also, as in the following screenshot, change the **LATITUDE** and **LONGITUDE** in both unions to a string, and crop them to eight characters only by adding two calculated fields (**Longitude Join** and **Latitude Join**):

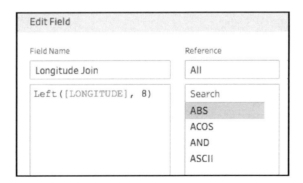

3. Rename our unions, as shown here:

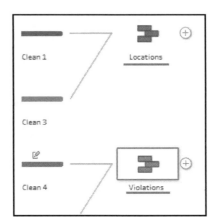

You can also add a description – all the extra effort you make now will help you later with documentation and explanation.

4. Drag **Locations** onto **Violations** and join the two.

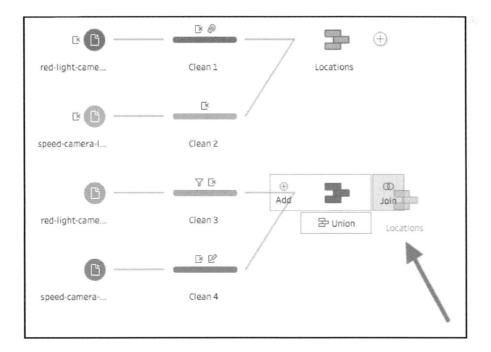

5. Select the following three fields (Table Names, Latitude Join, and Longitude Join) for an inner join and check the results:

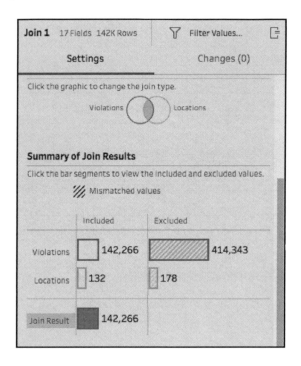

What this overview tells us is that from 557,000 rows of violations, we were only able to match **142K**. From 310 rows of locations, we were only able to match **132**. Our Join Result is **142,266** rows. This could be due to slightly different Longitudes and Latitudes – one file might have a NAD83 source and the other WGS84; however, we will continue for now. Change the join to a full outer join and dive deeper into the data later in Tableau Desktop.

Always wanted to know what the relation between Latitude, Longitude and actual km are?

- 1 degree Latitude is approximately 110.5 km
- 1 degree Longitude is approximately 111.3*cos(latitude) km
- WGS84 has 0.21mm longer ellipsoid than NAD83

In order to get to a full outer join, simply click on the outer edge of the two circles:

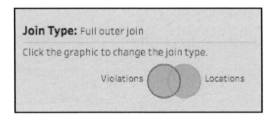

If you want to check immediate results, simply right-click on, for example, and the Join symbol (represented by the Venn diagram icon, as shown in the following screenshot), and you'll be able to check the data in Tableau Desktop:

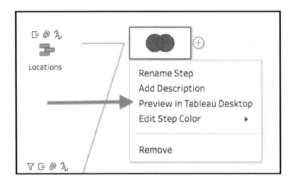

By now, we've seen how to clean data, and how to use unions and joins, so let's continue with the aggregation step.

Introduction to aggregating

An aggregation is used when you want to change the granularity of your data. In our dataset, we have one row per violation. However, we want to group them by camera in order to see where violations happen the most. Let's do it!

Exercise: aggregating

For aggregation,the following are the steps:

1. Our current flow pane looks like this:

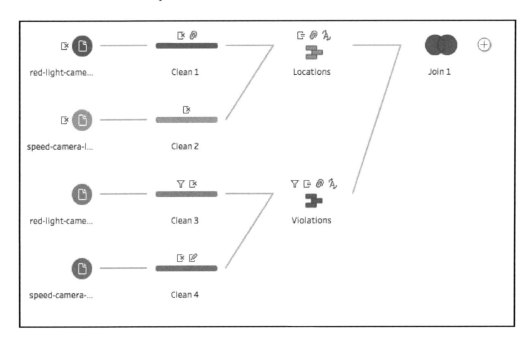

2. Now click on the **+** sign next to the **Join 1** and choose **Add Aggregate**:

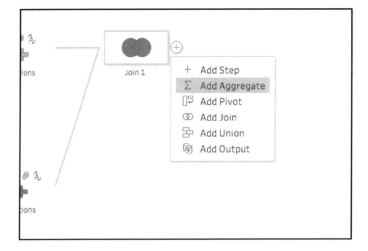

3. Our goal is to see violations per camera; therefore, we will add the sum of violations to **Aggregated Fields**, and other fields such as **LATITUDE, LONGITUDE, CAMERA ID** will be added to **Grouped Fields**:

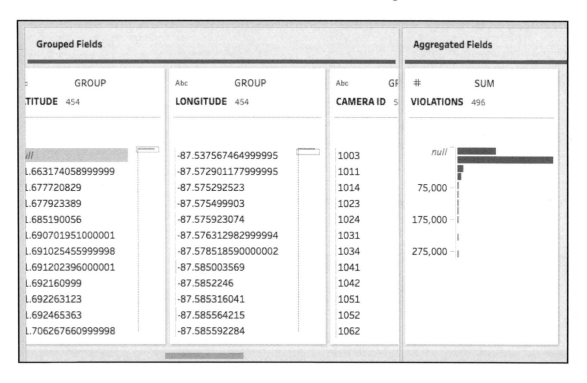

4. Let's have a look at the Tableau Desktop Preview by right-clicking on the Aggregate symbol and select **Preview in Tableau Desktop**:

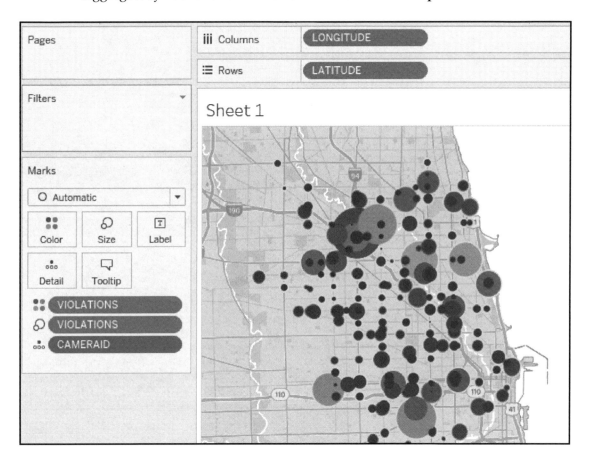

In the preceding screenshot, we can see the amount of violations per camera. Of course, Tableau Desktop will also sum up the violations per camera if those were the only fields dragged onto the view. But another benefit of aggregating it upfront is that you have less data to import; hence, it's possible to achieve better performance. If you want to continue analyzing the dataset, you can now ask further questions, such as the following:

- Do new cameras have an effect on the number of violations from older cameras?
- Is there a correlation between the number of violations from red-light and speeding cameras?
- In which months do the most violations happen and is it always the same location?

Good luck and happy dashboard building!

Pivoting

Our dataset on red-light and speed camera violations in Chicago does not really need any pivoting; therefore, we will have a look at another dataset. You can find it at `https://public.tableau.com/profile/marleen.meier`.

The dataset is very simple and looks like this:

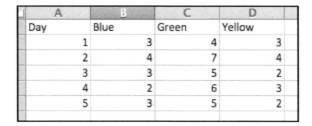

It has three different colors that were observed on five different days, x amount of times. This data is a typical example of when pivoting is helpful to tidy up the data because multiple columns have the same purpose – **B, C,** and **D** are all observation. We want to pivot this table in order for Tableau Desktop to be able to better process it. Let's start!

Exercise: pivoting

Please connect the **PivotDataSet** to Tableau Prep, and follow these steps to complete the pivot:

1. Add a **PivotDataSet** to the input:

2. Now, select all three colors and drag them onto the **Pivoted Fields** pane:

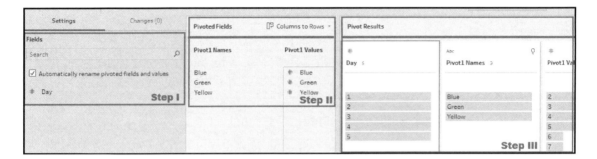

Now, have a look at the **Pivot Results** pane, and rename `Pivot1 Names` to `Colors` and `Pivot1 Values` to `Observations`. Et voilá, we now have a clean table:

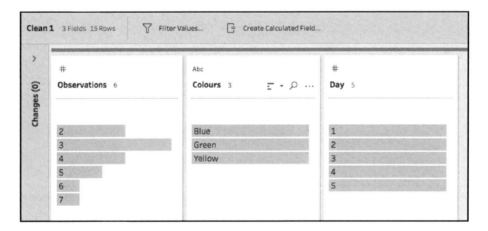

This is a simple use-case for pivoting, but the technique here can be transferred to any other dataset.

Exporting data

Last, but not least, we want to export our data. We have seen before that a right-click on a symbol in the flow pane offers the possibility to preview the data in Tableau Desktop:

1. If you want a flow to run according to a schedule or save it to a location, it's best to use **Add Output**:

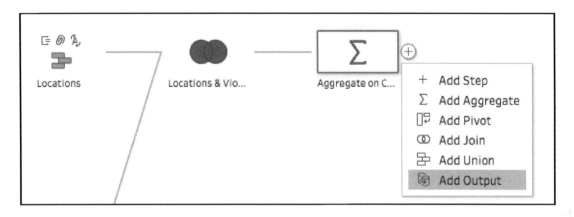

2. After you did this, the following screen will appear:

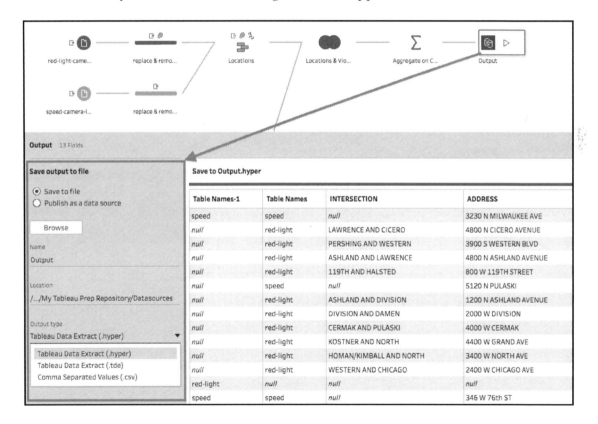

The user has now the option to save the data to a file, and also to save it in Hyper file format as `.hyper`, as a `.tde` file, or as a `.csv` file. Another option is to publish the newly generated data source directly to the Tableau server and make it available for other users. For this option, please select **Publish as a data source**. With version 2019.1, it will also be possible to schedule prep flows from the server.

Summary

We started this chapter with an introduction to Tableau Prep. We looked at the GUI and how we can connect data to it. After that, we did a lot of exercises regarding data preparation. This part can be divided in four parts: data cleaning, unions and joins, aggregation, and last but not least, pivoting. To round up this chapter on Tableau Prep, we looked at exporting data as the final topic. Here, we saw that the new dataset can be saved as a file, a data extract, or can be pushed directly to the Tableau Server.

Just like Tableau Desktop, Tableau Prep is very much self-explanatory and highly visual. Colors, symbols, and highlights make it easy to get used to this Extract, transform, and load tool. In the next chapter, we will focus on joins again, but this time, in Tableau Desktop itself. Along with this, we'll examine both data blending and data structures.

4
All About Data - Joins, Blends, and Data Structures

Connecting Tableau to data often means more than connecting to a single table in a single data source. You may need to use Tableau to join multiple tables from a single data source. You can also join tables from disparate data sources or union data with similar metadata structure. Sometimes, you may need to merge data that does not share a common row-level key. In such cases, you will need to blend the data. Also, you may find instances when it is necessary to create multiple connections to a single data source in order to pivot the data in different ways. This may be required in order to discover answers to questions that are difficult or simply not possible with a single data structure.

In this chapter, we will discuss the following topics:

- Introduction to joins
- Introduction to complex joins
- Introduction to join calculations
- Introduction to spatial joins
- Exercise: observing join culling
- Introduction to unions
- Understanding data blending
- Order of operations
- No dimensions from a secondary source
- Introduction to scaffolding
- Introduction to data structures
- Exercise: adjusting the data structure for different questions

Introduction to joins

This book assumes basic knowledge of joins, specifically inner, left outer, right outer, and full outer joins. If you are not familiar with the basics of joins, consider taking the SQL tutorial at www.w3schools.com. The basics are not difficult, so it won't take you long to get up to speed.

Introduction to complex joins

The terms simple join and complex join mean different things in different contexts. For our purposes, we will consider a simple join to be a single join between two tables. Every other instance of joining will be considered complex.

In the following screenshot, let's look at a star schema as an example of a complex join:

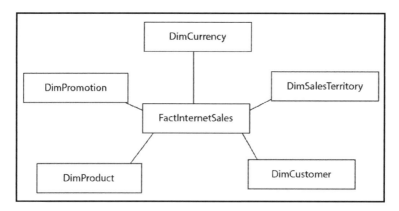

A star schema consists of a fact table that references one or more dimension tables. The fact table typically contains measures whereas the dimension tables, as the name suggests, contains dimensions. Star schema are an important part of data warehousing since their structure is optimal for reporting.

The star schema pictured here is based on the Adventure Works data warehouse for MS SQL Server 2014. The workbook associated with this chapter does not include the SQL Server database. Also, to keep the file size of the workbook small, the extract has been filtered to only include data for the United Kingdom. Access to the database may prove helpful when working through some of the exercises in this chapter.

Exercise: observing join culling

The following screenshot is a representation of the preceding star schema graphic in the Tableau Data Source Page:

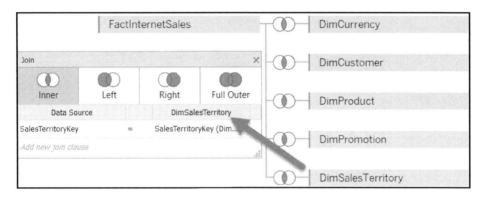

The preceding screenshot communicates an inner join between the fact table, **FactInternetSales** and various dimension tables. **FactInternetSales** and **DimSalesTerritory** are connected through an inner join on the common key, **SalesTerritoryKey**. In this exercise, we will look at the SQL generated by Tableau when building a simple view using these two tables.

Exercise: steps

Note that Tableau always denormalizes or flattens extracts; that is, no joins are included. The data you can access from the worksheet is an extract, therefore in order to be able to follow the steps of the exercise, please download the data and put it in separate sheets.

In the following screenshot, you can separate them based on the table structure in the worksheets:

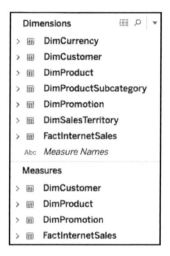

Open the tables and place the columns into separate files:

0	2319.99	2319.99		1	10	353	2	10	15668	20131222	#########	1	98
0	2319.99	2319.99		1	10	353	2	10	11568	20130302	#########	1	98
DimCurrency	DimCustomer	DimPromotion	DimProduct	FactInternetSales	FactInternetSalesPartII	DimSalesTeritory	DimProductSubcategory	+

Once you have done so, please follow these steps:

1. Locate and download the workbook associated with this chapter.
2. Select the **Joins w/o Snowflaking** worksheet and click on the **AdventureWorks_wo_Snowflaking** data source.
3. Drag **Sales Territory Country** to the **Rows** shelf and place **SalesAmount** on the **Text** Shelf.
4. From the menu, select **Help**, then **Settings and Performance**, and then **Start Performance Recording**.
5. Press *F5* on your keyboard to refresh the view.
6. Stop the recording with **Help**, then **Settings and Performance,** and finally **Stop Performance Recording.**
7. In the resulting **Performance Summary** dashboard, drag the time slider to **0.0000** and select **Executing Query**.

Now you see the SQL generated by Tableau:

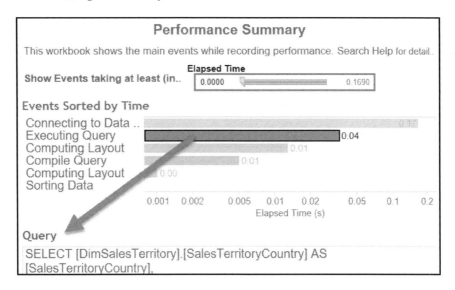

Exercise: commentary

Let's look at the SQL query in detail in the following code block:

```
SELECT "DimSalesTerritory"."SalesTerritoryCountry" AS
"SalesTerritoryCountry",
"FactInternetSales"."SalesAmount" AS "SalesAmount"
FROM "TableauTemp"."FactInternetSales$" "FactInternetSales"
INNER JOIN "TableauTemp"."DimSalesTerritory$" "DimSalesTerritory" ON
("FactInternetSales"."SalesTerritoryKey" =
"DimSalesTerritory"."SalesTerritoryKey")
GROUP BY 1, 2
```

Note that a single inner join was generated, between FactInternetSales and DimSalesTerritory. Despite the presence of a complex join, Tableau only generated the SQL necessary to create the view. This is join culling in action.

 In Tableau, join culling assumes tables in the database have referential integrity; that is, a join between the fact table and a dimension table does not require joins to other dimension tables. Join culling ensures that if a query requires only data from one table, other joined tables will not be referenced. The end result is better performance.

Now let's make one small change to the star schema and add the **DimProductSubcategory** dimension. In the workbook provided with this chapter, the worksheet is entitled **Joins w/ Snowflaking**. Viewing the joins presupposes that you have connected to a database as opposed to using the extracted data sources provided with the workbook.

Let's look at the changes made in the following screenshot:

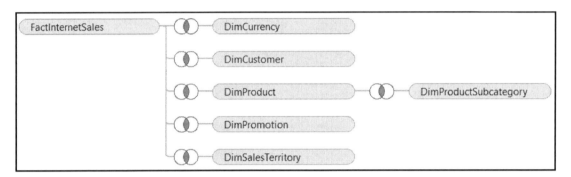

Note that there is no common key between **FactInternetSales** and **DimProductSubcategory**. The only way to join this additional table is to connect it to **DimProduct**.

Let's repeat the previous steps listed to observe the underlying SQL and consider the results in the following code block:

```
SELECT "DimSalesTerritory"."SalesTerritoryCountry" AS
"SalesTerritoryCountry",
"FactInternetSales"."SalesAmount" AS "SalesAmount"
FROM "TableauTemp"."FactInternetSales" "FactInternetSales"
INNER JOIN "TableauTemp"."DimProduct" "DimProduct" ON
("FactInternetSales"."ProductKey" = "DimProduct"."ProductKey")
INNER JOIN "TableauTemp"."DimSalesTerritory" "DimSalesTerritory" ON
("FactInternetSales"."SalesTerritoryKey" =
"DimSalesTerritory"."SalesTerritoryKey")
WHERE (NOT ("DimProduct"."ProductSubcategoryKey" IS NULL))
GROUP BY 1, 2
```

Although our view does not require the **DimProduct** table, an additional join was generated for the **DimProduct** table. Additionally, a `Where` clause was included. What's going on? The additional inner join was created because of snowflaking.

 Snowflaking normalizes a dimension table by moving attributes into one or more additional tables that are joined on a foreign key.

As a result of the snowflaking, Tableau is limited in its ability to exercise join culling. The resulting query is less efficient. The same is true for any secondary join.

 A materialized view is the result of a query that is physically stored in a database. It differs from a view in that a view requires the associated query to be run every time it needs to be accessed.

The important points to remember from this section are as follows:

- Using secondary joins limits Tableau's ability to employ join culling. This results in less efficient queries to the underlying data source.
- Creating an extract materializes all joins. Thus even if secondary joins are used when connecting to the data source, any extract from that data source will be denormalized or flattened. This means that any query to an extract will not include joins and may thus perform better.

Introduction to join calculations

In Tableau, it is also possible to join two files based on a calculation. You would use this functionality to resolve mismatches between two data sources. The calculated join can be accessed in the drop down of each join.

See the following screenshot:

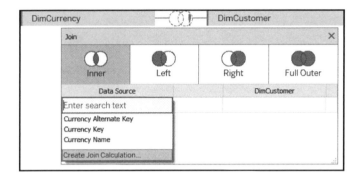

If you want to know more about calculated joins, please check the Tableau Help here: `https://onlinehelp.tableau.com/current/pro/desktop/en-us/joining_tables.htm` #*use-calculations-to-resolve-mismatches-between-fields-in-a-join*.

Introduction to spatial joins

In Tableau 2018.2, spatial joins were added. What this means is, that you can join spatial fields from Esri Shapefiles, KML, GeoJSON, MapInfo Tables, Tableau Extracts, and SQL Server. In order to do so, you have to select the `Intersects` field from the join dropdown. For more information please read `https://www.tableau.com/about/blog/2018/8/perform-advanced-spatial-analysis-spatial-join-now-available-tableau-92166`.

Introduction to unions

Sometimes you might want to analyze data with the same metadata structure, but it is stored in different files. For example, sales data from multiple year's, or different months, countries, and so on. Instead of copying and pasting the data, you can union it. We already touched upon this topic in `Chapter 3`, *Tableau Prep*. A union is basically appending rows, whereas Tableau will append all the rows of columns with the same header.

Understanding union

A union can be created by drag and drop.

1. Create the union by dragging and dropping it:

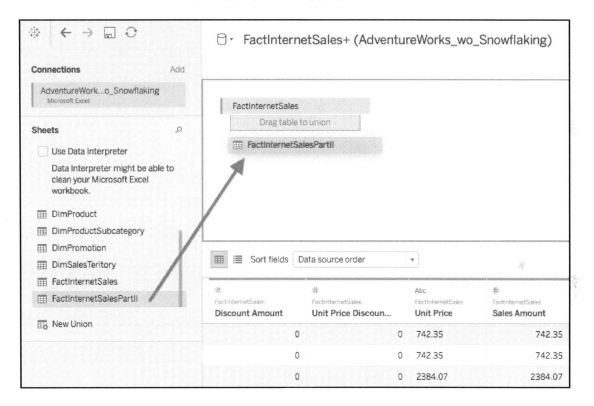

2. Or right-click on the primary dataset and select **Convert to Union**:

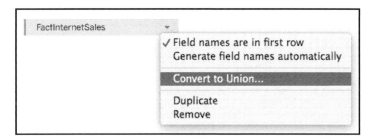

3. The user also has the option to select the files them self, or use a **Wildcard** union:

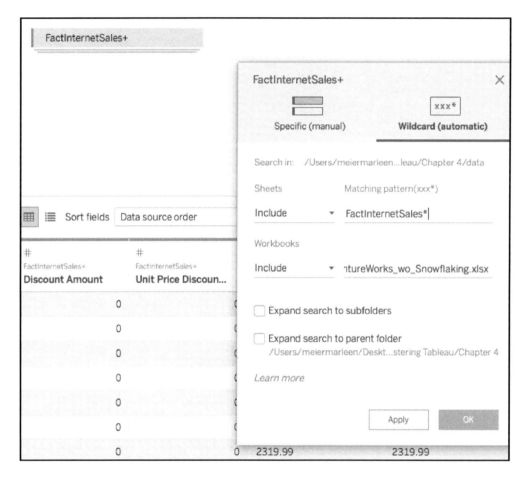

Let's look at the aspects we need to remember:

- Unions should only be used for same-structured data stored across multiple data sources.
- Keep an eye on performance when using an union.

Understanding data blending

In a nutshell, data blending allows you to merge multiple, disparate data sources into a single view. Understanding the four following points will give you a basic grasp on data blending.

- Data blending is typically used to merge data from multiple data sources. Although as of Tableau 10, joining is possible between multiple data sources, there are still cases when data blending is the only possible option to merge data from two or more sources. In the following sections, we will see a pants and shirts example that demonstrates such a case.

- Data blending requires a shared dimension. A date dimension is often a good candidate for blending multiple data sources.

- Data blending aggregates and then matches. Joining matches and then aggregates. This point will be covered in detail in a later section.

- Data blending does not enable dimensions from a secondary data source. Attempting to use dimensions from a secondary data source will result in a * or null in the view. There is an exception to this rule which we will discuss later.

Order of operations

Isn't a data blend the same thing as a left join? This is a question that new Tableau authors often ask. The answer, of course, is no, but let's explore the differences. The following example is simple, even lighthearted, but does demonstrate serious consequences that can result from incorrect aggregation resulting from an erroneous join.

Exercise: a data blend vs a left join

One day, in the near future, you may move to fulfill a lifelong desire to open a brick and mortar store:

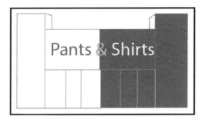

Let's assume that you will open a clothing store specializing in pants and shirts. Because of the fastidious tendencies you developed as a result of year's of working with data, you are planning to keep everything quite separate, that is, you plan to normalize your business. As evidenced by the preceding diagram, the pants and shirts you sell in your store will be quite separated. Also you intend to keep your data stored in separate tables, although these tables will exist in the same data source.

Let's view the segregation of the data in the following screenshot:

Pants Table		Shirts Table	
Sales Person	**Pants Amount**	**Sales Associate**	**Shirt Amount**
Tanya	100	Tanya	50
Zhang	100	Zhang	50
Tanya	100	Tanya	50
Zhang	100	Zhang	50

In these tables two people are listed: **Tanya** and **Zhang**. In one table, these people are members of the **Sales Person** dimension, and in the other they are members of the **Sales Associate** dimension. Furthermore, **Tanya** sold $200 in **pants** and $100 in **shirts**. Ditto for **Zhang**. Let's explore different ways Tableau could connect to this data to better understand joining and data blending.

When we look at the spreadsheets associated with this exercise, you will notice additional columns. These columns will be used in a later exercise.

Exercise: steps

Please continue reading the step-by-step instructions:

1. In the workbook associated with this chapter, right-click on the **Pants** data source and look at the data.
2. Do the same for the **Shirts** data source.
3. Open the **Join** data source and observe the join between the **Pants** and **Shirts** tables using **Sales Person/Sales Associate** as the common key:

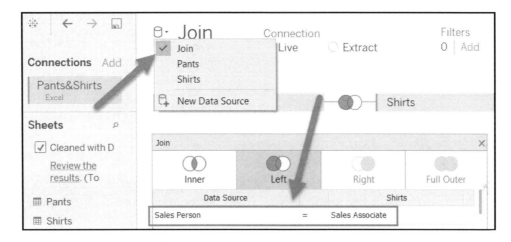

4. On the **Pants** worksheet, select the **Pants** data source and place **Sales Person** on the **Rows** shelf and **Pants Amount** on the **Text** shelf.
5. On the **Shirts** worksheet, select the **Shirts** data source and place **Sales Associate** on the **Rows** shelf and **Shirt Amount** on the **Text** shelf.
6. On the **Join** worksheet, select the **Join** data source and place **Sales Person** on the **Rows** shelf. Next, double-click **Pants Amount** and **Shirt Amount** to place both on the view.
7. On the **Blend – Pants Primary** worksheet, select the **Pants** data source and place **Sales Person** on the **Rows** shelf and **Pants Amount** on the **Text** shelf.
8. Select the **Shirts** data source and double-click on **Shirt Amount**.
9. Select **Data** then **Edit Relationships**.
10. In the resulting dialog box, click on the **Custom** radio button.
11. Click **Add**.
12. In the left column select **Sales Person**, and in the right column select **Sales Associate**.

13. Click **OK** and then remove the link between each instance of **Material Type**.

14. The results in the dialog box should match what is displayed in the following screenshot:

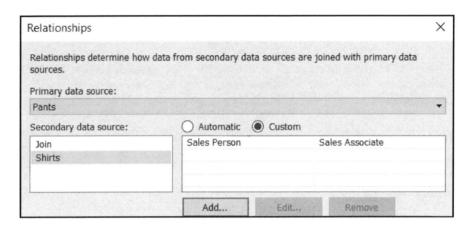

14. On the **Blend – Shirts Primary** worksheet, select the **Shirts** data source and place **Sales Associate** on the **Rows** shelf and **Shirt Amount** on the **Text** shelf.

15. Select the **Pants** data source and double click **Pants Amount**.

16. Place all five worksheets on a dashboard. Format and arrange as desired.

Now let's compare the results between the five worksheets, in the following screenshot:

Understanding the join

In the preceding screenshot, the **Join** worksheet has double the expected results. Why? Because a join first matches on the common key (in this case, **Sales Person/Sales Associate**) and then aggregates the results. The more matches found on a common key, the worse the problem will become. If multiple matches are found on a common key, the results will grow exponentially. Two matches will result in squared results, three matches will result in cubed results, and so forth.

This exponential effect is represented graphically in the following screenshot:

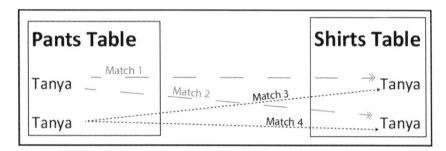

Understanding the data blend

Before the blend could function properly, we had to edit the data relationship so that Tableau could connect the two data sources using the **Sales Person** and **Sales Associate** fields. If the two fields had been identically named (for example, Sales Person), Tableau would have automatically provided an option to blend between the data sources using those fields.

The results for the **Blend – Pants Primary** and **Blend – Shirts Primary** worksheets are correct. There is no exponential effect. Why? Because data blending first aggregates the results from both data sources, and then matches the results on a common dimension.

In this case it is **Sales Person/Sales Associate**, as demonstrated in the following screenshot:

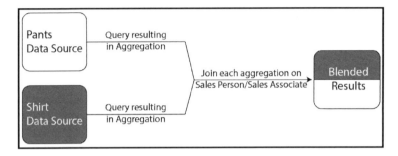

No dimensions from a secondary source

Data blending, although very useful for connecting disparate data sources, has limitations. The most important limitation to be aware of is that data blending does not enable dimensions from a secondary data source. There is an exception to this limitation; that is, there is one way you can add a dimension from a secondary data source. Let's explore further.

Exercise: adding secondary dimensions

There are other fields besides **Sales Person/Sales Associate** and **Shirt Amount/Pants Amount** in the data sources.

We will reference those fields in this exercise:

1. In the workbook associated with this chapter, select the **Adding Secondary Dimensions** worksheet.
2. Select the **Shirts** data source.
3. Add a relationship between the **Shirts** and **Pants** data sources for **Material Type**. Perform the following steps to do so:
    1. Select **Data** then **Edit Relationships.**
    2. Ensure that **Shirts** is the primary data source and **Pants** is the secondary data source.
    3. Select the **Custom** radio button.
    4. Click **Add.**
    5. Select **Material Type** in both the left and right columns.
    6. Click **OK** to return to the view.

4. Place **Material Type** on the **Rows** shelf.

5. Select the **Pants** data source and make sure that the chain-link icon next to **Material Type** in the **Data** pane is activated and that the chain-link icon next to **Sales Person** is deactivated. If the icon is a gray, broken chain-link, it is not activated. If it is an orange, connected chain-link, it is activated.

6. Place **Material Cat** before **Material Type** on the **Rows** shelf.

7. Place **Fastener** after **Material Type** on the **Rows** shelf:

Material Cat is a dimension from a secondary data source. Data blending does not enable dimensions from a secondary data source. Why does it work in this case? There are a few reasons:

- There is a one-to-many relationship between **Material Cat** and **Material Type**; that is, each member of the **Material Type** dimension is matched with one and only one member of the **Material Cat** dimension.

- The view is blended on **Material Type** not **Material Cat**. This is important because **Material Type** is at a lower level of granularity than **Material Cat**. Attempting to blend the view on **Material Cat** will not enable **Material Type** as a secondary dimension.

- Every member of the **Material Type** dimension within the primary data source also exists in the secondary data source.

Fastener is also a dimension from the secondary data source. In the preceding screenshot, it displays * in one of the cells, thus demonstrating that **Fastener** is not working as a dimension should; that is, it is not slicing the data as discussed in Chapter 1, *Getting Up to Speed - A Review of the Basics*. The reason an asterisk displays is because there are multiple fastener types associated with **Wool**. **Button** and **Velcro** display because **Acrylic** and **Polyester** each have only one fastener type in the underlying data.

Introduction to scaffolding

Scaffolding is a technique that introduces a second data source through blending for the purpose of reshaping and/or extending the initial data source. Scaffolding enables capabilities that extend Tableau to meet visualization and analytical needs that may otherwise be very difficult or altogether impossible. Joe Mako, the gentleman who pioneered scaffolding in Tableau, tells a story in which he used the technique to recreate a dashboard using four worksheets. The original dashboard, which did not use scaffolding, required 80 worksheets painstakingly aligned pixel by pixel.

Exercise: enhanced forecasting through scaffolding

Among the many possibilities scaffolding enables is extending Tableau's forecasting functionality. Tableau's native forecasting capabilities are sometimes criticized for lacking sophistication. Scaffolding can be used to meet this criticism.

The following are the steps:

1. In the workbook associated with this chapter, select the scaffolding worksheet and connect to the World Indicators data source.
2. Using Excel or a text editor, create a Records dataset. The following two-row table represents the Records dataset in its entirety:

Records
1
2

3. Connect Tableau to the Records dataset.
4. To be expedient, consider copying the dataset by using *Ctrl + C* and pasting it directly into Tableau with *Ctrl + V*.
5. Create a `Start Date` parameter in Tableau, with the settings seen in the following screenshot. In particular, notice the highlighted sections in the screenshot by which you can set the desired display format:

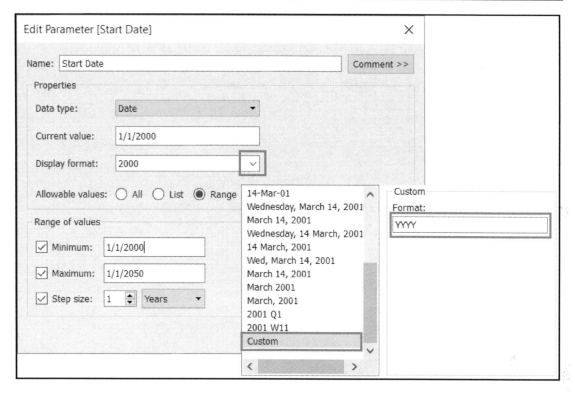

6. Create another parameter named **End Date** with identical settings.

7. In the **Data** pane, right-click on the **Start Date** and **End Date** parameters you just created and select **Show Parameter Control**.

8. Set the start and end dates as desired, for example, 2000 - 2005.

9. Select the **Records** data source and create the following calculated field:

Calculated field name	Calculated field code
Date	IIF([Records]=1,[Start Date],[End Date])

10. Place the **Date** field on the **Rows** shelf.

11. Right-click on the **Date** field on the **Rows** shelf and select **Show Missing Values**.

12. Note that all the dates between the start and end date settings now display:

13. Create a parameter named **Select Country A** with the settings shown in the following screenshot. In particular, note that the list of countries was added with the **Add from Field** button:

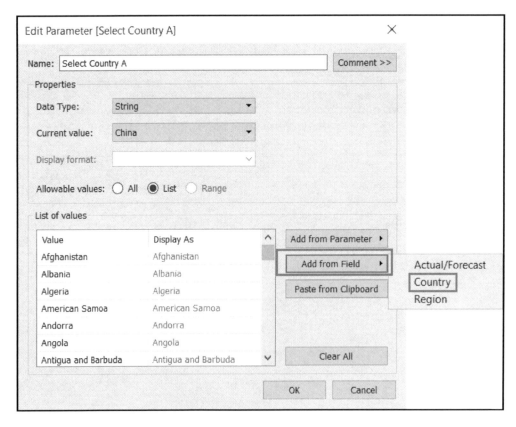

14. Create another parameter named **Select Country B** with identical settings.

15. Create a parameter named `Select Country A Forecast` with the settings given in the following screenshot. In particular, notice the highlighted sections by which you can set the desired display format:

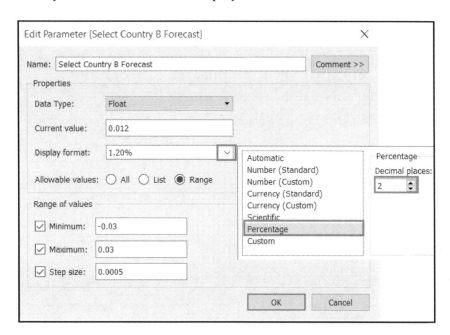

16. Create another parameter named **Select Country B Forecast** with identical settings.

17. In the **Data** pane, right-click on the four parameters you just created (**Select Country A**, **Select Country B**, **Select Country A Forecast**, and **Select Country B Forecast**) and select **Show Parameter Control**.

18. Make sure that the **Date** field in the **World Indicators** data source has the orange chain icon deployed. This indicates it's used as a linking field:

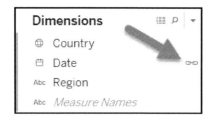

19. Within the **World Indicators** dataset, create the following calculated fields:

Calculated field name	Calculated field code
Country A Population	`IIF([Country] = [Select Country    A],[Population Total],NULL)`
Country B Population	`IIF([Country] = [Select Country    B],[Population Total],NULL)`

20. Within the `Records` dataset, create the following calculated fields:

Calculated field name	Calculated field code
Actual/Forecast	`IIF(ISNULL(AVG([World    Indicators].[Population Total])),"Forecast","Actual")`

Country A Population	`IF [Actual/Forecast] = "Actual"    THEN`
	`SUM([World Indicators].[Country A    Population])`
	`ELSE PREVIOUS_VALUE(0)`
	` *[Select Country A Forecast] +    PREVIOUS_VALUE(0)`
	`END`

Country A YOY Change	`([Country A Population] -`
	`LOOKUP([Country A Population], -1))    /`
	`ABS(LOOKUP([Country A Population],    -1))`

Country B Population	`IF [Actual/Forecast] = "Actual"    THEN`
	`SUM([World Indicators].[Country B    Population])`
	`ELSE PREVIOUS_VALUE(0)`
	` *[Select Country B Forecast] +    PREVIOUS_VALUE(0)`
	`END`

Country B YOY Change	`([Country B Population] -`
	`LOOKUP([Country B Population], -1))    /`
	`ABS(LOOKUP([Country B Population],    -1))`

Country A-B Diff	`[Country A Population] - [Country    B Population]`
Country A-B % Diff	`[Country A-B Diff]/[Country A    Population]`

21. Within the **Data** pane, right-click on **Country A YOY Change**, **Country B YOY Change**, and **Country A-B % Diff** and select **Default Properties** | **Number Format** to change the default number format to percentage, as shown in the following screenshot:

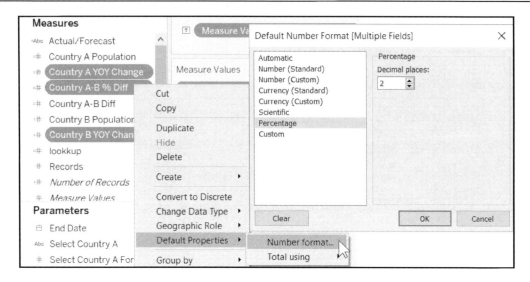

22. With the selected `Records` data source, place the following fields on their respective shelves:

Field	Shelf
Actual/Forecast	Color
Measure Values	Label/Text
Measure Names	Columns

23. Adjust the **Measure Values** shelf so that the fields that display are identical to the following screenshot. Also ensure that **Compute Using** for each of these fields is set to **Table (down):**

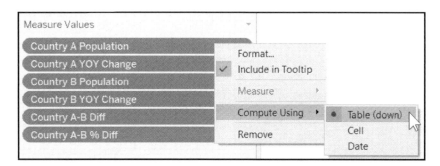

24. Let's ask, "When will the population of India overtake that of China?" Set the parameters as desired and observe the results. My results are the year **2024**. What are yours?

You can view my result in the following screenshot:

Year of D..	Country A Pop..	Country A YOY..	Country B Pop..	Country B YOY..	Country A-B Di..	Country A-B %..
2000	1,262,645,000		1,042,261,758		220,383,242	17.45%
2001	1,271,850,000	0.73%	1,059,500,888	1.65%	212,349,112	16.70%
2002	1,280,400,000	0.67%	1,076,705,723	1.62%	203,694,277	15.91%
2003	1,288,400,000	0.62%	1,093,786,762	1.59%	194,613,238	15.11%
2004	1,296,075,000	0.60%	1,110,626,108	1.54%	185,448,892	14.31%
2005	1,303,720,000	0.59%	1,127,143,548	1.49%	176,576,452	13.54%
2006	1,311,020,000	0.56%	1,143,289,350	1.43%	167,730,650	12.79%
2007	1,317,885,000	0.52%	1,159,095,250	1.38%	158,789,750	12.05%
2008	1,324,655,000	0.51%	1,174,662,334	1.34%	149,992,666	11.32%
2009	1,331,260,000	0.50%	1,190,138,069	1.32%	141,121,931	10.60%
2010	1,337,705,000	0.48%	1,205,624,648	1.30%	132,080,352	9.87%
2011	1,344,130,000	0.48%	1,221,156,319	1.29%	122,973,681	9.15%
2012	1,350,695,000	0.49%	1,236,686,732	1.27%	114,008,268	8.44%
2013	1,356,773,128	0.45%	1,251,526,973	1.20%	105,246,155	7.76%
2014	1,362,878,607	0.45%	1,266,545,296	1.20%	96,333,310	7.07%
2015	1,369,011,560	0.45%	1,281,743,840	1.20%	87,267,720	6.37%
2016	1,375,172,112	0.45%	1,297,124,766	1.20%	78,047,346	5.68%
2017	1,381,360,387	0.45%	1,312,690,263	1.20%	68,670,124	4.97%
2018	1,387,576,509	0.45%	1,328,442,546	1.20%	59,133,962	4.26%
2019	1,393,820,603	0.45%	1,344,383,857	1.20%	49,436,746	3.55%
2020	1,400,092,796	0.45%	1,360,516,463	1.20%	39,576,332	2.83%
2021	1,406,393,213	0.45%	1,376,842,661	1.20%	29,550,552	2.10%
2022	1,412,721,983	0.45%	1,393,364,773	1.20%	19,357,210	1.37%
2023	1,419,079,232	0.45%	1,410,085,150	1.20%	8,994,081	0.63%
2024	1,425,465,088	0.45%	1,427,006,172	1.20%	-1,541,084	-0.11%

Select Country A: China
Select Country B: India
Start Date: 2000
End Date: 2024
Select Country A Forecast: 0.45%
Select Country B Forecast: 1.20%

One key to this exercise is data densification. Data densification produces data that doesn't exist in the data source. The **World Indicators** dataset only includes dates from 2000 - 2012 and obviously the `Record` dataset does not contain any dates. By using the **Start Date** and **End Date** parameters coupled with the calculated `Date` field, we were able to produce any set of dates desired. The actual data densification occurred upon selecting **Show Missing Values** from the Date field dropdown after it was placed on the **Rows** Shelf. This allowed every year between **Start Date** and **End Date** to display even when there were no matching year's in the underlying data. The `Chapter 5`, *All About Data - Data Densification, Cubes, and Big Data*, will explore data densification in more detail.

Let's look at a few of the calculated fields in more depth to better understand how the forecasting works in this exercise.

Calculated Field: `Actual/Forecast`:

```
IIF(ISNULL(AVG([World Indicators].[Population Total])),"Forecast","Actual")
```

This preceding code determines whether data exists in the `World Indicators` dataset. If the date is after 2012, no data exists and thus `Forecast` is returned.

Calculated Field: `Country A Population`:

```
IF [Actual/Forecast] = "Actual" THEN
SUM([World Indicators].[Country A Population])
ELSE PREVIOUS_VALUE(0)
 *[Select Country A Forecast] + PREVIOUS_VALUE(0)
END
```

If forecasting is necessary to determine the value (that is, if the date is after 2012), the `ELSE` portion of this code is exercised. The `PREVIOUS_VALUE` function returns the value of the previous row and multiplies the results by the forecast and then adds the previous row.

Let's look at an example in the following table:

Previous Row Value (PRV)	1,000
Forecast (F)	0.01
PRV * F	10
Current Row Value	1,010

One important thing to note in the `Country A Population` calculated field is that the forecast is quite simple: multiply the previous population by a given forecast number and tally the results.

Without changing the overall structure of the logic, this section of code could be modified with more sophisticated forecasting.

Introduction to data structures

The right data structure is not easily definable. True, there are ground rules. For instance, tall data is generally better than wide data. A wide dataset with lots of columns can be difficult to work with, whereas the same data structured in a tall format with fewer columns but more rows is usually easier to work with. But this isn't always the case! Some business questions are more easily answered with wide data structures. And that's the crux of the matter. Business questions determine the right data structure. If one structure answers all questions, great! However, your questions may require multiple data structures. The pivot feature in Tableau helps you adjust data structures on the fly in order to answer different business questions.

Before beginning the exercise, make sure you understand the following points:

- Pivoting in Tableau is limited to Excel, Text Files, and Google Sheets, otherwise you have to use Custom SQL or Tableau Prep.
- Pivot in Tableau is referred to as unpivot in database terminology.

Exercise: adjusting the data structure for different questions

As a business analyst for a hospital, you are connecting Tableau to a daily snapshot of patient data. You have two questions:

- How many events occur on any given date? For example, how many patients check in on a given day?
- How much time expires between events? For example, what is the average stay for those patients who are in the hospital for multiple days?

Exercise steps: part I

The following are the steps:

1. In the starter workbook associated with this chapter, select the **Time Frames** worksheet, and within the **Data** pane select the **Patient_Snapshot** data source.
2. Click on the **dropdown** in the **Marks View** card and select **Bar**.
3. Right-click in the **Data** pane to create a parameter named **Select Time Frame** with the settings displayed in the following screenshot:

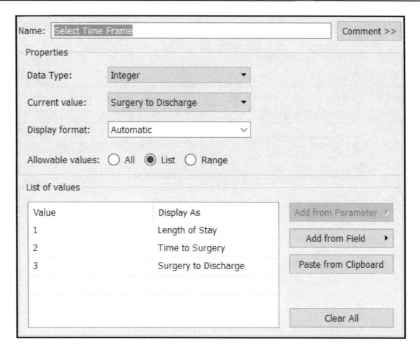

4. Right-click on the parameter we just created and select **Show Parameter Control**.
5. Right-click in the **Data** pane to create the following calculated field:

Calculated field name	Calculated field code
Selected Time Frame	CASE [Select Time Frame] WHEN 1 THEN DATEDIFF('day',[Check-in Date],[Discharge Date]) WHEN 2 THEN DATEDIFF('day',[Surgery Date],[Discharge Date]) WHEN 3 THEN DATEDIFF('day',[Check-in Date],[Surgery Date]) END

6. Drag the following fields to the associated shelves and define them as directed:

Field name	Shelf directions
Patient Type	Drag to the **Filter** shelf and check **Inpatient**.
Check-in Date	Drag to the **Filter** shelf and Select **Range of dates**. Also right-click on the resulting filter and select **Show Filter**.
Check-in Date	Right-click and drag to the Columns **Shelf** and select **MDY**.
Selected Time Frame	Right-click and drag to the **Rows** shelf and select **AVG**.
Selected Time Frame	Right-click and drag to the **Color** shelf and select **AVG**. Set colors as desired.

7. Right-click on the **Avg Selected Time Frame axis** and select **Edit Axis....** and then delete the title:

8. Select **Worksheet** | **Show Title**. Edit the title by inserting the parameter, as shown in the following screenshot:

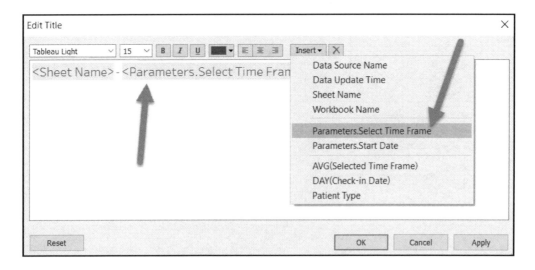

The data structure was ideal for the first part of this exercise. You were probably able to create the visualization quickly. The only section of moderate interest was setting up the **Selected Time Frame** calculated field with the associated parameter. This allows the end user to choose which time frame they would like to view.

But what happens if you need to find out how much time expires between events? This question is rather difficult to answer using the current data structure. (Try it and you will understand!)

Exercise steps: part II

In the second part of this exercise, we'll try a different approach by pivoting the data:

1. In the starter workbook associated with this chapter, select the **Events Per Date** worksheet.
2. In the **Data** pane, right-click the **Patient_Snapshot** data source and choose **Duplicate**.
3. Rename the duplicate **Events**.
4. Right-click on the **Events** data source and choose **Edit Data Source...**:

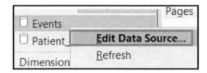

5. Review the highlighted areas of the following screenshot and take the following steps:
    1. Click on the **Manage metadata** icon.
    2. Select all five of the date fields with *Shift* or *Ctrl* click.
    3. Select the drop-down option for any of the selected fields and choose **Pivot**:

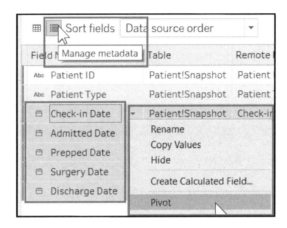

6. Rename the pivoted fields to **Event Type** and **Event Date**.
7. Select the **Events Per Date** worksheet and place the following fields on the associated shelves and define as directed:

Field name	Shelf directions
Event Date	Right-click and drag to the **Rows** shelf and select MDY.
Event Type	Place after **Event Date** on the **Rows** shelf.
Patient Type	Right-click and select **Show Filter**.
Number of Records	Drag to **Columns** shelf.

The original data structure was not well-suited for this exercise; however, after duplicating the data source and pivoting, the task was quite simple. That's the main takeaway. If you find yourself struggling to create a visualization to answer a seemingly-simple business question, consider pivoting.

Summary

We began this chapter with a discussion on complex joins and discovered that, when possible, Tableau uses join culling to generate efficient queries to the data source. A secondary join, however, limits Tableau's ability to employ join culling. An extract results in a materialized, flattened view that eliminates the need for joins to be included in any queries. Unions come in handy if identically-formatted data, stored in multiple sheets or data sources, needs to be appended. We showed how to do so in this chapter. Then, we reviewed data blending to clearly understand how it differs from joining. We discovered that the primary limitation in data blending is that no dimensions are allowed from a secondary source; however, we also discovered that there are exceptions to this rule. We also discussed scaffolding, which can make data blending surprisingly fruitful. Finally, we discussed data structures and learned how pivoting can make difficult or impossible visualizations easy.

Having completed our second data-centric discussion, in the next chapter, we will explore data densification, cubes, and big data.

5
All About Data - Data Densification, Cubes, and Big Data

Many questions that Tableau newbies have are neither related to Data Preparation, joins, unions, Data Blending, or data structures, and those are questions as follows:

- I just created a table calculation and observe that the view displays numbers that don't exist in the underlying data. Why?
- We use SAP BW in my organization. What should I know about how Tableau works with cubes?
- Can you tell me how Tableau works with big data?

This chapter will continue the data discussion from the previous chapters by addressing the topics these three preceding questions target, respectively:

- Data densification
- Working with cubes
- Tableau and big data

There are a few people who have worked diligently to provide resources that were very helpful while writing this chapter. Joe Mako has championed data densification – be sure to check out his video on Vimeo for a deep dive into this challenging topic. The Tableau Online Help has an invaluable series of articles and accompanying workbooks for understanding the ins and outs of working with OLAP Cubes, and lastly, Ben Sullins has provided an excellent resource on Tableau and big data at Pluralsight.

In this chapter, we will discuss the following topics:

- Introduction to data densification
- Domain completion
- Deployment of domain completion
- Usefulness of domain completion
- Domain padding
- Working with cubes
- Exercise: Using a data blend for continuous months when accessing a cube
- Exercise: Using a data blend for hierarchies, aliasing, and grouping when accessing a cube
- The deprecation of cubes
- Tableau and big data
- Exercise: a strategy for addressing excel's row limitation
- Massively parallel processing
- Exercise: building a visualization with Google BigQuery

Introduction to data densification

Data densification is a largely undocumented aspect of Tableau that can be useful in many circumstances, but can also be confusing when encountered unexpectedly. This section will provide information about data densification with the intent of dispelling confusion and providing the Tableau author with sufficient knowledge to use this feature to their advantage.

To begin understanding data densification, four terms should be defined: Data Densification, Sparse Data, Domain Completion, and Domain Padding. In addition to the definitions, each term will be discussed in detail by using examples to help improve understanding.

- **Data densification**: A behavior wherein Tableau displays marks in the view for which there is no corresponding underlying data.

- **Sparse data**: An intersection of one or more dimensions and one measure for which there is no value.

Domain completion

There are two types of data densification: domain completion and domain padding. Domain completion is the more complex of the two and can be deployed cleverly to solve sparse data issues, but may also appear unexpectedly and prove a challenge to address.

- **Domain completion**: The addition of marks on a sparsely-populated view that cause all possible dimension/measure combinations to display results.

Grasping domain completion requires a good understanding of dimensions and measures – discrete and continuous – and partitioning and addressing within table calculations. The first two sets of terms, dimensions/measures and discrete/continuous, are discussed in Chapter 1, *Getting Up to Speed – A Review of the Basics*. The last set of terms, partitioning and addressing, is discussed in detail in Chapter 6, *Table Calculations*.

Now, let's consider how domain completion can be deployed, when it's helpful, and when it's a problem.

Deployment of domain completion

Domain completion can be activated in numerous and sometimes perhaps surprising and confusing ways. Adjusting the arrangement of pills on the shelves, toggling dimensions between discrete and continuous, switching view types on the **Marks** view card, adjusting partitioning, addressing, and other changes can impact domain-completion activation. Although examples for every activation possibility will not be covered in this book, a review of typical domain completion scenarios should prove helpful.

Exercise: activating domain completion in a crosstab part I

The following steps will guide you through the Exercise of Domain Completion:

1. Navigate to `https://public.tableau.com/profile/marleen.meier` to locate and download the workbook associated with this chapter.
2. Navigate to the entitled **DC - Crosstab** worksheet.
3. Ensure that **Analysis** > **Table Layout** > **Show Empty Rows** and **Show Empty Columns** are both deselected.

4. In the Blockbuster data source, create a calculated field named Index with the `INDEX()` code.

5. Place **Title** on the **Rows** shelf and add a filter to view only a few movies.

6. Place **Year** on the **Columns** shelf. Note, as shown in the following screenshot, the view is sparsely populated:

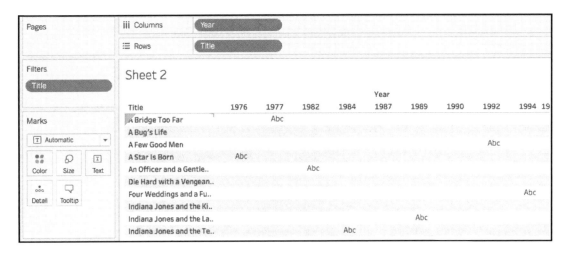

7. Place **Index** on the **Detail** shelf. Note that in the following screenshot the view now reflects domain completion, that is, the view is fully populated:

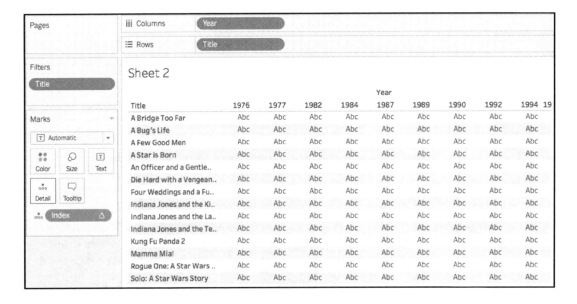

8. Right-click on **Year** and select **Continuous**. Note that data densification is deactivated:

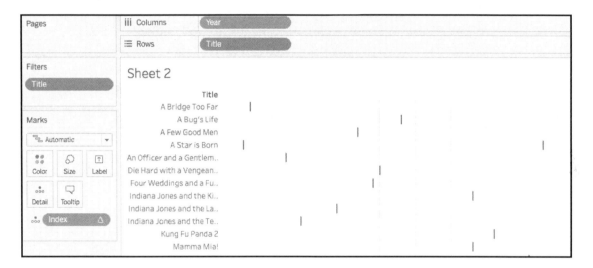

9. Reset **Year** to **Discrete** and then right-click on **Index** and select **Edit Table Calculation**.

10. In the resulting dialog box, select **Specific Dimensions** and then observe the results for each of the following selections:

Select Specific Dimension	Data Densification Activated/Deactivated
Title	Activated
Year	Activated
Title and Year	Deactivated
No selection	Deactivated

 The preceding exercise illustrates the following rule for deploying domain completion: given a crosstab with discrete dimensions on the **Rows** and **Columns** shelves, utilizing a table calculation in which at least one dimension is addressed (but not all dimensions) activates domain completion.

One word in the preceding rule may have been confusing: addressed. Partitioning and addressing were briefly mentioned above and will be defined here to ensure understanding.

Consider the following, from the Tableau documentation:

The dimensions that define how to group the calculation, that is, that define the scope of the data it is performed on, are called partitioning fields. The table calculation is performed separately within each partition. The remaining dimensions, upon which the table calculation is performed, are called addressing fields, and determine the direction of the calculation.

When editing a table calculation, you can choose to select/deselect specific dimensions. When a dimension is selected, that dimension is used to address the table calculation. When a dimension is not selected, the dimension is used to partition the table calculation. The following screenshot demonstrates partitioning on **Year** and addressing **Title**:

This is an example of the dialog box that is used to edit a **Table Calculation**.

Exercise: activating domain completion in a crosstab part II

We will now look at the remaining steps involved in activating domain completion in a crosstab Part II:

1. Duplicate the worksheet from the previous exercise, **DC – Crosstab**. Name the new worksheet DC – Crosstab II.
2. Right-click on **Index** and select **Compute Using** > **Cell**. Note that the view is sparsely populated.
3. Select **Analysis** > **Table Layout** > **Show Empty Columns**. The view is now fully populated.

This exercise illustrates the following rules for deploying domain completion:

- Given a crosstab with discrete dimensions on the **Rows** and **Columns** shelves, selecting **Compute Using** > **Cell** deactivates domain completion.
- Given a crosstab with discrete dimensions on the **Rows** and **Columns** shelves, selecting **Analysis | Table Layout** > **Show Empty Rows/Columns** activates domain completion.

Setting Compute Using to **Cell** may raise a question: what about the other **Compute Using** options, such as **Table (across)**, and **Table (down)**? These options are actually all variations on partitioning and addressing.

Exercise: activating domain completion through view types

We will now look into activating domain completion through View Types.

1. Duplicate the worksheet from the previous exercise, **DC – Crosstab II**. Name the new worksheet **DC – View Types**.
2. Remove **Index** from the **Marks** view card and deselect **Analysis** > **Table Layout** > **Show Empty Columns**. The view is now sparsely populated.

3. Change the **Marks** view card from **Automatic** to **Line**. The view is now fully populated with more marks:

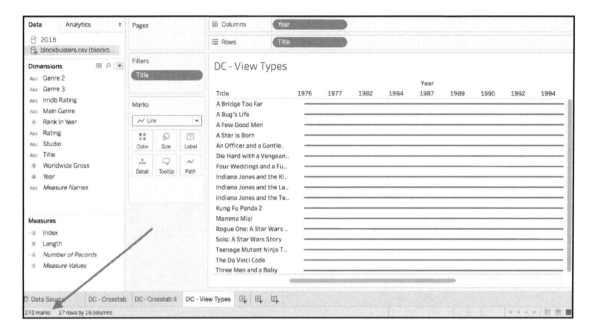

4. Choose each view type option on the **Marks View** card and observe which view types activate domain completion and which do not.

The preceding exercise illustrates the following rule for deploying data completion: given a view with discrete dimensions on the **Rows** and **Columns** shelves, selecting the **Line**, **Area**, and **Polygon** view types from the **Marks** view card activates domain completion.

Usefulness of domain completion

Domain completion can be useful in many circumstances. In fact, you may have gleaned some uses from the previous exercises even though they were designed merely for illustration purposes. The following exercise demonstrates using domain completion to display No Data for cells without a value in a sparsely-populated view.

Exercise: labelling nulls

Let us look at the following steps to begin with the exercise:

1. Duplicate the worksheet from the previous exercise, **DC – View Types**. Name the new worksheet DC – Labelling Nulls.

2. Adjust the duplicated worksheet so that the view type is set to **Text**. Also insure that only **Title** and **Year** are deployed on the view. Be sure to leave **Title** on the **Filters** shelf so that a few movies are displayed.

3. Create a calculated field named No Data with the following code:

```
IF ISNULL(SUM([Sales])) THEN 'No Data' END
```

4. Place **Worldwide Gross** and **No Data** on the **Text** shelf. Note that the text **No Data** does not display:

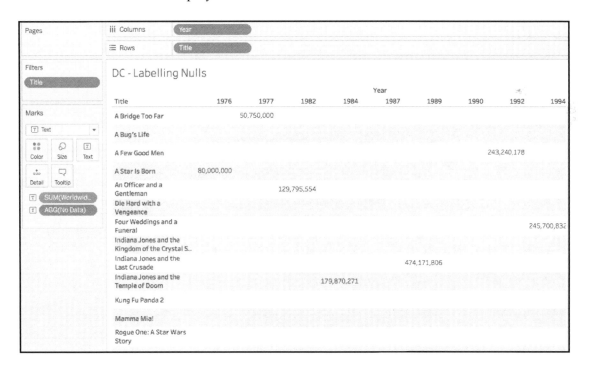

5. Place **Index** on the **Detail** shelf. Note that the text **No Data** does display. The domain completion portion of the exercise is now complete but consider making the visualization more appealing by utilizing a shape:

Problems of domain completion

After being made aware of domain completion, a user will no longer be confused when unwanted marks display in the view. But how to get those unwanted marks to not display can be a challenge. The following exercise shows a scenario of undesired domain completion and how to address the problem. The goal of the exercise is to display each year that a given country reported tourism revenue with an accompanying filter to adjust the countries that display, based on the number of year's data is available.

Exercise: unwanted domain completion

We will now look into unwanted domain completion:

1. In the workbook associated with this chapter, navigate to the **DC - Year Count** worksheet.

2. Select the **World Happiness** dataset in the **Data** pane.

3. Place **Country** and **Year** on the **Rows** shelf and **Whisker** high on the **Text** shelf. Format as desired. Note the missing values as shown in the following screenshot. This is not an instance of data densification since the dataset actually has these null values:

4. In order to remove the **Null values**, click on the drop-down menu associated with **SUM(Whisker high)** and select **Filter**. In the resulting dialog box, select **Special** and **Non-null values**:

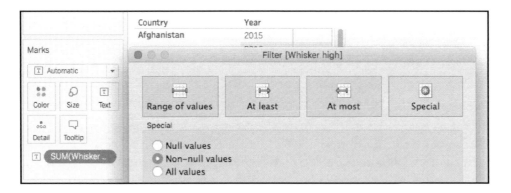

5. Create a table calculation named `Year Count` with the following code:

   ```
   SIZE()
   ```

6. Place a discrete instance of **Year Count** on the **Columns** shelf to the right of **Country** and **Year**. Note that the resulting number represents every column in the view.

7. Right-click on **Year Count** and select **Compute Using > Year**. It appears as if the problem discussed in the *step 2* has returned. However, although the issue looks the same in the view, the underlying problem differs. **Year Count** is a table calculation and has caused domain completion.

8. Right-click on **Year Count** and select **Edit Table Calculation**.

9. In the resulting dialog box, select **Specific Dimensions**. Make sure that **Country** and **Year** are both checked and in the order shown in the following dialog box. Leave **At the level** at **Deepest** and set **Restarting every** to **Country**:

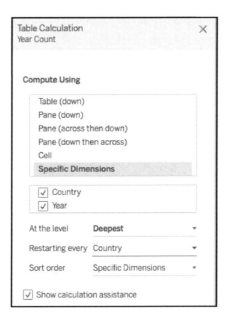

The following step is optional:

10. If you have more than one value for **Year Count**, complete the exercise by moving **Year Count** from the **Columns** shelf to the **Filters** shelf. Change **Year Count** to continuous and display the filter. Format as desired. (This allows you to filter on dimensions with the same number of rows in the partition.)

This exercise illustrates the first rule of domain completion: given a crosstab with discrete dimensions on the **Rows** and **Columns** shelves, utilizing a table calculation in which at least one dimension is addressed (but not all dimensions) activates domain completion.

The relevant section in the preceding rule for this exercise is a table calculation in which at least one dimension is addressed (but not all dimensions) activates domain completion. The domain completion occurred when first deploying **Year Count**, which is a table calculation. Upon changing the addressing and partitioning of **Year Count** so that all dimensions were addressed (that is, no dimensions were partitioned), the issue was resolved.

Domain padding

The second type of data densification is known as domain padding. It is fairly straightforward and, unlike domain completion, is discussed in Tableau documentation. We will proceed with a definition and then consider how domain padding is deployed and when it's useful.

 Domain padding: The addition of marks to the view through the Show Missing Values option on range-aware dimensions (that is, date and bin) and **Analysis > Table Layout > Show Empty Rows/Columns** even when there is no underlying data associated with those marks.

Deploying domain padding through Show Empty Rows/Columns

You may recall that one of the ways to deploy domain completion was **Analysis > Table Layout > Show Empty Rows/Columns**. The same is true of domain padding, as is illustrated in the following exercise.

Exercise: activating domain padding through Show Empty Rows/Columns

This exercise demonstrates how to toggle domain padding on and off:

1. In the workbook associated with this chapter, select **Data > New Data Source** and connect to the **Superstore** Excel workbook that ships with Tableau. It is located in **My Tableau Repository > Datasources+**.

2. In the resulting instance of the **Data Source** page, double-click on **Orders and Returns**. This will cause an inner join to be created on the field **Order ID**.

3. Name the data source **Superstore – Returns**.

4. Navigate to the worksheet entitled **DP – Show Missing Values** and select the **Superstore – Returns** data source that was just created.

5. Place **Ship Mode** and **Region** on the **Rows** shelf. Next, place Sales on the **Text** shelf. Note that the **South** region does not display for **Same Day**.

6. Select **Analysis** > **Table Layout** > **Show Missing Rows**:

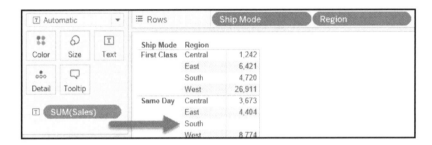

Initially, it was necessary to point to a live data source, such as the instance of **Superstore** that ships with Tableau, because using an extract would not, in this case, activate domain padding even if **Analysis** > **Table Layout** > **Show Missing Rows** was selected. The end result of the exercise, as displayed in the screenshot, is that the South region now displays even though there is no associated value.

Usefulness of domain padding

Domain padding is often useful when working with dates with gaps. Such gaps occur when some dates have associated values and some dates do not. As shown in the following example, returns do not occur every day in the Superstore dataset. Since a visualization that displays dates with gaps could be confusing, it might be helpful to fill in those gaps.

Exercise: domain padding – filling date gaps

We will now try to fill date gaps:

1. In the workbook associated with this chapter, navigate to the worksheet entitled **DP – Filling Date Gaps**.

2. Select the **Superstore – Returns** data source that was created in the previous exercise.

3. Place a discrete instance of **MDY(Order Date)** on the **Columns** shelf and place **Sales** on the **Rows** shelf. Note that every mark in the view is equally spaced regardless of the length of time between dates:

4. Right-click on **MDY(Order Date)** and select **Show Missing Values**.
5. Right-click on **SUM(Sales)** in the **Rows** shelf and select **Format**. In the resulting format window, choose the **Pane** tab and select **Marks: Show at Default Value**. Note that the distance between marks is now based on the length of time between dates. All dates with no value display at the zero line:

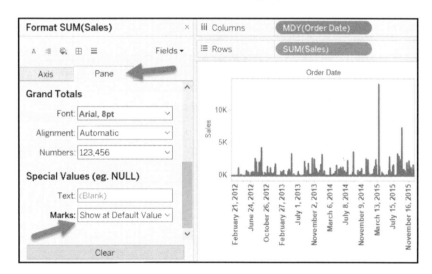

Problematic domain padding

Since domain padding can be toggled on or off through specific commands in Tableau (that is, Show Missing Values and Show Empty Rows/Columns), it's typically not a problem. There are a few scenarios, however, when domain padding may cause confusion, one of which is covered in the following example.

Exercise: from a domain-padded visualization to a crosstab

Let's have a look at creating a crosstab from a domain-padded visualization:

1. In the workbook associated with this chapter, navigate to the worksheet entitled **DP – From Viz to Crosstab**.
2. Select the **Superstore** dataset.
3. Right-click on **Discount** and select **Create | Bins**. In the resulting dialog box, choose a bin size of 0.05.
4. Place the newly-created **Discount (bin)** dimension on the **Columns** shelf.
5. Right-click on **Discount (bin)** and ensure that **Show Missing Values** is selected.
6. Right-click and drag the **Discount** measure from the **Data** pane to the **Rows** shelf. Select **CNT** in the resulting dialog box. Note that some of the bins have no values. For example, as shown in the following screenshot, the **35%** bin has no associated value:

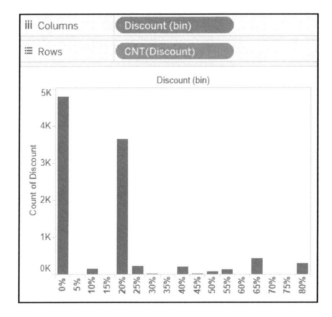

7. Duplicate the sheet as a crosstab by right-clicking on the worksheet tab and selecting Duplicate as Crosstab. Note that **Show Missing Values** is still activated:

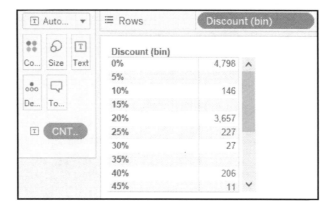

8. Complete the exercise by right-clicking on **Discount (bin)** and deselecting **Show Missing Values**.

Utilizing **Show Missing Values** for bins or dates is often helpful in a visualization, but may not be helpful in a crosstab view. This is especially true if there are many rows or columns without values.

Working with cubes

For the most part, Tableau behavior is uniform across data sources. For example, the experience of working with an Access database and an Oracle database is very similar. Of course, different data sources will have different nuances but, in general, Tableau attempts to make working with different data sources a seamless experience. However, working with cubes (that is, multidimensional data sources) is quite different. Major differences include the inability to alias, create calculated fields on dimensions, create groups or hierarchies, change aggregation types, and generate extracts. The Tableau Online Help provides many workarounds for these shortcomings.

As of this writing, the central cube-related article is located at `https://onlinehelp.tableau.com/current/pro/desktop/en-us/cubes.htm`.

The preceding article provides detailed information and is worth studying in detail if you work with cubes. Provided with the article are many links and examples on how to reproduce typical Tableau behavior when working in a cube environment. Although this material is excellent, we want to mention the topic of using data blending to work more effectively with cubes. This section addresses that shortcoming.

In order to complete the following cube-related exercises, you must have access to Microsoft Analysis Services with an instance of the Adventure Works cube (Adventure Works is the sample cube that ships with Microsoft Analysis Services). Detailed instructions for installing SQL Server, Analysis Services, and the accompanying Adventure Works cube are available at MSDN. A search engine query on `hh403424` will return the link to these instructions.

Data blending for continuous months

Typically, a cube includes one or more date hierarchies. When Tableau is connected to a cube, the members of a date hierarchy that display in the **Data** pane behave such as strings. Thus, Tableau's built-in hierarchy capabilities that are usually available when working with dates in relational data sources are not available. This limitation can be partially overcome by coding **Multidimensional Expressions (MDX)** queries in Tableau, but to achieve all the Tableau date capabilities a data blend is necessary.

Exercise: data blending for continuous months

We will now look into data blending and cubes:

1. In the workbook associated with this chapter, navigate to the worksheet entitled **Cube – Continuous Days**.
2. Connect to the **Adventure Works** data source through **Data** > **New Data Source** > **Microsoft Analysis Services** (see notes *Working with Cubes* to learn how to install Analysis Services and the Adventure Works cube).
3. In the dimension portion of the **Data** pane, expand **Date** and locate the **Date** field.
4. Note that different versions of the Adventure Works cube have slightly different naming conventions.
5. Right-click on **Date** and select **Change Data Type** > **Date**.
6. Drag **Date** to the **Columns** shelf.

7. Place **Internet Sales Amount** on the **Rows** shelf:

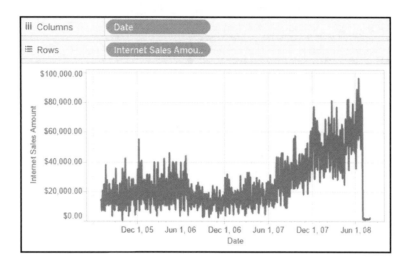

8. Select the worksheet entitled **Cube – Preparing Dates**.
9. Expand **Date** and then **Calendar** and lastly **Date.Calendar**:

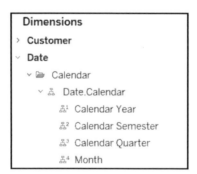

10. Drag **Calendar Year** and **Month** to the **Rows** shelf. Also drag **Internet Sales Amount** to the **Text** shelf.

11. Note that including **Internet Sales Amount** forces every month to display.

12. Select **Worksheet** > **Export** > **Crosstab to Excel**.

13. Adjust the Excel spreadsheet to look like the following screenshot. Be sure to replace the **Internet Sales Amount** column with a column named **Blended Month** which should include first-of-the-month date information for each row, for example, **06/01/2011**. Also, copy and paste **Calendar Year** so that every cell is populated:

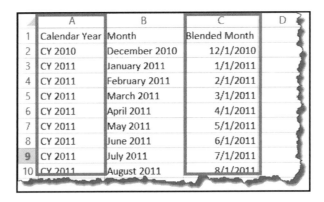

14. Save the Excel spreadsheet as `AWDates.xlsx`.

15. In Tableau, select the worksheet entitled **Cube – Continuous Months**.

16. Select the Adventure Works (**AdventureWorksMultiDimensional**) dataset and drag **Internet Sales Amount** to the **Rows** shelf.

17. Add `AWDates.xlsx` as a new dataset.

18. Select **Data** > **Edit Data Relationships** and set the relationships so that **Date.Date.Calendar.Calendar Year** blends to **Calendar Year** and **Date.Date.Calendar.Month** blends to **Month**:

19. In the **Data** pane, select the **AWDates** data source and blend on **Calendar Year** and **Month** by clicking the grey broken chainlink icons.

20. Right-click and drag **Blended Month** to the **Columns** shelf and select **month continuous**:

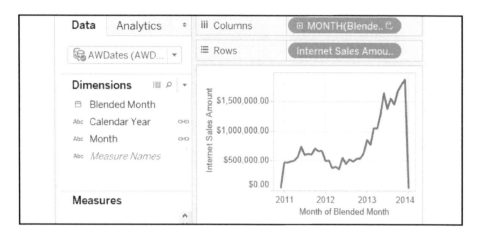

In *Steps 1-5*, we demonstrated a simple way to create a view with a continuous date when connected to a cube. No MDX code was necessary. However, these same steps also reveal the shortcomings of working with a cube: that many of the choices normally available for dates in Tableau are not accessible. This is a problem that cannot be overcome by restructuring the cube or writing MDX code. The remaining steps in the exercise demonstrate how this problem can be overcome through data-blending. Although the data blend created in the exercise only provides month-level granularity, it would not be difficult to include day-level granularity. The end result is a demonstration that the date capabilities normally expected in Tableau can be made available when connected to a cube. Furthermore, if the blended data source remains small, the impact on performance should be negligible.

Data blending for hierarchies, aliasing, and grouping

MDX can be used to provide some of the functionality normally available in Tableau that is otherwise missing when connected to a cube. For example, although you cannot create groups in Tableau when accessing a cube data source, MDX can be passed to the cube by using a calculated member to create groups. Instructions for how to do this are provided in the aforementioned knowledge-based articles. Similarly, it is possible to use MDX to create hierarchies or to alias dimension members, but that requires knowledge of MDX that most Tableau authors do not possess.

Exercise: demonstrating data blending for hierarchies, aliasing, and grouping

This exercise will demonstrate how to use data-blending to accomplish hierarchies, aliasing, and grouping when accessing a cube:

1. Create an Excel spreadsheet named **Aliasing**, with the following data:

Group	Hemispheres
Europe	Eastern Hemisphere
North America	Western Hemisphere
Pacific	Eastern Hemisphere

2. In the workbook associated with this chapter, navigate to the **Cube – Hierarchy** worksheet.

3. If you have not already added the Adventure Works dataset, connect through **Data** > **New Data Source** > **Microsoft Analysis Services** (see *Working with Cubes* to learn how to install Analysis Services and the Adventure Works cube).

4. Select the Adventure Works dataset and place **Internet Sales Amount** on the **Text** shelf.

5. Add the newly-created Excel spreadsheet, **Aliasing**, as a data source.

6. In the **Aliasing** source, blend on **Group** by clicking the grey broken chainlink icon.

7. Create a hierarchy on **Group** and **Hemispheres** by selecting both in the **Data** pane, right-clicking, and selecting **Hierarchy** > **Create Hierarchy**. Name the hierarchy as desired.

8. Make **Hemispheres** the first dimension in the hierarchy by dragging it above **Group**.

9. Place **Hemispheres** and **Group** on the **Rows** shelf:

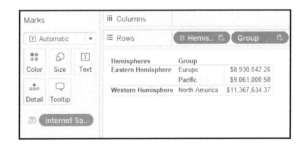

10. Navigate to the worksheet entitled **Cube – Aliasing and Grouping**.

11. Select the Adventure Works dataset and place **Internet Sales Amount** on the **Text** shelf.

12. Select the **Aliasing** dataset, right-click on **Group** and select **Duplicate**. Name the duplicate field `Regional Groups`.

13. Right-click on **Regional Groups** and select **Aliases**. Adjust the aliasing so that Europe is aliased as **EMEA**, Pacific is aliased as **AsiaPac**, and **North America** is left unchanged.

14. Blend on **Group** by clicking the grey broken chainlink icon.

15. Place **Hemispheres** and **Regional Groups** on the **Rows** shelf:

Typically, dimensions are not enabled for secondary data sources in a data blend; however, in the preceding case, since the secondary data source is blended on **Group** and there is a one-to-many relationship between **Hemispheres** and **Group**, both of these fields can be used as dimensions in the view. Nonetheless, for unrestricted use of dimensions, always use the primary data source. Thus, to further extend the exercise, select the Adventure Works data source and drag various dimensions to the **Rows** or **Columns** shelves, including **Country** and **Region**.

One point of interest in the preceding exercise is the necessity of creating **Regional Groups** in the secondary data source by duplicating **Group**. This was required to successfully alias the dimension members. Attempting to alias members directly within **Group** breaks the data blend, as shown in the following screenshot:

The deprecation of cubes

Are cubes here to stay? Maybe not. The advent of big data solutions and the continued evolution of **Relational Database Management Systems (RDBMSs)** may make cubes obsolete. Cubes pre-aggregate data, which can make certain analytic and reporting needs very quick; however, as RDBMS and big data solutions become faster, easier to query, and more sophisticated, the pre-aggregation paradigm may become obsolete. Some argue that cubes are already obsolete. Also, cubes have serious drawbacks, including no performance advantage for non-aggregated data (which is typical at lower levels of granularity), challenges with more complex analytic needs, difficulty mastering the MDX language, and many BI vendors do not cater to cubes. This last point is true of Tableau. Although Tableau can be used with cubes, there are challenges to overcome.

Tableau and big data

Perhaps the first challenge of big data is defining it adequately. It's a term so widely used as to be almost meaningless. For example, some may refer to data exceeding 1,048,576 rows as big data (that is, the row limit in Excel 2010 and 2013) while others would only apply the term to datasets in the multiple petabyte range. Definitions found on Wikipedia and Webopedia are so broad as to encompass both of these examples. You can find them in the following links, `https://en.wikipedia.org/wiki/Big_data` and `https://www.webopedia.com/TERM/B/big_data.html`.

True, we should probably not consider data that merely exceeds Excel's row limitation as big data; nevertheless, from the perspective of the individual for whom Excel is the traditional data-processing application, the preceding definitions fit.

Rather than try to provide an adequately narrow definition to what is essentially a buzzword, this section will primarily focus on one aspect of big data: massively parallel processing. However, before we begin, let's consider a couple of housekeeping items. First, when I have been asked about Tableau and big data, the intent of the question has invariably been about Tableau performance when working with large datasets. Since `Chapter 13`, *Improving Performance*, is dedicated to Tableau performance, this section will not address performance thoroughly. Second, for the user who works predominately or exclusively with Excel, exceeding the row limit is a real problem for which a solution may proof helpful.

Addressing Excel's row limitation

As mentioned in the section *Tableau and Big Data*, exceeding Excel's row limitation should not be considered big data. Nevertheless, that limitation can be an issue, and telling a Tableau author to use a database is often not helpful. A Tableau author may indeed want to utilize a database but may not have direct access. For example, the data that resides in the database may be exported through a web application and then imported into an Excel workbook that Tableau utilizes as a data source. If this process is performed weekly or monthly and each import involves 10,000+ rows, it won't be long before the Excel row limit is hit. In the next exercise, we will see one strategy for addressing this issue.

Exercise: Excel's row limitation

Note that this exercise is Windows-centric. Similar tasks can be implemented in a macOS environment. Follow the steps to learn more about how to work around Excel's row limitation:

1. In the workbook associated with this chapter, navigate to the dashboard entitled **Excel Row Limit**. That dashboard includes a link (`https://github.com/ PacktPublishing/Mastering-Tableau-2019.1-Second-Edition/tree/master/ Chapter05`) to GitHub where you can find the files necessary to complete this exercise.
2. Download the files.
3. Open `Spreadsheet_2` in Excel or a text editor and remove the header, that is, the first row. Save the spreadsheet as a `.csv` file.
4. Place copies of the two files in a new directory.
5. Open Command Prompt. This can be quickly done by pressing the Windows key + *R* and then entering `cmd`.
6. In Command Prompt, type the following:

```
cd [filepath to the newly created directory]
```

7. An example `filepath` -
   `C:\Users\MarleenMeier\Desktop\New_Directory`
8. Press *Enter*.

9. In Command Prompt, enter the following:

```
for %f in (*.csv) do type "%f" >> output.csv
```

10. Press *Enter*. Note that the resulting .csv file (that is, output.csv) will not open successfully in Excel but, as shown in the following steps, it can be used as a data source in Tableau.

11. In Tableau, press *Ctrl + D* to open a new data source.

12. In the resulting window, select **Text File**:

13. Connect to the output.csv data source.

14. Place **Number of Records** on the **Text** shelf and observe that the total equals the number of rows in **Spreadsheet_1** plus the number of rows in **Spreadsheet_2**:

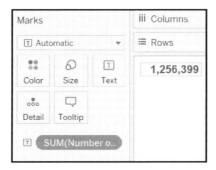

This exercise could also be replaced by Tableau's built-in union function.

The scheduling of wildcard unions through the command line are available in Tableau Prep. You can find documentation about it here: https://onlinehelp.tableau.com/current/prep/en-us/prep_save_share.htm#commandline.

Massively parallel processing

Big data may be semi-structured or unstructured. The **massively parallel processing** (**MPP**) architecture structures big data to enable easy querying for reporting and analytic purposes. MPP systems are sometimes referred to as shared nothing systems. This means that data is partitioned across many servers (otherwise known as nodes) and each server processes queries locally.

Let's explore MPP in detail using the following diagram as a point of reference:

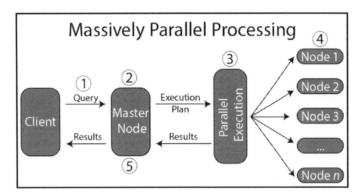

Please see following, an explanation of the diagram:

- The process begins by the **Client** issuing a query that is then passed to the **Master Node**.
- The **Master Node** contains information, such as the data dictionary and session information, which it uses to generate an execution plan designed to retrieve the needed information from each underlying **Node**.
- **Parallel Execution** represents the implementation of the execution plan generated by the **Master Node**.
- Each underlying Node executes the unique query it has received and then passes the results to the **Master Node**. Each **Node** is actually a standalone server with its own RAM, disk space, and operating system.
- The **Master Node** assembles the results, which are then passed to the **Client**.

On the plus side, MPP systems are easily scalable. Once the initial architecture is set up, adding additional hard drive space and processing power can be as easy as adding additional servers. On the downside, MPP systems can be costly to implement—requiring thousands or even tens of thousands of servers, along with associated failover requirements and highly-skilled, costly labor for support. As a result of the expense, many organizations opt for a cloud-based solution, such as Amazon Redshift or Google BigQuery. Amazon Redshift uses an MPP system, while Google BigQuery uses Tree Architecture which is a little different but still takes advantage of MPP techniques.

Building a visualization with Google BigQuery

In order to build a visualization with Google BigQuery, you will need to first set up access to BigQuery. The following exercise will point you in the right direction. Once you have set up access to BigQuery, you will be able to connect to the BigQuery sample datasets. In the remainder of the exercise, you will build a visualization while connected to BigQuery. Assuming you have a good internet connection, the performance will likely exceed what you experience when working with a local copy of an extracted data source of similar size.

Exercise: building a visualization with Google BigQuery

Let us have a look at how we can use Google BigQuery in our Tableau Dashboard.

1. Log into your Google account.
2. Navigate to `https://cloud.google.com/bigquery/` and follow the provided instructions to try **BigQuery** for free.
3. In the workbook associated with this chapter, navigate to the **BigQuery** worksheet.
4. Press *Ctrl + D* to connect to a data source. In the resulting window, select **Google BigQuery** and, when prompted, provide your login information.
5. In the **Data Source** page, choose the **publicdata** project, the **samples** dataset, and the **natality** table.
6. The **natality** table provides birth demographics for the United States from 1969 to 2008:

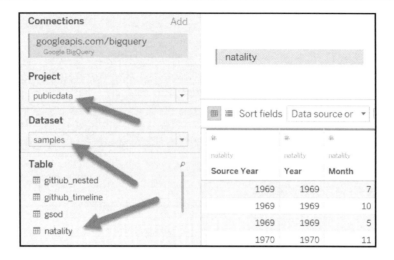

7. In the **Data** pane, double-click **Number of Records**.
8. From the **Data** pane, drag **Month** to the **Columns** shelf.
9. Set **Month** to **Discrete**.
10. Right-click on the axis and select **Edit Axis**.
11. Deselect **Include Zero**.
12. Format as desired. This visualization displays the number of infants born in each month from 1969 to 2008:

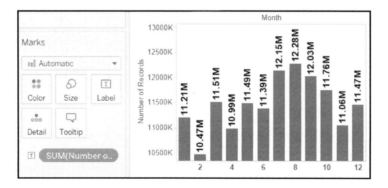

Knowing the fields on which the big data engine is partitioned will help a lot when facing performance issues. If, for example, your data is partitioned on Year, always make use of this field in filters and calculations. Chapter 13, *Improving Performance*, contains more information on this topic.

Summary

We began this chapter with a discussion of data densification, and discovered that there are two types of data densification: domain completion and domain padding. When reviewing these two types of data densification, we learned how to how each can be deployed, when each is useful, and when each can be a problem. Next, we learned how to work with cubes. We discussed the Tableau Online Help articles as well as how to use data-blend and cubes. Finally, we explored big data. We also surveyed MPP and walked through an example of using Tableau to connect to Google BigQuery.

Having competed three chapters of data-centric discussion, we will discuss Table calculations in the next chapter, as well as partitioning and addressing.

6

Table Calculations

The topic of table calculations in Tableau is so rich and deep that it alone could legitimately be the subject of an entire book. Exploring the various options that are available for each table-calculation function and the various ways that table calculations can be applied is an interesting and rewarding endeavor.

As you review the examples in this chapter, you will undoubtedly encounter techniques that you can apply in your day-to-day work; however, you may struggle to understand why some of these techniques work. This chapter has been written with the intent of providing ways of thinking about table calculations that will prove useful in your journey toward mastering this fascinating topic. Along the way, some practical examples will be considered as well.

The structure of this chapter was created with the intent of providing a simple schema for understanding table calculations. This is communicated through two questions:

- What is the function?
- How is the function applied?

These two questions are inexorably connected. You cannot reliably apply something until you know what it is. And you cannot get useful results from something until you correctly apply it. The *Introduction to Functions* section explores each unique table-calculation function, and how each can be considered directional or non-directional. The *Application of Functions* section explores how table calculations are applied to the view via partitioning and addressing dimensions.

I would like to draw your attention to the work of three individuals who helped to make this chapter possible. Joshua Milligan provided the idea of directional and non-directional as a taxonomy for considering how Tableau table-calculation functions are applied. Of the dozens of blogs, forum posts, conference sessions, articles, and white papers reviewed for this chapter, Jonathan Drummy's blog post (`http://drawingwithnumbers.artisart.org/ at-the-level-unlocking-the-mystery-part-1-ordinal-calcs/_`) *At the Level – Unlocking the Mystery Part 1: Ordinal Calcs*, was the clearest and most insightful for understanding the various nuances of partitioning and addressing. Lastly, Joe Mako's unsurpassed understanding of the inner workings of Tableau and his willingness to share that insight through the Tableau forums was very helpful.

In this chapter, we will discuss the following topics:

- A definition and two questions
- Introduction to functions
- Directional and non-directional table calculations
- Application of functions

A definition and two questions

As discussed in `Chapter 1`, *Getting Up to Speed – A Review of the Basics*, calculated fields can be categorized as either row-level, aggregate-level, and table-level. For row- and aggregate-level calculations, the underlying data source engine does most (if not all) of the computational work and Tableau merely visualizes the results. For table calculations, Tableau also relies on the underlying data source engine to execute computational tasks; however, after that work is completed and a dataset is returned, Tableau performs additional processing before rendering the results.

The following process-flow diagram shows were the table calculations are being performed:

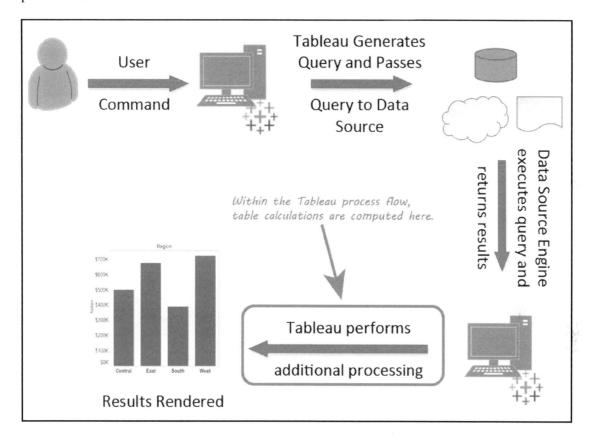

Let us look at the definition of table calculation, in the following information box:

 A table calculation is a function performed on a dataset in cache that has been generated as a result of a query from Tableau to the data source.

Let's consider a couple of points regarding the dataset-in-cache mentioned in the preceding definition:

- This cache is not simply the returned results of a query. Tableau may adjust the returned results. For example, as discussed in Chapter 5, *All About Data – Data Densification, Cubes, and Big Data*, Tableau may expand the cache through data densification.
- It's important to consider how the cache is structured. Basically, the dataset-in-cache is a table and, like all tables, is made up of rows and columns. This is particularly important for table calculations since a table calculation may be computed as it moves along the cache. Such a table calculation is directional.
- Alternatively, a table calculation may be computed based on the entire cache with no directional consideration. These table calculations are non-directional. Directional and non-directional table calculations will be explored more fully in the *Exercise: Directional and Non-Directional Table Calculations*.

 Note that in the Tableau documentation, the dataset-in-cache is typically referred to as a partition. This chapter will often use both terms side-by-side for clarity.

Introduction to functions

As discussed in the introduction to this chapter, it may be helpful to enhance your understanding of table calculations with the following two questions: What is the function? And, How is the function applied? We will begin by grouping each table-calculation function to be directional or non-directional.

Directional and non-directional

Tableau offers a wide range of table calculations, but if we narrow our consideration to unique groups of table-calculations functions, we will discover that there are only 11.

The following table shows those 11 functions organized into two categories:

Directional Table-calculation Functions	Non-Directional Table-calculation Functions
LOOKUP	SCRIPT_STR
PREVIOUS VALUE	SIZE
RUNNING	TOTAL

WINDOW	
FIRST	
INDEX	
LAST	
RANK	

As mentioned in *A definition and two questions*, non-directional table-calculation functions operate on the entire cache and thus are not computed based on movement through the cache. For example, the SIZE function doesn't change based on the value of a previous row in the cache. On the other hand, RUNNING_SUM does change based on previous rows in the cache and is therefore considered directional. In the following example, we'll see directional and non-directional table-calculation functions in action.

Directional and non-directional table calculations

Let us have a closer look at directional and non-directional table calculations:

1. Navigate to https://public.tableau.com/profile/marleen.meier to locate and download the workbook associated with this chapter.
2. Navigate to the **Directional/Non-Directional** worksheet.
3. Create the calculated fields, as shown in the following table:

Name	Calculation	Notes
Lookup	LOOKUP(SUM([Sales]),-1)	Notice the -1 included in this calculation. This instructs Tableau to retrieve the value from the previous row.
Size	SIZE()	As Tableau help states, the SIZE function returns the number of rows in the partition. Therefore, as can be seen in the following screenshot, the size equals the total number of rows.

Window Sum	`WINDOW_SUM(SUM([Sales]))`	The Window sum functions (`WINDOW_SUM(expression, [start, end])`) can operate either directionally or non-directionally. Since this example does not include the [`start`, `end`] option, it operates non-directionally.
Window Sum w/ Start&End	`WINDOW_SUM(SUM([Sales]),0,1)`	This example of a window function is operating directionally, as can be seen by the inclusion of the [`start`, `end`] option.
Running Sum	`RUNNING_SUM(SUM([Sales]))`	By their nature, `RUNNING` functions operate directionally since they consider previous rows in order to compute.

4. Place **Category** and **Ship Mode** on the **Rows** shelf.
5. Double-click on **Sales, Lookup, Size, Window Sum, Window Sum w/ Start&End**, and **Running Sum** to populate the view as shown in the following screenshot:

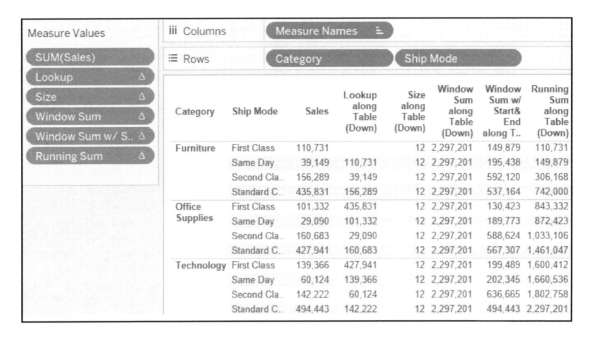

6. In answer to the question, What is the function? we have considered a taxonomy composed of two categories: directional and non-directional. Now, we will move to considering the table-calculation functions individually. Regretfully, space does not allow us to explore all table calculations; however, to gain a working understanding, it should suffice to consider all but one of the unique groups of options. The four table calculations that begin with **Script_** are covered in Chapter 15, *Programming Tool Integration*.

7. Although some effort has been made to make the following exercises useful for real-world scenarios, each is focused on demonstrating table-calculation functionality while considering how each interacts directionally or non-directionally with the dataset-in-cache (also known as the partition).

Exercises: exploring each unique table calculation function

The following exercises will show us each table calculation individually, based on an example.

Lookup and Total

The objectives of the following worksheet displays those customers who made purchases in the last 2 days of 2013, and the associated absolute as well as relative sales of the month of December.

In the following table, notice in the results how LOOKUP behaves directional whereas TOTAL is non-directional. Follow the steps in order to do so:

1. In the workbook associated with this chapter, navigate to the **Lookup/Total** worksheet.
2. Drag **Customer Name** and **Order Date** to the **Rows** shelf. Set **Order Date** to **Month/Day/Year** discrete.
3. Place **Order Date** on the **Filters** shelf and choose to view only December 2013.
4. Create the following calculated fields:

Name	Calculation
Lookup Intervening Time	DATEDIFF(day,LOOKUP(Max([Order Date]),0), DATE(12/31/2013))
% Total Sales	SUM(Sales)/TOTAL(SUM([Sales]))

5. Right-click on **% Total Sales** and select **Default Properties** > **Number format** to set the number format to percentage with two decimal places.

6. Place **Lookup Intervening Time** on the **Filters** shelf and choose a range from 0 - 1.

7. Double-click on **Sales** and **% Total Sales** to place both fields on the view.

8. Format as desired, as seen in the following screenshot:

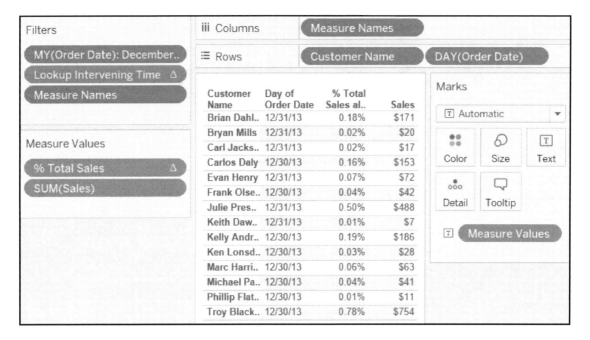

9. Let's consider how the preceding worksheet functions:

   - The **filter on Order Date** ensures that the dataset returned to Tableau only includes data from the month of December 2013.
   - The **% Total Sales** SUM(Sales)/TOTAL(SUM([Sales])) includes the TOTAL(SUM([Sales])) code, which returns the total sales for the entire dataset. Dividing SUM([Sales]) by this total returns the percentage of total.

- The **Lookup Intervening Time**: `DATEDIFF(day,LOOKUP(Max([Order Date]),0), DATE(12/31/2013))` will return an integer that reflects the difference between the date returned by the `LOOKUP` function and **12/31/2013**. Note that the `LOOKUP` function has an offset of zero. This results in each row returning the date associated with that row. This is different from *Directional and Non-Directional Table Calculations*, which included a `LOOKUP` function with an offset of -1, which caused each row in the view to return data associated with the previous row. At first glance, you might think that you could simplify this workbook by removing Lookup Intervening Time from the **Filters** shelf and adjusting the filter on [Order Date] to display only the last two days of December. However, if you do this, **% Total Sales** will add up to 100% across all rows in the view, which would not satisfy the workbook's objectives. Think of **Lookup Intervening Time** as not filtering but hiding all but the last two days in December. This hiding ensures that the data necessary to calculate **% Total Sales** is in the dataset-in-cache/partition.

Previous Value

The objectives of the following worksheet are to return the aggregate value of sales for each year and set next year's sales' goal. Note that two options have been provided for determining next year's sales' goal in order to demonstrate how `PREVIOUS_VALUE` differs from `LOOKUP`. Also note that `PREVIOUS_VALUE` behaves directionally.

Let us have a look at the steps:

1. In the workbook associated with this chapter, navigate to the **Previous Value** worksheet.
2. Create the following calculated fields:

Name	Calculation
Next Year Goal Prv_Val	PREVIOUS_VALUE(SUM([Sales])) * 1.05
Next Year Goal Lkup	LOOKUP(SUM([Sales]),0) * 1.05

3. Place **Order Date** on the **Rows** shelf.
4. Double-click **Sales** and **Next Year Goal Prv_Val** to place each on the view.

5. Format as desired, as seen in the following screenshot:

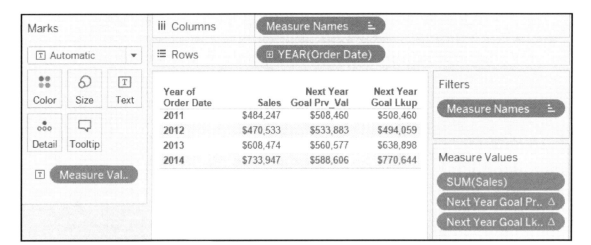

6. Let's consider how the preceding worksheet functions.

- The **Next Year Goal Prv_Val**: PREVIOUS_VALUE(SUM([Sales])) * 1.05 is applied in this worksheet, this calculation retrieves the results from each previous row and adds 5%. In other words, the goal is a steady state growth rate of 5% per year over all years.
- The **Next Year Goal Lkup**: LOOKUP(SUM([Sales]),0) * 1.05 is applied in this worksheet, this calculation adds 5% to the current year's sales. In other words, the goal for next year is for sales that are 5% greater than this year. Previous years are not considered.

To better understand this exercise, consider the values associated with **2014** in the preceding screenshot. **Next Year Goal Prv_Val** is calculated via the **2013 Next Year Goal Prv_Val**; that is, **$560,577** * 1.05. On the other hand, **Next Year Goal Lkup** is calculated via the **2014** sales; that is, $733,947 * 1.05.

Running

The objective of the following worksheet is to display the running minimum profit, running average profit, and running maximum profit compared with **SUM(Profit)** for each month in the dataset.

This following example demonstrates how the Running functions behave directionally:

1. In the workbook associated with this chapter, navigate to the **Running** worksheet.
2. Create the following calculated fields:

Name	Calculation
Running Min	`RUNNING_MIN(SUM([Profit]))`
Running Max	`RUNNING_MAX(SUM([Profit]))`
Running Avg	`RUNNING_AVG(SUM([Profit]))`

3. Place **Order Date** on the **Columns** shelf and set to **Month/Year** continuous.
4. Place **Measure Values** on the **Rows** shelf.
5. Remove all instances of measures from the **Measure Values** shelf except for **Running Min**, **Running Max**, **Running Avg**, and **Profit**.
6. Move **SUM(Profit)** from the **Measure Values** shelf to the **Rows** shelf.
7. Right-click on **SUM(Profit)** and select **Dual Axis**.
8. Format as desired, as seen in the following screenshot:

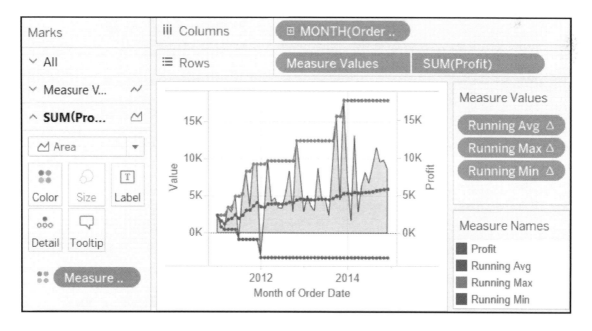

9. Let's consider how the preceding worksheet functions:

- The **Running Min**: `RUNNING_MIN(SUM([Profit]))` is visible in the preceding screenshot, **Running Min** compares the current **SUM(Profit)** with the least **SUM(Profit)** recorded to that point in time. If the current **SUM(Profit)** is less than the least **SUM(Profit)** recorded to date, the current **SUM(Profit)** replaces the least **SUM(Profit)**.
- The **Running Max**: `RUNNING_MAX(SUM([Profit]))` operates similarly to **Running Min** only, of course, it looks for maximum values.
- The **Running Avg**: `RUNNING_AVG(SUM([Profit]))` calculates the average **SUM(Profit)** based on every month to the current month.

Window

The objective of the following worksheet is to display a directional instance of a `WINDOW` function and a non-directional instance.

Please follow the steps:

1. In the workbook associated with this chapter, navigate to the **Window** worksheet.
2. Create the following calculated fields:

Name	Calculation
Win Avg Directional	`WINDOW_AVG(SUM([Profit]),-2,0)`
Win Avg Non-Directional	`WINDOW_AVG(SUM([Profit]))`

3. Place **Order Date** on the **Columns** shelf and set to **Month/Year** continuous.
4. Place **Measure Values** on the **Rows** shelf.
5. Remove all instances of measures from the **Measure Values** shelf except **Win Avg Directional**, **Win Avg Non-Directional**, and **Profit**.
6. From the **Data** pane, drag another instance of Profit to the **Rows** shelf.
7. Right-click on the instance of Profit on the **Rows** shelf and select **Quick Table Calculation** > **Moving Average**.
8. Right-click on the instance of **Profit** on the **Rows** shelf and select **Dual Axis**.
9. Right-click on the axis labeled **Moving Average of Profit** and select **Synchronize Axis**.

10. Format as desired, as seen in the following screenshot:

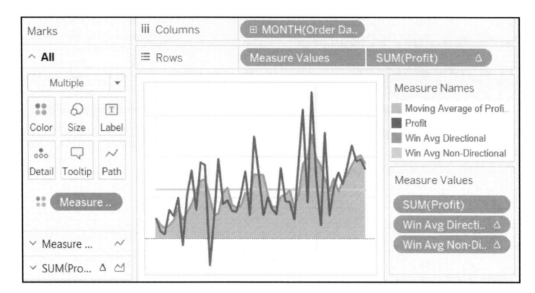

11. Let's consider how the preceding worksheet functions:

- The **Win Avg Directional**: Window_AVG(SUM([Profit]),-2,0) has a start point of -2 and end point of 0 signifies that Tableau will create a point based off the average of the **SUM([Profit])** calculated on the current month and the previous two months. Changing the 0 to 2 would cause the average of each point to be calculated on the previous 2 months, the current month, and the next 2 months. Double-click on the instance of Profit on the **Rows** shelf to view the underlying code. (This is the instance of Profit that was changed into a table calculation by right-clicking and selecting **Quick Table Calculation** > **Moving Average**.) Note that the code is identical to the code created for Win Avg Directional. However, if you right-click on both pills and select Edit Table Calculation, you will notice that the resulting dialog boxes differ. The dialog box associated with Profit has more options, including the ability to change the previous and next values. Changing the previous and next values for Win Avg Direction requires adjusting the calculated field.

- The **Win Avg Non-Directional**: WINDOW_AVG(SUM([Profit])) is associated with the horizontal line across the view. Note that it is not dependent on direction. Instead, it is a single value generated by the average of all aggregated Profit values in the dataset-in-cache/partition.

First and Last

The objective of the following worksheet is to display the first and last instance of the best-selling item in the Superstore dataset. Notice how the following example demonstrates that the FIRST and LAST functions behave directionally.

Please follow along:

1. In the workbook associated with this chapter, navigate to the **First/Last** worksheet.
2. Create the following calculated fields:

Name	Calculation
First	FIRST()
Last	LAST()
First or Last	FIRST() = 0 OR LAST() = 0

3. Place **Product Name** on the **Filters** shelf, select the **Top** tab, and choose **Top** 1 by **Sum** of **Sales**, as shown in the following screenshot:

4. Place **First** or **Last** on the **Filters** shelf and select **True** in the resulting dialog box.
5. Drag **Product Name**, **Order Date**, and **Row ID** to the **Rows** shelf.
6. Set **Order Date** to **Month/Day/Year** discrete.
7. Double-click on **Sales**, **First**, and **Last** to place each on the view.
8. Right-click on **First**, **Last**, and **First** or **Last** and select **Compute Using** > **Table (down)**.

9. Format as desired:

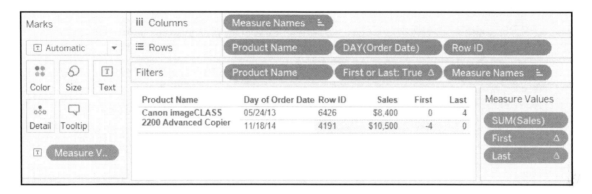

10. Let's consider how the preceding worksheet functions:

- **First:** FIRST() starts at 0 and counts down to the last row of the dataset-in-cache. In the preceding screenshot, note that the first instance of **Canon imageCLASS** occurs on **05/24/13**. The fact that FIRST() ranges from **0** to **-4** communicates that there are five instances of **Canon imageCLASS** in the dataset-in-cache.

- **Last:** LAST() starts at the last row of the dataset in cache and counts down to the 0. In the preceding screenshot, note that the last instance of **Canon imageCLASS** occurs on **11/18/14**. The fact that **LAST()** ranges from **4** to **0** communicates that there are five instances of **Canon imageCLASS** in the dataset-in-cache.

- **First:** FIRST() = 0 OR LAST() = 0, when placed on the **Filters** shelf and set to **True**, hides all instances of matching rows except the first and last.

- The **Row ID** field is included in the view to make sure that the very first and last instance of **Canon imageCLASS** display. Otherwise, if there are multiple instances of **Canon imageCLASS** on the first or last date, sales numbers will reflect multiple values. It's important to set **Compute Using** to **Table (down)** for each table calculation in the view. **Compute Using** is the same as **Addressing,** which will be discussed in detail in the *Index* section.

Index

The objective of the following worksheet is to list those states in the USA with over 50 postal codes represented in the underlying dataset.

Notice how the following example demonstrates that the INDEX function behaves directionally:

1. In the workbook associated with this chapter, navigate to the **Index** worksheet.
2. Set the **Marks View** card to **Circle**.
3. Place **State** on the **Rows** shelf and **Postal Code** on the **Detail** shelf.
4. Create a calculated field named Index with the INDEX() code.
5. Drag **Index** to the **Filters** shelf and choose to view only values that are 50 or greater.
6. Right-click on **Index** and select **Edit Table Calculation**. Select **Specific Dimensions** and check **Postal Code**.
7. Select **Analysis > Stack Marks > Off**, as seen in the following screenshot:

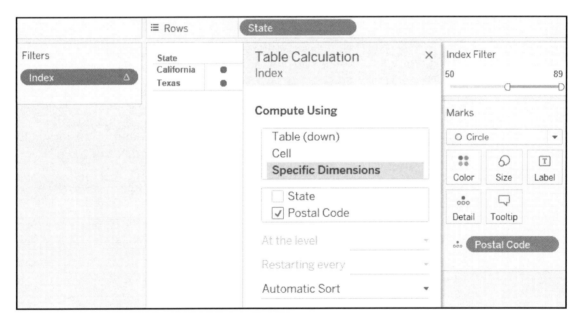

8. Let's consider how the preceding worksheet functions:

- An **Index**: INDEX() counts from 1 to n. As such, it behaves directionally. In this case, as a result of the partitioning and addressing settings, Index is counting postal codes. (Partitioning and addressing will be discussed in detail in the *Rank* section.) Setting the Index filter to display only values of 50 or more insures that only those states with 50 or more postal codes in the partition/dataset-in-cache display.

Rank

The objective of the following worksheet is to display the top-three-selling items in each region. This example will demonstrate how RANK interacts directionally with the dataset in cache:

1. In the workbook associated with this chapter, navigate to the **Rank** worksheet.
2. Place **Product Name** on the **Filters** shelf, select the **Top** tab, and choose **Top 3** by **Sum of Sales**.
3. Place **Region** and **Product Name** on the **Rows** shelf and **Sales** on the **Columns** shelf.
4. Note that only two items display for each region.
5. Create a calculated field named **Rank** with the Rank(SUM(Sales)) code.
6. Drag **Rank** between **Region** and **Product Name** on the **Rows** shelf.
7. Note that before you can place **Rank** between the two pills on the **Rows** shelf, you have to cast it as discrete. One way to accomplish this is by placing **Rank** on the **Detail** shelf, right-clicking on the pill, and selecting **Discrete**.
8. Right-click on Rank and select **Compute Using** > **Product Name**.
9. Remove **Product Name** from the **Filters** shelf.
10. Press *Ctrl* and right-mouse-click and drag **Rank** from the **Rows** shelf to the **Filters** shelf.
11. Pressing the *Ctrl* key while dragging a pill from one shelf to another will create a copy of that pill. Failing to press the *Ctrl* key will, of course, simply result in moving the pill.
12. In the resulting dialog box, select **1**, **2**, and **3**.

13. Format as desired:

If you followed the step-by-step instructions for this exercise, you noticed that after placing **Region** and **Product Name** on the **Rows** shelf and filtering to show only the top 3 product names, the resulting visualization only showed two products in each region. This is because the filter on **Product Name** showed the top three products overall but only two were present in each region. To fix this issue, we employed the Rank table-calculation function. Following an explanation:

Instead of the Rank(Sum(Sales)) function, the same code will be automatically generated by right-clicking on an instance of **Sales** on any shelf and selecting **Quick Table Calculation** > **Rank**. Note that **Rank** is counting the product names within each region. This demonstrates that the Rank table calculation operates directionally on the dataset-in-cache/partition.

Size

The objective of the following worksheet is to display all states with 5 or fewer cities in the **Superstore** dataset. This example will demonstrate how SIZE utilizes the entire partition/dataset-in-cache and is thus non-directional. We will also use the FIRST table-calculation function, which *is* directional in order to clean up the view.

Please follow along the steps:

1. In the workbook associated with this chapter, navigate to the **Size** worksheet.
2. Set **Analysis** > **Stack Marks** to **Off**.

3. Create the following calculated fields:

Name	Calculation
Size	SIZE()
City Count	IF FIRST() = 0 THEN [Size] ELSE NULL END

4. Drag State to the **Rows** shelf, **City** to the **Detail** shelf, **City Count** to the **Text/Label** shelf, and **Size** to the **Detail** shelf.
5. Right-click on the **Size** filter and select **Compute Using** > **City**.
6. Move **Size** from the **Marks View** card to the **Filters** shelf.
7. In the resulting dialog box, select an **At most value of 5**.
8. On the **Marks View** card, right-click on **City Count** and select **Edit Table Calculation**.
9. Under **Nested Calculations**, select **City Count**.
10. Select **Compute Using** > **Specific Dimensions** and check **City**.
11. Under **Nested Calculations**, select **Size**.
12. Select **Compute Using** > **Specific Dimensions** and check **City**, as seen in the following screenshot:

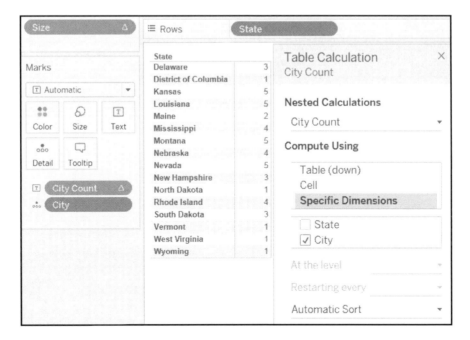

13. Let's consider how the preceding worksheet functions.

- `Size`: `Size()` generates a single number based on the partition/dataset-in-cache. That number can change depending on partitioning and addressing settings, but does not change based on movement across the partition. As such, it behaves non-directionally.

- `City Count`: `IF FIRST() = 0 THEN LOOKUP([Size],0) ELSE NULL END` field is not strictly necessary. You could, instead, simply place **Size** on the **Text/Label** shelf. However, if you do so, you will note that the numbers in the view will look bolded. This occurs because the numbers are actually repeated and then layered on top of each other. Utilizing `FIRST() = 0` causes only one set of numbers to display. Perhaps the most difficult thing to grasp about this exercise is the use of partitioning and addressing. We will discuss partitioning and addressing in the *Application of Functions* section. Note that the preceding exercise had an option for **Nested Calculations**, this is because the `Size` calculated field was referenced within the `City Count` calculated field.

Application of functions

So far, we have covered the first of our two major questions: What is the function? Now we will proceed to the next question: How is the function applied?

Let's try to understand that question via the following three options:

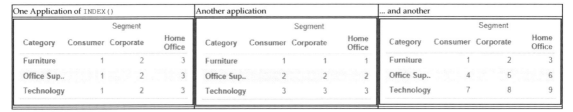

The `INDEX` function is used in each of these three screenshots; however, it is applied differently in each. The first and second screenshots both display **1,2,** and **3**, but differ directionally. The third screenshot ranges from 1 to 9. How is Index being applied in each case? Answering this question can be confusing because Tableau uses different terminology. Within Tableau itself, the way a table calculation is applied may be referred to as running along, moving along, compute using, or partitioning and addressing. For our purposes, we will utilize the terms **partitioning** and **addressing**, which we will define here according to the Tableau documentation:

The dimensions that define how to group the calculation, that is, define the scope of data it is performed on, are called partitioning fields. The table calculation is performed separately within each partition. The remaining dimensions, upon which the table calculation is performed, are called addressing fields, and determine the direction of the calculation.

Before Tableau 10, the terms partitioning and addressing could be readily seen when editing a table calculation. As of Tableau 10, these terms are someone difficult to find in the interface. They are only viewable through a link that displays when you are working with a table calculation in the calculated field editor. The link is default **Table Calculation**. If you click on that link and then in the resulting dialog box select the Advanced option, you will see these two terms. The important thing, however, is that the concept is alive and well in Tableau 10. It's simply represented differently. If a table calculation is utilized in the view, you can right-click on it and select **Edit Table Calculation**. Upon doing so, you will see a dialog box that will allow you to choose specific dimensions. If a dimension is checked, it is addressed. If it is unchecked, it is partitioned.

See an example in the following screenshot:

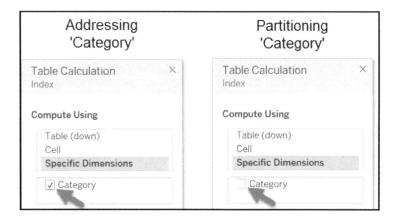

Tableau provides many out-of-the-box partitioning and addressing settings, including **Table (down)**, **Table (across)**, **Pane (down)**, and **Cell**. We will reference these options occasionally but will not give a detailed review. This leads us to our first partitioning and addressing guideline.

Partitioning/Addressing guideline

Don't use the out-of-the-box partitioning and addressing settings provided by Tableau, including **Table (across)** and **Pane (down)**. Force yourself to click **Specific Dimensions** and manually define the partitioning and addressing so that you clearly understand how every table calculation is applied.

There are a couple of caveats to the preceding guideline:

- There's an exception, which is **Cell**. It is not possible to address individual cells in a view using partitioning and addressing. Instead, it is necessary to use **Compute Using** as **Cell** or, within the **Table Calculation** dialog box, to select **Cell**. Surprisingly, addressing a table calculation along each cell can be useful. An example is provided in the workbook associated with this chapter.
- If you set partitioning and addressing for a given table calculation and then add dimensions to the view, usually Tableau will not automatically adjust the partitioning and addressing settings; they are locked down. However, when using **Table (down)**, **Pane (across)**, and the like, Tableau will make automatic adjustments as dimensions are added to the view. This leads us to our next guideline.

Partitioning/Addressing guideline
Place all needed dimensions on the desired shelves before setting partitioning and addressing for table calculations.

Following these guidelines will help ensure that you are always clear about how your table calculations are being applied.

Building a playground

Let's set up a simple playground environment to quickly and efficiently explore partitioning and addressing:

1. In the workbook associated with this chapter, navigate to the **Playground** worksheet.
2. Place **Category** on the **Rows** shelf and the **Index** calculation on the **Text/Label** shelf.
3. The **Index** calculation is simply `Index()`.
4. Click on the drop-down menu associated with **Index** and select **Edit Table Calculation**.
5. In the resulting dialog box, click **Specific Dimensions**.

6. Position the screen components optimally. See the following screenshot for one possible setup:

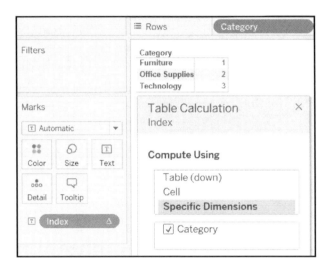

In the following pages, we will utilize our playground extensively and modify it as necessary. However, for the sake of efficiency, we will need to keep the focus of the playground and the accompanying discussion narrow. The discussion will be confined to dimensions on the **Rows** and **Columns** shelves and the INDEX function on the **Text** shelf. We could explore different functions on various shelves and the different options that affords. For instance, placing a date field on the **Pages** shelf will cause a table calculation that uses the TOTAL function to display an option to compute the total across all pages. Regretfully, exploring every possible nuance is simply not possible due to space constraints.

Partitioning and addressing with one dimension

Let's use our playground to start exploring partitioning and addressing with the simplest possible example:

	Partitioning: Category Addressing: Null			Partitioning: Null Addressing: Category	
1A	Category Furniture 1 Office Supplies 1 Technology 1		1B	Category Furniture 1 Office Supplies 2 Technology 3	

In this simple example, Addressing **Category** causes each member of the **Category** dimension to be counted. This demonstrates that addressing a dimension determines the direction of the calculation.

Partitioning and addressing with two dimensions

Two additional options are made available when partitioning and addressing two or more dimensions: **At the level** and **Restarting every**:

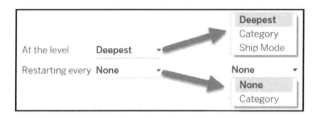

Both **At the level** and **Restarting every** allows the author to choose dimensions from a drop-down menu. **At the level** allows the author to choose what level to increment at and, as the name suggests, **Restarting every** allows the author to choose which dimensions to restart on. The many examples here will provide context for your understanding.

Note that **At the level** has one additional choice: **Deepest**. In this case, setting **At the level** to **Deepest** is the same as selecting **Ship Mode**. This leads us to our next guideline.

Partitioning/Addressing guideline
 It is not necessary to choose the bottom dimension in the **At the level** drop-down menu. It is always identical to **Deepest**.

To recreate the iterations listed here, you will need to make some changes to the playground environment. In addition to **Category** on the **Rows** shelf and **Index** on the **Text/Label** shelf, also place **Ship Mode** on the **Rows** shelf. We will not cover iterations that include one or more dimensions on the **Columns** shelf since the behavior of these possibilities are much the same.

As you consider and/or reproduce the following options, note that the **Addressing** order is important. For options 3 - 5, **Category** is first on the addressing list. For options 6 - 8, **Ship Mode** is first on the list:

ID	Partitioning	Addressing	At the level	Restarting every	Results		
1	Category	Ship Mode			**Category**	**Ship Mode**	
					Furniture	First Class	1
						Same Day	2
						Second Class	3
						Standard Class	4
					Office Supplies	First Class	1
						Same Day	2
						Second Class	3
						Standard Class	4
					Technology	First Class	1
						Same Day	2
						Second Class	3
						Standard Class	4
2	Ship Mode	Category			**Category**	**Ship Mode**	
					Furniture	First Class	1
						Same Day	1
						Second Class	1
						Standard Class	1
					Office Supplies	First Class	2
						Same Day	2
						Second Class	2
						Standard Class	2
					Technology	First Class	3
						Same Day	3
						Second Class	3
						Standard Class	3
3		Category Ship Mode	Deepest	None	**Category**	**Ship Mode**	
					Furniture	First Class	1
						Same Day	2
						Second Class	3
						Standard Class	4
					Office Supplies	First Class	5
						Same Day	6
						Second Class	7
						Standard Class	8
					Technology	First Class	9
						Same Day	10
						Second Class	11
						Standard Class	12

ID	Partitioning	Addressing	At the level	Restarting every	Results
4		Category Ship Mode	Deepest	Category	Category / Ship Mode Furniture — First Class 1, Same Day 2, Second Class 3, Standard Class 4 Office Supplies — First Class 1, Same Day 2, Second Class 3, Standard Class 4 Technology — First Class 1, Same Day 2, Second Class 3, Standard Class 4
5		Category Ship Mode	Category	None	Category / Ship Mode Furniture — First Class 1, Same Day 2, Second Class 3, Standard Class 4 Office Supplies — First Class 1, Same Day 2, Second Class 3, Standard Class 4 Technology — First Class 1, Same Day 2, Second Class 3, Standard Class 4
6		Ship Mode Category	Deepest	None	Category / Ship Mode Furniture — First Class 1, Same Day 4, Second Class 7, Standard Class 10 Office Supplies — First Class 2, Same Day 5, Second Class 8, Standard Class 11 Technology — First Class 3, Same Day 6, Second Class 9, Standard Class 12

ID	Partitioning	Addressing	At the level	Restarting every	Results
7		Ship Mode Category	Deepest	Ship Mode	Category — Ship Mode Furniture — First Class 1, Same Day 1, Second Class 1, Standard Class 1 Office Supplies — First Class 2, Same Day 2, Second Class 2, Standard Class 2 Technology — First Class 3, Same Day 3, Second Class 3, Standard Class 3
8		Ship Mode Category	Ship Mode	None	Category — Ship Mode Furniture — First Class 1, Same Day 2, Second Class 3, Standard Class 4 Office Supplies — First Class 1, Same Day 2, Second Class 3, Standard Class 4 Technology — First Class 1, Same Day 2, Second Class 3, Standard Class 4

Let's consider some of the possibilities presented here in more detail.

Some of the options are identical. In fact, out of the nine options, only four are unique. Let's consider options 1, 4, and 8, each of which have identical end results. Does this mean that each is truly identical? Options 1 and 4 are identical. Option 8, however, is slightly different. To understand this, note the description within the table calculation dialog box for option 4:

[Index]

Index
Results are computed along Ship Mode for each Category.

Results are computed along Ship Mode for each Category can be translated as Partitioning Category and Addressing Ship Mode. This translation is identical to the actual partitioning/addressing setup accomplished in option 1. Furthermore, the text in the description box for option 1 is identical to that for option 4. Therefore, options 1 and 4 are identical. Option 8, however, is slightly different in that the description reads Results are computed along Ship Mode, Category. But does this mean there are practical differences? Personally, I do not know of any.

Option 6 may seem confusing at first. Why has the odd numbering sequence occurred? Because the order in which the dimensions are addressed differs from the order of dimensions on the **Rows** shelf. The addressing order is **Ship Mode, Category**. The order on the **Rows** shelf is Category, Ship Mode. Simply reversing the position of **Category** and **Ship Mode** on the **Rows** shelf and noting the change in the number sequence should help dispel any confusion:

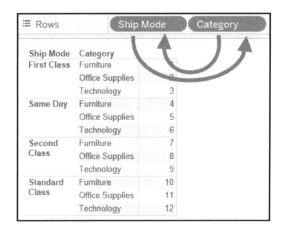

Is there any practical use for option 6? Yes. From time to time, it may be necessary to address dimensions in a different order than they are listed on a shelf. But this is not usually the case. This leads us to our next guideline.

Partitioning/Addressing guideline
When addressing multiple dimensions for a table calculation, the order of addressing will usually reflect the order of dimensions on the **Rows** and/or **Columns** shelves.

Partitioning and addressing with three dimensions

Let's add another dimension to our playground and reorder thing slightly. Place **Category** and **Region** on the **Rows** shelf and **Ship Mode** on the **Columns** shelf. **Index** should remain on the **Text** shelf. Also add two filters. Filter **Region** to **East**, **South**, and **West**. Filter **Ship Mode** to **First Class**, **Second Class**, and **Standard Class**.

When partitioning and addressing three dimensions, the number of possible iterations jumps to 57; however, only 14 of these are unique. Here is a listing of those unique possibilities:

ID	Partitioning	Addressing	At the level	Restarting every	Results
1	Category Region	Ship Mode			<table><tr><td></td><td></td><td colspan="3">Ship Mode</td></tr><tr><td>Category</td><td>Region</td><td>First Class</td><td>Second Class</td><td>Standard Class</td></tr><tr><td>Furniture</td><td>East</td><td>1</td><td>2</td><td>3</td></tr><tr><td></td><td>South</td><td>1</td><td>2</td><td>3</td></tr><tr><td></td><td>West</td><td>1</td><td>2</td><td>3</td></tr><tr><td>Office Supplies</td><td>East</td><td>1</td><td>2</td><td>3</td></tr><tr><td></td><td>South</td><td>1</td><td>2</td><td>3</td></tr><tr><td></td><td>West</td><td>1</td><td>2</td><td>3</td></tr><tr><td>Technology</td><td>East</td><td>1</td><td>2</td><td>3</td></tr><tr><td></td><td>South</td><td>1</td><td>2</td><td>3</td></tr><tr><td></td><td>West</td><td>1</td><td>2</td><td>3</td></tr></table>
2	Category Ship Mode	Region			<table><tr><td></td><td></td><td colspan="3">Ship Mode</td></tr><tr><td>Category</td><td>Region</td><td>First Class</td><td>Second Class</td><td>Standard Class</td></tr><tr><td>Furniture</td><td>East</td><td>1</td><td>1</td><td>1</td></tr><tr><td></td><td>South</td><td>2</td><td>2</td><td>2</td></tr><tr><td></td><td>West</td><td>3</td><td>3</td><td>3</td></tr><tr><td>Office Supplies</td><td>East</td><td>1</td><td>1</td><td>1</td></tr><tr><td></td><td>South</td><td>2</td><td>2</td><td>2</td></tr><tr><td></td><td>West</td><td>3</td><td>3</td><td>3</td></tr><tr><td>Technology</td><td>East</td><td>1</td><td>1</td><td>1</td></tr><tr><td></td><td>South</td><td>2</td><td>2</td><td>2</td></tr><tr><td></td><td>West</td><td>3</td><td>3</td><td>3</td></tr></table>

ID	Partitioning	Addressing	At the level	Restarting every	Results
3	Category	Region Ship Mode			*See sub-table below*
4	Category	Region Ship Mode	Deepest	None	*See sub-table below*
5	Category	Ship Mode Region	Deepest	None	*See sub-table below*

Results for ID 3:

		Ship Mode		
Category	Region	First Class	Second Class	Standard Class
Furniture	East	1	1	1
	South	1	1	1
	West	1	1	1
Office Supplies	East	2	2	2
	South	2	2	2
	West	2	2	2
Technology	East	3	3	3
	South	3	3	3
	West	3	3	3

Results for ID 4:

		Ship Mode		
Category	Region	First Class	Second Class	Standard Class
Furniture	East	1	2	3
	South	4	5	6
	West	7	8	9
Office Supplies	East	1	2	3
	South	4	5	6
	West	7	8	9
Technology	East	1	2	3
	South	4	5	6
	West	7	8	9

Results for ID 5:

		Ship Mode		
Category	Region	First Class	Second Class	Standard Class
Furniture	East	1	4	7
	South	2	5	8
	West	3	6	9
Office Supplies	East	1	4	7
	South	2	5	8
	West	3	6	9
Technology	East	1	4	7
	South	2	5	8
	West	3	6	9

ID	Partitioning	Addressing	At the level	Restarting every	Results
6	Region	Category Ship Mode	Deepest	None	*See table below*
7	Ship Mode	Category Region	Deepest	None	*See table below*
8	Ship Mode	Region Category	Deepest	None	*See table below*

Results for ID 6:

		Ship Mode		
Category	Region	First Class	Second Class	Standard Class
Furniture	East	1	2	3
	South	1	2	3
	West	1	2	3
Office Supplies	East	4	5	6
	South	4	5	6
	West	4	5	6
Technology	East	7	8	9
	South	7	8	9
	West	7	8	9

Results for ID 7:

		Ship Mode		
Category	Region	First Class	Second Class	Standard Class
Furniture	East	1	1	1
	South	2	2	2
	West	3	3	3
Office Supplies	East	4	4	4
	South	5	5	5
	West	6	6	6
Technology	East	7	7	7
	South	8	8	8
	West	9	9	9

Results for ID 8:

		Ship Mode		
Category	Region	First Class	Second Class	Standard Class
Furniture	East	1	1	1
	South	4	4	4
	West	7	7	7
Office Supplies	East	2	2	2
	South	5	5	5
	West	8	8	8
Technology	East	3	3	3
	South	6	6	6
	West	9	9	9

ID	Partitioning	Addressing	At the level	Restarting every	Results
9		Category Ship Mode Region	Deepest	None	See table below
10		Ship Mode Category Region	Deepest	None	See table below
11		Ship Mode Category Region	Category	None	See table below

ID 9 Results

Category	Region	Ship Mode		
		First Class	Second Class	Standard Class
Furniture	East	1	4	7
	South	2	5	8
	West	3	6	9
Office Supplies	East	10	13	16
	South	11	14	17
	West	12	15	18
Technology	East	19	22	25
	South	20	23	26
	West	21	24	27

ID 10 Results

Category	Region	Ship Mode		
		First Class	Second Class	Standard Class
Furniture	East	1	10	19
	South	2	11	20
	West	3	12	21
Office Supplies	East	4	13	22
	South	5	14	23
	West	6	15	24
Technology	East	7	16	25
	South	8	17	26
	West	9	18	27

ID 11 Results

Category	Region	Ship Mode		
		First Class	Second Class	Standard Class
Furniture	East	1	4	7
	South	1	4	7
	West	1	4	7
Office Supplies	East	2	5	8
	South	2	5	8
	West	2	5	8
Technology	East	3	6	9
	South	3	6	9
	West	3	6	9

ID	Partitioning	Addressing	At the level	Restarting every	Results
12		Ship Mode Region Category	Deepest	None	*(see table below)*
13		Ship Mode Region Category	Deepest	Ship Mode	*(see table below)*
14		Region Ship Mode Category	Deepest	None	*(see table below)*

Results for ID 12:

		Ship Mode		
Category	Region	First Class	Second Class	Standard Class
Furniture	East	1	10	19
	South	4	13	22
	West	7	16	25
Office Supplies	East	2	11	20
	South	5	14	23
	West	8	17	26
Technology	East	3	12	21
	South	6	15	24
	West	9	18	27

Results for ID 13:

		Ship Mode		
Category	Region	First Class	Second Class	Standard Class
Furniture	East	1	1	1
	South	4	4	4
	West	7	7	7
Office Supplies	East	2	2	2
	South	5	5	5
	West	8	8	8
Technology	East	3	3	3
	South	6	6	6
	West	9	9	9

Results for ID 14:

		Ship Mode		
Category	Region	First Class	Second Class	Standard Class
Furniture	East	1	4	7
	South	10	13	16
	West	19	22	25
Office Supplies	East	2	5	8
	South	11	14	17
	West	20	23	26
Technology	East	3	6	9
	South	12	15	18
	West	21	24	27

We will not address the various instances of these possibilities. Instead, the reader is encouraged to recreate these 14 possibilities in Tableau in order to solidify their understanding of partitioning and addressing. Even better, consider recreating all 57 possible iterations and working to understand how Tableau is producing each end result. The process may be tedious but the resulting understanding is invaluable.

Summary

In this chapter, we explored the inner workings of table calculations. We began by considering two questions:

- What is the function?
- How is the functions applied?

As we explored these two questions, we surveyed each unique group of table-calculation functions with the exception of the Script_ functions, which will be covered in `Chapter 15`, *Programming Tool Integration*. We also learned how to apply these functions to a view through partitioning and addressing.

In the next chapter, we will explore a new functionality: **level-of-detail (LOD)** calculations. We will discover how LOD calculations can easily accomplish tasks that were previously only possible through complex table calculations. It's important to note, however, that even though LOD calculations can, in some cases, replace table calculations, they by no means replace every instance of table calculations. Table calculations remain an important part of everyday Tableau usage.

Level of Detail Calculations

7

When we talk about **Level of Detail (LOD)** calculations in Tableau, we usually mean three expressions: FIXED, INCLUDE, and EXCLUDE. These three expressions open a world of options by providing the ability to create calculations that target specific levels of granularity. In older versions of Tableau, data granularity for a worksheet was established by the dimensions in a view. If the view contained dimensions for Region, State, and Postal Code but the author wanted to create a City level calculation, the City dimension would need to be included on the view. Furthermore, there was no mechanism for excluding or ignoring a given dimension on a view. Admittedly, the desired results could normally be obtained through some complex and sometimes convoluted use of table calculations, data blends, and so on. Fortunately, LOD calculations greatly simplify these use case scenarios and, in some cases, enable what was previously impossible.

In this chapter, we will discuss the following topics:

- Building playgrounds
- Playground I: FIXED and EXCLUDE
- Playground II: INCLUDE
- Practical application
- Exercise: practical FIXED
- Exercise: practical INCLUDE
- Exercise: practical EXCLUDE

Building playgrounds

Delivering reports as required by one's job duties may lead to a thorough knowledge of a limited set of capabilities; that is, a deep but narrow understanding. It can be difficult to set aside time (and also justify that time to the boss!) to explore capabilities of Tableau that on the surface may seem to have no direct correlation to job duties. Playground environments can help overcome any difficulties and objections, by providing efficient avenues of exploration. In this chapter, we'll build two playground environments to help make the task of deep and broad understanding easier by providing an efficient avenue for exploration and understanding.

Playground I: FIXED and EXCLUDE

The first playground we will build will be for the purpose of exploring two of the three LOD functions: `FIXED` and `EXCLUDE`. We will use a set of parameters and associated calculated fields to efficiently explore how these functions work.

Exercise: exploring Fixed and Exclude and setting up the workbook

Much of the groundwork for this exercise has already been completed in the workbook associated with this chapter. If you do not have ready access to the workbook, you should be able to construct a similar one by referencing the following information.

Inspecting the worksheet and initial setup

We will now look into the initial setup of a worksheet:

1. Navigate to `https://public.tableau.com/profile/marleen.meier` to locate and download the workbook associated with this chapter.
2. Open the workbook associated with this chapter and navigate to the Fixed and Exclude worksheet.

3. Select the Superstore data source and inspect the parameter named 1st Dim. Note the following:
    - Data Type: Integer
    - Allowable Values: List
    - Value and Display As:

Value	Display As	Value	Display As	Value	Display As
1	Category	6	Order ID	11	Segment
2	City	7	Postal Code	12	Ship Mode
3	Country	8	Product ID	13	State
4	Customer ID	9	Product Name	14	Sub-Category
5	Customer Name	10	Region	15	Null

4. The parameters named 2nd Dim, 3rd Dim, and 4th Dim are identical to 1st Dim.

5. Note that except for Order Date and Ship Date, every dimension in the dataset is included in the List of values. For the purposes of this exercise, Category, Region, Segment, Ship Mode, and Sub-Category are particularly important because those are dimensions with fewer members. Dimensions with many members are more difficult to use in this context.

6. Inspect the following parameters included in the workbook and note the Value and Display As values:

Parameter	Value	Display As
Choose Fixed Dims	1	1st
2	2nd	
3	3rd	
4	4th	
5	Fixed: Nothing	
6	0	
Choose Excluded Dims 1	1	1st
2	2nd	
3	3rd	
4	4th	
5	0	
Choose Excluded Dims 2	1	1st
2	1st-2nd	

3	1st-3rd	
4	1st-4th	
5	Exclude nothing	
6	0	

7. Inspect the calculated field named 1st Dim (it is located under the Practical: All folder). The code is as follows:

```
Case [Parameters].[1st Dim] WHEN 1 THEN [Category] WHEN 2 THEN
[City] WHEN 3 THEN [Country] WHEN 4 THEN [Customer ID] WHEN 5 THEN
[Customer Name] WHEN 6 THEN [Order ID] WHEN 7 THEN STR([Postal
Code]) WHEN 8 THEN [Product ID] WHEN 9 THEN [Product Name] WHEN 10
THEN [Region] WHEN 11 THEN [Segment] WHEN 12 THEN [Ship Mode] WHEN
13 THEN [State] WHEN 14 THEN [Sub-Category] WHEN 15 THEN "" END
```

8. The calculated fields named 2nd Dim, 3rd Dim, and 4th Dim are identical to 1st Dim except that each references the parameter bearing its name; for example, the 2nd Dim calculated field utilizes [Parameters].[2nd Dim].

9. These Case statements, in conjunction with the associated parameters, allow the author to choose which dimensions to view from a dropdown in the view.

10. Inspect the following calculated fields, which enable the author to choose which LOD calculations to employ and thus to compare and contrast differences and similarities:

   • Case Fixed:

```
CASE [Choose Fixed Dims]
WHEN 1 THEN SUM({FIXED [1st Dim]: SUM([Sales])})
WHEN 2 THEN SUM({FIXED [2nd Dim]: SUM([Sales])})
WHEN 3 THEN SUM({FIXED [3rd Dim]: SUM([Sales])})
WHEN 4 THEN SUM({FIXED [4th Dim]: SUM([Sales])})
WHEN 5 THEN SUM({FIXED : SUM([Sales])})
WHEN 6 THEN 0
END
```

- Case Exclude 1:

```
CASE [Choose Excluded Dims 1]
WHEN 1 THEN SUM({EXCLUDE [1st Dim]: SUM([Sales])})
WHEN 2 THEN SUM({EXCLUDE [2nd Dim] : SUM([Sales])})
WHEN 3 THEN SUM({EXCLUDE [3rd Dim] : SUM([Sales])})
WHEN 4 THEN SUM({EXCLUDE [4th Dim]: SUM([Sales])})
WHEN 5 THEN 0
END
```

- Case Exclude 2:

```
CASE [Choose Fixed Dims]
WHEN 1 THEN SUM({EXCLUDE [1st Dim]: SUM([Sales])})
WHEN 2 THEN SUM({EXCLUDE [1st Dim],[2nd Dim] : SUM([Sales])})
WHEN 3 THEN SUM({EXCLUDE [1st Dim],[2nd Dim],[3rd Dim] :
SUM([Sales])})
WHEN 4 THEN SUM({EXCLUDE [1st Dim],[2nd Dim],[3rd Dim], [4th
Dim]: SUM([Sales])})
WHEN 5 THEN SUM({EXCLUDE : SUM([Sales])})
WHEN 6 THEN 0
END
```

11. Note the context filter on Product Name.
12. Open the filter for inspection.
13. In the resulting dialog box, click the **Wildcard** tab and note the settings as shown in the following screenshot.

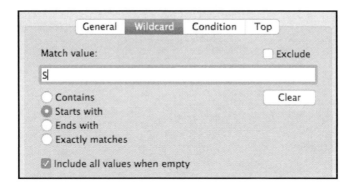

14. After clicking OK, right-click on the filter and note that it is a context filter. As you can see, context filters are denoted in gray:

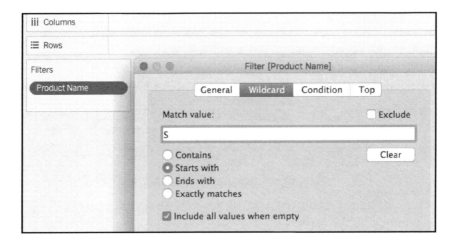

15. Place the following dimensions on the **Rows** shelf: 1st Dim, 2nd Dim, 3rd Dim, and 4th Dim.

16. Double-click on Measure Names. Remove measures from the **Measure Values** shelf until only the following displays:

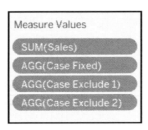

17. Display each parameter by right-clicking **Show Parameter Control**. Order the parameter controls as follows:
    - 1st Dim
    - 2nd Dim
    - 3rd Dim
    - 4th Dim
    - Choose Fixed Dims
    - Choose Excluded Dims 1
    - Choose Excluded Dims 2

Understanding FIXED

Now that the playground environment is complete, let's build scenarios to better understand FIXED and EXCLUDE. We'll begin with FIXED:

1. Using the worksheet described previously, set the following parameters as shown here:

Parameter	Setting
1st Dim	Region
2nd Dim	Category
3rd Dim	Null
4th Dim	Null
Choose Fixed Dims	2nd
Choose Exclude Dims 1	0
Choose Exclude Dims 2	0

2. Observe that the **Case Fixed** column displays the totals for each Category and ignores region:

1st Dim	2nd Dim	Sales	Case Fixed
Central	Furniture	$10,072	47,379
	Office Supplies	$16,340	70,596
	Technology	$13,995	76,801
East	Furniture	$14,249	47,379
	Office Supplies	$21,560	70,596
	Technology	$20,646	76,801
South	Furniture	$4,494	47,379
	Office Supplies	$8,721	70,596
	Technology	$17,451	76,801
West	Furniture	$18,564	47,379
	Office Supplies	$23,975	70,596
	Technology	$24,710	76,801

3. Change the Choose Fixed Dims parameter to 1st and note that **Case Fixed** now displays the totals for each region:

1st Dim	2nd Dim	Sales	Case Fixed
Central	Furniture	$10,072	40,406
	Office Supplies	$16,340	40,406
	Technology	$13,995	40,406
East	Furniture	$14,249	56,455
	Office Supplies	$21,560	56,455
	Technology	$20,646	56,455
South	Furniture	$4,494	30,666
	Office Supplies	$8,721	30,666
	Technology	$17,451	30,666
West	Furniture	$18,564	67,249
	Office Supplies	$23,975	67,249
	Technology	$24,710	67,249

4. Change the Choose Fixed Dims parameter to Fixed: Nothing and note that the amount reflects the total allowed by the context filter:

1st Dim	2nd Dim	Sales	Case Fixed
Central	Furniture	$10,072	194,776
	Office Supplies	$16,340	194,776
	Technology	$13,995	194,776
East	Furniture	$14,249	194,776
	Office Supplies	$21,560	194,776
	Technology	$20,646	194,776
South	Furniture	$4,494	194,776
	Office Supplies	$8,721	194,776
	Technology	$17,451	194,776
West	Furniture	$18,564	194,776
	Office Supplies	$23,975	194,776
	Technology	$24,710	194,776

As is evident, the Fixed LOD considers only the dimensions to which it is directed. Thus, when fixed on Category, Region is ignored. And, as demonstrated, when fixed on Region, Category is ignored. Lastly, when Choose Fixed Dims is set to Fixed: Nothing, the entire dataset that is not restricted by the context filter on Product Name is displayed.

Understanding EXCLUDE

Let us start understanding the EXCLUDE LOD:

1. Set the parameters as shown in the following table:

Parameter	Setting
1st Dim	Region
2nd Dim	Category
3rd Dim	Segment
4th Dim	Null
Choose Fixed Dims	0
Choose Exclude Dims 1	1st
Choose Exclude Dims 2	0

2. You can observe the following results:

1st Dim	2nd Dim	3rd Dim	Sales	Case Exclude 1
Central	Furniture	Consumer	$5,444	26,738
		Corporate	$2,779	13,050
		Home Office	$1,849	7,592
	Office Supplies	Consumer	$9,085	31,861
		Corporate	$3,462	24,179
		Home Office	$3,793	14,556
	Technology	Consumer	$5,144	39,955
		Corporate	$3,848	23,766
		Home Office	$5,003	13,081
East	Furniture	Consumer	$6,941	26,738
		Corporate	$4,415	13,050
		Home Office	$2,893	7,592
	Office Supplies	Consumer	$11,361	31,861
		Corporate	$7,217	24,179

3. Case Exclude 1 displays the total of each Category and Segment and ignores Region. For example, the total of the Segment Consumer within the Category Furniture is $26,738. That total is repeated for each Region. The relevant code that is generating these results is

```
SUM({EXCLUDE [Region] : SUM([Sales])}).
```

4. Make the following changes to the parameters:

Parameter	Setting
Choose Fixed Dims	3rd
Choose Exclude Dims 1	1st
Choose Exclude Dims 2	1st-2nd

5. You can observe the results in the following screenshot:

1st Dim	2nd Dim	3rd Dim	Sales	Case Fixed	Case Exclude 1	Case Exclude 2
Central	Furniture	Consum..	$5,444	98,554	26,738	98,554
		Corpora..	$2,779	60,994	13,050	60,994
		Home O..	$1,849	35,228	7,592	35,228
	Office Supplies	Consum..	$9,085	98,554	31,861	98,554
		Corpora..	$3,462	60,994	24,179	60,994
		Home O..	$3,793	35,228	14,556	35,228
	Technol..	Consum..	$5,144	98,554	39,955	98,554
		Corpora..	$3,848	60,994	23,766	60,994
		Home O..	$5,003	35,228	13,081	35,228
East	Furniture	Consum..	$6,941	98,554	26,738	98,554

6. LOD calculations may be used to consider multiple dimensions in a view. In this case, Case Exclude Dims 2 ignores 1st Dim and 2nd Dim, which are associated with Region and Category. The associated code is therefore `SUM({EXCLUDE [Region],[Category] : SUM([Sales])})`. Note that **Case Exclude 2** and **Case Fixed** have identical results. This is because, in this case, excluding the first two dimensions is the same as fixing on the third dimension.

7. Make the following changes to the parameters.

Parameter	Setting
4th Dim	Ship Mode

8. You can observe the results in the following table:

1st Dim	2nd Dim	3rd Dim	4th Dim	Sales	Case Fixed	Case Exclude 1	Case Exclude 2
Central	Furniture	Consumer	First Class	$740	98,554	2,961	8,843
			Second Class	$313	98,554	6,493	24,765
			Standard Class	$4,391	98,554	17,147	62,011
		Corporate	First Class	$164	60,994	779	10,622
			Second Class	$801	60,994	3,139	8,818
			Standard Class	$1,813	60,994	8,934	38,997
		Home Office	First Class	$746	35,228	1,202	3,121
			Same Day	$106	35,228	517	2,616
			Second Class	$24	35,228	2,286	6,953
			Standard Class	$973	35,228	3,586	22,537
	Office Supplies	Consumer	First Class	$251	98,554	1,854	8,843
			Same Day	$160	98,554	2,165	2,935

9. Note that **Case Exclude 2** and **Case Fixed** no longer have identical results. This is because Ship Mode was introduced and **Case Exclude 2** considers Ship Mode whereas **Case Fixed** does not.

10. Experiment with other settings to further enhance your understanding of the Fixed and Exclude LODs.

Understanding order of filtering

Let's have a look at the order of filtering.

1. Set the parameters as shown in the following table:

Parameter	Setting
1st Dim	Region
2nd Dim	Category
3rd Dim	Segment
4th Dim	Null
Choose Fixed Dims	3rd
Choose Exclude Dims 1	1st
Choose Exclude Dims 2	1st-2nd

2. Observe the results.

1st Dim	2nd Dim	3rd Dim	Sales	Case Fixed	Case Exclude 1	Case Exclude 2
Central	Furniture	Consumer	$5,444	98,554	26,738	98,554
		Corporate	$2,779	60,994	13,050	60,994
		Home Office	$1,849	35,228	7,592	35,228
	Office Supplies	Consumer	$9,085	98,554	31,861	98,554
		Corporate	$3,462	60,994	24,179	60,994
		Home Office	$3,793	35,228	14,556	35,228
	Technology	Consumer	$5,144	98,554	39,955	98,554
		Corporate	$3,848	60,994	23,766	60,994
		Home Office	$5,003	35,228	13,081	35,228
East	Furniture	Consumer	$6,941	98,554	26,738	98,554
		Corporate	$4,415	60,994	13,050	60,994
		Home Office	$2,893	35,228	7,592	35,228
	Office	Consumer	$11.361	98.554	31,861	98.554

3. Note that, as seen in the previous exercise, **Case Exclude 2** and **Case Fixed** are identical.

4. Right-click on the Product Name filter and select **Remove from Context**:

5. Observe the results in the following screenshot:

1st Dim	2nd Dim	3rd Dim	Sales	Case Fixed	Case Exclude 1	Case Exclude 2
Central	Furniture	Consumer	$5,444	1,161,401	26,738	98,554
		Corporate	$2,779	706,146	13,050	60,994
		Home Office	$1,849	429,653	7,592	35,228
	Office Supplies	Consumer	$9,085	1,161,401	31,861	98,554
		Corporate	$3,462	706,146	24,179	60,994
		Home Office	$3,793	429,653	14,556	35,228
	Technology	Consumer	$5,144	1,161,401	39,955	98,554
		Corporate	$3,848	706,146	23,766	60,994
		Home Office	$5,003	429,653	13,081	35,228
East	Furniture	Consumer	$6,941	1,161,401	26,738	98,554
		Corporate	$4,415	706,146	13,050	60,994
		Home Office	$2,893	429,653	7,592	35,228
	Office	Consumer	$11.361	1.161.401	31.861	98.554

6. **Case Exclude 2** and **Case Fixed** are no longer identical. **Case Fixed** is no longer impacted by the Product Name filter because the context was removed.

Exercise: commentary

The behavior difference observed between **EXCLUDE** and FIXED in the preceding exercise reflects the underlying filter order of operation. As shown in the following screenshot, **Context Filters** will impact Fixed, Exclude, and Include. Dimension Filters, however, will only impact Exclude and Include.

Please see following diagram, a schematic representation of order of operations in Tableau:

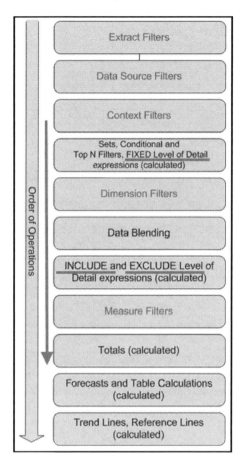

 You can find more information here: `https://onlinehelp.tableau.com/ current/pro/desktop/en-us/order_of_operations.htm`.

Playground II: INCLUDE

The second playground we will build will be for the purpose of exploring INCLUDE. Like in Playground I, we'll start with setting up the workbook for effective exploration. If you do not have ready access to the workbook, you should be able to construct a similar one by referencing the following information.

Inspecting the worksheet and initial setup

Following, we will setup a worksheet with which we can practice the INCLUDE Level of detail calculations.

1. Open the workbook associated with this chapter and navigate to the Exploring Include worksheet.

2. The parameters and calculated fields named 1st Dim, 2nd Dim, 3rd Dim, and 4th Dim created in the previous exercises are also utilized for this worksheet.

3. Right-click on the 1st Dim parameter and choose Duplicate.

4. Rename the duplicate Choose Included Dims.

5. Create a new calculated field named Case Include with the following code:

```
CASE [Choose Included Dims]
WHEN 1 THEN AVG({INCLUDE [Category]: SUM([Sales])})
WHEN 2 THEN AVG({INCLUDE [City]: SUM([Sales])})
WHEN 3 THEN AVG({INCLUDE [Country]: SUM([Sales])})
WHEN 4 THEN AVG({INCLUDE [Customer ID]: SUM([Sales])})
WHEN 5 THEN AVG({INCLUDE [Customer Name]: SUM([Sales])})
WHEN 6 THEN AVG({INCLUDE [Order ID]: SUM([Sales])})
WHEN 7 THEN AVG({INCLUDE [Postal Code]: SUM([Sales])})
WHEN 8 THEN AVG({INCLUDE [Product ID]: SUM([Sales])})
WHEN 9 THEN AVG({INCLUDE [Product Name]: SUM([Sales])})
WHEN 10 THEN AVG({INCLUDE [Region]: SUM([Sales])})
WHEN 11 THEN AVG({INCLUDE [Segment]: SUM([Sales])})
WHEN 12 THEN AVG({INCLUDE [Ship Mode]: SUM([Sales])})
WHEN 13 THEN AVG({INCLUDE [State]: SUM([Sales])})
WHEN 14 THEN AVG({INCLUDE [Sub-Category]: SUM([Sales])})
WHEN 15 THEN 0
END
```

6. Place the following measures and dimensions in their respective shelves, as seen in the following table:

Field(s)	Shelf
Case Include	Detail
Sum(Sales)	Columns
1st Dim, 2nd Dim, 3rd Dim, 4th Dim	Rows

7. Display each of the following parameters by right-clicking **Show Parameter Control**:

1st Dim
2nd Dim
3rd Dim
4th Dim
Choose Included Dims

Exercise steps: exploring INCLUDE

Now that the playground environment is complete, let's build scenarios to better understand INCLUDE:

1. Set the parameters as shown here:

Parameter	Setting
1st Dim	Region
2nd Dim	Null
3rd Dim	Null
4th Dim	Null
Choose Included Dims	Region

2. Add two reference lines with the following settings:

	Scope	Value	Label
Reference Line 1	Entire Table	SUM(Sales) and Average	Custom, Overall Avg: <Value>
Reference Line 2	Entire Table	AGG(Case Include)	Custom, Include Dim Avg: <Value>

Let us look at the following screenshot for more details:

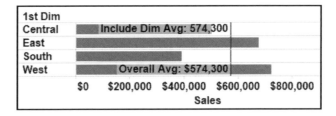

3. Note that both reference lines are equal.

4. If the reference lines are overlapping each other, edit the formatting and set the Alignment to Top. To access the formatting, click on the **Reference Line** in the view:

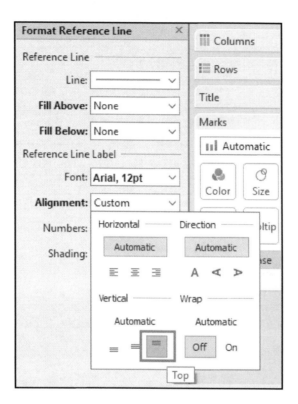

5. Set the parameters as shown here:

Parameter	Setting
1st Dim	Region
2nd Dim	Category
3rd Dim	Ship Mode
4th Dim	Segment
Choose Included Dims	Region

In Tableau Desktop, you should see the following now:

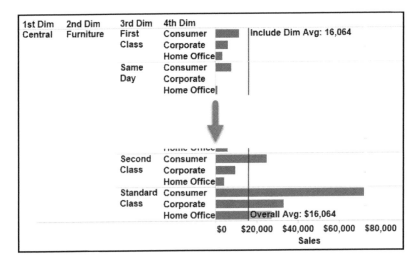

6. As before, both reference lines are equal.

7. Change the Choose Included Dims parameter to Category, Ship Mode, and Segment, respectively.

8. Note that the reference lines equal one another for each of these settings. This is because Choose Included Dims is only introducing dimensions already represented in the view.

9. Change the Choose Included Dims parameter to Sub-Category:

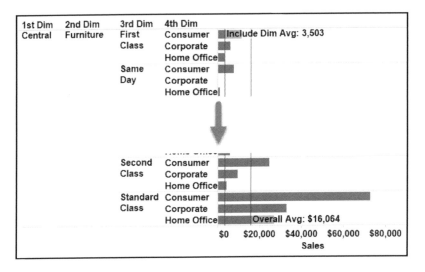

Note: The **Include Dim Avg** reference line now includes Sub-Category in the average and so differs from the **Overall Avg** reference line. Furthermore, note that the Sub-Category dimension is not used in the view. LOD calculations do not require a calculation to reside in the view.

Practical application

The first portion of this chapter was designed to demonstrate how LOD calculations work. The remainder will be dedicated to practical applications. Specifically, we will consider three typical challenges that previously were solved using other Tableau capabilities, such as table calculations and data blending.

Exercise: practical FIXED

This exercise will look at a problem that occurs when mixing a table calculation that calculates the percentage of the total with a dimension filter. We will consider the problem, a workaround used in previous versions of Tableau, and a solution using an LOD calculation. After covering these three options, a commentary section will discuss the germane points of each.

Exercise steps: practical FIXED – the problem

The following steps will guide you through the exercise:

1. Open the workbook associated with this chapter and navigate to the worksheet entitled The Problem.
2. Select the 2012_World_Pop dataset.
3. Create a calculated field named **Percent of Total** with the following code:

```
SUM([Population]) / TOTAL(SUM([Population]))
```

4. Right-click on Percent of Total and select **Default Properties** > **Number Format** > **Percentage**.

5. Place **Country** on the **Columns** shelf, **Measure Names** on the **Rows** shelf, and Measure Vales on the **Text** Shelf.

6. Remove Number of Records from the **Measure Values** shelf.

7. Right-click on **Percent of Total** and set to **Compute Using** > **Country**.

8. Create a filter on **Country** such that only **Afghanistan** displays:

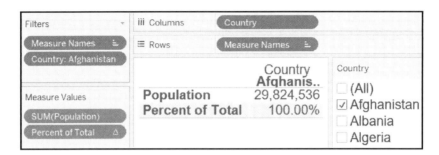

Afghanistan displays a percentage of the total of 100%. Obviously, this does not represent Afghanistan's percentage of the total population of the world.

Exercise steps: practical FIXED – table calc solution

Follow along the exercise steps:

1. Duplicate the previous worksheet (the one named The Problem) and entitle it Solution: Table Calc.

2. Create a calculated field named Country – Table Calc Filter with the following code:

```
LOOKUP( MAX( [Country] ),0 )
```

3. Remove **Country** from the **Filter** shelf.

4. Create a filter on Country – Table Calc Filter and display only **Afghanistan**.

5. Note that **Afghanistan** displays a percent of the total of **0.43%**:

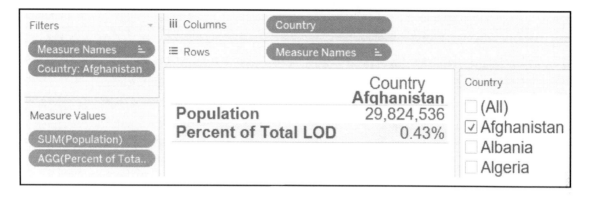

Exercise steps: practical FIXED – LOD solution

Follow along the exercise steps:

1. Duplicate the worksheet entitled The Problem and rename it Solution LOD.
2. Create a calculated field named **Percent of Total LOD** with the following code:

```
SUM([Population])/SUM({ FIXED : SUM([Population])})
```

3. Place **Percent of Total LOD** on the **Measure Values** shelf and note that the displayed percentage equals 0.43%. If 0 displays, change the number formatting to percentage.
4. Remove the **Percent of Total** table calculation that was previously created from the **Measure Values** shelf:

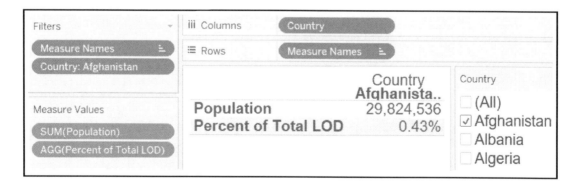

Exercise: commentary

Assuming an SQL data source, let's look at a query that Tableau generates for the worksheet entitled The Problem. Generated queries can be viewed By **Help** > **Settings and Performance** > **Start Performance Recording**. (See Chapter 11, *Visualization Best Practices and Dashboard Design*, for additional information regarding viewing Tableau generated queries).

The SQL statement is as follows:

```
SELECT ['2012_World_Pop$'].[Country] AS [Country],
SUM(['2012_World_Pop$'].[Population]) AS [sum:Population:ok] FROM
[dbo].['2012_World_Pop$'] ['2012_World_Pop$'] WHERE
(['2012_World_Pop$'].[Country] = 'Afghanistan') GROUP BY
['2012_World_Pop$'].[Country]]
```

Note that the WHERE clause in the query is limiting the returned dataset to only those rows that have 'Afghanistan' as Country. This WHERE clause was generated as a result of placing Country on the filters shelf. By limiting the returned data, the processing requirements are shifted from Tableau to the underlying data source engine. In other words, the data source engine does the work of executing the query, and Tableau thus works with a smaller dataset. The reasoning behind this design is that data source engines are specifically engineered to efficiently query large datasets and also typically have underlying hardware to support such activities. Furthermore, limiting the rows of data returned to Tableau can reduce inefficiencies due to latency.

Inefficiencies are further reduced because Tableau works from cache whenever possible. Often a user can perform various operations without generating a call to the underlying data source. However, in the preceding case, if a user were to select a different country from the filter, Tableau would generate a new query to the data source. For example, if a user interacts with the filter and deselects 'Afghanistan' and selects 'Albania', a new query with a corresponding WHERE clause is generated.

Although the logic of Tableau's reliance on the data source engine is demonstrable, the problem proposed in the preceding example still remains. What can a Tableau author do to calculate the percent of the whole regardless of filtering? Prior to Tableau 9.0, a common solution was to create a table calculation like we did for the Solution: Table Calc worksheet. The code, LOOKUP (MAX ([Country]), 0), simply references each country in the underlying dataset and can thus be used to display the list of countries. It can also be used as a filter. The difference is that, unlike in the previous worksheet (The Problem), the query generated by Tableau to the data source returns the entire dataset.

We can see this in the underlying SQL:

```
SELECT ['2012_World_Pop$'].[Country] AS [Country],
MIN(['2012_World_Pop$'].[Country]) AS [TEMP(TC_)(1470307846)(0)],
SUM(['2012_World_Pop$'].[Population]) AS [TEMP(TC_)(616435453)(0)]
FROM [dbo].['2012_World_Pop$'] ['2012_World_Pop$']
GROUP BY ['2012_World_Pop$'].[Country]
```

The preceding query does not include a WHERE clause. No filtering occurs at the data source. When a table calculation is used in a filter, the filtering does not take place until the underlying data is returned. In other words, Tableau performs the filtering. This preserves percent of total percentages regardless of which country population totals the user chooses to view.

A potential issue with this table calculation solution is that the returned dataset may be quite large, which may cause performance challenges. Latency may be experienced due to increased time required to return a large dataset and Tableau may perform more slowly because of additional processing responsibilities to filter the dataset. An LOD calculation can address these challenges. Let's take a look at the SQL queries created by the Percent of Total LOD calculated field in the Solution: LOD worksheet:

```
SELECT [t0].[Country] AS [Country], [t1].[__measure__0] AS
[TEMP(Calculation_418553293854285824)(2417030171)(0)],
[t0].[TEMP(Calculation_418553293854285824)(616435453)(0)] AS
[TEMP(Calculation_418553293854285824)(616435453)(0)] FROM ( SELECT
['2012_World_Pop$'].[Country] AS [Country],
SUM(['2012_World_Pop$'].[Population]) AS
[TEMP(Calculation_418553293854285824)(616435453)(0)] FROM
[dbo].['2012_World_Pop$'] ['2012_World_Pop$'] WHERE
(['2012_World_Pop$'].[Country] = 'Afghanistan') GROUP BY
['2012_World_Pop$'].[Country] ) [t0] CROSS JOIN ( SELECT
SUM(['2012_World_Pop$'].[Population]) AS [__measure__0] FROM
[dbo].['2012_World_Pop$'] ['2012_World_Pop$'] GROUP BY () ) [t1]
```

Note CROSS JOIN; the LOD calculation generates a query that instructs the underlying data source engine to return data in such a way as to allow Tableau to divide the population values of one or more countries by the world population total thus returning the correct percentage of total.

Exercise: practical INCLUDE

In this exercise, we will create a worksheet that displays the following:

- Total sales per region
- The average of total sales across all regions
- The average of total sales across all states in each region

Using an LOD calculation to display these values is pretty straightforward. Prior to 9.0, however, such a worksheet could be rather convoluted. Let's explore.

Exercise steps part I – solving using an LOD calculation

Follow along the exercise steps:

1. Select the Practical Include worksheet.
2. Select the Superstore dataset.
3. Create a calculated field named Per State INCLUDE with the following code:

```
{INCLUDE [State]:SUM([Sales])}
```

4. Drag Region to the **Columns** shelf, **SUM(Sales)** to the **Rows** shelf, and AVG(Per State INCLUDE) to the **Details** shelf. Be sure to change Per State INCLUDE to an average aggregation.
5. Add two reference lines by right-clicking on the sales axis and selecting Add Reference Line. Use the following settings:

	Scope	Value	Label
Reference Line 1	Per Pane	SUM(Sales) and Average	Custom: Avg per Region: <Value>
Reference Line 2	Per Cell	AVG(Per State INCLUDE) and Average	Custom: Avg Per State: <Value>

6. Complete the worksheet by formatting as desired.

Exercise steps part II – solving without an LOD calculation

Follow along the exercise steps:

1. In a new worksheet, create a calculated field named **Window_AVG** with the following code:

```
WINDOW_AVG(SUM([Sales]))
```

2. Place Region on the **Columns** shelf, Sales on the **Rows** shelf, and Window Avg on the **Rows** shelf.
3. Select the Window Avg pane in the Marks View Card and add State to the **Detail** shelf.

4. Right-click on Window Avg and select **Compute Using** > **State**.
5. Select the Window Avg pane in the **Marks View** card and select Gantt Bar as the view type:

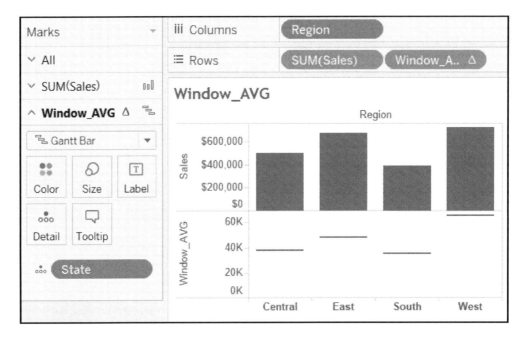

6. Adjust the color of the Gantt Bar to contrast with the bar chart associated with **SUM(Sales)**.
7. Right-click on the Window Avg pill in the **Rows** shelf and select Dual Axis.
8. Select the **SUM(Sales)** pane in the **Marks View** card and select Bar Chart as the view type.
9. Right-click on the Window Avg axis and select Synchronize Axis.
10. Right-click on the Windows Avg axis and deselect Show Header.
11. Add a reference line by right-clicking on the Sales axis and selecting Add Reference Line. Use the following settings:

Scope	Value	Label
Per Pane	SUM(Sales) and Average	Custom: Avg per Region: <Value>

12. Complete the worksheet by formatting as desired:

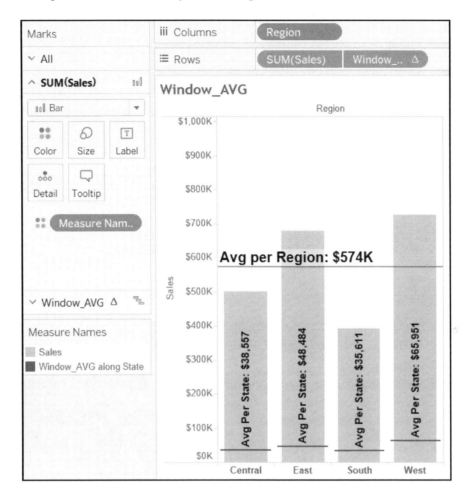

Exercise: commentary

Part 1 of this exercise is mostly self-explanatory. The one point to stress is that the INCLUDE statement does not require State to be in the view. State is simply declared within the calculation.

Part 2 of the exercise is more complicated and less intuitive, and requires many more steps. The key thing to note is that the State dimension has to be on the view in order to be referenced to correctly calculate the average of each state per region. That's the nature of table calculations. In order to use 'Compute Using' for any given dimension, that dimension must be in the view.

Exercise: practical EXCLUDE

In this exercise, we will create two worksheets using the Superstore dataset. Each will calculate the percentage of sales generated by each city in a region. In the first solution, we will use LOD calculations. In the second solution, we will use a data blend.

Exercise steps part I: solving using an LOD calculation

Follow along the exercise steps:

1. Select the Practical Exclude worksheet.
2. Select the Superstore dataset.
3. Create the following calculated fields:

Region Values	% Per Region LOD
`{ EXCLUDE [City],[State]:ZN( SUM([Sales]) ) }`	`SUM([Sales])/SUM( [Region Values] )`

4. Place Region and City on the **Rows** shelf.
5. Place Measure Names on the **Columns** shelf and Measure Values on the **Text** shelf.

6. Remove all instances of measures from the **Measure Values** shelf except **Sales**, **Region Values**, and % Per Region LOD.

7. In order for % Per Region LOD to display as a percentage, the number formatting must be adjusted. Simply right-click on the calculation in the **Data** pane and select **Default Properties** > **Number Format** > **Percentage**.

8. Place an instance of SUM(% Per Region LOD) on the **Filter** shelf and adjust to display **At Least** 10%:

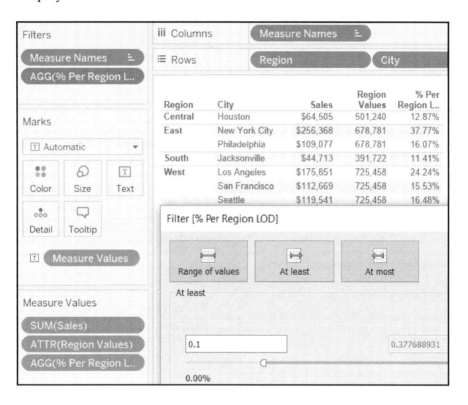

9. Place State on the **Rows** shelf between **Region** and **City**. Note that **Jacksonville** disappears:

Region	City	Sales	Region Values	% Per Region LOD
Central	Houston	$64,505	501,240	12.87%
East	New York City	$256,368	678,781	37.77%
	Philadelphia	$109,077	678,781	16.07%
South	Jacksonville	$44,713	391,722	11.41%
West	Los Angeles	$175,851	725,458	24.24%
	San Francisco	$112,669	725,458	15.53%
	Seattle	$119,541	725,458	16.48%

Region	State	City	Sales	Region Values	% Per Region L..
Central	Texas	Houston	$64,505	501,240	12.87%
East	New York	New York ..	$256,368	678,781	37.77%
	Pennsylvan..	Philadelphia	$109,077	678,781	16.07%
West	California	Los Angeles	$175,851	725,458	24.24%
		San Franci..	$112,669	725,458	15.53%
	Washington	Seattle	$119,541	725,458	16.48%

10. Right-click on **State** in the **Rows** shelf and deselect Show Header:

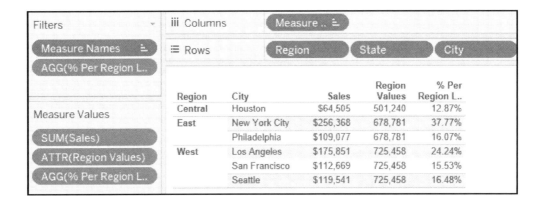

Exercise steps part II: solving using blending

Follow along the exercise steps:

1. Create a new worksheet.
2. Place Region and City on the **Rows** shelf.
3. Place Measure Names on the **Columns** shelf and Measure Values on the **Text** shelf.
4. Remove all instances of measures except Sales, City Values, and Region Values.
5. Right-click on the **Superstore** dataset and **Duplicate**:

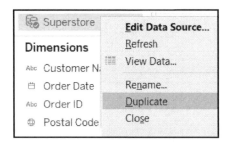

6. Name the duplicated data source **Superstore** Blend.
7. Select Superstore Blend and link on **Region**. Ensure that no other fields are linked:

8. Double-click on Sales in the Superstore Blend data source to place Sales in the view.
9. Alternately link on **Region**, State, and City and observe changes. Make sure that Region is the only option selected when you're done.
10. In the primary data source (Superstore), create a calculated field named % Blend:

```
SUM([Sales])/SUM([Superstore Blend].[Sales])
```

11. Place % Blend on the **Measure Values** shelf and adjust the formatting to display the percentage.
12. Place an instance of % Blend on the **Filter** shelf and adjust to display At Least 10%.
13. Remove City Values and Region Values from the **Measure Values** shelf.
14. Rename the instance of Sales from the secondary data source to Sales by Region.
15. Note that Jacksonville is displaying. It should not because there are actually two different cities named Jacksonville in the South Region.
16. From the primary data source, place State between Region and City on the **Rows** shelf.
17. If the view expands to include more cities, check the secondary data source to insure that the blend is only on Region.
18. Right-click on State in the **Rows** shelf and deselect **Show Header**.

Exercise: commentary

The first part of this exercise utilized an LOD calculation to arrive at a fairly simple solution. The only tricky part was catching the fact that two cities named Jacksonville exist in the South Region. The blended solution also worked fairly well although it took more steps. So, which solution is better? The LOD solution wins out because it will likely perform better. Any solution that requires a data blend necessitates querying another data source and then blending the results from the two data sources, which impacts performance.

Summary

We began this chapter exploring why LOD calculations are so impactful and why their inclusion in Tableau was so lauded. Next, we built a couple of playgrounds to explore how the three LOD calculations – FIXED, EXCLUDE, and INCLUDE – work. Finally, we covered three common scenarios that might utilize LOD calculations and explored alternative solutions using table calculations and data blending.

In the next chapter, we'll turn our attention to the visual side of Tableau and explore chart types that go beyond the out-of-the-box possibilities provided by Tableau.

2
Section 2: Advanced Calculations, Mapping, Visualizations

Part 2 of this book will cover advanced calculations, mappings, and visual design.

The following chapters are in this section:

- Chapter 8, *Beyond the Basic Chart Types*
- Chapter 9, *Mapping*
- Chapter 10, *Tableau for Presentations*
- Chapter 11, *Visualization Best Practices and Dashboard Design*
- Chapter 12, *Advanced Analytics*
- Chapter 13, *Improving Performance*

Beyond the Basic Chart Types

8

The assumption behind this chapter is that the reader is familiar with basic chart types such as bar, line graph, treemap, pie, and area. The focus will be on the middle ground, with the intent of relating how to improve visualization types you may already use on a regular basis, as well as introducing chart types with which you may be unfamiliar, but which are, nonetheless, widely useful. And, finally, I will introduce you to Tableau extensions, which offer some more exotic chart types.

Perhaps the most useful part of this chapter is actually not contained in the book at all, but rather in the workbook associated with the chapter. Be sure to download that workbook (the link is provided in the following section) to check out a wider range of visualization types.

This chapter will explore the following visualization types and topics:

- Improving popular visualizations
- Custom background images
- Tableau extensions

Improving popular visualizations

Most popular visualizations are popular for good reasons. Basic bar charts and line graphs are familiar, intuitive, and flexible and are thus widely used in data visualization. Other less basic visualizations such as bullet graphs and Pareto charts may not be something you use every day but are nonetheless useful additions to the data analyst's toolbox. In this section, we will explore ideas for how to tweak, extend, and even overhaul a few popular chart types.

Bullet graphs

The **bullet graph** was invented by *Stephen Few* and communicated publicly in 2006 through his book *Information Dashboard Design: The Effective Visual Communication of Data*. Stephen Few continues to be a strong voice in the data visualization space through his books and his blog, www.perceptualedge.com. Bullet graphs communicate efficiently and intuitively by packing a lot of information into a small space while remaining attractive and easy to read. Understandably, they have gained much popularity and are being utilized for many purposes, as can be readily seen through a web search. The following two exercises communicate the basics of bullet graphs and how to improve on those basics. That is not to say that I have improved on the bullet graph in this chapter! The intent is merely to relay how this important visualization type can be more effectively used in Tableau.

Exercise steps for the bullet graph: the basics

The following are the steps:

1. Navigate to https://public.tableau.com/profile/marleen.meier to locate and download the workbook associated with this chapter.
2. Navigate to the worksheet entitled **Bullet Graph** and select the **CoffeeChain** data source.
3. Place these fields on their respective shelves:

Field	Shelf
Profit	Columns
Market	Rows
Budget Profit	Detail

4. Right-click on the axis and select **Add Reference Line**.
5. Within the upper left-hand corner of the **Edit Reference Line, Band or Box** dialog box, select **Line**. Also, set **Scope** to **Per Cell**, **Value** to **SUM(Budget Profit)**, and **Label** to **None**. Click **OK**:

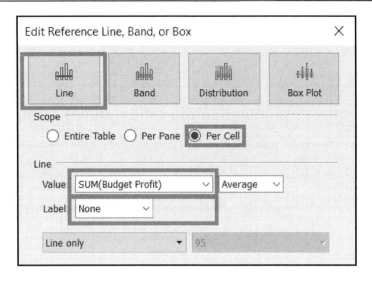

6. Once again, right-click on the axis and select **Add Reference Line**.
7. Within the dialog box, select **Distribution** and set the **Scope** to **Per Cell**.
8. Under **Computation**, set the **Value** to **Percentages** with 90, 95, 100 and **Percent of:** to **SUM(Budget Profit)** (as shown in the following screenshot).
9. Set **Label** to **None**:

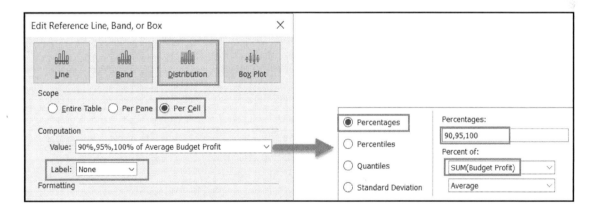

10. Create the following calculated fields:

Name	Code
Profit to Budget Profit Ratio	SUM([Profit])/SUM([Budget Profit])
Quota Met?	SUM([Profit])>=SUM([Budget Profit])

11. Right-click on **Profit to Budget Profit Ratio** and select **Default Properties** > **Number Format** > **Percentage**.

12. Place **AGG(Profit to Budget Profit Ratio)** on the **Label** shelf and **AGG(Quota Met?)** on the **Color** shelf:

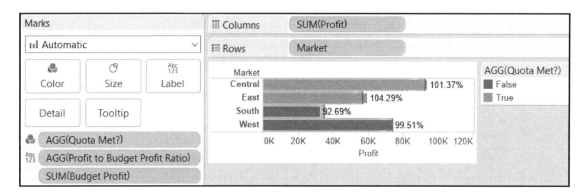

As you survey our results thus far, you will notice that there are positive aspects to this visualization. For example, the reference lines and the colored bars clearly delineate when a quota was met and missed. Furthermore, the percentages communicate how close the actual profit was to the budgeted profit for each market. However, there are also some problems to address:

1. The percentage associated with the South market is partially obscured.
2. The background colors represented by the reference distribution are obscured.
3. The colors of the bars are not intuitive. Orange is set to True, which signifies, in this case, the markets that made the quota. However, psychologically speaking, orange is a warning color used to communicate problems and therefore would be more intuitively associated with those markets that failed to make the quota. Furthermore, these colors are not easily distinguishable when presented in grayscale.
4. The words False and True in the legend are not immediately intuitive.

Exercise steps for bullet graph: beyond the basics

The following are the steps for the exercise:

1. Continuing from the previous exercise, access the **Data** pane on the left-hand portion of the screen and right-click on Quota Met? and adjust the calculation as follows:

```
IF SUM([Profit])>=SUM([Budget Profit])
THEN 'Quota Met'
ELSE 'Quota Missed'
END
```

Note that the legend is more intuitive than the previous True and False.

2. Create a calculated field named **Greater of** Profit or Budget Profit with the following code:

```
IF SUM(Profit) > SUM([Budget Profit])
THEN SUM(Profit)
ELSE SUM([Budget Profit])
END
```

3. Place Greater of Profit or Budget Profit on the **Columns** shelf after Profit. Also, right-click on the pill and select **Dual Axis**.
4. Right-click on the axis for Greater of Profit or Budget Profit and select Synchronize Axis.
5. Within the **Marks View** card, select the pane labeled All.
6. Set the view type to Bar.
7. Remove Measure Names.
8. Within the **Marks View** card, select the pane labeled AGG(Greater of Profit or Budget Profit).
9. Click on the **Color** shelf and set Transparency to 0%.
10. Within the **Marks View** card, select the pane labeled **SUM(Profit)**.
11. Remove AGG(Profit to Budget Profit Ratio) from the **Marks View** card.

Note that the percentage labels are no longer obscured.

12. Click on the **Color** shelf and select Edit Colors. Within the resulting dialog box, complete the following steps:
    1. Double-click on Quota Met and set the HTML to # FFFFFF.
    2. Double-click on Quota Missed and set the HTML to #000000.

13. After you have clicked OK for each dialog box and returned to the main screen, once again click on the **Color** shelf and select black for the border:

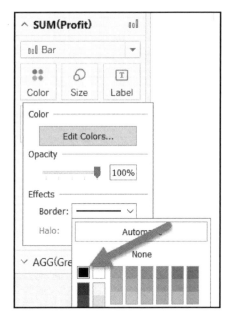

14. Click on the **Size** shelf to narrow the width of the bars.

15. Right-click on the Profit axis and select **Edit Reference Line** > 90%,95%,100% of **Average Budget Profit**:
    1. Click the **Fill Below** checkbox.
    2. Set the fill color to **Gray**.
    3. Select the **Reverse** checkbox. Note that the background colors are now more easily distinguished:

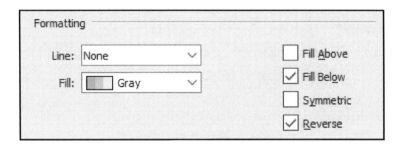

16. Right-click on the axis labeled Greater of Profit or Budget Profit and deselect Show Header.

17. You may wish to make some additional tweaks:

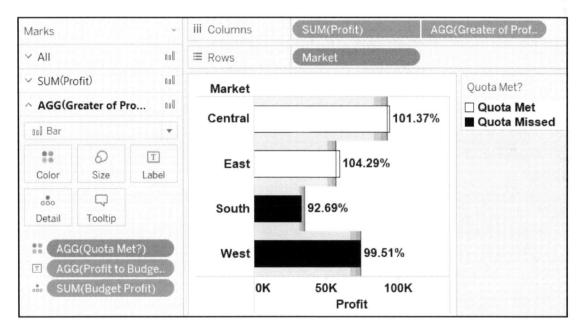

Note that each of the aforementioned problems have now been addressed:

1. The percentage numbers are no longer obscured.
2. The background colors are easier to distinguish due to having narrowed the bars.
3. The color of the bars is more intuitive. Furthermore, using black, white, and gray has circumvented any readability problems arising from color blindness or grayscale print.
4. The words False and True in the legend have been replaced with the more descriptive terms **Quota Met** and **Quota Missed**.

Making useful pies and donuts

Pie charts are normally frowned upon in data visualization circles. They simply have too many drawbacks. For instance, pie charts don't utilize space well on a rectangular screen. Treemaps fit much better. Also, the number of slices that are reasonable on a pie chart is fairly limited; perhaps six to eight at best. Once again, treemaps are superior because they can be sliced at a finer level of granularity while remaining useful. Lastly, when using pie charts it can be difficult to discern which of two similarly sized slices is largest. Treemaps are no better in this regard; however, if the viewer understands that treemap sorting is from top-left to bottom-right, that knowledge can be used to distinguish size differences. Of course, bar charts circumvent that particular problem entirely, since the eye can easily distinguish widths and heights but struggles with angles (pie charts) and volume (treemaps).

Despite these drawbacks, because of their popularity pie charts will likely continue to be widely used in data visualization for years to come. For the pessimistic Tableau author, the best course of action is to grin and bear it. But for one willing to explore and push frontier boundaries, good uses for pie charts can be discovered. The following exercise is one contribution to that exploration.

Exercise: pies and donuts on maps

Occasionally, there is a need (or perceived need) to construct pie charts atop a map. The process is not difficult (as you will see in the following exercise), but there are some shortcomings that cannot be easily overcome. We will discuss those shortcomings after the exercise.

Exercise: steps for pies and donuts

The following are the steps:

1. Within the workbook associated with this chapter, navigate to the worksheet entitled Pie Map and select the Superstore data source.
2. In the **Data** pane, double-click on State to create a map of the United States.
3. Place Sales on the **Color** shelf.
4. Click on the **Color** shelf and change the palette to Gray.

5. Drag an additional copy of **Latitude (generated)** on the **Rows** shelf to create two rows, each of which displays a map:

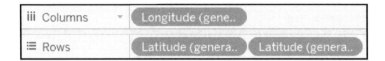

6. In the **MarksView** card, you will note that there are now three panes: All, **Latitude (generated)** and **Latitude (generated)** (2). Click on **Latitude (generated)** (2) and set the view type to **Pie**.
7. Place Category on the **Color** shelf and Sales on the **Size** shelf.
8. Right-click on the second instance of **Latitude (generated)** in the **Rows** shelf and select Dual Axis:

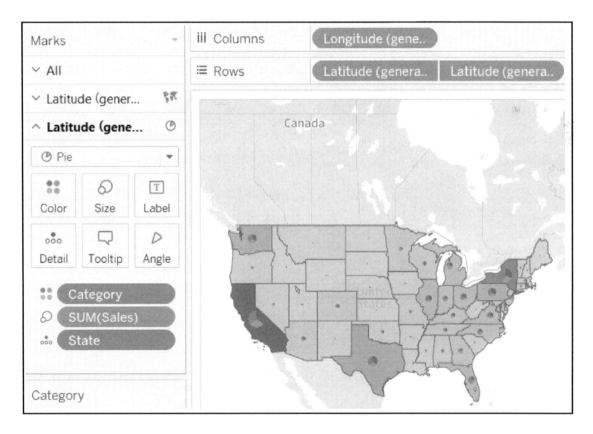

Can you see issues in the visualization? Two should be immediately apparent. First, the smaller pies are difficult to see. Clicking on the drop down menu for the Size legend and selecting Edit Sizes could partially address this problem, but pies on smaller states such as Rhode Island will continue to be problematic. Second, many states have the same light gray background despite widely varying sales amounts. The following approach will address these issues while adding additional functionality.

Exercise: steps for pies and donuts – beyond the basics

The following are the steps:

1. Within the workbook associated with this chapter, navigate to the worksheet entitled Altered Pie Map and select the Superstore data source.
2. Create the following calculated fields:

Name	Code
Log Sales	LOG(SUM(Sales))
Category State Sales	{FIXED State, Category: SUM(Sales)}
State Max	{FIXED State : MAX([Category State Sales])}
Top Selling Category per State	MAX(If [State Max] = [Category State Sales] then Category END)

3. Within the **MarksView** card, set the view type to Pie.
4. Place Log Sales on the **Size** shelf.
5. Within the **Data** pane, select the States data source.
6. Click the chain link next to State in the **Data** pane in order to use State as a linking field.
7. Drag Column to the **Columns** shelf and Row to the **Rows** shelf.
8. From the Superstore data source, place Category on the **Color** shelf and Sales on the **Angle** shelf.
9. Click on the **Size** shelf and adjust the size as desired.
10. At this point, you should see a rough map of the United States made up of pie charts. Next, we will further enhance the graphic by changing the pies into donuts.
11. Return to the States data source and place another instance of Row on the **Rows** shelf.

12. In the **MarksView** card, select Row (2).
13. Change the view type to Circle.
14. From the Superstore dataset, place Top Selling Category per State on the **Color** shelf.
15. Place Sales on the **Label** shelf.
16. Right-click on the instance of Sales you just placed on the **Label** shelf and select 'Format'. Make the following adjustments in the **Format** window.
17. Set the numbers formatting to **Currency (Custom)** with 0 decimal places and **Units** set to Thousands (K):

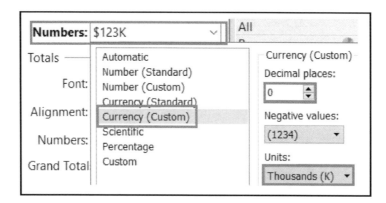

18. Set the alignment to **Middle Center** as shown in the following screenshot, so that the numbers are centered over the circles:

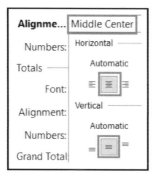

19. In the **Rows** shelf, right-click on the second instance of Row and select Dual Axis.
20. Right-click on the instance of the Row axis located at the far right-hand side of your screen and select Synchronize Axis.

21. Within the Row (2) instance of the **MarksView** card, click on the **Color** shelf and select Edit Colors. Adjust the color settings as desired so that the color of the overlaying circle (the hole of the donut) differs from underlying colors and yet retains the same hue. One way to accomplish this is by double-clicking on each color and changing the Saturation and Value numbers but leaving the Hue numbers the same.

22. Also within the **Color** shelf, set the border to the desired color.

23. Right-click on each axis and deselect Show Header.

24. Select **Format** | **Lines** and set Grid Lines to None.

25. Make other formatting changes as desired:

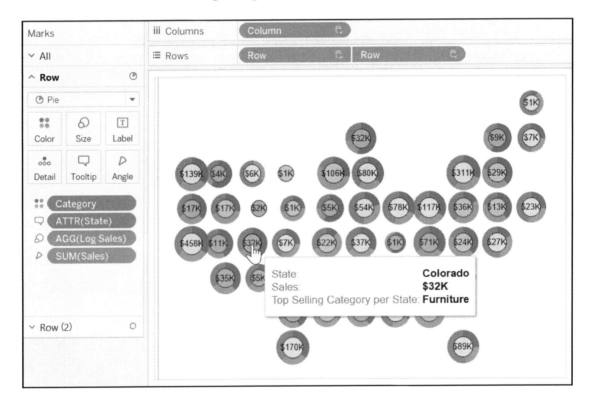

At first glance, the visualization may look peculiar. It's called a Tile Grid Map and although it's fairly new to the data visualization scene, it has begun to see usage at media outlets such as NPR. In the right setting, a Tile Grid Map can be advantageous. Let's consider a couple of the advantages the preceding exercise gives us. First, the grid layout in combination with the Log Sales calculated field creates a map immediately evident as the United States, while ensuring that the sizing of the various pie charts changes only moderately from greatest to least. Thus, each slice of each pie is reasonably visible; for example, District of Columbia sales are as easily visible as California sales. Second, the end user can clearly see the top-selling category for each state via the color of the inner circle (that is, the hole of the donut). This was accomplished with the LOD calculations. The end result is an information-dense visualization that uses pie charts in a practical, intuitive manner.

Pareto charts

In the late 19th century, an Italian economist named Vilfredo Pareto observed that 80% of the land in Italy was owned by 20% of the people. As he looked around, he observed this mathematical phenomena in many unexpected places. For example, he noted that 80% of the peas in his garden were produced from 20% of the peapods. As a result, although Vilfredo Pareto is not a household name, the 80/20 rule has found its way into the popular vernacular. In the following exercise, we'll discuss how to build a basic Pareto chart and then how to expand that chart to make it even more useful.

Of course, not every dataset is going to adhere to the 80/20 rule. Accordingly, the following exercise considers loan data from a community bank where 80% of the loan balance is *not* held by 20% of the bank's customers. Nonetheless, a Pareto chart can still be a very helpful analytical tool.

Exercise: steps for a Pareto chart – the basics

The following are the steps:

1. Within the workbook associated with this chapter, navigate to the worksheet entitled Pareto - Basic and select the Bank data source.
2. In the **Data** pane, change **Account #** to a dimension.
3. Place **Account #** on the **Columns** shelf and Current Loan Balance on the **Rows** shelf.

4. Click on the **Fit** drop-down menu and choose Entire View.

5. Right-click on the **Account** # pill and select Sort. Set the sort to Descending by the aggregated sum of the field Current Loan Balance.

6. Right-click on SUM(Current Loan Balance) located on the **Rows** shelf and select Add **Table Calculation**. Choose the settings as shown in the following screenshot:

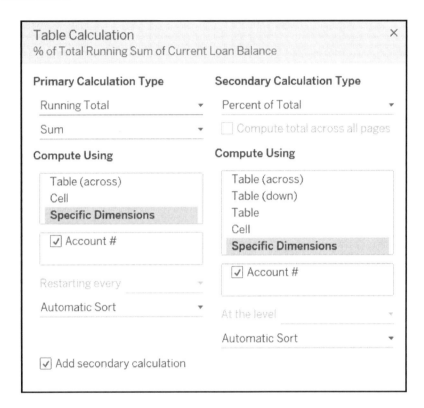

7. Drag an instance of **Account** # to the **Detail** shelf.

8. Click on the **Color** shelf and set Border to None.

9. Right-click on the instance of **Account** # that is on the **Columns** shelf and select **Measure | Count (Distinct)**. Note that a single vertical line displays.

10. Once again, right-click on the instance of **Account** # on the **Columns** shelf and select Add Table Calculation. Deploy the settings listed in the following screenshot:

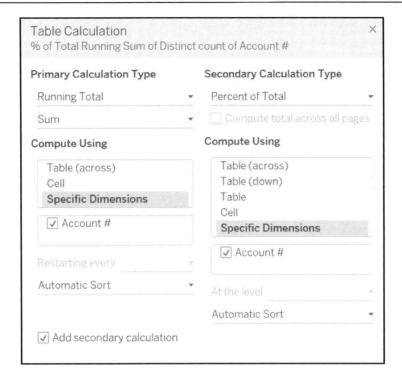

11. Click the **Analytics** tab in the upper left-hand corner of the screen and perform the following two steps:

    1. Drag Constant Line to Table > **SUM(Current Loan Balance)**.

    2. In the resulting dialog box, select **Constant** and set the **Value** to 0.8 as shown in the following screenshot:

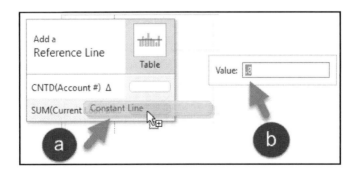

12. Repeat the previous step with the following differences:
    1. Drag **Constant Line** to **Table | CNTD(Account #).**
    2. In the resulting dialog box, select Constant and set the value to 0.2.

13. Drag Current Loan Balance to the **Rows** shelf. Place it to the right of **SUM(Current Loan Balance)** Δ that is currently on the **Rows** shelf. Note that the axis is affected by a single loan with a much larger balance than the other loans.

14. Right-click on the Current Loan Balance axis and select edit axis.

15. In the resulting dialog box, set the Scale to Logarithmic and click OK. This addresses the problem of the single large loan affecting the axis and thus obscuring the view of the other loans.

16. Within the **MarksView** card, select the second instance of **SUM(Current Loan Balance)** and set the view type to bar:

17. Right-click on **SUM(Current Loan Balance)** on the **Rows** shelf and select Dual Axis.

18. Right-click on the % of Total Running Sum of Current Loan Balance axes and select 'Move Marks to Front'.

19. Change colors, tooltip, and formatting as desired:

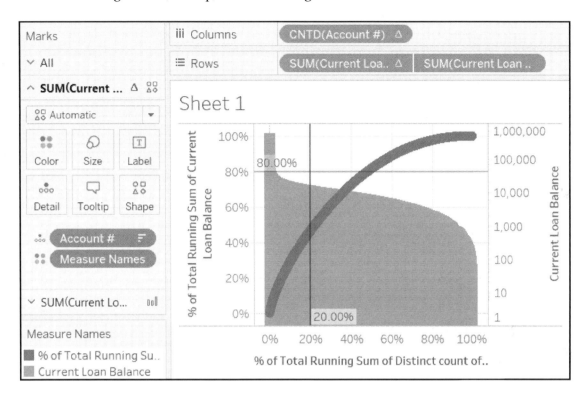

There are positive aspects of this visualization to consider. First, the end user can quickly gain initial understanding simply by observing both portions of the graph in conjunction with the values on the axes. Furthermore, the end user can hover the cursor over any part of the curve and see the resulting tooltip. Adding parameters to the two reference lines would be a quick way to add additional value. But let's see if we can go a little beyond that.

Exercise: steps for a Pareto chart – beyond the basics

The following are the steps:

1. Duplicate the sheet from the previous exercise and name the duplicate 'Pareto - Improved'.
2. Remove both reference lines.
3. Drag 'SUM(Current Loan Balance) Δ' (i.e., the table calculation) from the **Rows** shelf to the **Data** pane. When prompted, name the field 'Running % of Balance'.

4. Create and display a parameter with the following settings:

Field Name	Field Value
Name	% of Balance
Data Type	Float
Display Format	Percentage
Allowable Values	Range
Minimum	0
Maximum	1
Step size	0.01

5. Create the following calculated fields:

Name	Code
Running % of Loans	`RUNNING_SUM(COUNTD([Account #]) / TOTAL(COUNTD([Account #])))`
Pareto Split	`IF [Running % of Balance] < [% of Balance] THEN "Makes up X% of Balance" ELSE "Makes up rest of Balance" END`

Pareto Split (label)	`IF LOOKUP([Pareto Split], -1) != LOOKUP([Pareto Split], 0)`
	`THEN`
	`MID(STR([Running % of Loans] * 100), 1, 5) +`
	`"% of loans make up " +`
	`MID(STR([% of Balance] * 100), 1, 5) +`
	`"% of balance"`
	`END`

6. Select the **All** portion of the **MarksView** Card.

7. Drag **Pareto Split** to the **Detail** shelf.

8. Click on the drop-down menu to the left of the 'Pareto Split' pill on the **MarksView** Card and select **Color**:

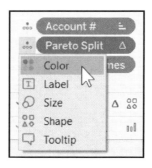

9. Select the Running % of Balance Δ portion of the **Marks View** Card.

10. Set the Mark type to Line.

11. Drag Pareto Split (label) to the **Label** shelf. Note that the expected label does not display. The next two steps will address that.

12. Click on the **Label** shelf and select Allow labels to overlap other marks.

13. Right click Pareto Split (label) on the **Marks View** card and select **Compute Using** à Account #.

14. Click the **Analytics** tab in the upper left-hand corner of the screen and perform the following two steps:

    1. Drag **Reference Line** to Table à Δ Running % of Balance.

    2. In the resulting dialog box, select % of Balance (Parameters) from the **Value** drop-down menu and set the **Label** to None.

15. Change colors, tooltip, and formatting as desired:

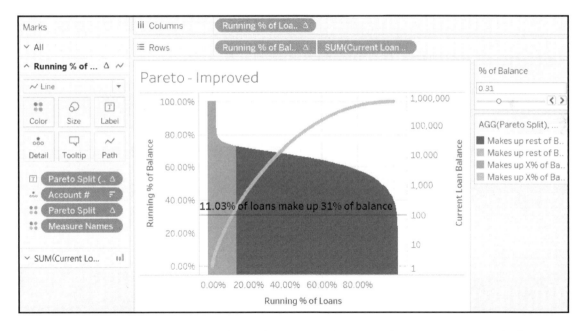

As you will see in the screenshot, the end user now has a single parameter to slide that moves the horizontal reference line on the chart. As the end user moves the reference line, the text updates to display loan and balance percentages. The colors also update as the end user adjusts the parameter to vertically communicate the percentage of loans under consideration.

Custom background images

Custom background images in Tableau open a world of potential. Imagine the ability to visualize any space. Possibilities encompass sports, health care, engineering, architecture, interior design, and much, much more. Despite this wealth of potential, background images in Tableau seem to me to be underutilized. Why? Part of the reason is because of the difficulty of generating datasets that can be used with background images.

Like the Tile Grid Map discussed before, background images require a grid layout to pinpoint X, Y coordinates. In the following section, we will address how to use Tableau to create a grid that can be superimposed on an image to instantly identify locations associated with X and Y coordinates and relatively quickly produce datasets that can be accessed by Tableau for visualization purposes. Specifically, we will use Tableau to generate the XML required to construct an SVG file that can be opened with a vector graphic tool. The tool that will be referenced in the exercise is Inkscape. **Inkscape** is open source and is thus available free of charge. Visit `inkscape.org` to download the latest version.

 Note that a grid with only 10 rows and columns is used in the following examples. Of course, 10 rows and columns generate a grid of 100 cells. This will perform satisfactorily in Inkscape. However, if a large cell count is required, a professional graphics tool such as Adobe Illustrator may be required. I tested grids with up to 10,000 cells and found the performance in Inkscape unacceptable. The same grids performed adequately in Illustrator; that is, Illustrator remained stable, and manipulating the grid was reasonably quick.

Exercise: creating a grid

The following exercise serves multiple purposes. The first purpose is, of course, to demonstrate how to use Tableau to create a grid. Additionally, this exercise requires many table calculations that will help reinforce lessons learned in Chapter 6, *Table Calculations*. Also, this chapter provides another opportunity to use data scaffolding, which was discussed in Chapter 4, *All About Data – Joins, Blends, and Data Structures*. The difference is that in Chapter 4, *All About Data – Joins, Blends, and Data Structures* dates were used for scaffolding purposes whereas in the following section bins are utilized. Lastly, this exercise makes use of data densification, which was discussed in Chapter 5, *All About Data – Data Densification, Cubes, and Big Data*.

Exercise: steps for creating a grid

The following are the steps:

1. Open a new Tableau workbook and name the first sheet Header.
2. Using Excel or a text editor, create a Records dataset. The following two row table represents the 'Records' data set in its entirety:

Records
1
2

3. Connect Tableau to the Records dataset.
   - To be expedient, consider copying the dataset using *Ctrl* + *C* and pasting it directly in Tableau using *Ctrl* + *V*.
   - Tableau will likely consider Records a measure. Drag Records to the dimensions portion of the **Data** pane.
4. Create two parameters. Entitle one Overall Pixel Count and the other Rows Down/Columns Across. The settings for both are as follows:
   - Data type: Integer
   - Allowable values: All
5. Show both parameters. Set Rows Down/Columns Across to 10 and Overall Pixel Count to 1000.
6. Create a calculated field named Concatenate Header with the following code:

Note that entering line breaks in the Calculated Field dialog box may make the results difficult to extract from Tableau. In other words, remove all line breaks.

```
'<?xml version="1.0" encoding="utf-8"?> <svg version="1.1" id="Squares"
xmlns="http://www.w3.org/2000/svg"
xmlns:xlink="http://www.w3.org/1999/xlink" x="0px" y="0px" viewBox="0 0 ' +
STR( [Overall Pixel Count] ) + " " + STR([Overall Pixel Count])+ '"
style="enable-background:new 0 0 '+ STR([Overall Pixel Count]) + ' ' +
STR([Overall Pixel Count]) + ';" xml:space="preserve"> <style
type="text/css"> .st0{fill:none;stroke:#000000;stroke-miterlimit:10;}
</style>'
```

7. Place the newly created calculated field on the **Text** shelf.

8. In the toolbar, choose to fit to 'Entire View' to view the results.
9. Create a new worksheet named 'Location Codes'.
10. Create the following calculated fields:

Name	Code
Rows Down/Columns Across	`[Parameters].[Rows Down/Columns Across]`
Which Column?	`LAST()+1`
Which Row?	`INDEX()`
Grid Size	`[Overall Pixel Count]/LOOKUP([Which Column?],FIRST())`
X	`[Overall Pixel Count] - ([Grid Size] * ([Which Row?]))`
Y	`[Overall Pixel Count] - ([Grid Size] * ([Which Column?]-1))`
Count	`If [Records] = 1 THEN 1 ELSE [Rows Down/Columns Across] END`
Decicount	`If [Records] = 1 THEN 1 ELSE [Rows Down/Columns Across] END`
Location Codes	`Index()`
Concatenate Locations	`'<text transform="matrix(1 0 0 1 ' + STR([X]) + " " + STR([Y]) +')">' + STR( [Location Codes] ) + '</text>'`

11. Right-click on Count and select **Create > Bins**. In the resulting dialog box, set the size of the bin to 1.
12. Right-click on Decicount and select **Create > Bins**. In the resulting dialog box, set the size of the bin to 1.
13. Place Count (bin), Decicount (bin), Location Codes, X, and Y on the **Rows** shelf. Be sure to place those fields in the order listed here.
14. Right-click on each field on the **Rows** shelf and set to 'Discrete'.
15. Right-click on Count (bin) and Decicount (bin) and ensure that 'Show Missing Values' is selected.
16. Right-click on Location Code and select **Compute Using > Table (Down)**.
17. Set the Compute Using value for X to Count (bin).
18. Set the Compute Using value for Y to Decicount (bin).
19. Place Concatenate Locations on the **Text** shelf.

20. Right-click on the instance of Concatenate Locations you just placed on the **Text** shelf and select Edit Table Calculations. At the top of the resulting dialog box, note that there are four options under **Nested Calculations**: Grid Size, Which Column?, Which Row?, and 'Location Codes'. Set the Compute Using definition for each as follows:

Name	Compute Using Setting
Grid Size	Table (Down)
Which Column?	Discount (bin)
Which Row	Count (bin)
Location Codes	Table (Down)

21. In the toolbar, choose to fit to Fit Width to view the results.

22. Create a new worksheet named Lines.

23. Select **Analysis** > **Table Layout** > **Advanced** and set maximum values for rows and columns to 16:

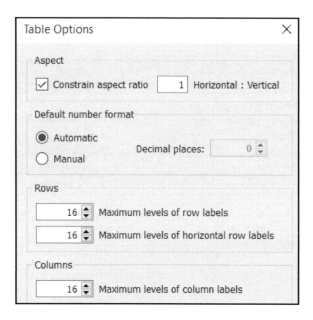

24. Create the following calculated fields:

Name	Compute Using Setting
H Then V	Index()
HLine	Last()

VLine	`Index()-1`
X1	`IF [H Then V] = 1 THEN 0 ELSE` `[Overall Pixel Count] - ([Grid Size] * ([VLine])) END`
Y1	`IF [H Then V] = 2 THEN 0 ELSE` `[Overall Pixel Count] - ([Grid Size] * ([VLine])) END`
X2	`IF [H Then V] = 1 THEN [Overall Pixel Count] ELSE [Overall Pixel` `Count] - ([Grid Size] * ([VLine])) END`
Y2	`IF [H Then V] = 2 THEN [Overall Pixel Count] ELSE [Overall Pixel` `Count] - ([Grid Size] * ([VLine])) END`

25. Next, place the following eight fields on the **Rows** shelf. Note that each should be cast as discrete:

Count (bin)	Decicount (bin)	H Then V	HLine	VLine
Grid Size	X1	Y1	X2	Y2

26. Right-click on Count(bin) and Decicount(bin) and set each to Show Missing Values.
27. Right-click on each of the remaining fields on the **Rows** shelf and select Edit Table Calculations. Set the Compute Using definition of each field as shown in the following table:

Name	Nested Calculation	Compute Using Setting
H then V	N/A	Count (bin)
HLine	N/A	Count (bin)
VLine	N/A	Decicount (bin)
Grid Size	Grid Size	Table (Down)
	Which Column?	Decicount (bin)
X1, Y1, X2, Y2	H Then V	Count (bin)
	Grid Size	Count (bin)
	Which Column?	Count (bin)
	VLine	Decicount (bin)

Note that some of the fields include nested table calculations. In such cases, the Table Calculations dialog box will include an extra option at the top entitled Nested Calculation as can be seen in the following screenshot:

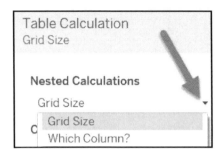

28. Filter H Then V to display only 1 and 2.
29. Create the following calculated field:

Name	Code
Concatenate Lines	`'<line class="st0" x1="' + STR([X1]) + '" y1="' + STR([Y1]) + '" x2="' + STR( [X2] ) + '" y2="' + STR([Y2]) + '"/>'`

30. Place Concatenate Lines on the **Text** shelf.
31. Export the code from the three worksheets just created.

> Exporting the code from the three worksheets can be tricky since Tableau may try to input additional quote marks. I found the following approach works best:
>
> 1. Select the Header worksheet.
> 2. Press *Control + A* to select all the contents of the worksheet.
> 3. Hover the cursor over the selected text in the view and pause until the tooltip command buttons appear.
> 4. Select the View Data icon at the right-hand side of the tooltip.
> 5. In the resulting View Data dialog box, select Export All.
> 6. Save the CSV file using the same name as each worksheet; for instance, the data exported from the Header worksheet will be named `Header.csv`.
> 7. Repeat the steps for the remaining worksheets.

32. Open an instance of Notepad (or your favorite text editor) and save it as `Grid and Location Codes.svg`.
33. Using Excel, copy the data from `Header.csv` and paste it into `Grid and Location Codes.svg`. Be sure not to include the header information. Include only the XML code.

34. Using Excel, copy the required data from `Location.csv` and paste into `Grid and Location Codes.svg`. The required data only includes the column labeled Concatenate Locations. Do not include the other columns or the header. Include only the XML code.

35. Using Excel, copy the required data from `Lines.csv` and paste into `Grid and Location Codes.svg`. The required data only includes the column labeled Concatenate Lines. Do not include the other columns or the header. Include only the XML code.

36. Lastly, complete the SVG file by entering the `</svg>` closing tag.

Now, open the SVG file in Inkscape and observe the grid. We'll cover an example of how to use the grid in the next exercise.

Exercise: steps for using a grid to generate a dataset

Skilled chess players will complete a game in about 40 moves. In chess tournaments, data is routinely captured for each game, which provides opportunities for data visualization. In this exercise, we will use data from a chess game to visualize how often each square of a chessboard is occupied:

1. Within the workbook associated with this chapter, navigate to the worksheet entitled Chessboard.
2. Download the pictures provided from the link in the caption. Unzip the contents to a directory of your choosing.
3. Open the SVG file created from the previous exercise in Inkscape.

 If you did not complete the previous exercise, you can copy the XML code located on the dashboard entitled Generated SVG Code in the solution workbook associated with this chapter. Paste that code in a text editor and save it with an SVG extension. Lastly, open the file with Inkscape.

4. Within Inkscape, Press *Ctrl + A* to select all.
5. Group the selection using *Ctrl + G*.
6. From the Inkscape menu, select **Layer** > **Layers**. The Keyboard shortcut is **Shift + Ctrl + L**.
7. Within the Layers palette that displays on the right-hand side of the screen, Press the + icon to create a layer. Name the layer **Chessboard**.

8. Create another layer named 'Grid':

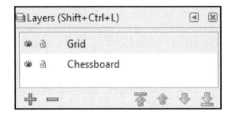

9. Click on any line or number in the view.
10. Right-click on that same line or number and select Move to layer. Chose the layer Grid.
11. Select **File à Import** and choose the Chessboard image included in the zip file previously downloaded.

Make sure that the image is placed on the Chessboard layer so that the location code numbers are not obscured. Position the chessboard image such that location code 81 is centered over the top left-hand square of the chessboard. Since the chessboard is only composed of 64 squares, it will not encompass all 100 squares the grid provides.

At this point, you can generate a dataset based on how often each location is occupied. For example, you might note that for one game position, 81 was occupied for 40 moves, in which case the player may simply have never moved that rook. However, in another game the position may be occupied for only 10 moves, perhaps indicating the player performed a castle early in the game.

For the next exercise, we will take a look at a dataset generated from a chess game and discover how to visualize the results based on the work done in the previous exercises.

Exercise: visualizing a chess game

The following are the steps:

1. Within the workbook associated with this chapter, navigate to the worksheet entitled Chessboard and select the Chessboard data source.

Note: In order to follow the next step, you will need to download the assets associated with this chapter. To do so, simply follow the link in the caption of the worksheet.

2. Right-click on the Chessboard data source and select Edit Data Source in order to examine the dataset.

3. In the dialog box asking Where is the data file?, steer to the `Chessboard.xlsx` provided with the assets associated with this chapter.

The table named Board Grid contains each location code and the X and Y coordinates associated with each location code. This dataset was taken from the Location Codes worksheet created earlier in this chapter. The table named Squares Occupied contains the fields Location Code and Moves Occupied. Board Grid and Squares Occupied are connected using a left join on Location Code:

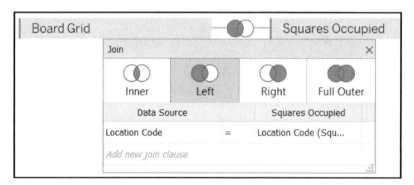

4. On the Chessboard worksheet, select **Map à Background Images à Chessboard**.

5. In the resulting dialog box, click Add Image to add a background image.

6. Fill out the Add Background Image dialog box as shown:

Field	Content
Name	Chessboard
File or URL	*Click Browse to choose a path to the Chessboard image previously downloaded.*
X Field	X
Left	0
Right	1000
Y Field	Y
Bottom	1000
Top	0

7. Place these fields on their respective shelves:

Field	Shelf
X	Columns
Y	Rows
Moves Occupied	Color
Moves Occupied	Size
Location Code	Detail

8. Right-click on the X and Y axes and set both to **Fixed** with a **Fixed start** of **0** and a **Fixed end** of **875**:

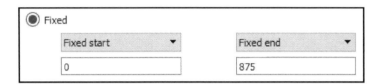

9. Edit the Y axis and set it to Reversed. Do not reverse the X axis.

 This last step was performed because the data has been structured to mirror the X and Y coordinate setup that is the default in most graphic tools. In these, the upper left-hand corner is where X and Y both equal 0.

10. Adjust color, size and shapes, and so on as desired:

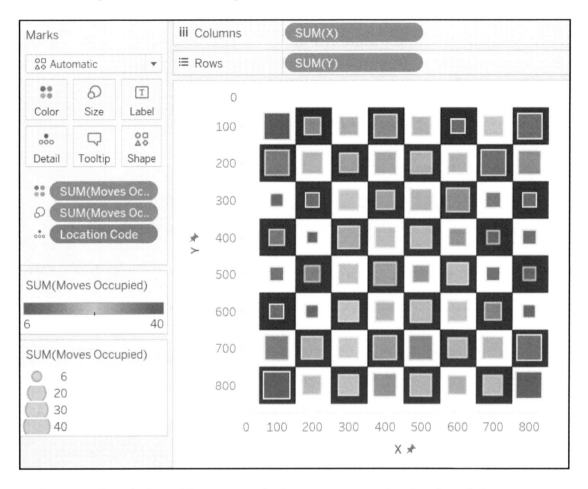

In the screenshot, the large blue squares designate spaces on the chessboard that were most frequently occupied. The small orange squares designate squares less frequently occupied.

Exercise: creating polygons on a background image

Utilizing shapes on specific points of a visualization was sufficient for the previous exercise, but sometimes it may be advantageous to use polygons to outline shapes. Polygons are natively used in Tableau in geocoding when using country, state, and other geocoded data; however, there are geocoded elements (such as cities) that are not natively available in Tableau. In the next chapter, we will discuss techniques for drawing polygons on a map. In the following section, we will discuss how to utilize polygons on a background image.

Exercise: steps for creating polygons on a background image

The following are the steps:

1. Within the workbook associated with this chapter, navigate to the worksheet entitled Dashboard - Polygon and select the DartBoard_W_Polygons data source.

 If you have not already done so when completing the previous exercise, download pictures provided from the link in the caption. Unzip the contents to a directory of your choosing.

2. Select Map > Background Images à Dartboard_W_Polygons. In the Background Images dialog box, select 'Add Image'. Fill out the dialog box as shown:

Dialog Box Field	Contents
Name	Dartboard_Blank
File or URL	Click browse and navigate to the directory where you unzipped the compressed file just downloaded. Select `Dartboard_Blank.png`.
X Field	X
X Field Left	0
X Field Right	646
Y Field	Y
Y Field Bottom	0
Y Field Top	655

3. Create a parameter with the following information:

Dialog Box Field	Contents
Name	Select Player
Data type	Integer
Allowable Values	List
List of Values	Value | Display As 1 | Matthew 2 | David 3 | Total Hits

4. Display the parameter created in the previous step by right clicking on it at the bottom of the **Data** pane and selecting Show Parameter Control.
5. Create the following calculated fields:

Name	Code
Total Hits	[David]+[Matthew]
Case	CASE [Select Player] WHEN 1 THEN SUM([Matthew]) WHEN 2 THEN SUM([David]) WHEN 3 THEN SUM([Total Hits]) END

6. Set the **Marks View** card to Polygon.
7. Survey the **Data** pane to ensure that Point and Shape are both dimensions. The other fields are measures.
8. Place these fields on their respective shelves:

Field	Shelf
X	Columns
Y	Rows
Point	Path
Shape	Detail
Case	Color

9. Right-click on each axis and set the range from **0** to **650**:

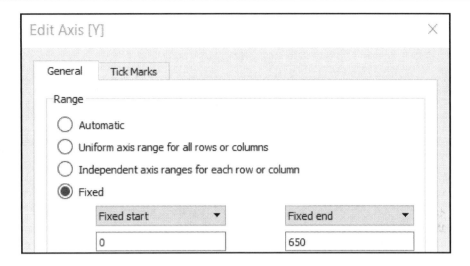

10. Click on the **Color** shelf and select **Edit Colors**. Adjust color as desired. One possibility is represented in the following screenshot:

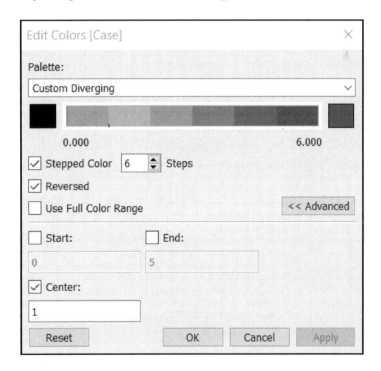

It is likely that you found completing this exercise in Tableau relatively easy. The challenge is in getting the data right; particularly the polygon points. A useful (and free) tool for generating polygon data can be found at `http://powertoolsfortableau.com/tools/drawing-tool`. This is one of many tools created by InterWorks that are helpful for addressing common Tableau challenges.

You may have noticed that the curved sections of the polygons in this exercise aren't quite perfect. That's simply the nature of working with points on a Cartesian grid in Tableau. Vector graphic applications such as Inkscape and Illustrator have Bézier drawing tools with which you can create a very precise dartboard. It's not possible in Tableau to draw Bézier curves using X and Y coordinates atop a background map. However, if your graphing needs require precisely drawn curves, check out the Circular and Hive Plot Network Graphing article by Chris DeMartini at DataBlick for techniques utilizing math that very closely approximates Bézier curves in Tableau.

Tableau extensions

Another very helpful tool when it comes to 'Beyond the Basic Chart Types' is the Tableau Extensions API, which was released for public in 2018. What does the Extensions API do? Basically, it allows you to use third-party tools directly in Tableau. Some selected extensions are available here: `https://extensiongallery.tableau.com`. Let's have a look at one example from Infotopics.

Show me More

In the associated workbook, navigate to **Show me More** and select the **Coffee** Chain Dataset. Now please reproduce the following:

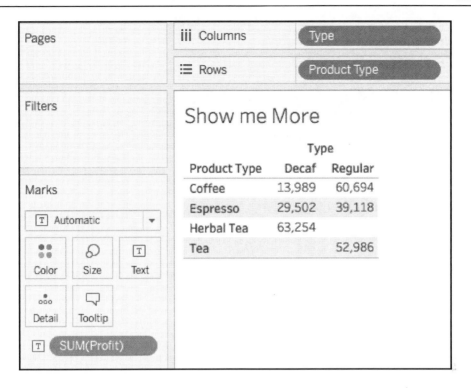

Your Stakeholder really wants to see this as a Sankey Chart. You know how to do it with calculated fields, but you have heard that there is also an Extension to do so.

Extensions API exercise

The following are the steps:

1. In the associated workbook, open a Dashboard tab.
2. Drag the Show me More Sheet onto the Dashboard.

3. Now also drag the **Extension** Object on to the Dashboard:

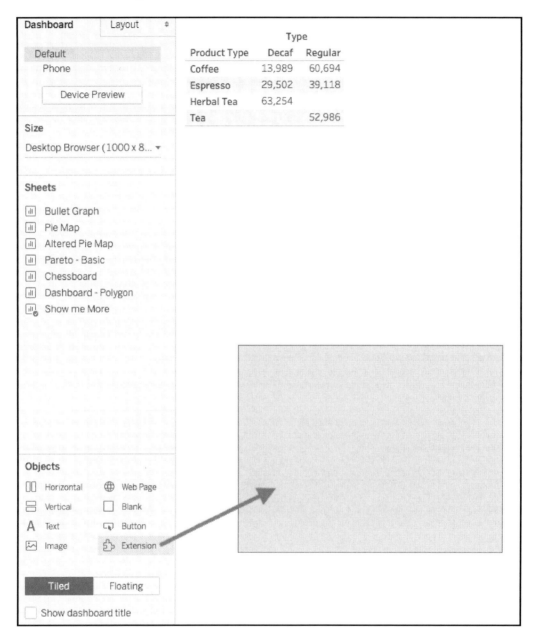

Another window will open up:

4. Click on **Extension Gallery** and select the Show me More Extension.
5. Then click **Download**. Once you have downloaded the `.trex` file, choose **My Extensions** in the popup.

The Extension will open on the Dashboard and is ready to use.

6. Configure the variables as follows:

7. Hit the **Ok** button and voilà, you have your **Sankey** chart:

Besides this Sankey chart, I would highly recommend you have a look at the Extensions library. There are many extensions for multiple different use cases; some are for free, some have to be paid for, but, you can also, you can build your own. It is worth taking a look!

Summary

We began this chapter by considering how to tweak popular visualization types. Specifically, we fine-tuned a bullet graph, considered a very different approach for using pie charts in mapping, and we ended by tweaking a Pareto chart. Next, we turned our attention to custom background images where we considered how to build a grid using XML to generate an SVG file to expedite generating data necessary to use with background images. Then, we completed the chapter by building polygons on a background image and had a quick excursion in to the world of Tableau Extensions.

In the next chapter, we will turn our attention to mapping, where we will consider how to extend Tableau's native mapping capabilities without ever leaving the interface, as well as how to extend Tableau's mapping capabilities with other technology.

9
Mapping

When I conducted Tableau classes and workshops for people who were seeing Tableau for the first time, I found that demonstrating mapping is always a big hit, sometimes resulting in murmurs of appreciation and surprise. People have told me on multiple occasions that Tableau's mapping capability was the key feature that caused them to take notice and consider Tableau's offerings more seriously. Tableau's out-of-the-box mapping capabilities are powerful and flexible. You may be surprised at how much you can accomplish without ever leaving the user interface. But these out-of-the-box capabilities are just the tip of the iceberg. With proper guidance (which I will attempt to provide in this chapter), you can expand beyond the native mapping functionality and explore techniques that will greatly enhance your workbooks' functionality and aesthetics.

In this chapter, we will discuss the following topics:

- Extending Tableau's mapping capabilities without leaving Tableau
- Extending Tableau mapping with other technology
- Exercise: connecting to a WMS server
- Exploring the TMS file
- Exploring Mapbox
- Accessing different maps with a dashboard
- Creating custom polygons
- Converting shape files for Tableau
- Exercise: polygons for Texas
- Heatmaps

Extending Tableau's mapping capabilities without leaving Tableau

In our everyday lives, a map can be helpful for better understanding the world around us. For instance, maps are often used on websites, television, or in printed media to present demographic information. In such instances, the mapping requirement is **static** since the immediate goal does not require movement. Often, however, a map is needed to navigate from point A to point B. This kind of mapping requirement is more complicated, because it encompasses static needs (what restaurant is nearby?), but must also deliver additional information, such as routes and distances (how can I get to that restaurant?). These **dynamic** mapping needs assume that movement is required to fulfill a demand. Similarly, some businesses only have what might be referred to as static mapping requirements. For example, a retail chain might create a visualization that includes a map to better understand sales performance in a given region. In such cases, movement between locations is not a direct need. Many businesses, however, need to understand routes and mileages, that is, how to get from point A to point B and the distances involved. These dynamic mapping requirements can vary greatly but most of these needs share at least two things in common: routes and distances.

Exercise: displaying routes and calculating distances

In this exercise, we will consider flight routes and associated distances in Australia. Specifically, we will cover how to extract longitude and latitude numbers from Tableau, and use that information in conjunction with trigonometry to calculate mileage between various points. Along the way, we will utilize data blending, table calculations, mapping, and LOD calculations for a robust exercise that touches on many advanced features.

Please follow along the steps:

1. Navigate to https://public.tableau.com/profile/marleen.meier to locate and download the workbook associated with this chapter.
2. Open the workbook and navigate to the Map worksheet.
3. Select the Transit Data data source in the **Data** pane and double-click on City, then change City from **Detail** to Text in the Mark-shelf.

In the following screenshot, note that the cities Mackay and Brisbane are the only cities that display. Click on **14 unknown**:

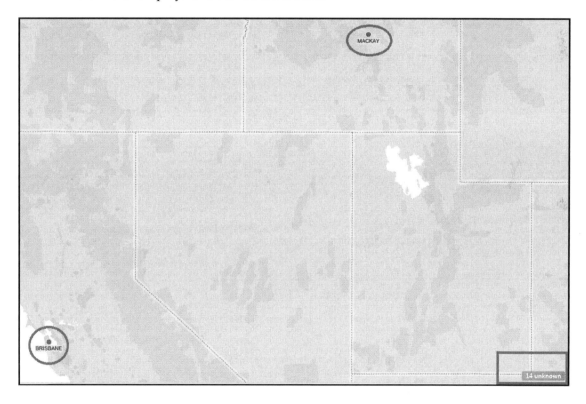

Caveat: If you are in the **United States**, Melbourne in Florida will display. If you are in another country, you may get different results.

4. Select **Edit Locations...**:

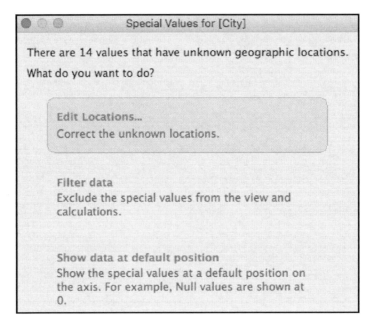

5. Change the **Country/Region** to **Australia**:

6. **Australia** is now displayed on the map:

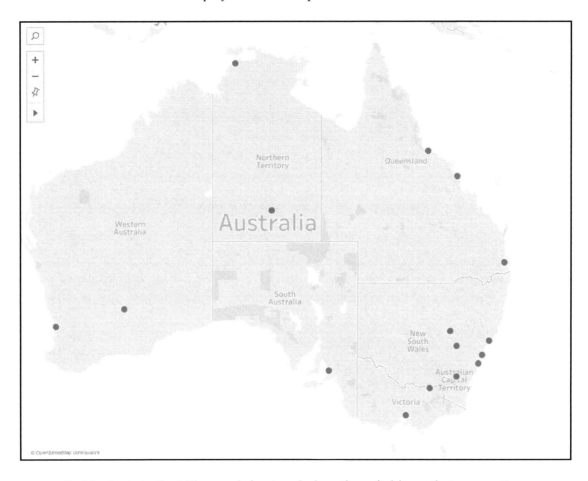

7. Navigate to the Miles worksheet and place these fields on their respective shelves, as seen in the following table:

Field	Shelf
Trip ID	Rows
City	Rows
Latitude (generated)	Text
Longitude (generated)	Text

8. Your screen should look like the preceding screenshot. Note that the cross tab is pretty cluttered. Ideally, Latitude and Longitude should display in separate columns. Unfortunately, we can't do this with the generated Latitude and Longitude because, although they are listed under the Measures portion of the **Data** pane, Tableau doesn't treat them as measures. In order to complete the exercise, we will need to be able to access the Latitude and Longitude coordinates from a separate data source.

   To do this, extract the coordinates and create a data blend, as seen in the following screenshot:

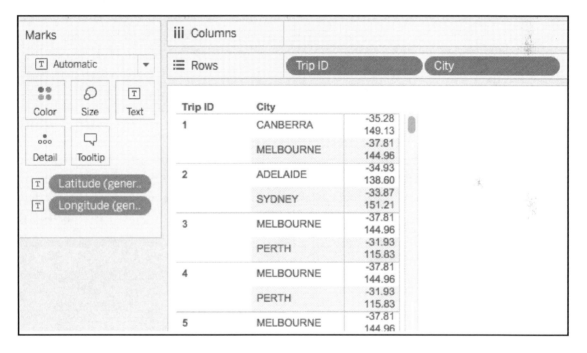

9. Click on the Map worksheet tab.
10. Right-click on the visualization and select View Data.
11. Copy all the data in the resulting dialog box.
12. Close the dialog box and press *Control + v* to create a new dataset in Tableau.
13. Rename the resulting dataset Lat Long. Also name the worksheet Lat Long.
14. In the Lat Long worksheet, rename **Latitude (generated)** and **Longitude (generated)** to Lat and Long.

15. Return to the Miles worksheet and, within the Transit Data data source, create the calculated fields present in the following table:

Name	Code
LAT	AVG([Lat Long].[Lat])
LONG	AVG([Lat Long].[Long])

16. Remove **Latitude (generated)** and **Longitude (generated)** from the **Marks View** card.
17. Place Measure Names on the **Columns** shelf and Measure Values on the **Text/Label** shelf. Now, we have the ability to treat Latitude and Longitude as true measures.
18. Remove all measures from the **Measure Values** shelf except Lat and Long.
19. Create the following calculated fields:

Name	Code
Lookup Lat	Lookup(Lat,-1)
Lookup Long	Lookup(Long, -1)

20. Place the two newly-created calculated fields on the **Measure Values** shelf.
21. Create a calculated field named Great Circle Distance Formula with the following code:

```
3959 * ACOS
(
SIN(RADIAN([Lat])) * SIN(RADIANS([Lookup Lat]))+
COS(RADIANS([Lat])) * COS(RADIANS([Lookup Lat])) *
COS(RADIANS([Lookup Long]) - RADIANS([Long]))
 )
```

For kilometers, change 3959 to 6378.

22. Place the newly-created calculated field on the **Measure Values** shelf.
23. Change the calculation so that it computes using City.
24. Adjust the following calculations accordingly:

Name	Code
Lookup Lat	IFNULL(LOOKUP(Lat,-1), LOOKUP(Lat,1))
Lookup Long	IFNULL(LOOKUP(Long,-1), LOOKUP(Long,1))

26. Select the Map worksheet and set the **Marks View** card to Line.
27. Place Trip ID on the **Detail** Shelf.
28. Drag City to the bottom of the **Marks View** card.
29. Place the Great Circle Distance formula on the **Tooltip** shelf.
30. Set the Great Circle Distance formula to Compute Using City.
31. Create the following calculated fields:

Name	Code
Source City	{ FIXED [Trip ID]:MIN(IF [Dest/Orig]='Source' THEN City END) }
Destination City	{ FIXED [Trip ID]:MIN(IF [Dest/Orig]='Destination' THEN City END) }

32. Use the newly-created calculated fields to format as desired. In particular, notice in that **Source City** is on the **Color** shelf and Destination City is used on the **Tooltip** shelf:

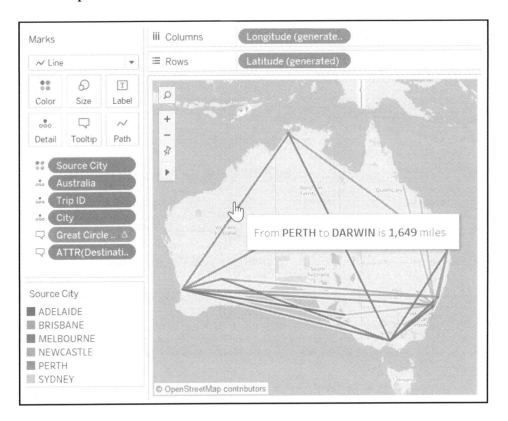

Extending Tableau mapping with other technology

Next we will consider how to extend Tableau's mapping capabilities with other tools. Tableau developers were careful to create a mapping interface that is readily extensible. Some areas of this extensibility, such as connecting to a Web Map Service (WMS) Server, are available directly from the interface. Other areas require delving into the rarely-explored Tile Map Service (TMS) file. And still others require the author to provide latitude and longitude points – perhaps millions of points – to create complicated polygons on a map or background image.

Exercise: connecting to a WMS server

The easiest way to bring a custom map into Tableau is directly from Desktop. We need a properly-formatted URL that points to a WMS server.

> A good place to find a list of such URLs is http://directory.spatineo.com, which provides information for about 101,500 mapping services, as of this writing.

The following exercise was inspired by Jeffrey A. Shaffer's article at http://www.dataplusscience.com, Building weather radar in Tableau in under 1 minute:

1. Open the workbook associated with this chapter and navigate to the **WMS Server** worksheet via Desktop.
2. Select the Superstore data source.
3. Place State on the **Detail** shelf.
4. Copy the http://nowcoast.noaa.gov/arcgis/services/nowcoast/radar_ meteo_imagery_nexrad_time/MapServer/WMSServer? URL.
5. In Tableau, navigate to **Map** > **Background Maps** > **Map Services**.
6. Select Add, choose **WMS Servers**, and paste the URL:

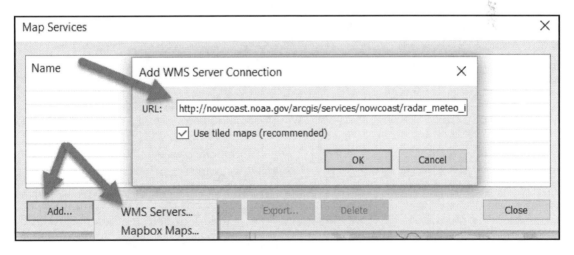

7. In the **Marks View** card, set the view type to Map.

8. Click on the Color shelf to turn on borders and set the opacity to 0%:

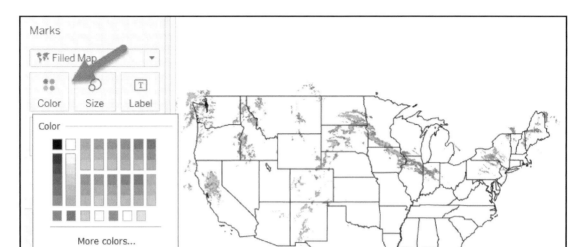

Tableau Desktop can connect to any WMS Server that supports the WMS 1.0.0, 1.1.0, or 1.1.1 standard. If you need to connect to a map server using a different protocol, such as a tile server, you can do so by creating a TMS file. We'll take a look at the structure of a TMS file in the next section.

Before we proceed, here's a note on tiling and zooming before proceeding. Since high resolution maps may be many gigabytes, it's impractical to require you to download an entire map in order to zoom in on one small area. Tiles solve this problem by enabling multiple zoom levels. A zoom level of 0 results in a single tile (often a 256 x 256 pixel PNG image) that displays the entire map. As the zoom levels increase, the number of map tiles increases exponentially. Also, a proportionally smaller section of the map displays; that is, as the zoom level increases, the area of the entire map that displays decreases and the total number of tiles required to fill the display remains constant. This helps control the amount of data downloaded at any given time.

Exploring the TMS file

By default, TMS files are located on the C drive in `Documents\My Tableau Repository\Mapsources`. After installing Tableau Desktop, this directory is blank; however, the directory may be populated with any number of TMS files. Note that in order for a TMS file to become available after placing it in the Mapsources directory, Tableau must be restarted.

A good way to explore the various TMS options is via the `Tableau.tms` file located in the Program Files directory. The default location for the `Tableau.tms` file is `C:\Program Files\Tableau\Tableau x.x\Mapsources`. The following TMS example is an abbreviated version of the `Tableau.tms` file.

The TMS file structure

Check the file structure in the following code block:

```
<?xml version = '1.0' encoding = 'utf-8'?>
<mapsource inline ='true' version = '8.2'>
<connection class = 'OpenStreetMap' max-scale-level = '16.0' max-stretch =
'1.0' min-shrink = '1.0' port = '80' server = ' maps.tableausoftware.com'
url-format = ' tile/d/{L}/ol/{Z}/{X}/{Y}{D}.png?apikey = {K}&amp;size={P}'
  Username = 'tabmapbeta'/>
  <layers>
<layer display-name = 'Base' name = 'base' show-ui = 'true'
 type = 'features' request-string = '/' />
<layer current-id='...' display-
 name = 'Population' group = 'US Population' name = '...' prepend-
 date = 'true' show-ui = 'true' type = 'data'/>
  </layers>
  <map-styles>
     <map-style display-name = 'Light' name = '...'>
     <map-layer-style name = '...' request-string = '...'/>
     </map-style>
  <map-styles>
     <mapsource-defaults version='8.2'>
     <style>
        <style-rule element='map-layer'>
<format attr='enabled' id='tab_coastline' value='false' />
        </style-rule>
           <style-rule element='map'>
           <format attr='washout' value='0.0' />
        </style-rule>
     </style>
```

```
</mapsource-defaults>
```

Let's consider various features of the preceding TMS file:

- **Inline**: This required attribute must include True or False. Typically, True is desirable since this will embed the TMS information in the Tableau Workbook File (TWB) file. Thus, the map referenced by the TMS file will continue to work when uploaded to Tableau Server. Selecting False will cause the TMS information to not be included with the TWB file, which will then require the author to upload a separate TMS file to Tableau Server in order for the map to display.
- **Class**: This required attribute communicates the server type. The OpenStreetMap term is simply communicating that a tile server is being accessed. Another term is OGC-WMS, which communicates that the server under consideration is using the Open Geospatial Consortium WMS standard.
- **Max-scale-level**: This optional attribute can be used to set the maximum zoom allowable. Note that the `Tableau.tms` file utilizes the `maps.tableausoftware.com` server, which supports a max-scale-level of 16. Other map servers support different levels of magnification that may exceed 16 levels.
- **Max-stretch/shrink**: These optional attributes allow Tableau to stretch or shrink map tiles. If the values are set to 1.0, no stretching or shrinking occurs; instead, each tile is sized exactly as dictated by the zoom level.
- **Port**: This optional attribute communicates which port to access. Port 80 is the typical port for HTTP servers. If omitted, port 80 is assumed.
- **Server**: This required attribute must include the URL to the map server.
- **Url-format**: This optional attribute includes additional URL fragments that the map server may require. {Z},{X} and {Y} are of particular interest. These URL fragments, also known as Slippy Map Tilenames, direct Tableau to the appropriate directories:
    - {Z} indicates the zoom level. Zoom levels range from 0 - 20+. Tableau documentation states that the maximum zoom level is 16, but this limit can be surpassed if the map server supports a higher zoom level.
    - {X} indicates a column of map tiles.
    - {Y} indicates a specific map tile.

- **Layers**: This required tag must include **layer display-name** and may include the **layer current-id** attribute. The layer display-name attribute controls what displays in Tableau within **Map > Map Layers**. Note that if the show-ui tag is set to true, at least one of the map layers must be selected before the map will display. The layer current-id attribute enables access to data layers provided by the map server within the **Map Layers** window.

  See following a comparison:

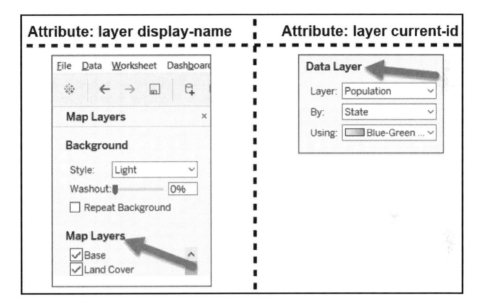

- **Map-styles**: This optional tag determines the options in Tableau within **Map > Map Layers > Background**.
- **Mapsource-defaults**: This optional tag determines default values for various attributes, such as which **Map Layers** display and **washout**. Washout can have a value ranging from 0 - 1, with 1 equal to 100%.

Following, a comparison screenshot:

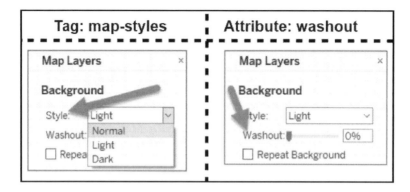

Accessing popular map servers

A TMS file may point to any one of many publicly-available map servers, commercial map servers, or an in-house map server. Setting up a map server in-house is, of course, beyond the scope of this book; however, it's important to note that this can be done if security needs dictate. In this section, we will confine ourselves to discussing three mapping services you may wish to consider for your mapping needs: ArcGIS, Stamen, and Mapbox.

ArcGIS

ArcGIS is a **geographic information system** (GIS). As the name suggest, a GIS is intended for working with geographic information; however, ArcGIS also supports other types of maps, such as street maps. Although the ArcGIS infrastructure includes various commercial packages, the platform enables the creation of maps that can be accessed without charge. As a result, many ArcGIS maps are freely available for Tableau.

You can access several ArcGIS maps via `http://www.arcgis.com/home/gallery.html`. Once you've constructed a basic TMS file, you can access many of the maps provided in the ArcGIS gallery simply by making a small adjustment to the url-format attribute, as shown here:

url-format: `/ArcGIS/rest/services/{map name here}/MapServer/tile/{Z}/{Y}/{X}`

Here's the basic information needed to create a TMS file that points to the ArcGIS World Street Map:

- **Server**: `http://services.arcgisonline.com`
- **URL Format**:
  `/ArcGIS/rest/services/World_Street_Map/MapServer/tile/{Z}/{Y}/{X}`

Can you create a TMS file using this basic information? You should be able to do so by referencing the TMS File Structure section above. Regardless, the code for a barebones TMS file is provided for ArcGIS World Street Map in the Dashboarding exercise presented later in this chapter.

Stamen

Stamen is a design firm that works on a broad variety of projects. You can know more about Stamen's mission statement and their work on their website: (`www.stamen.com`).

Stamen has various maps available at `maps.stamen.com`. The toner map is particularly good for Tableau. Since it's strictly black and white, you can create visualizations on top of the toner map using a wide variety of color schemes without clashing with the map colors.

Here's the basic information needed to create a TMS file that points to the Stamen Toner map:

- **Server**: `http://a.tile.stamen.com`
- **URL Format**: `/toner/{Z}/{X}/{Y}.png`

Can you create a TMS file using this basic information? You should be able to do so by referencing the TMS File Structure discussion above. Regardless, the code for a barebones TMS file is provided for Stamen Toner in the Dashboarding exercise presented later in this chapter.

Exploring Mapbox

Mapbox provides a mapping service with an accompanying web application that enables users to customize maps. This customizability encompasses fonts, colors, background images, and more. Mapbox provides basic services free of charge but, of course, more maps and greater bandwidth needs will require an upgrade with an accompanying fee. Be sure to visit Mapbox.com to learn how to build your own custom maps.

Exercise: Mapbox Classic

This exercise will show you how to connect to Mapbox, but does not include instructions for customizing maps through Mapbox:

1. Navigate to Mapbox.com and create an account.
2. After completing the sign up and logging into **Mapbox**, click on the Studio link located at the top of the page.
3. On the right side of the page, copy the **Access token**:

4. In the workbook associated with this chapter, navigate to the Mapbox Classic worksheet.
5. Select **Map > Background Maps > Map Services** to bring up the **Map Services** dialog box.
6. Click Add and choose **Mapbox Maps**.
7. Click on **Classic**.

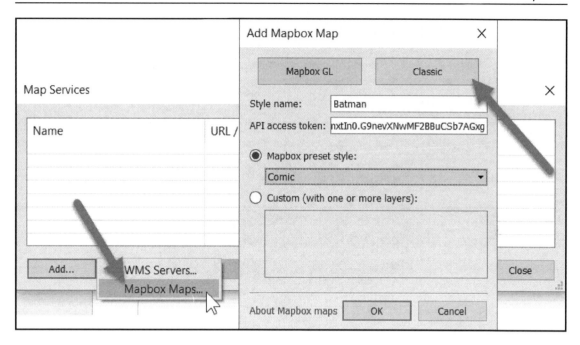

8. Name the map.
9. Paste in the API access token.
10. Select a Mapbox preset style:

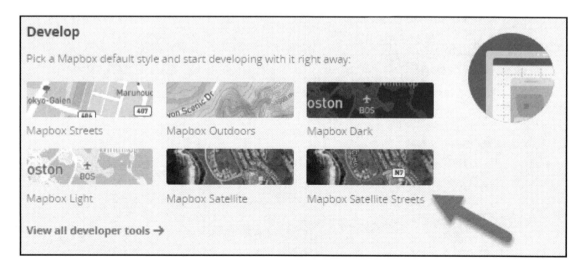

11. Close out of these dialog boxes, select the Superstore data source, and double-click on State to see the **Mapbox Map**.

Exercise: Mapbox GL

This exercise assumes that you have already created a Mapbox account. The following are the steps:

1. Log into `Mapbox.com` and click on **Products > Studio > Get Started.**
2. Select **New Style > Satellite:**

3. In the resulting webpage, under select **Share > Use > Third Party > Tableau** and click the **Copy** icon:

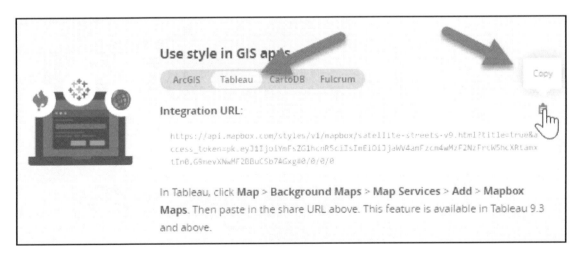

4. In the workbook associated with this chapter, navigate to the Mapbox GL worksheet.
5. Select **Map > Background Maps > Map Services** to bring up the **Map Services** dialog box.
6. Click Add and choose **Mapbox Maps**.
7. Click on **Mapbox GL**.
8. Name the map.
9. Paste in the URL that was copied from **mapbox**.
10. Tableau will fill out the remaining portion of the dialog box:

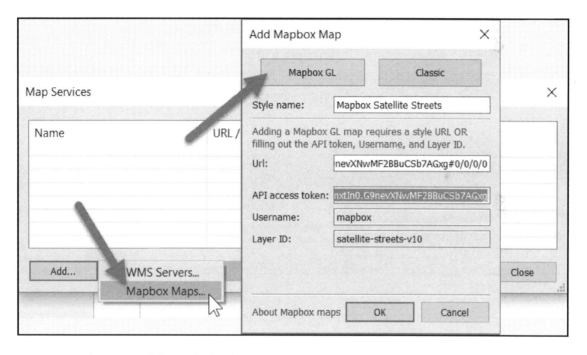

11. Close out of these dialog boxes, select the Superstore data source, and double-click on State to see the Mapbox map.

Accessing different maps with a dashboard

We will create a Dashboard that allows the end user to choose between the various maps we just discussed. The exercise assumes you've completed the exercises in the *Extending Tableau mapping with other technology* section.

Exercise: swapping maps

The technique used for this exercise is known as **Sheet Swapping**. However, a deeper dive into this technique is presented in `Chapter 11`, *Visualization Best Practices and Dashboard Design*.

Let's look at the necessary steps (the Mapbox Classic and Mapbox GL worksheets are assumed to have been completed via the Mapbox centric exercises presented earlier in this chapter):

1. Access the TMS files for ArcGIS World Street Map and Stamen Toner that you created earlier in this chapter. If you did not create the TMS files, you can use the XML presented here. Simply copy this code into a text editor for both files and then save those files with a TMS extension. Note that this code is very abbreviated but functional.

> If you choose to copy the following code, be aware that Tableau requires straight quotes; curly or slanted quotes will likely not work.

See the following code:

ArcGIS World Street Map code for the TMS file	```<?xml version="1.0" encoding="utf-8"?>```
	```<mapsource inline="true" version="8.2">```
	``` <connection class="OpenStreetMap" server='http://services.arcgisonline.com'```
	```url-format='/ArcGIS/rest/services/World_Street_Map/MapServer/tile/{Z}/{Y}/{X}'/>```
	``` <layers>```
	``` <layer display-name="World_Street_Map" name="World_Street_Map" show-```
	```ui="false" type="features" />```
	``` </layers>```
	```</mapsource>```

Stamen Toner code for the TMS file	```<?xml version="1.0" encoding="utf-8"?>```
	```<mapsource inline="true" version="8.2">```
	``` <connection class="OpenStreetMap" server='http://a.tile.stamen.com' url-```
	```format='/toner/{Z}/{X}/{Y}.png'/>```
	``` <layers>```
	``` <layer display-name="toner" name="toner" show-ui="false" type="features"```
	```/>```
	``` </layers>```
	```</mapsource>```

2. Place the newly-created TMS files in `My Tableau Repository\Mapsources` and restart Tableau.
3. Open the workbook associated with this chapter. Select the 'ArcGIS' worksheet.
4. Select the **Superstore** data source and place State on the **Detail** shelf.

5. Navigate to **Map > Background Maps** and select the **ArcGIS** map.
6. Navigate to the **StamenToner** worksheet and repeat the last two steps except, of course, choosing the **StamenToner** map.
7. Create a parameter for **ArcGIS**, **StamenToner**, **Mapbox Classic**, and **Mapbox GL**, as shown in the following screenshot:

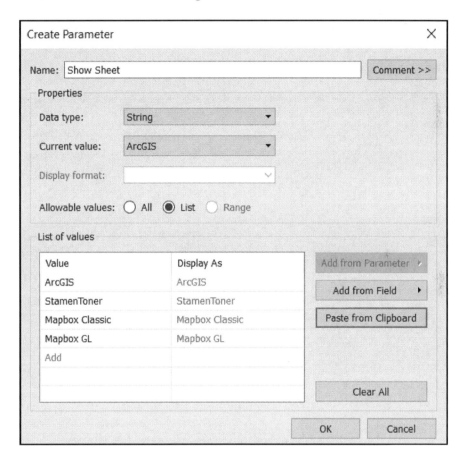

8. In the **Superstore** data source, create a calculated field named Show Sheet Filter with the [Show Sheet] code.
9. Select the **ArcGIS** worksheet.
10. Drag the **Show Sheet** Filter calculated field to the **Filters** shelf and select **ArcGIS** in the resulting dialog box.
11. Right-click on the Parameter in the **Data** pane and select Show Parameter Control.

12. Interact with the **Show Sheet** parameter on the view and select **StamenToner**. Notice that the view goes blank:

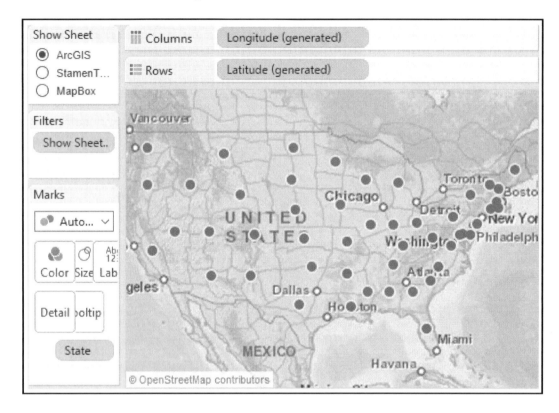

13. On the **Mapbox Classic** worksheet, show the parameter control.
14. On the **Show Sheet** parameter, select **Mapbox Classic**.
15. Drag the **Show Sheet** Filter calculated field to the **Filters** shelf and select **Mapbox GL**.
16. Repeat the last three steps for the **StamenToner** and **Mapbox GL** worksheets. Of course, be sure to set the parameter and filter to use the appropriate names for both worksheets.
17. Create a Dashboard.
18. Place a horizontal container on the Dashboard.
19. Drag the **ArcGIS** worksheet into the horizontal container.
20. Note that the worksheet does not display.
21. If the **Show Sheet** parameter does not display, click on the dropdown associated with the worksheet and choose **Show Sheet**:

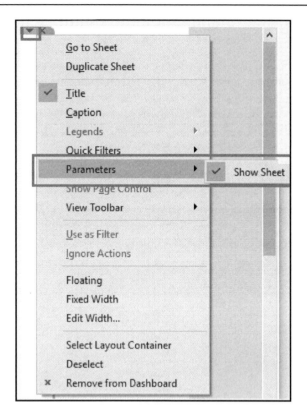

22. In the parameter dropdown, choose **ArcGIS**. The **ArcGIS** worksheet should display in the Dashboard.
23. In the Show Sheet parameter, select **StamenToner**. Note that the Dashboard goes blank.
24. Drag **StamenToner** onto the Dashboard under **ArcGIS**. The **StamenToner** worksheet now displays.
25. In the Show Sheet parameter, select **Mapbox Classic**. The Dashboard displays nothing.
26. Drag **Mapbox Classic** onto the Dashboard under **StamenToner**. The **Mapbox Classic** worksheet now displays.
27. In the Show Sheet parameter, select **Mapbox GL**. The Dashboard displays nothing.
28. Drag **Mapbox GL** onto the Dashboard under **Mapbox Classic**. The **Mapbox GL** worksheet now displays.
29. Right-click on each of the worksheet titles and select Hide Title.

Creating custom polygons

Geographic areas for which Tableau natively provides polygons include country, state/province, county, and postcode/ZIP code. This means, for example, that a filled map can easily be created for the countries of the world. Simply copy a list of the world's countries and paste that list into Tableau. Next, set the View type in Tableau to 'Filled Map' and place the country list on the details shelf. Tableau will automatically draw polygons for each of those countries.

There are some geo types for which Tableau will not automatically provide polygons. These include telephone area code and city. For these geo types, Tableau will draw a symbol map but not a filled map. Furthermore, special mapping needs may arise that require polygons to be drawn for areas that are not typically included on maps. For example, an organization may define sales regions that don't follow usual map boundaries.

Lastly, mapping needs may arise for custom images. A Tableau author may import an image of a basketball court or football pitch into Tableau and draw polygons to represent particular parts of the playing area.

To create a filled map for each of these examples for which Tableau does not natively provide polygons, custom polygons must be created. In this section, we will start with the basics by drawing a simple square around the mythical Republic of Null Island, which is located at the intersection of the prime meridian and the equator.

Exercise: Drawing a square around Null Island

We will progress to a more robust example that requires drawing polygons for every city in Texas. There is an option in Tableau that allows an author to Show Data at Default Position for unknown locations. Selecting this option will cause Tableau to set latitude and longitude coordinates of 0 (zero) for all unknown locations, thus creating a symbol on the world map 1,600 kilometers off the western coast of Africa. Tableau developers affectionately refer to this area as The Republic of Null Island and it even has its own YouTube video: https://www.youtube.com/watch?v=bjvIpI-1w84.

Exercise: steps

In this exercise, we will draw a square around Null Island:

1. Recreate the following dataset in Excel:

Point	Latitude	Longitude
0	-1	-1
1	-1	1
2	1	1
3	1	-1
4	-1	-1

2. Copy and paste the dataset into Tableau.
3. Clear the sheet by clicking on the Clear Sheet icon:

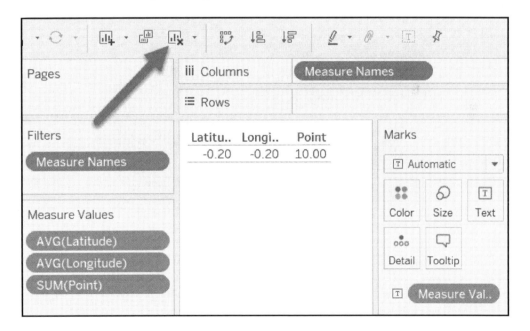

4. Convert Point to a dimension.

5. This can be accomplished by either right-clicking on Point and selecting Convert to dimension, or by dragging it to the dimensions portion of the **Data** pane.

6. Select the StamenToner map from the previous exercise or a map of your choosing.

7. Double-click on latitude and longitude. It doesn't matter in which order, Tableau will automatically place longitude on the **Columns** shelf and latitude on the **Rows** shelf.

8. Change the View type to Line.

9. Drop Point on the **Path** shelf. You should see the following results:

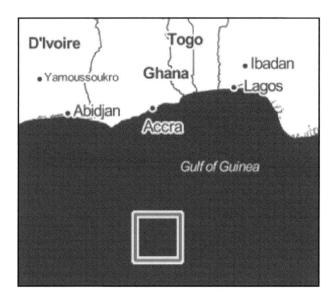

10. Create another dataset, as seen in the following table:

Point	Latitude	Longitude
0	-1	-1
1	1	1
2	-1	1
3	1	-1
4	-1	-1

11. Follow steps 2 - 8 and observe the resulting image:

This interesting but incorrect image occurred because of incorrect point ordering. As a rule of thumb, when determining point order, select an order that would make sense if you were physically drawing the polygon. If you cannot draw the desired polygon on a sheet of paper using a given point order, neither can Tableau.

Converting shape files for Tableau

A GIS file utilizes a standard format to encode geographic data. There are many GIS applications that use various flavors of this format. One popular version (or flavor) is the shape file format developed by ESRI. As of this writing, Tableau can directly read the following shape files:

- ESRI
- MapInfo
- KLM
- GeoJSON
- TopoJSON

For some shape files, there is a constraint to have other files in the same directory, in order for Tableau to process them. Please check out the Online Help for more information: `https://onlinehelp.tableau.com/current/pro/desktop/en-us/maps_shapefiles.htm`.

Exercise: polygons for Texas

As mentioned in the section *Creating custom polygons*, Tableau does natively provide polygons for several shape files.

Exercise: steps

In this exercise, we will use a `.shp` file to show the population of Texas:

1. Google the Texas City Limits Shape file and open the **Texas Department of Transportation** page.
2. On the right side, use the download dropdown and download the shape file.
3. In your download directory you should find multiple files:

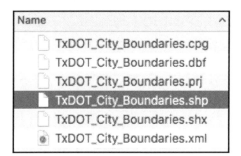

4. In the workbook associated with this chapter, navigate to the Texas_Cities worksheet and select **Data > New Data Source > Text File**.
5. Navigate to the download directory and select the `.shp` file (which is also selected in the latest screenshot).
6. Double-click Geometry. Your polygon map is ready:

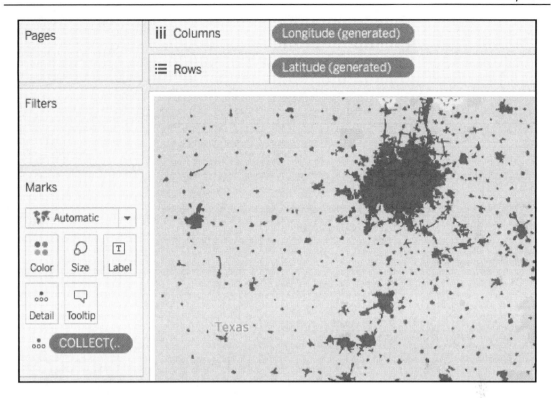

 Note that Tableau created the Geometry field and that it choose the
COLLECT measure by Default.

Heatmaps

I want to share a feature with you that was part of the Tableau 2018.3 release, and has been
proven to be very useful when working with geographical data. It is the mark-type **density**
with which you can create heatmaps. This new feature is not limited to maps; you can also
use it for any other type of chart, however it is most efficient for dense data where patterns
cannot be spotted easily.

Example

The following steps will illustrate an example of creating a heatmap:

1. Open the Citylimits tab in the workbook related to this chapter.
2. Duplicate the worksheet and name it Density.
3. Set the mark-type to **density**:

You can use the size slider for the density around the marks, you can choose different colors, and, on the color mark you can define the intensity, which will lead to a use of more or fewer spots.

Heatmaps can show you a spatial concentration, and are perfect for very dense datasets. It will be much easier to spot patterns using this fairly new functionality.

Summary

In this chapter, we explored how to extend Tableau's mapping capabilities without leaving the interface by capturing Tableau-generated latitude and longitude data, and then feeding that data back into the interface through data blending. Next, we explored various ways to extend Tableau's mapping using other technology. We connected to a WMS server, explored the structure of a TMS file, created our own TMS files, and then explored the Mapbox offering. Finally, we covered the topic of shape files.

In the next chapter, we will explore using Tableau for presentations. Specifically, we will look at how to get the best images out of Tableau, how to effectively and efficiently use Tableau with PowerPoint, and how to use Tableau directly for presentations without relying on third-party tools.

10
Tableau for Presentations

All Tableau authors are essentially storytellers. Analyzing data is more than just puzzle-solving, it is a search for a story that will make a difference. Topics can range from Airbnb to Zinka, and may be pleasantly diverting or life-changing, but they all serve a common need: to tell a story. This chapter is dedicated to helping you stock your toolkit of knowledge with ideas and methods for using Tableau to make presentations that engage, delight, and make a difference.

This chapter will explore the following presentation-centric topics:

- Getting the best images out of Tableau
- From Tableau to PowerPoint
- Embedding Tableau in PowerPoint
- Animating Tableau
- Story points and dashboards for presentations

For the content of this chapter, I'm particularly indebted to Robert Mundigl and Cathy Bridges.

Getting the best images out of Tableau

In this section, we will review options for porting an image from Tableau into other applications and discuss the pros and cons of each method. We'll begin by surveying various screenshot applications and then we will consider methods available directly in Tableau.

A brief survey of screen capture tools

Perhaps the easiest way to capture an image in Tableau is to use a screen capture tool. The following are some screen capture tools that won't impact your pocketbook:

- Snipping Tool is installed by default with Windows and, although a very simple tool with few bells and whistles, is easy to use and effective.
- Greenshot is an open source screen capture tool with many features similar to SnagIt. Visit http://getgreenshot.org/ to download the application and learn more.
- Microsoft Office OneNote includes a screen capture feature. If you have OneNote installed with Windows 7 or earlier, simply press Windows + *s* to activate the screen capture. If you are on Windows 8 or 10, press Windows + *n* and then the s key for activation.
- Grab is a screen capture utility natively available on macOS. Grab is located in the Utilities folder under applications.

Tableau's native export capabilities

One of the shortcomings of screen capture tools is that they are limited to raster images. Raster images are often sufficient for documentation or a PowerPoint presentation but are subject to pixilation if enlarged. Vector images, on the other hand, do not pixilate when enlarged and may therefore provide sharper image quality. Natively, Tableau includes both raster and vector export options. These options are discussed in the following section.

The five export types

Tableau can export images in five formats, each of which is described in the following table:

File format	Access	Pros and cons
JPEG		JPEG is a raster image format that is good for high resolution images such as photographs but does not work very well for low color images, like those typically deployed in Tableau. Export an image from Tableau in the JPEG format and then zoom in close. Note that the white Space (especially white space surrounding text) includes stray pixels of various colors. These are known as artifacts or **noise**. Although these pixels are not visible unless zoomed in, the overall impact on an exported image is that it can look blurry. Thus, there is rarely, if ever, a reason to export to JPEG from Tableau.
PNG	Worksheet > Export > Image	Like JPEG images, PNG images are raster. The advantage of the PNG format is that it works well with both high color images such as photographs and low color images like those typically used in Tableau. Export an image from Tableau in PNG format and zoom in to observe that, although pixilation occurs, the white space is comprised of only white. Unlike JPEG images, no artifacts or Noise appears. PNG should be considered the format of choice when using a raster image.
BMP		BMP is a raster image format that looks quite nice but is uncompressed and can thus result in large image files. Today, the BMP format is considered antiquated and should typically be avoided.
EMF		Since the EMF format is vector (as opposed to raster), it will not pixilate. Export an image from Tableau in EMF format and zoom in close to observe. There are drawbacks, however, to using EMF. Some images (especially fonts) will look jagged when used in Microsoft Office. Thus, to effectively use an EMF image, a vector graphic tool such as Adobe Illustrator may be needed. If the intent is to alter an image with a vector graphic tool once it's exported from Tableau, an EMF format may be warranted. However, since the post-Tableau alteration possibilities are much the same for a PDF and, as will be discussed, PDF files have additional advantages, EMF should not typically be considered.

PDF	File > Print to PDF	PDF files handle a wide variety of graphic types including vector and raster. When files are exported from Tableau using Illustrator, Tableau uses the vector type when possible. Export a worksheet using the PDF option and zoom in using Adobe Reader (or another PDF-centric application) to observe that the image will not pixilate. Adobe Reader handles images differently than Microsoft Office. The jagged results that can be seen when using EMF files in an Office document (as per the previous discussion of the EMF file type) does not occur with Adobe Reader. Furthermore, the **Print to PDF** feature has the added advantage of allowing the exportation of the entire workbook to one PDF file. As will be shown later in this chapter, this can be quite useful.

From Tableau to PowerPoint

PowerPoint is ubiquitous. Some may argue that other presentation tools such as Prezi are superior, but for many organizations (probably the vast majority) PowerPoint remains the software of choice. As such, it's important to integrate Tableau and PowerPoint efficiently and effectively. The following exercises explore various techniques for doing so.

Exercise: creating a template

For this first PowerPoint-centric exercise, a template is created that will be utilized in future exercises. It will include common PowerPoint elements such as a header and a footer. The size of the template will be 1200 x 900, which adheres to the 4:3 aspect ratio typically used for PowerPoint presentations. Of course, other sizes may be targeted, but aspect ratio should always be kept in mind. Let us look at the following steps:

1. Navigate to `https://public.tableau.com/profile/marleen.meier` to locate and download the workbook associated with this chapter.
2. Create a new worksheet and select the Superstore dataset.
3. Create the header asset.
4. Name the worksheet Header.
   - Place **Sales** on the **Color shelf**.
   - Click on the **Color shelf** and click **Edit Colors...**
   - In the resulting dialog box, click on the color box located at the right-hand side. In the resulting secondary dialog box that appears, set the HTML hex color value to **#000000**.

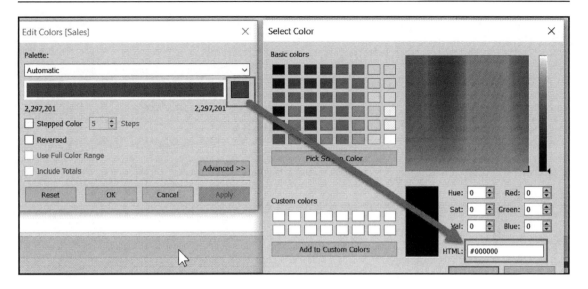

5. Create the first footer asset:
    - Duplicate the Header worksheet and name the duplicate **Footer1**.
    - Set the hex color value to #34959e. If needed, refer to the instructions used to create the Header worksheet as a guide.

6. Create the second footer asset:
    - Duplicate the **Footer1** worksheet and name the duplicate **Footer2**.
    - Set the hex color value to #4cdbe8. If needed, use the instructions used to create the Header worksheet as a guide.

7. Create the margins for the template:
    - Create a new **Dashboard** called **Template**.
    - Within the **Dashboard** pane, set the size to 1200 x 900. Note that 1200 x 900 is a 4:3 aspect ratio.
    - Display the **Dashboard** title via **Dashboard > Show Title**.
    - Double-click on the title. In the resulting dialog box, left-justify the **Text** if needed.
    - In the **Dashboard** pane, make sure that **Tiled** is selected.
    - From the **Dashboard** pane, drag **Blank** from the Objects panel and place it on the left-hand side of the Dashboard.

Be careful to place it so that it stretches from the top to the bottom of the dashboard, as shown in the following screenshot:

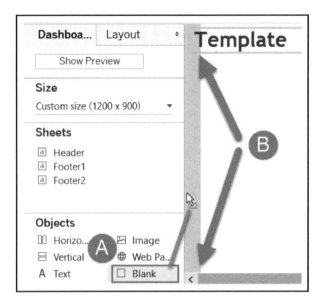

8. Repeat the previous step for the right-hand side and the bottom of the dashboard. When creating the bottom margin, be sure to position the object so that it stretches from the far right to the far left of the dashboard.

9. Size the left and right **Blank** objects to create appropriate margins. This can be accomplished by dragging the inner edge of each blank object (that is, the edges facing the center) as far to the right or left as possible:

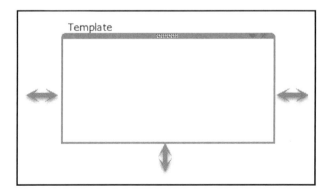

10. Create the bottom margin by clicking on the top edge of the bottom blank object and dragging it toward the title. When completed, the bottom blank object should occupy about one quarter of the vertical space. See the previous screenshot as an example.

11. Deploy the assets:
    - In the Objects portion of the **Dashboard** pane, click Floating.
    - Drag the **Header, Footer1**, and **Footer2** assets onto to the dashboard.
    - If a Sales legend appears, delete it.
    - Right-click on the title of each asset and select Hide title.
    - In the **Layout** pane enter the following values for each asset:

Header	Size				Footer1	Size				Footer2	Size			
	w	960	h	3		w	1212	h	70		w	1212	h	11
	Position					Position					Position			
	x	40	y	45		x	-6	y	828		x	-6	y	817

12. Set each asset to Entire View by clicking in the toolbar on the fit drop-down menu next to the word Standard and selecting Entire view. The results should be a line just under the title stretching across 4/5s of the dashboard and two bars at the bottom stretching across the entire dashboard:
    - Click on the container located underneath the title Template.
    - Drag the bottom edge of the container so that it is even with the top edge of **Footer2**.
    - If you have not already done so, download the assets associated with this chapter. A link is provided in the workbook.
    - Drag an **Image** container from the **Objects** portion of the **Dashboard** pane onto the dashboard. When prompted, select the bw_globe.png image supplied with this chapter. Note the globe logo that appears.
    - Drag another **Image** container from the **Objects** portion of the **Dashboard** pane onto the dashboard. When prompted, select the Mastering-Tableau.png image supplied with this chapter. Note that the text represented by the .png image is white, so it will be necessary to drag it over a colored section of the dashboard in order to see it.

- Position the containers via the **Layout** pane as shown in the following table:

Globe Logo	Size				Text Logo	Size			
	w	68	h	62		252	h	46	46
	Position					Position			
		43	y	833		x	910	y	843

Exercise: creating two dashboards

This exercise will utilize the template created previously to make two dashboards. Basic instructions are provided, but specifics are left to individual preference:

1. Right-click on the tab entitled Template created in the previous exercise, *Creating a template*, and select Duplicate sheet.
2. Repeat the previous step.
3. Rename the first duplicate sheet Superstore Loss Leaders. Rename the second duplicate sheet Map Loss Leaders.
4. Populate the Superstore Loss Leaders dashboard with the worksheets Loss Leaders Regions, Loss Leaders Cities, Loss Leaders Zip, and Filter. Arrange as desired.
5. Populate the Map Loss Leaders dashboard with the worksheets Map, Loss Leaders Cities, Loss Leaders Zip, and Filter. Arrange as desired.
6. Consider hiding some of the titles for the worksheets. For instance, the title for Filter is not necessary nor is the title for Map Loss Leaders.
7. On each dashboard select the Filter worksheet and click the Use as Filter icon.
8. On each dashboard, select both Bookcases and Tables from the Filter worksheet. Note that a worksheet with an associated action is used in place of a quick filter because the light outline used for checkboxes may not successfully make the transition to PowerPoint.
9. Right-click on Superstore Loss Leaders and Map Loss Leaders respectively and select Hide all sheets.
10. Select **File > Print to PDF**.
11. In the resulting dialog box, select the options shown in the following screenshot:

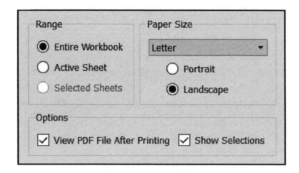

12. Click **OK** to generate a PDF and save the results.

13. Complete the exercise by saving the Tableau workbook as `PowerPoint Approaches.twbx`.

Before moving to the next step of creating a PowerPoint presentation from the dashboards we have just created, there are a few things to note about the provided worksheets. Consider Loss Leader Regions. Note that axis lines and gridlines are missing. Also note that the lines between rows for Loss Leader Cities are relatively thick and colored a dark grey. Lastly, consider Loss Leader Zip. The axis lines denoting 0 are solid instead of dotted. Tableau uses dotted lines by default.

The reason the various adjustments were made to the default lines used by Tableau is much the same as why quick filters were not used in either dashboard; that is, lightly colored lines may not successfully make the transition to PowerPoint. If it is absolutely essential that dotted and lightly colored lines display in a PowerPoint presentation, a more image-based approach may be necessary. Image-centric options are considered in the following section, but first we'll consider how to generate a PowerPoint presentation that maintains as much editable text as possible.

Exercise: creating a PowerPoint presentation

Various tools can be used to generate a PowerPoint presentation from a PDF file. Popular choices include Adobe Acrobat Pro DC and Nitro. These applications are powerful but are also relatively expensive. Also, note that the results achieved by these tools may not be any better than the results of the free online services suggested later in the chapter. In other words, be sure to download trial versions before purchasing.

The first of the services to be used, PDFResizer, is used to crop PDF files. Natively, Tableau creates a PDF with margins that does not lead to visually appealing results in PowerPoint. PDFResizer removes unwanted margins. The second service, PDF to PowerPoint, generates the PowerPoint from the PDF. The advantage of this service is that editable text is maintained in PowerPoint. The disadvantage is that the formatting may not translate as desired. Thus, additional tweaking may be needed in the Tableau workbook or in the generated PowerPoint presentation to achieve the desired results. The third service, PDF to PNG, generates PNG files. Since each PNG file represents an entire dashboard, each could be quickly placed on a PowerPoint slide to produce a presentation. The advantage to this approach is that the look of the dashboard is maintained exactly.

Unfortunately, editable text is not maintained:

1. Navigate to `https://pdfresizer.com/crop`.
2. Upload the PDF file created in the previous exercise.
3. On the web page, use the cursor to draw a marquee around the image displayed from the PDF. Be sure to include a margin at the top but no margin at the bottom or sides.
4. Crop and download the resulting PDF.

 Press *Ctrl* + mouse wheel to zoom in and more carefully set the crop.

5. Inspect the downloaded PDF to ensure the results are as desired. Pay particular attention to the margins and make sure that no white space appears on either side or the bottom.
6. Navigate to `https://www.pdftoppt.com/`.
7. Upload the PDF generated by PDFResizer and convert to PowerPoint. An email will be sent a few minutes after conversion.
8. Navigate to `http://pdf2png.com/`.
9. Upload the PDF file generated by PDFResizer and convert to PNG. The results are immediately available for download.

Exercise: automating a weekly PowerPoint presentation

The previous exercises (*Creating a Template and Creating two dashboards*) demonstrated two methods for generating a PowerPoint presentation. The methods were identical until the final steps. One approach resulted in a PowerPoint presentation with editable text. The other approach resulted in PNG images where each image represents a single slide. This exercise will consider a hybrid approach.

 Because of the shortcomings of creating a PowerPoint presentation that includes editable text but has inconsistent formatting or a PowerPoint presentation that is simply a raster image of the dashboard, a hybrid approach combining the best of both approaches often provides more consistency and better versatility.

Follow along the exercise steps:

1. Open the workbook created previously entitled `PowerPoint Approaches.twbx`.
2. Navigate to Map Loss Leaders and right-click on Map in the **Dashboard** pane and deselect Hide Sheet.
3. Navigate to the Map worksheet.
4. Remove any pills on the **Filters shelf**.
5. Right click on Sub-Category in the **Data** pane and select 'Show filter'.
6. Select **Worksheet > Export > Image...**
7. Click OK and in the resulting dialog box choose to save the image as `Map.png`.
8. Open the PowerPoint presentation generated in the previous exercise by the PDF to PowerPoint website.
9. Navigate to the first slide entitled Template.
10. Select the Insert ribbon and choose Pictures.
11. Navigate to the PNG image you just exported.

12. In the Insert dialog box, choose the drop-down selector next to **Insert** and select **Insert and Link** as shown in the following screenshot. Note that this step is important because it will allow pictures to be swapped out easily as will be demonstrated:

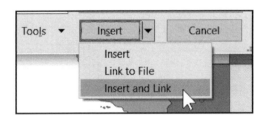

13. Save the PowerPoint presentation as `Auto Update.pptx`.
14. Close PowerPoint.
15. In Tableau, modify the Map worksheet by changing the filter.
16. Overwrite the previously exported `Map.png` image via **Worksheet > Export > Image...**
17. Open `Auto Update.pptx` and note that the new image of the map displays.

Something I come across frequently when I teach in Tableau classes, is that I encounter people who are responsible for providing PowerPoint presentations on a weekly or monthly basis. These presentations include charts and graphs that are updated along with a few annotations but the overall layout remains unchanged. The technique covered in the preceding exercise can make that process much quicker. Although Tableau Desktop only allows the author to update one image at a time, Tableau Server can be configured to export multiple images simultaneously thus making the process even more efficient. Exporting images from Tableau Server is discussed in the `Chapter 14`, *Interacting with Tableau Server* dedicated to Tableau Server.

Embedding Tableau in PowerPoint

It is possible to embed Tableau directly in a PowerPoint presentation. Or, to be more accurate, it's possible to embed a web browser through which an instance of Tableau Server may be accessed. There are various methods for accomplishing this including the Web Viewer app, a third party add-in called LiveWeb, and VBA code.

The Web Viewer app is available at `https://appsource.microsoft.com/en-us/product/office/WA104295828?tab=Overview`. Although it works well for Tableau Public, the default Tableau Server settings disallow access via Web View. LiveWeb works well but requires an additional installation. The third method mentioned previously, using VBA, is perhaps the most workable method and will be discussed next.

Exercise: creating an interactive PowerPoint presentation

The steps below utilize PowerPoint 2013 on Windows. Other versions of PowerPoint may require a slightly different approach but any differences should be relatively easy to figure out. Also, the exercise assumes that the Developer toolbar is activated. If the Developer toolbar is not activated for your instance of PowerPoint, a quick search on developer tab PowerPoint will provide instructions.

Follow along the exercise steps:

1. Create a new PowerPoint file with a single blank slide.
2. Select the Developer tab in the ribbon and click on the Command Button icon located in the **Controls** group:

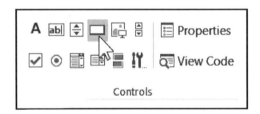

3. In the lower left-hand portion of the slide, create a **CommandButton** by clicking and dragging.
4. Right-click on the **CommandButton** just created and select Property Sheet.

5. Within the property sheet locate **Caption** and set the text to **Launch Workbook**. The command button should now be labelled **Launch Workbook**:

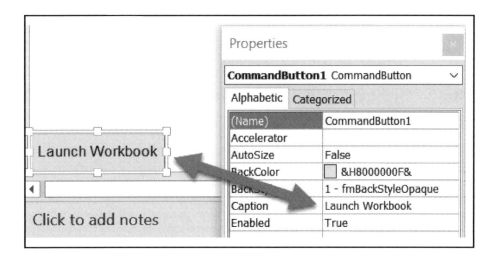

6. Within the Controls group in the Developer ribbon, select **More Controls**:

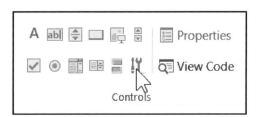

7. Within the resulting dialog box, choose **Microsoft Web Browser** and click **OK**. If a warning dialog box displays stating that **The ActiveX control cannot be inserted**, continue reading. This problem will be discussed and resolved in step 9:

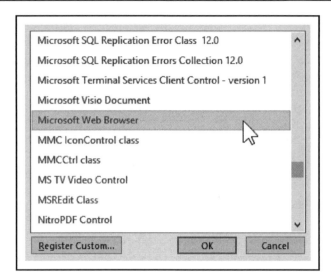

8. Drag a marquee over most of the slide allowing only enough room for the Launch Workbook command button previously created.

9. If you receive the error message displayed in the following screenshot, proceed to steps a–i. If not, skip to step 10. Note that steps a–i provide instructions regarding adjusting registry settings. Adjusting registry settings can be tricky business! Proceed at your own risk:

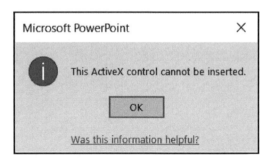

10. Save the file and close PowerPoint.

11. Press the Windows + *r*.

12. Within the Run dialog box, type Regedit.

13. In the Registry Editor, locate the following ClassID: **8856F961-340A-11D0-A96B-00C04FD705A2**. This ClassID will be located differently based on different installation methods for Office. The following three locations are likely candidates:

    - `HKEY_LOCAL_MACHINE\SOFTWARE\Microsoft\Office\15.0\Common\COM Compatibility\`

    - `HKEY_LOCAL_MACHINE\SOFTWARE\Microsoft\Office\15.0\ClickToRun\REGISTRY\MACHINE\Software\Wow6432Node\Microsoft\Office\15.0\Common\COM Compatibility\`

    - `HKEY_LOCAL_MACHINE\SOFTWARE\Wow6432Node\Microsoft\Office\15.0\Common\COM Compatibility`

14. Click on the ClassID and note the type **REG_DWORD** in the right panel.

15. Right-click on **REG_DWORD** and select Modify.

16. Change the text box labelled **Value data** to **0** and click **OK**.

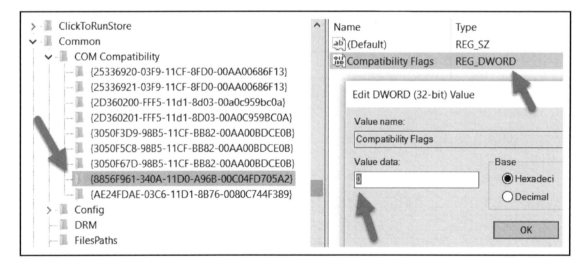

17. Start PowerPoint and open the file saved previously.

18. Now you should be able to add the Microsoft Web Browser control as described previously.

19. Right-click on the Launch Workbook command button and select View Code.

20. Within the VBA console that appears, delete any existing code and enter the following code:

```
Private Sub CommandButton1_Click()
'Begin Comment:  The above line of code gives instructions
```

```
regarding what action to take when clicking on the command button.
End Comment.
WebBrowser1.Navigate
("https://public.tableau.com/profile/david.baldwin#!/vizhome/1_Star
ter/SampleWorksheet")
'Begin Comment:  WebBrowser1 is the name of the Microsoft
WebBrowser control that the command button controls.  End Comment.
'Begin Comment:  The URL can be replaced with a URL of your
choosing.  End Comment.
'Begin Comment:  '"Navigate" is the Property/Method that accepts
the URL.  End Comment.
End Sub
```

21. Close the Visual Basic for Applications (VBA) console.
22. Press *F5* and click the Launch Workbook command button. An instance of a Tableau workbook should now display in PowerPoint.

 Note that the preceding VBA code includes comments. The statements Begin Comment and End Comment are included for clarity but are not required.

Robert Mundigl explores various techniques for embedding Tableau in PowerPoint similar to the preceding example on his blog `clearlyandsimply.com`. Perform a search on the blog for PowerPoint to explore these methods. Robert's creative ideas include a technique for accessing multiple workbooks on a single PowerPoint slide and a technique for embedding the Tableau Desktop authoring environment in PowerPoint for on-the-fly authoring without leaving the presentation interface.

Animating Tableau

Including animation in a presentation can be very effective for engaging an audience. Hans Rosling accomplishes this admirably with his popular YouTube video (`https://www.youtube.com/watch?v=jbkSRLYSojo&t=4s`), 200 Countries, 200 Years, 4 Minutes. In this video, Rosling uses data visualization to track wealth and life expectancy over time. His combination of data visualization with insightful commentary and a passion for his message makes Rosling's video a must-see for anyone interested in making appealing presentations using data.

Animation is easy to implement in Tableau but has a curious shortcoming. It is available via Tableau Reader but not Tableau Server. A worksheet with animation that is uploaded to Tableau Server will provide the end user with an option to click through each frame of the animation or access any given frame through a drop-down menu, but there is no option to play from beginning to end. With HTML5, a play option would probably not be difficult for Tableau developers to implement. So, why hasn't this been done? The following answer is speculative but perhaps defensible.

Animation is great for presentations but not well-suited for analysis. To put it another way, an animation can certainly make for engaging communication but does not work well for deeper dives into the data. Tableau Server is more geared toward analysis than making presentations in group settings. This bent toward analysis can be seen in the fact that Tableau Server allows direct viewing and exportation of underlying data. Note that Tableau Reader does not offer this capability. Also, Tableau Server can connect, of course, to external data sources whereas Tableau Reader is limited to self-contained TWBX files with no external connections. In presentation settings, this is actually an advantage for Tableau Reader, since relying on an internet connection when speaking to groups adds an extra element of risk. Therefore, Tableau Reader is more geared toward presentation than analysis and is thus better suited for animation than Tableau Server is.

Exercise: creating an animation with Tableau

The following exercise tracks ACT testing scores from 1991 to 2015. Complete the exercise to learn how to create an animation in Tableau and also discover if standardized testing results in the United States have improved over time.

Follow along the exercise steps:

1. Open the workbook associated with this chapter and navigate to the worksheet entitled ACT 1991–2015.
2. Select the ACT data source.
3. Place Year on the **Columns shelf**, Score Value on the Rows shelf, and Score Type on the **Color shelf**.
4. Right-click on the Score Value axis and select Edit Axis.
5. In the resulting dialog box, deselect Include zero.
6. Place Year on the **Pages** shelf.
7. In the **Current Page** panel that appears on the worksheet, check Show history and click on the drop-down menu. Note that neither the Show options nor the Trails options are available.

8. In the **Marks View** card, click on the drop-down menu to change the view type from Automatic to Circle.

9. Click on the **Show history** drop-down menu again and note that both the Show options and the Trails options are now available.

10. Under **Marks to Show history for** select **All**.

11. Under **Show** select **Both**.

12. Ensure that **Fade** is deselected.

13. Click on the **Format** drop-down menu under **Trails** and select the dotted line option:

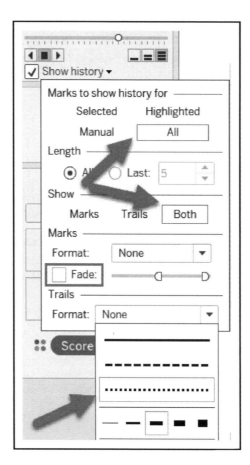

14. Interface with the Current page panel to play the animation.

Sometimes, the question 'how can I create a dashed line in Tableau?' arises. One method is demonstrated in the preceding exercise. By setting the view type to **Circle** and adjusting the **Show history** options, a dashed line was created. If a dashed line without animation is required, simply hide the Current page panel (that is, the video control panel).

To briefly extend the theme of creating dashed lines in Tableau, the shortcoming of using the **Pages** shelf is that only one line type is available per visualization. To discover how to create multiple lines with varying dash types, check out `https://boraberan.wordpress.com/2015/11/22/quick-tip-creating-your-own-dashed-line-styles-in-tableau/`, where Bora Beran has pioneered a method using calculated fields to insert NULLs to achieve differing line effects.

Exercise: using an animation to export many images

There are at least two reasons it may be necessary to export many images from a timeline. First, it may be analytically advantageous to see separate images for each time snapshot; for example, a separate image for each day in a month. Second, it may be necessary to create an animation outside of Tableau; perhaps in PowerPoint.

The next two exercises (*Using an animation to export many images* and *Using an animation in Tableau to create an animation in Power Point*), cover both scenarios:

1. Open the workbook associated with this chapter and navigate to the worksheet entitled ACT 1991 - 2015. Note that the following steps assume that the previous exercise was completed.
2. Select **File > Page Setup...**
3. At the bottom of the resulting dialog box, under **Pages Shelf** select **Show all pages**:

4. Select **File > Print to PDF**.

5. In the resulting dialog box, set Range to Active Sheet. Also set the orientation to Landscape.

6. Click OK and save the PDF as `Animation.pdf` to a location of your choice.

7. Navigate to `https://www.pdftoppt.com/`.

8. Upload `Animation.pdf` and convert it to PowerPoint. An email will be sent a few minutes after conversion.

9. Download the file via the link provided in the email.

10. Open the file in PowerPoint.

11. Within PowerPoint, select **File > Save As**.

12. Within the Save as type drop-down menu, select ***.png**:

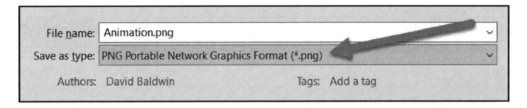

13. When prompted, choose to export all slides.

14. Save the PowerPoint presentation. Note that when PowerPoint finishes saving, a dialog box will display stating that each slide in the presentation has been saved as a separate file.

15. Open and inspect the saved PNG files as desired.

Exercise: using an animation in Tableau to create an animation in PowerPoint

1. Access the PowerPoint presentation downloaded from `https://www.pdftoppt.com/` in the previous exercise.

2. In the **View** ribbon, select **Slide Sorter** under the **Presentation Views** group.

3. Select all slides in the PowerPoint presentation except for the last one.

4. On the **Transition** ribbon under the **Timing** group, set to advance the slide after 0.10 seconds:

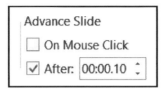

5. Press *F5* to see the animation.

To further improve the animation in PowerPoint consider the following additional steps:

1. Upload the PDF to `https://pdfresizer.com/crop` and crop the size as desired. PDFResizer was covered earlier in this chapter.
2. If the animation is too slow in PowerPoint, it is likely because all text and drawing elements are maintained. For example, the background grid is made up of individual lines. Rendering all text and drawing elements is resource intensive.

Consider creating a separate PowerPoint presentation using the PNG images created in the *Using an animation to export many images* exercise. This will lead to a quicker, smoother running animation.

Story points and dashboards for Presentations

Story points are Tableau's answer to PowerPoint. As such, each shares fundamental similarities. A PowerPoint presentation provides a linear approach to communication. So do story points in Tableau. A PowerPoint presentation provides slides, each of which is a blank canvas that provides a user with infinite possibilities to communicate ideas. A story in Tableau provides story points for the same purpose.

Although there are fundamental similarities, it is important to understand that Tableau story points and PowerPoint presentations often do not fulfill the same role. Each has advantages over the other and thus a list of pros and cons should be considered.

We can view the pros and cons of PowerPoint and Tableau story points in the following table:

Pros/Cons of PowerPoint	Pros/Cons of Tableau story points
Can be quick and easy to create	Can be more difficult to create
Easily fits different resolutions	Requires forethought regarding resolution size
Difficult to automate based on changes to underlying data	Automatically updates as underlying data changes
Difficult to create a presentation that allows for departure from linear thought	Easily allows nonlinear exploration in the middle of a presentation

So how does one decide between using PowerPoint and Tableau when making presentations? Perhaps the following list will help.

When to Use PowerPoint	When to Use Tableau story points
A presentation where the audience has little opportunity for immediate feedback	A presentation where immediate feedback is likely and exploratory questions may be asked
A one-time presentation comprised of clearly delineated points	A reusable presentation with updates mostly based on changes to underlying data
A presentation where the monitor resolution size may not be known in advance	A presentation where the monitor resolution size is known or assumed

The basics of creating and using story points are straightforward; nor as of this writing is there much beyond the basics. Since the focus of this book is on more advanced Tableau ideas and concepts, those basics will not be considered here. If you need to quickly understand story point basics, I recommend watching the six-minute video entitled Story Points located at `http://www.tableau.com/learn/tutorials/on-demand/story-points`.

Presentation resources

Using story points effectively in Tableau is perhaps more of an artistic consideration than a technical one. Although this book attempts to consistently consider best practices for data visualization and to encourage attractive and user-friendly worksheets and dashboards, a discussion of effective presentation techniques is out of its scope.

If you would like to improve your ability to create effective presentations consider the following resources:

- **Presentation Zen**: Garr Reynolds is a bestselling author and a repeat speaker at Tableau Conferences. His books and website (`https://presentationzen.com`) provide provocative ideas for effective presentations.

- **Tableau Public**: Learning by example is invaluable. Fine examples of story points can be found on Tableau Public. To learn from one of the most engaging, navigate to `https://public.tableau.com` and search for KPMG's Global Automotive Executive Survey 2016.

- **Blogs**: As of this writing, the blogosphere seems a bit light on Tableau story points; especially from the perspective of making quality presentations. One of the more interesting posts discussing Tableau story points in combination with good presentation methodology can be found on Matt Frances' blog `wannabedatarockstar.blogspot.com`. The post is entitled, Five Tips For Better Tableau Story Points.

Exercise: using Tableau dashboards to create a PowerPoint-like presentation

As discussed previously, story points are Tableau's answer to PowerPoint. However, there is one aspect to story points that Tableau authors sometimes consider a negative; that is, the ever-present Navigator bar.

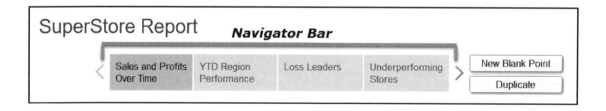

Aspects of the Navigator bar can be formatted such as font, shading, alignment, and sizing; however, it cannot be hidden or deleted. One workaround is to create linked dashboards as shown in the following exercise. Be sure to read `Chapter 11`, *Visualization Best Practices and Dashboard Design*, to learn other valuable dashboarding tips and tricks.

Note that the following steps assume that previous exercises in this chapter have been completed; specifically, the exercises entitled *Create a Template, Create Two Dashboards*, and *Creating an Animation with Tableau*.

1. Open the workbook associated with this chapter.
2. Duplicate the Template dashboard and name the duplicate Animated Dashboard.
3. Place ACT 1991–2015 on Animated Dashboard and format as desired.
4. Create a worksheet named Frt Arrow.
5. Create an ad hoc calculation by double-clicking in the bottom portion of the **Marks View** card. Enter the `Index()` code.
6. In the **Marks View** card drop-down menu, set the visualization type to Shape.
7. Click on the **Shape** shelf and select More shapes.
8. In the resulting dialog box, click on the **Select Shape Palette** drop-down menu and select the palette called **Arrows**.
9. Choose the circular, black, front arrow:

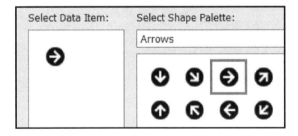

10. Set the fit of the worksheet to Entire View.
11. Click on the **Size** shelf to adjust the size of the arrow so that it uses the entire view. Be sure not to make the sizing so large that clipping occurs.
12. Select **Format > Borders**.

13. Within the Format Borders window, set **Row Divider** and **Column Divider** to **None**. This will ensure that no borders display around the arrows when they are placed on the dashboard:

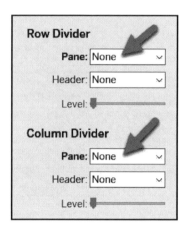

14. Select **Format > Shading**.
15. Within the **Format Shading** window, under **Default** click on the drop-down menu for Worksheet and select **More colors...**:

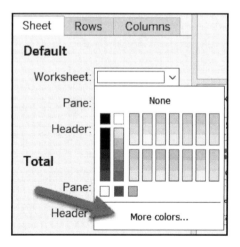

16. Within the resulting dialog box, set the shading to #34959e. This will cause the background color around the arrow to match the background color on the dashboard.

17. Select **Worksheet > Tooltip...** and deselect the Show Tooltips option.

18. Duplicate the Frt Arrow worksheet and name the duplicate Bk Arrow.

19. Click on the **Shape** shelf to swap the front arrow for the back arrow.

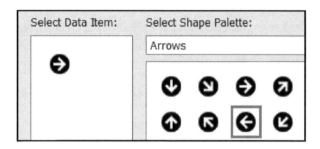

20. Open the dashboard entitled Map Loss Leaders.

21. Within the **Objects** section of the **Dashboard** Pane, click on the Floating button.

22. Place Frt Arrow and Bk Arrow on the dashboard.

23. Hide the titles for both Frt Arrow and Bk Arrow.

24. Select the **Layout** Pane and set the positioning as follows:

	Size						Size				
Frt Arrow	w	60	h	30		Bk Arrow	w	60	h	30	
	Position						Position				
	x	1145	y	835			x	1145	y	865	

25. Right-click on the **Mastering Tableau** image and select **Floating Order > Bring to Front**. The results should look like the following screenshot:

26. Select **Dashboard > Actions** and click on the Add Action button to create the filter actions pictured in the following screenshot. Pay special attention to selecting the Source and Target sheets correctly:

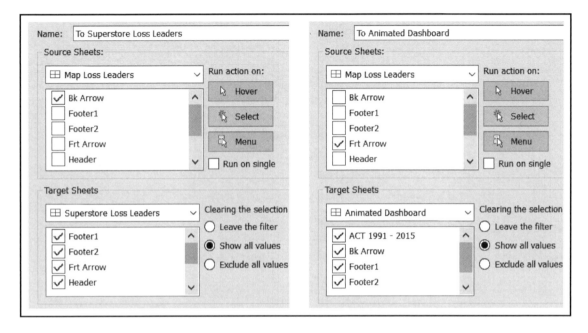

27. Open the **Superstore Loss Leaders** dashboard and place the **Frt Arrow** worksheet (but not **Bk Arrow**) on the dashboard.

28. Hide the title for **Frt Arrow**.

29. Set the positioning to be the same as the **Frt Arrow** positioning listed previously: so, w: 60 h: 30 x: 1145 y: 835.

30. Set the float order of the **Mastering Tableau** image to Front.

31. Select **Dashboard > Actions** and click on the Add Action button to create the filter action described in the following table:

Field	Selection
Name	To Map Loss Leaders
Source Sheets (Dropdown)	Superstore Loss Leaders
Source Sheets (Checkbox)	Frt Arrow
Target Sheets (Dropdown)	Map Loss Leaders
Target Sheets (Checkboxes)	All
Run action on	Select
Clearing the selection will	Show all values

32. Open Animated Dashboard and place the **Bk Arrow** worksheet (but not **Frt Arrow**) on the dashboard.

33. Hide the title for **Bk Arrow**.

34. Set the positioning to be the same as the Bk Arrow positioning listed in step 17: so, w: 60 h: 30 x: 1145 y: 865.

35. Set the float order of the **Mastering Tableau** image to Front.

36. Select **Dashboard > Actions** and click on the Add Action button to create the filter action described in the following table:

Field	Selection
Name	To Map Loss Leaders
Source Sheets (Dropdown)	Animated Dashboard
Source Sheets (Checkbox)	Bk Arrow
Target Sheets (Dropdown)	Map Loss Leaders
Target Sheets (Checkboxes)	All
Run action on:	Select
Clearing the selection will	Show all values

37. In the toolbar, click on the Presentation Mode icon or Press *F7* to enter presentation mode and test the buttons.

Summary

We began this chapter by exploring various screen capture tools as well as Tableau's native export capabilities. Next, we turned our consideration to PowerPoint, where we explored various methods for creating PowerPoint presentations from Tableau workbooks, and even explored how to embed a live instance of Tableau in PowerPoint. Next, we considered Tableau animation. Lastly, we explored how to use story points and dashboards for presentations. Since Tableau 2019.1 you can also create an export directly to Power Point through File > Export as PowerPoint. Try it and see what you like better.

In the Chapter 11, *Visualization Best Practices and Dashboard Design*, we will turn our attention to dashboarding, where we will push beyond the normal boundaries of the typical dashboard but not lose focus on the practical applications.

11
Visualization Best Practices and Dashboard Design

This chapter was particularly influenced by the giants in data visualization and dashboard design – Edward Tufte and Stephen Few. I would also like to draw attention to Alberto Cairo – a relatively new voice who is providing new insights. Each of these authors should be considered a must read for anyone working in data visualization.

This chapter will address three main categories with the intent of empowering the reader with design knowledge and Tableau-centric techniques for creating effective dashboards.

In this chapter, we will cover the following topics:

- Visualization design theory
- Formatting rules
- Color rules
- Visualization type rules
- Compromises
- Keeping visualizations simple
- Dashboard design
- Dashboard layout
- Sheet Selection

Visualization design theory

Any discussion about designing dashboards should begin with information about constructing well-designed content. The quality of the dashboard layout, and the utilization of technical tips and tricks, do not matter if the content is subpar. In other words, we should consider the worksheets displayed on dashboards and ensure that those worksheets are well-designed. Therefore, our discussion will begin with a consideration of visualization design principles. Regarding these principles, it's tempting to declare a set of rules, such as the following:

- To plot change over time, use a line graph
- To show breakdowns of the whole, use a treemap
- To compare discrete elements, use a bar chart
- To visualize correlations, use a scatter plot

But of course, even a cursory review of this list brings to mind many variations and alternatives! Thus, in the next section, *Formatting Rules*, we will consider various rules, while keeping in mind that rules (at least rules such as these) are meant to be broken.

Formatting rules

The following formatting rules encompass fonts, lines, and bands. Fonts are, of course, an obvious formatting consideration. Lines and bands, however, may not be something you typically think of when formatting – especially when considering formatting from the perspective of Microsoft Word. But if we broaden formatting considerations to think of Adobe Illustrator, InDesign, and other graphic design tools, lines and bands are certainly considered. This illustrates that data visualization is closely related to graphic design and that formatting considers much more than just textual layout.

Rule: keep the font choice simple

Typically, using one or two fonts on a dashboard is advisable. More fonts can create a confusing environment and interfere with readability. Fonts chosen for titles should be thick and solid, while the body fonts should be easy to read. As of Tableau 10.0, choosing appropriate fonts is simple because of the new Tableau Font Family. Select **Format > Font** to display the **Format Font** window to see and choose these new fonts.

Assuming your dashboard is primarily intended for the screen, sans-serif fonts are best. On the rare occasion that a dashboard is primarily intended for print, you may consider serif fonts, particularly if the print resolution is high.

Rule: using lines in order of visibility

The pseudo-formula Trend line > Fever line > Reference line > Drop line > Zero line > Grid line is intended to communicate line visibility. For example, trend-line visibility should be greater than fever-line visibility. Visibility is usually enhanced by increasing line thickness, but may be enhanced via color saturation or by choosing a dotted or dashed line over a solid line. Let's look at each of the line types:

- **Trend lines**: The trend line, if present, is usually the most visible line on the graph. Trend lines are displayed via the **Analytics** pane and can be adjusted via **Format > Lines**.

- **Fever lines**: The fever line (for example, the line used on a time-series chart) should not be so heavy as to obscure twists and turns in the data. Although a fever line may be displayed as dotted or dashed by utilizing the **Pages** shelf, this is usually not advisable because it may obscure visibility. The thickness of a fever line can be adjusted by clicking on the **Size** shelf in the **Marks View** card.

- **Reference lines**: Usually less prevalent than fever or trend lines and can be formatted via **Format > Reference lines**.

- **Drop lines**: Not frequently used. To deploy drop lines, right-click in a blank portion of the view and select **Drop lines > Show drop lines**. Next, click a point in the view to display a drop line. To format drop lines, select **Format > Droplines**. Drop lines are relevant only if at least one axis is utilized in the visualization.

- **Zero lines**: These are sometimes referred to as base lines, and only display if zero or negative values are included in the view, or positive numerical values are relatively close to zero. Format zero lines via **Format > Lines**.

- **Grid lines**: These should be the most muted lines on the view and may be dispensed with altogether. Format grid lines via **Format > Lines**.

Rule: band in groups of three to five

Visualizations composed of a tall table of text or horizontal bars should segment dimension members in groups of three to five.

Exercise: banding

Please follow along the steps:

1. Navigate to `https://public.tableau.com/profile/marleen.meier` to locate and download the workbook associated with this chapter.
2. Navigate to the Banding worksheet.
3. Select the Superstore data source and place Product Name on the **Rows** shelf.
4. Double-click on Discount, Profit, Quantity, and Sales.
5. Navigate to **Format > Shading** and set **Band Size** under **Row Banding** so that three to five lines of text are encompassed by each band. Be sure to set an appropriate color for both **Pane** and **Header**:

Note that after completing *step 4*, Tableau defaulted to banding every other row. This default formatting is fine for a short table, but is quite busy for a tall table.

 The Band in Groups of Three to Five rule is influenced by Dona W. Wong, who, in her book *The Wall Street Journal Guide to Information Graphics*, recommends separating long tables or bar charts with thin rules to separate the bars in groups of three to five to help readers read across.

Color rules

It seems slightly ironic to discuss color rules in a book that will be printed in black and white (of course that may not be true if you are reading this book on an electronic device). Nevertheless, even in a monochromatic setting, a discussion of color is relevant. For example, exclusive use of black text communicates something different than using variations of gray. The following survey of color rules should be helpful for insuring that you use colors effectively in a variety of settings.

Rule: keep colors simple and limited

Stick to the basic hues and provide only a few (perhaps three to five) hue variations. In his book, *The Functional Art: An Introduction to Information Graphics and Visualization*, Alberto Cairo provides insight as to why this is important:

> *The limited capacity of our visual working memory helps explain why it's not advisable to use more than four or five colors or pictograms to identify different phenomena on maps and charts.*

Rule: respect the psychological implications of colors

In western society, there is a color vocabulary so pervasive that it's second nature. Exit signs marking stairwell locations are red. Traffic cones are orange. Baby boys are traditionally dressed in blue, while baby girls wear pink. Similarly, in Tableau, reds and oranges should usually be associated with negative performance while blues and greens should be associated with positive performance. Using colors counterintuitively can cause confusion.

Rule: be colorblind friendly

Colorblindness is usually manifested as an inability to distinguish red and green, or blue and yellow. Red/green and blue/yellow are on opposite sides of the color wheel. Consequently, the challenges these color combinations present for colorblind individuals can be easily recreated with image-editing software such as Photoshop. If you are not colorblind, convert an image with these color combinations to greyscale and observe. The challenge presented to the 8.0% of men and 0.5% of women who are colorblind becomes immediately obvious!

Rule: use pure colors sparingly

The resulting colors from the following exercise should be a very vibrant red, green, and blue. Depending on the monitor, you may even find it difficult to stare directly at the colors. These are known as **pure colors** and should be used sparingly, perhaps only to highlight particularly important items.

Exercise: using pure colors

Please follow along the exercise steps:

1. Open the workbook associated with this chapter and navigate to the Pure Colors worksheet.
2. Select the Superstore data source and place Category on both the **Rows** shelf and the **Color** shelf.
3. Set the Fit to Entire View.
4. Click on the **Color** shelf and choose **Edit Colors**....
5. In the **Edit Colors** dialog box, double-click on the color icons to the left of each dimension member, that is, **Furniture**, **Office Supplies**, and **Technology**:

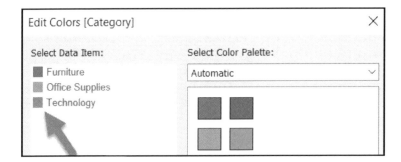

6. Within the resulting dialog box, set furniture to an HTML value of #0000ff, Office Supplies to #ff0000, and Technology to #00ff00.

Rule: color variations over symbol variation

Deciphering different symbols takes more mental energy for the end user than distinguishing color. Therefore, color variation should be used over symbol variation. This rule can actually be observed in Tableau defaults. Create a scatter plot and place a dimension with many members on the **Color** shelf and **Shape** shelf, respectively. Note that by default, the view will display 20 unique colors but only 10 unique shapes. Older versions of Tableau (such as Tableau 9.0) display warnings that include text such as ...the recommended maximum for this shelf is 10.

See the following screenshot as an example of symbol variation:

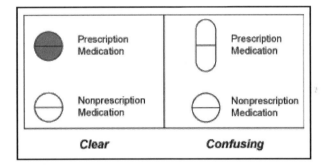

Visualization type rules

Since there's a chapter dedicated to visualization types, Chapter 8, *Beyond the Basic Chart Types*, and since much of this book explores various visualizations, we won't take the time here to delve into a lengthy list of visualization type rules. However, it does seem appropriate to review at least a couple of rules. Here, we will consider keeping shapes simple and effectively using pie charts.

Rule: keep shapes simple

Too many shape details impede comprehension. This is because shape details draw the user's focus away from the data. Consider the following exercise using two different shopping cart images.

Exercise: shapes

Let us look at the following exercise steps:

1. Open the workbook associated with this chapter and navigate to the **Simple Shopping Cart** worksheet.
2. Note that the visualization is a scatterplot that shows the top-10-selling Sub-Categories in terms of total sales and profits.
3. Navigate to the Shapes directory located in the My Tableau Repository. On my computer, the path is `C:\Users\Marleen Meier\Documents\My Tableau Repository\Shapes`.
4. Within the Shapes directory, create a folder named My Shapes.
5. Reference the link included in the comment section of the worksheet to download assets associated with this chapter.
6. In the downloaded material, find the images entitled Shopping_Cart and Shopping_Cart_3D, then copy those images into the My Shapes directory.
7. In Tableau, access the **Simple Shopping Cart** worksheet.
8. Click on the **Shape** shelf and then select More Shapes.
9. Within the **Edit Shape** dialog box, click the Reload Shapes button.
10. Select the My Shapes palette and set the shape to the simple shopping cart.
11. After closing the dialog box, click on the **Size** shelf and adjust as desired. Also adjust other aspects of the visualization as desired.
12. Navigate to the **3D Shopping Cart** worksheet and then repeat steps 8 - 11 above. Instead of using the **Simple Shopping Cart**, use the **3D Shopping Cart**:

See following, a comparison of simple and 3D shopping carts:

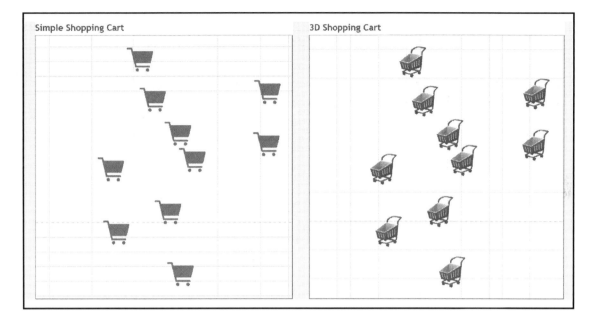

From the preceding screenshot, compare the two visualizations. Which version of the shopping cart is more attractive? Likely the cart with the 3D look was your choice. Why not choose the more attractive image? Making visualizations attractive is only of secondary concern. The primary goal is to display the data as clearly and efficiently as possible. A simple shape is grasped more quickly and intuitively than a complex shape. Besides, the cuteness of the 3D image will quickly wear off.

Rule: use pie charts sparingly

Edward Tufte makes an acrid (and somewhat humorous) comment against the use of pie charts in his book, *The Visual Display of Quantitative Information*, saying that a table is always better than a pie chart, because we humans fail to interpret the visual dimension of pie charts.

The present sentiment in data-visualization circles is largely sympathetic to Tufte's criticism. There may, however, be some exceptions, that is, some circumstances where a pie chart is optimal. Consider the following visualization:

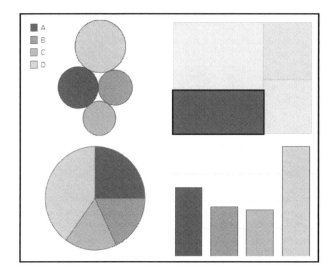

Which of the four visualizations best demonstrates that **A** accounts for 25% of the whole? Clearly it's the pie chart! Therefore, perhaps it is fairer to refer to pie charts as limited and to use them sparingly, as opposed to considering them inherently evil.

Compromises

In this section, we will transition from more or less strict rules to compromises. Often, building visualizations is a balancing act. It's not uncommon to encounter contradictory direction from books, blogs, consultants, and within organizations. One person may insist on utilizing every pixel of space while another advocates simplicity and whitespace. One counsels a guided approach while another recommends building wide-open dashboards that allow end users to discover their own path. Avant-guard types may crave esoteric visualizations, while those of a more conservative bent prefer to stay with convention. Let's explore a few of the more common competing requests and then suggest compromises.

Making the dashboard simple and dashboard robust

Recently a colleague showed me a complex dashboard he had just completed. Although he was pleased that he had managed to get it working well, he felt the need to apologize by saying, I know it's dense and complex but it's what the client wanted. Occam's Razor encourages the simplest possible solution for any problem. For my colleague's dashboard, the simplest solution was rather complex. This is OK! Complexity in Tableau dashboarding need not be shunned. But a clear understanding of some basic guidelines can help the author intelligently determine how to compromise between demands for simplicity and demands for robustness.

- *More frequent data updates necessitate simpler design:* Some Tableau dashboards may be near real-time. Third-party technology may be utilized to force a browser that displays a dashboard via Tableau Server to refresh every few minutes to ensure the latest data displays. In such cases, the design should be quite simple. The end user must be able to see at a glance all pertinent data and should not use that dashboard for extensive analysis. Conversely, a dashboard that is refreshed monthly can support high complexity and thus may be used for deep exploration.

- *Greater end user expertise supports greater dashboard complexity:* Know thy users. If they want easy, at-a-glance visualizations, keep the dashboards simple. If they like deep dives, design accordingly.

- *Smaller audiences require more precise design:* If only a few people monitor a given dashboard, it may require a highly customized approach. In such cases, specifications may be detailed, which are complex and difficult to execute and maintain because the small user base has expectations that may not be natively easy to produce in Tableau.

- *Screen resolution and visualization complexity are proportional:* Users with low-resolution devices will need to interact fairly simply with a dashboard. Thus the design of such a dashboard will likely be correspondingly uncomplicated. Conversely, high-resolution devices support greater complexity.

- *Greater distance from the screen requires larger dashboard elements:* If the dashboard is designed for conference-room viewing, the elements on the dashboard may need to be fairly large to meet the viewing needs of those far from the screen. Thus, the dashboard will likely be relatively simple. Conversely, a dashboard to be viewed primarily on end users' desktops can be more complex.

Although these points are all about simple versus complex, do not equate simple with easy. A simple and elegantly-designed dashboard can be more difficult to create than a complex dashboard.

Steve Jobs already said, that the simple way can be harder than the complex, however, simple can move mountains.

Presenting dense information and sparse Information

Normally, a line graph should have a max of four or five lines. However, there are times when you may wish to display many lines. A compromise can be achieved by presenting many lines and empowering the end user to highlight as desired. The following line graph displays the percentage of Internet usage by country from 2000 - 2012. Those countries with the largest increases have been highlighted. Assuming that Highlight Selected Items has been activated within the Color legend, the end user can select items (countries in this case) from the legend to highlight as desired. Or, even better, a worksheet can be created that lists all countries and is used in conjunction with a highlight action on a dashboard to focus attention on selected items on the line graph.

We can see the example in the following screenshot:

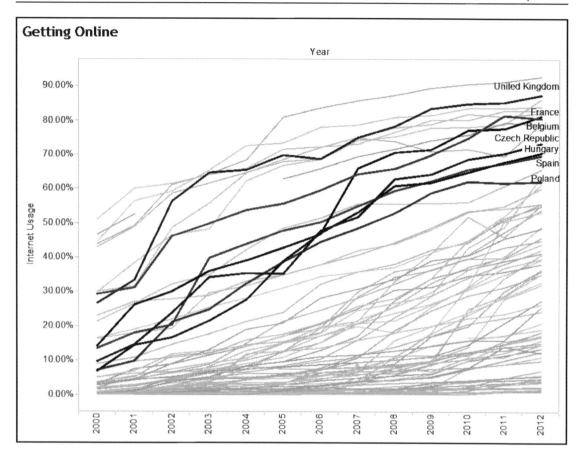

Getting Online

Telling a story

In his excellent book, *The Functional Art: An Introduction to Information Graphics and Visualization*, Albert Cairo includes a section where he interviews prominent data visualization and information graphics professionals. Two of these interviews are remarkable for their opposing views. Jim Grimwade mentions that, visualization designers should not try to make editors out of users, expecting them to make up a story on their own is not the approach he likes. On the contrary, Moritz Stefaner is fascinated by being able to explore key insights on big data sets on his own.

Fortunately, the compromise position can be found in the Jim Grimwade interview where he states that the New York Times let you explore complex data sets, but that beforehand, they give the reader some context.

Although the scenarios considered here are likely quite different from the Tableau work you are involved in, the underlying principles remain the same. You can choose to tell a story or build a platform that allows the discovery of numerous stories. Your choice will differ depending on the given dataset and audience. If you choose to create a platform for story discovery, be sure to take the New York Times approach suggested by Grimwade. Provide hints, pointers, and good documentation to lead your end user to successfully interact with the story you wish to tell or to successfully discover their own story.

Documenting

In the *Telling a story* section, we considered the suggestion of providing hints, pointers, and good documentation, but there's an issue. These things take up space. Dashboard space is precious. Often, Tableau authors are asked to squeeze more and more stuff on a dashboard and are hence looking for ways to conserve space. Here are some suggestions for maximizing documentation on a dashboard while minimally impacting screen real-estate:

- **Craft titles for clear communication**: Titles are expected. Not just a title for a dashboard and worksheets on the dashboard, but also titles for legends, filters, and other objects. These titles can be used for effective and efficient documentation. For instance, a filter should not just read Market. Instead it should say something such as Select a Market. Notice the imperative statement. The user is being told to do something and this is a helpful hint. Adding a couple of words to a title will usually not impact dashboard space.

- **Use subtitles to relay instructions**: A subtitle will take up some extra space, but it does not have to be much. A small, italicized font immediately underneath a title is an obvious place a user will look for guidance. Consider an example: Red represents loss. This short sentence could be used as a subtitle that may eliminate the need for a legend and thus actually save space.

- **Use intuitive icons**: Consider a use case of navigating from one dashboard to another. Of course, you could associate an action with some hyperlinked text that states Click here to navigate to another dashboard. But this seems unnecessary when an action can be associated with a small, innocuous arrow, such as is natively used in PowerPoint, to communicate the same thing.

- **Store more extensive documentation in a tooltip associated with a help icon**: A small question mark in the upper-right corner of an application is common. Currently, I'm composing this chapter in Word 2013, which has such a question mark. This clearly communicates where to go if additional help is required. As shown in the following exercise, it's easy to create a similar feature on a Tableau dashboard.

Exercise: tooltips for extensive help

Follow along the steps:

1. Open the workbook associated with this chapter and navigate to the Help worksheet.
2. Hover over the question mark on the worksheet and note the text that appears.

 Note that Lorem ipsum... is commonly used by web designers, who borrowed it from typesetters, who have been using this Latin text as a placeholder for centuries. Visit `www.loremipsum.io` to learn more.

3. The text in this worksheet was deployed via **Worksheet > Tooltip**. This worksheet could be thoughtfully placed on a dashboard (for example, in the upper-right corner) to give very detailed documentation that minimally impacts space.

Keeping visualizations simple

Some people tire of seeing the same chart types over and over. This leads to requests such as, Can we spice up the dashboard a bit? Normally such sentiments should be resisted. As stated at the beginning of this chapter, introducing variety for its own sake is counterproductive. Nevertheless, there are times when a less common visualization type may be a better choice than a more popular type. When are those times?

Use less common Chart Types in the following scenarios:

- The chart is used to catch the end user's attention
- The chart type presents the data more effectively

Sometimes a less common chart type can be effectively used to catch the end user's attention for some particular goal, such as humor, making a salient point, or making the visualization more memorable. One such example can be found on the Tableau 404 error page. Navigate to `http://www.tableau.com/asdf` and observe Sasquatch in a packed bubble chart. Note that this page changes from time to time so you may see Elvis, aliens, or some other visualization.

An example of the second point is using a treemap over a pie chart. Both are non-Cartesian chart types (visualizations with no fields on the **Rows** or **Columns** shelves) used to show parts of a whole. Pie charts are the more common of the two, but treemaps usually present the data better. There are at least three reasons for this:

- A treemap can represent more data points
- The rectangular nature of a treemap fits monitor space more efficiently
- Pie slice sizes are more difficult to distinguish than sizes of treemap segments

Sometimes using a less common visualization type may elicit complaints. I like pie charts. Give me a pie chart! In such cases, a compromise may be possible. Later in this chapter we will consider sheet swapping. As you will learn, sheet swapping can allow the end user to determine which visualization type to view. In the end, if a compromise is not possible and the person responsible for your paycheck desires a less-than-ideal chart type... well, I recommend a chipper you got it!

Dashboard design

Now that we have completed our discussion of visualization theory, let's turn our attention to dashboard design. We'll begin by asking the question, what is a dashboard? This is rather difficult to answer; however, its usage in everyday conversation in many organizations would suggest that people have a definite idea as to what a dashboard is. Furthermore, search engine results provide no shortage of definitions. But those definitions can differ significantly and even be contradictory.

Why is it so difficult to define dashboard? In part, it is because data visualization as a whole, and dashboarding specifically, is an emerging field that combines many other disciplines. These disciplines include statistical analysis, graphic and web design, computer science, and even journalism. An emerging field with so many components is a moving target, and as such is difficult to define.

For our purposes, we will begin with Stephen Few's definition as it first appeared in an issue of *Intelligent Enterprise* in 2004. He states that a dashboard is a visual display of vital statistics we need to reach, and how all these details are present on a sole screen, so that this information can be observed at first sight. Then we'll extend and adapt that definition for Tableau dashboards.

Although this definition is good, Tableau takes a broader approach. For instance, a Tableau dashboard may be contained on a single screen, but can be designed (and quite effectively designed) to require scrolling. More importantly, Tableau dashboards are typically interactive, which opens a world of exploration, analysis, and design options. Therefore, let's attempt a Tableau-centric dashboard definition.

> A Tableau dashboard is a display that contains one or more data visualizations designed to enable a user to quickly view metrics. This display may provide interactive elements, such as filtering, highlighting, and drill down capabilities that enable further exploration and analysis.

Dashboard layout

The layout of a dashboard is important for the same reason that the layout of a magazine foldout or a webpage is important. Placing the right information in the right place helps the viewer quickly and efficiently gather information and draw conclusions. In order to appreciate this fact, consider the last time you had to hunt through a poorly-constructed web page to find important information. Your time could have been better used actually applying that important information!

The golden rectangle layout

You have probably heard of the Fibonacci Sequence, the Golden Rectangle, and the Golden Ratio. Since it may have been a few years since you attended a math class, a brief reminder may prove helpful.

The Fibonacci Sequence is a series of numbers where every number is the sum of the previous two numbers, for example, 1, 1, 2, 3, 5, 8, 13, 21.

A Golden Rectangle is achieved when the ratio of the longest side to the shortest side of a rectangle is approximately 1.618. This ratio is known as the Golden Ratio. Mathematically, the Golden Ratio is represented as follows:

$$\varphi = \frac{1 + \sqrt{5}}{2} \approx 1.61803398874989...$$

You can see the connection between the Fibonacci Sequence and the Golden Ratio when dividing each number of the Fibonacci Sequence by the previous number, for example, take the following sequence:

0, 1, 1, 2, 3, 5, 8, 13, 21, 34

This leads to the following:

1/1=1, 2/1=2, 3/2=1.5, 5/3=1.67, 8/5=1.6, 13/8=1.625, 21/13=1.615, 34/21=1.619

Now let's consider a dashboard layout using the Golden Rectangle. The layout shown here is constructed of rectangles such that each is 1.618 times longer or taller than the next. The spiral (known as the Golden Spiral) is displayed to demonstrate the order of the rectangles:

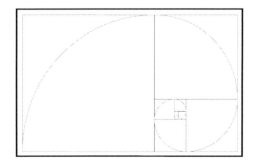

The Fibonacci Sequence/Golden Rectangle/Golden Ratio appears endlessly in nature and throughout history. Many sea shells and flowers adhere to the Fibonacci sequence. The Great Pyramid of Giza appears to have been constructed with the Golden Ratio in mind. Phidias likely used the Golden Ratio to design his statues for the Athenian Parthenon. Indeed the Parthenon itself was designed with Golden Rectangle proportions.

So does the Golden Rectangle, as pictured in the preceding diagram, represent the ideal dashboard layout? Perhaps it's truer to say that this image represents one acceptable dashboard layout. The ideal is not so much found in the abstract as it's found in the application. Dashboard layouts may sometimes approximate the Golden Rectangle but, as we will see, other dashboard layouts may be better for different scenarios.

The dashboard pictured here (which is also available in the Tableau workbook that accompanies this chapter) utilizes the Golden Rectangle:

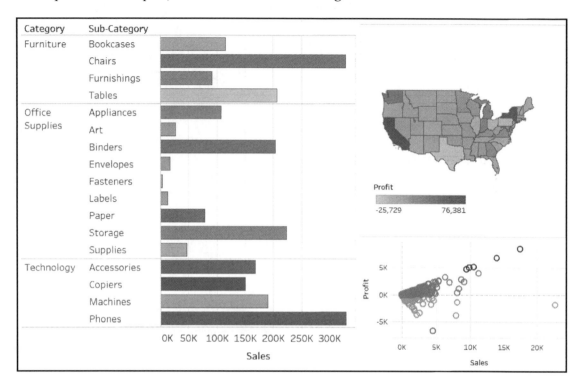

Notice that this example does not attempt to follow the Golden Spiral through to smaller and smaller rectangles. There are practical limits.

The Golden Rectangle layout is particularly good for guiding the viewer from courser to finer granularity. In this example, the left portion of the dashboard displays the coarsest granularity, 17 subcategories. The map is next. Finally, the scatterplot displays the finest granularity. Creating actions that follow this path would make a natural interaction for the end user. For example, an end user might first click on Tables and next click on the state of Pennsylvania in order to observe outliers in the scatterplot.

The quad layout

The Quad layout divides a dashboard into four more or less equal quadrants. It's easy to implement. On a blank dashboard, simply double-click on four worksheets in the **Dashboard** pane. The result is a Quad layout, though some small adjustments may need to be made to account for legends, filters, and parameters. To observe a Quad layout, refer to the diagram just before the *Rule – Use Pie Charts Sparingly* section.

The small multiple layout

A Small Multiple layout displays many views on a single dashboard. Like the Quad layout, a Small Multiple layout can be implemented simply by double-clicking on each desired worksheet in the **Dashboard** pane. Small Multiples are useful when viewing information that utilizes the same visualization type repeatedly. Also, a consistent theme is helpful; for example, the following screenshot demonstrates a theme of profit performance per state in the USA. Attempting to create a Small Multiple with multiple visualization types and multiple themes will likely be messy and difficult to interact with:

Some layouts are essentially variations on a theme. For instance, a layout that displays three views where one view on the dashboard covers double the real-estate of each of the other views may essentially be a variation of the Quad layout. Other layouts defy easy categorization and are unique to a given dashboard. Regardless, this will hopefully provide some food for thought as you design dashboards in the future.

Sheet selection

Sheet selection, often referred to as sheet swapping, allows the Tableau author to hide and display visualizations as well as move worksheets on and off the dashboard. These techniques have been used in creative ways with some very impressive results. For example, Tableau Zen Master Joshua Milligan has built various games, including Tic-Tac-Toe and Blackjack, using sheet selection. For our purposes, we will stick to using sheet selection to assist with creating dashboards that adhere to the design principles we've discussed.

In the section *Rule: use pie charts sparingly* we discussed pie charts and treemaps, we noted that a treemap is a better visualization but people are often more comfortable with pie charts. As a compromise, in the first exercise we will review an example that allows the end user to choose whether to see a pie chart or a treemap.

In the section *Documenting*, the point was made that dashboard space is precious. In the second exercise, we will review an example that will use sheet selection to allow the end user to show or hide filters, and thus make more efficient use of screen real-estate.

Exercise: sheet swapping pie charts and treemaps

Please follow along the exercise steps:

1. Open the workbook associated with this chapter and navigate to the Population Pie worksheet.
2. Select the World Indicators data source and note the calculated field, called Blank. The code is composed of single quotes with a space in between.
3. Place Blank on the **Columns** shelf.
4. Non-Cartesian visualization types (for example, visualizations with no fields on the **Rows** or **Columns** shelves) require this step for sheet swapping to work. Otherwise, when placing the worksheet in a Vertical container on a dashboard, the worksheet will not properly stretch to fill the width of the container.

5. In the view, select all pie slices via *Ctrl + A* or by dragging a marquee around the entire pie.
6. Right-click on any pie slice and choose **Annotate > Mark**.
7. In the resulting dialog box, delete all text except `<Country>`.
8. Position and format the annotations as desired. Note that additional adjustments may be required once the pie chart is deployed on a dashboard.
9. Create a parameter named Select Chart Type with the following settings:
   - **Data Type**: String
   - **Current Value**: Pie Chart
   - **Allowable Values**: List
   - Create the following for Value and Display As:

Value	Display As
Pie Chart	Pie Chart
Treemap	Treemap

 Note that the preceding Current Value setting is important.

10. Create a calculated field entitled Sheet Swap with the `[Select Chart Type]` code; that is, the calculated field will simply reference the parameter.
11. Place Sheet Swap on the **Filters** shelf and select Pie Chart in the resulting dialog box.
12. Display the parameter by right-clicking on Select Chart Type and choosing Show Parameter Control.
13. In the displayed parameter, toggle back and forth between Pie Chart and Treemap, then observe.
14. Navigate to the Population Tree worksheet.
15. Place Blank on the **Columns** shelf.
16. Place Sheet Swap on the **Filters** shelf and select Treemap in the resulting dialog box.
17. If Treemap does not display as a choice, make sure that the Select Chart Type parameter is toggled to Treemap.
18. Create a new dashboard entitled Latin American Population.
19. In the **Dashboard** pane, double-click on Vertical to place a vertical container on the dashboard.

20. In the **Dashboard** pane, double-click on Population Tree and Population Pie.
21. Right-click on the titles Population Tree and Population Pie, then select Hide Title.
22. Place Population Map and Population Line on the dashboard, then position as desired.
23. Shift-drag the Select Chart Type parameter over the treemap in order to float the control and position as desired.
24. Delete all legends and quick filters.
25. Format, document, and position all dashboard elements as desired. Now the end user can determine whether to view Treemap or Pie Chart.

See an example of the Dashboard:

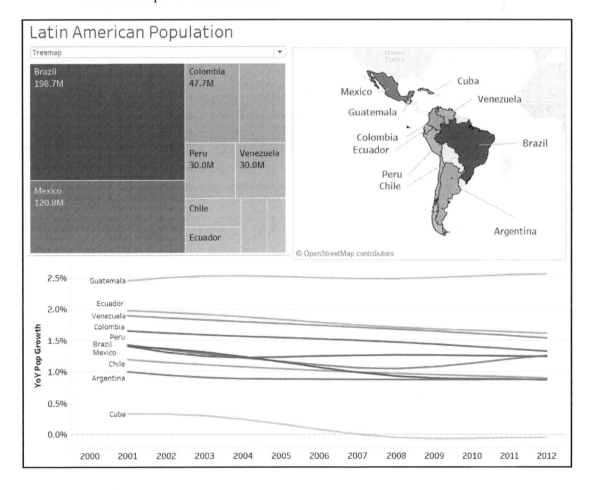

Exercise: collapsible menu

Please follow along the exercise steps:

1. Duplicate the dashboard created in the preceding exercise and name it Collapsible Menu. If you did not complete the preceding exercise, utilize the dashboard included with the Solution workbook provided with this chapter.
2. In the bottom portion of the **Dashboard** pane, select Floating.
3. Drag the Menu icon from the **Dashboard** pane onto the dashboard.
4. Right-click on the title and select Hide Title.
5. Set the fit of Menu icon to Entire View.
6. Size and position Menu icon so that it fits in the upper-right corner of the dashboard. The following dimensions can be entered in the **Layout** pane:

Position		Size	
X	927	w	47
Y	4	h	23

7. In the bottom portion of the **Dashboard** pane, select Tiled.
8. Place the Menu worksheet anywhere on the dashboard. The filters for Year and Country should display on the right side of the dashboard.
9. Navigate to the Menu worksheet and take a moment to explore the settings of each dimension on the **Filters** shelf. Note that the Latin America Countries filter is set to Context and that Country Copy is displayed as a quick filter. Also note that the Country Copy quick filter is set to Show All Values in Context. It is necessary to display the Country Copy filter as opposed to the Country filter because Country displays the condition (that is, AVG([Population Total]) > 1000000) in the quick filter.
10. Return to the Collapsible Menu dashboard.
11. Right-click on the Menu title and select Hide Title.
12. Make the Menu worksheet floating and then size and position with the following dimensions:

Position		Size	
X	1	w	1
Y	1	h	1

 Note that the goal of this step is to make the Menu worksheet as small as possible. It is necessary for the Menu worksheet to remain on the dashboard so that the accompanying Year and Country filters can be used.

13. On the **Dashboard** pane, select Floating and drag a horizontal container on to the view in approximately the middle of the dashboard.

14. Within the **Layout** pane, set the width of the horizontal container to 400.

15. In the lower-right section of the dashboard, right-click the container that houses the Country and Year filters. In the resulting pop-up menu, choose Edit Width and set the value to 200.

16. Drag the container selected in the previous step and place it in the container that is floating in the center of the dashboard.

17. From the **Dashboard** pane, press Shift to drag a vertical container and place it inside the left portion of the floating horizontal container.

18. Right-click on the newly-created vertical container and select Fixed Width. The width of the vertical container should now be 200 pixels.

19. Place the Expander worksheet in the newly-created vertical container; be sure to press Shift and drag.

20. The Expander worksheet contains a small, transparent image that will be used to expand and collapse the menu we are creating. An image does not have to be used. For example, text could be used instead. However, since small, transparent images are sometimes used in web design to stretch tables, one is used here to assist readers with a web design background.

21. Set the fit for the Expander worksheet to Entire View.

22. Right-click on the Expander worksheet title and select Hide Title. The results should look similar to the following screenshot:

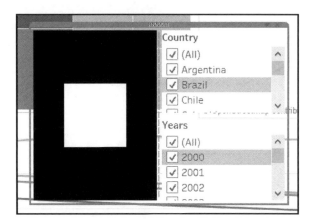

23. Within the **Layout** pane, select the horizontal container that contains the Country and Years filters and the Expander worksheet. Enter the following dimensions:

Position		Size	
X	800	w	400
Y	26	h	700

24. The results should look similar to this screenshot:

25. Select **Dashboard > Actions** and create the following filter action:

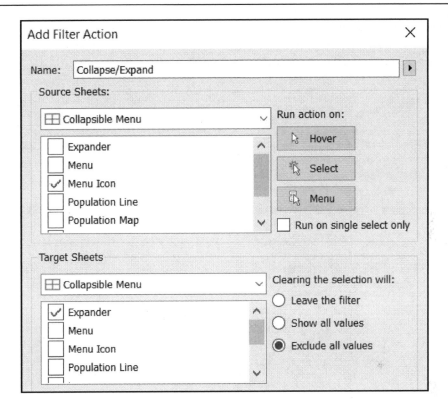

26. In the **Layout** pane, right-click on the vertical container that is housing the Expander worksheet and deselect fixed width. This step is necessary so that the Collapse/Expand action will work properly. It was necessary to fix the container width previously so as to properly align the contents of the container.

27. On the dashboard, click on the Menu Icon. The Expander worksheet should appear and disappear, causing the filters to move on and off the dashboard. When finished with this step, make sure that the Expander worksheet is visible.

28. From the **Dashboard** pane, Shift-drag two blank containers onto the dashboard. Position one directly above the Expander and one directly below. The results should look similar to the following screenshot:

29. Size the blank containers so that the black rectangle is as small as possible and is positioned so that it covers only a blank portion of the dashboard. Be sure to continually test the Menu action as you adjust the size so as to not inadvertently break the collapsing functionality of the container.

30. Navigate to the Expander worksheet and select **Format > Shading** and change the worksheet shading from black to none.

31. Navigate back to the Collapsible Menu dashboard and click the drop-down menus associated with both the Country and Year filter, then choose **Apply to Worksheets > Selected Worksheets....**

32. In the resulting dialog boxes, choose Population Line, Population Map, Population Pie and Population Tree.
33. Adjust formatting and positioning as desired.

After completing this exercise, you may think, OK. The filters do not technically display on the dashboard, but they are still visible to the side. While this is true in Tableau Desktop, if you are able to upload the workbook to an instance of Tableau Server, you will note that when clicking on the menu icon, the filters appear and disappear and do not display to the side. Note, however, that the same is not true of Tableau Reader. As in Tableau Desktop, in Tableau Reader, the end user will be able to see the filters to the side of the dashboard. Fortunately, this limitation is quite easy to overcome. In the solution workbook provided with this chapter, the Hider worksheet has been floated off the right side of the dashboard to completely hide the filters from view. Review the Hider approach if your design needs require completely hiding material that is beyond the confines of the dashboard.

Summary

We began this chapter by considering visualization design theory. We looked at formatting rules, color rules, and rules about which visualization types to use and which we need to avoid. We also explored how to compromise when contradictory design goals are expressed by end users. Then we discussed dashboard design principles. We covered three popular layouts: the Golden rectangle, Quad, and Small multiple.

Finally, we looked at how to use sheet selection techniques as an ally in good design. Specifically, we explored how to allow the end user to choose which visualization type to view, and how to hide and display filters so as to make the best use of screen real estate.

In the next chapter, we will focus on Use-Cases. From a dataset to a product will be the theme and you can practice doing so with a World Index data set and a Geo-Spatial one. The knowledge you gained from the previous chapters will very useful!

12
Advanced Analytics

Have you ever asked yourself how other people start working on a dashboard? How they clean data and how they come up with a dashboard design? If so, this is the right chapter for you! I want to share two use cases with you, written as a train of thought in order to give you an idea about how I work. Please note, this is my personal example and there are many different ways that can lead you to your goal.

Self-service Analytics

Self-Service Analytics can be seen as a form of business intelligence. People from the business are encouraged to execute queries on datasets themselves, instead of placing it in a backlog with an IT team. Based on this, query analysis can be done, which should lead to more insights and data-driven decision-making. But how do you start if it's your first time? How do you go from a dataset to a product? I usually start with a descriptive analysis, moving forward to a more quantitative part. I draw my dashboard ideas on a piece of paper but adjust my plan whenever needed. So, let's start with the use cases.

Use case – Self-service Analytics

Imagine your line manager gives you the following task:

> *Create a dashboard for me in which I can easily spot all correlated indices. I need it by tomorrow morning.*

Now, take a few minutes before you continue reading and think about how you would tackle this question. Write down your steps, open the workbook related to this chapter from `https://public.tableau.com/profile/marleen.meier`, and follow your steps; time how long it takes you.

And now, I will illustrate one way I could imagine solving this task:

1. First, I opened the file in Tableau Prep in order to get insights on the descriptive analytics:

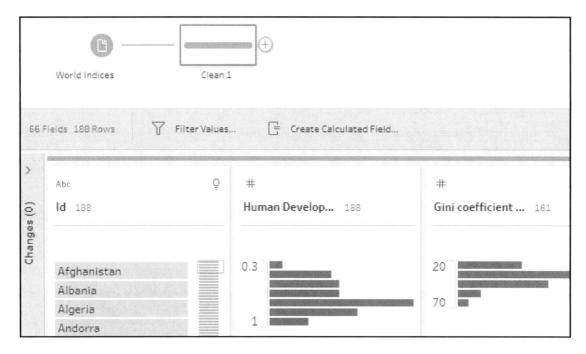

With this dataset, I actually didn't see too much in Prep. It's 1 row per country and another 65 columns with different indices. And because I know that my boss wants to see a quantitative analysis on the correlations, I can continue directly with Tableau Desktop.

2. My next thought was, how can I visualize all correlations at once, and won't it be too much information? And if I select some, is my boss more interested in a positive or negative correlation, or will I just take an absolute number and show the highest positive and negative correlation?

No, this won't work. The task was very generic, therefore I decided to go for a two-parameter approach, which will enable my end user to select each of index combinations them self.

3. I name the parameters **X-Axis** and **Y-Axis** because they will be used to define the **X-Axis** and the **Y-Axis**:

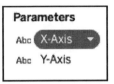

4. I defined both parameters as a **String** and pasted all field names from the clipboard. To do this, I opened the input file in Excel, transposed the header row to a column, and pressed *Ctrl + C*:

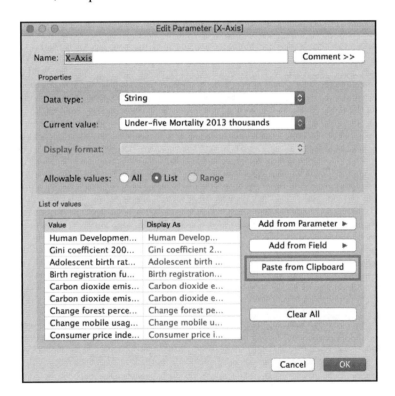

5. I also want the parameters to be visible on the dashboard, therefore I select **Show Parameter Control**:

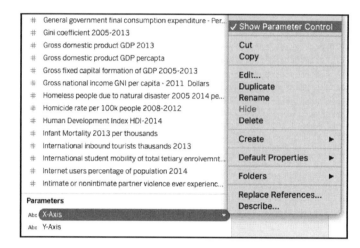

If you test the parameter now, you will be able to select values (the prior column headers), but nothing will happen. We need a calculated field that defines that, if a selection from the parameter has been made, it will select a field.

6. I create the following calculated field:

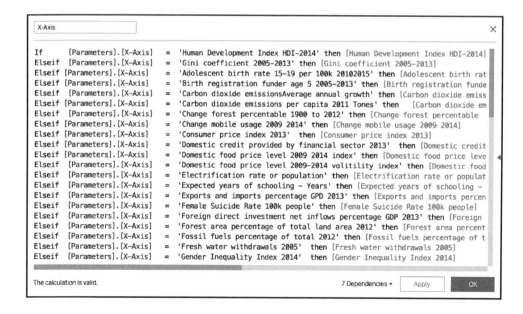

7. We will do the same thing for the **Y-Axis** Parameter.

In order to create the calculated field for **Y-Axis**, copy and paste the **X-Axis** calculated field into Excel and find and replace **[Parameters].[X-Axis]** with **[Parameters].[Y-Axis]**.

8. Drag the **X-Axis** calculated field to columns, and the **Y-Axis** to rows. Also, put the **ID** field on the details shelf:

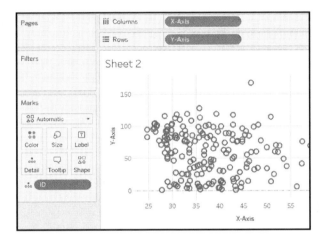

9. In order to see the correlation **Analytics** from Tableau, drag a **Trend Line** onto the sheet:

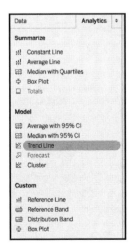

The sheet with the Trend Line looks as follows:

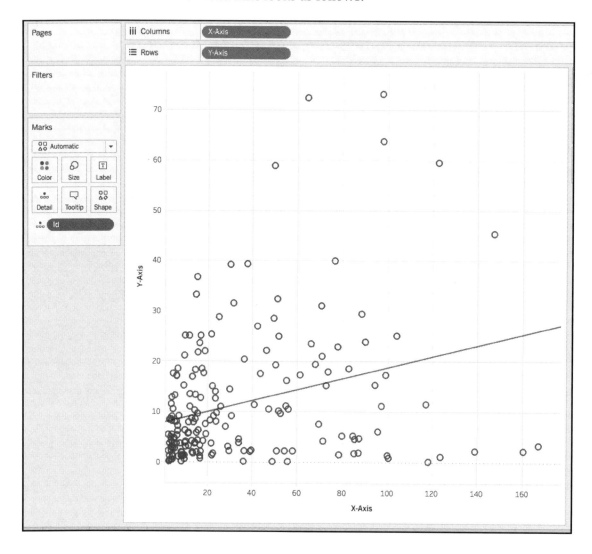

When hovering over the trend line, you will see the equation of the line, the **R-Squared**, and the **P-value**:

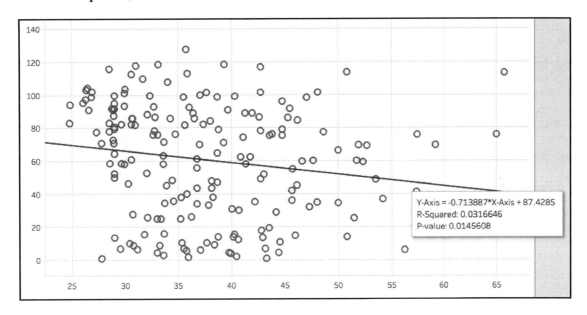

Y-Axis = -0.713887*X-Axis + 87.4285
R-Squared: 0.0316646
P-value: 0.0145608

10. In order to see more coefficients, right-click on the line and select **Describe Trend Line**:

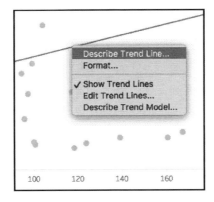

The following window will appear:

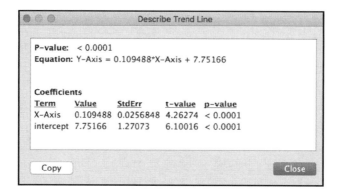

Alternatively, you can select the **Describe Trend Model** option and you will see this:

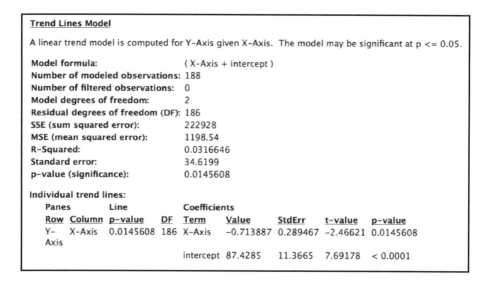

If you want to learn more about the interpretation, please read the following article: https://onlinehelp.tableau.com/current/pro/desktop/en-us/trendlines_add.htm.

11. At this point, I get a bit distracted by the grid lines, so I decide to remove them by right-clicking > **Format**:

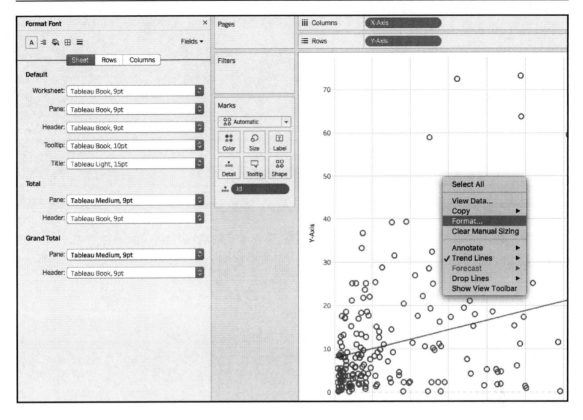

12. Select the fifth option, the dashes, and remove the **Grid Lines**:

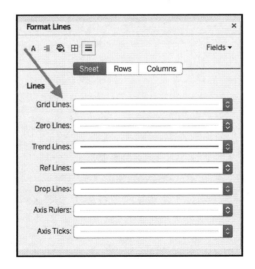

13. I also changed the **Marks** from automatic to **Circle**:

14. Now, I thought it would be helpful if someone wanted to see where on the scatterplot a specific country is located, so I changed the **Id** field from detail to text, however this looks a bit too chaotic:

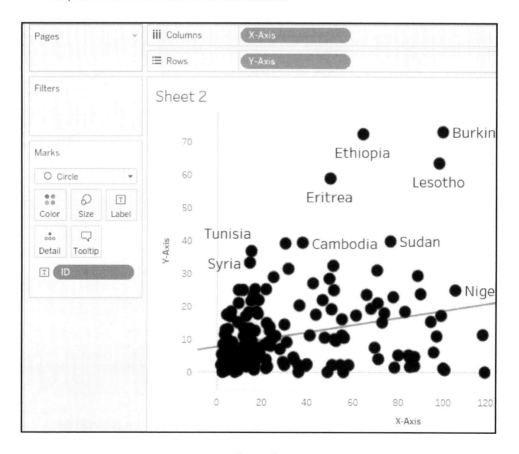

15. Instead I add a `highlighter` function. Now, the end user will see the country when hovering over a dot:

16. I also wanted it to pop out a bit more and changed the **Id** color in the **Tooltip** to red and increased the size:

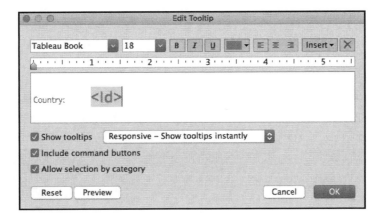

The result looks as follows:

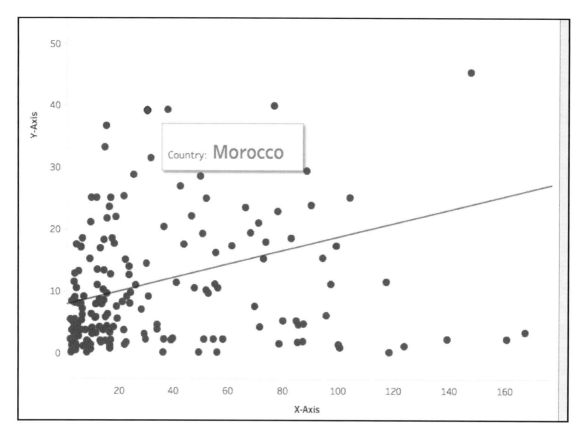

17. A few steps back I added the trend line, and I now want to show the **Pearson R** or R-squared value in the view; however, it is not possible without selecting the **Describe Trend Line** or **Describe Trend Model** option. Hence, I calculated it myself:

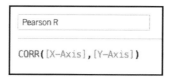

18. But, I want you to immediately know what you are looking at, therefore I create another calculated field:

```
Correlation yes or no                                                                    ×

IF [Pearson R] > 0.7 then 'The two variables have a very strong positive correlation.'
ELSEIF [Pearson R] < 0.7 and [Pearson R] > 0.4 then 'The two variables have a strong positive correlation.'
ELSEIF [Pearson R] < 0.4 and [Pearson R] > 0.2 then 'The two variables have a moderate positive correlation.'
ELSEIF  [Pearson R] <0.2 and [Pearson R] > -0.2 then 'The two variables have no or a weak correlation.'
ELSEIF [Pearson R] < -0.2 and [Pearson R] >-0.4 then 'The two variables have a moderate negative correlation.'
ELSEIF [Pearson R] < -0.4 and [Pearson R] > -0.7 then 'The two variables have a strong negative correlation.'
ELSEIF [Pearson R] < -0.7 THEN 'The two variables have a very strong negative correlation.'
END
```

19. And I put it on a separate sheet as Text:

The sheet will look as simple as:

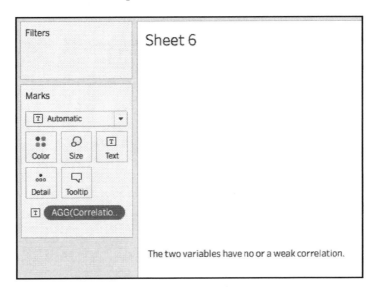

20. I finally have everything ready to build the dashboard I was thinking about in the beginning. But now that it is almost done, I think it would help my user to also see a **Top** n of the two selected Indices, giving the information more context. So I create a **Top** 10 **Filter** on **Id**:

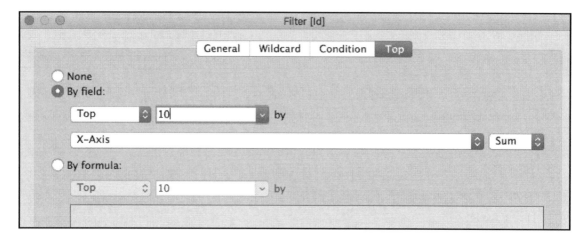

21. And I drag **Id** to columns and **X-Axis** to rows:

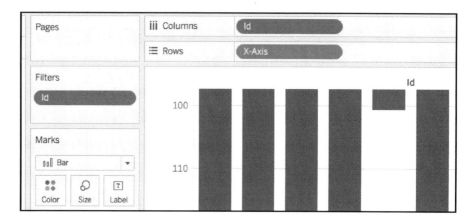

22. Then we will do the same for the **Y-Axis** and I'll **Rename Id** to Country:

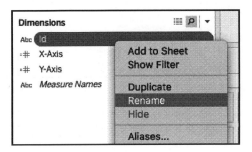

23. On my scatterplot sheet, I then removed the header:

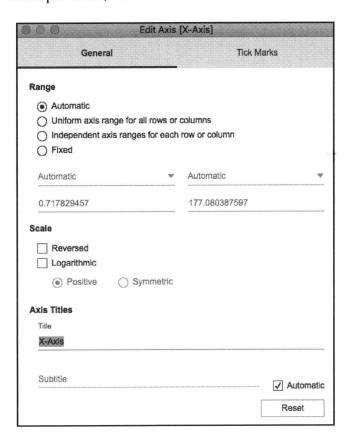

24. I put two the scatterplot as well as the correlation text sheet on the dashboard canvas:

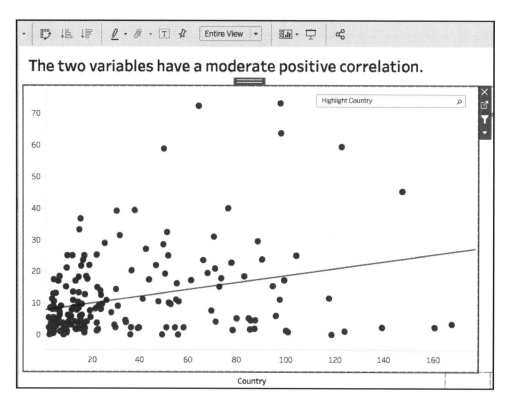

25. I make the country highlighter **Floating**:

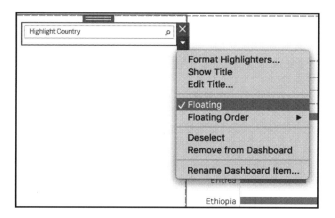

26. Last but not least, I make the correlation text red, add the parameter, and add the top n to the related site of the scatterplot. Then we add some blanks to make the canvas look as per the following screenshot:

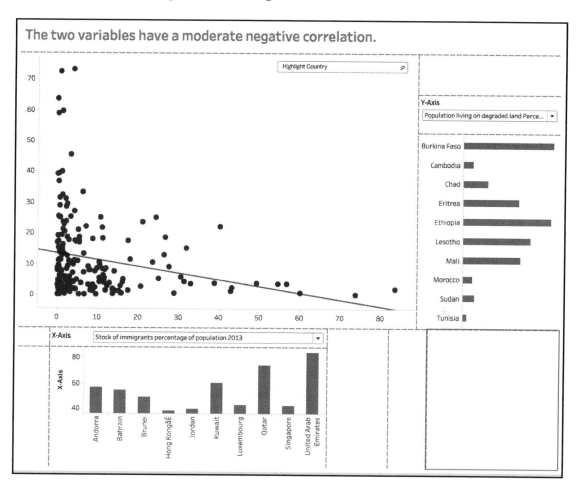

27. I notice that the title of the parameter could be better used to explain as such that users know what to do with it:

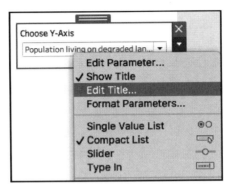

28. Then we add some text with borders to explain the top 10 histogram:

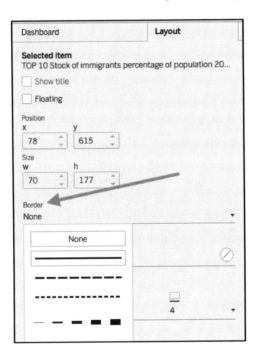

And the final result looks such as this:

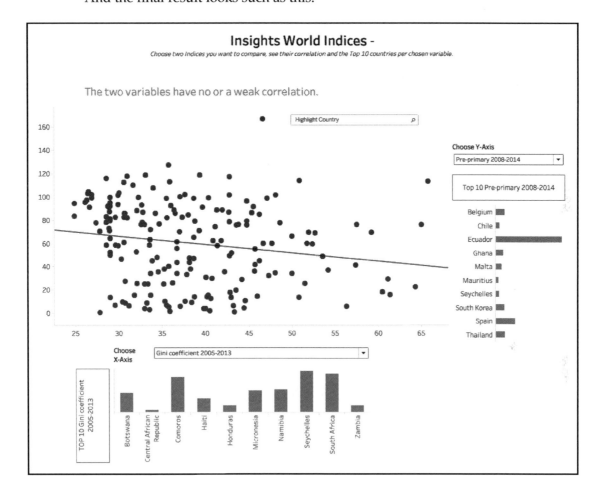

When hovering over the dots, you can see the country highlighted:

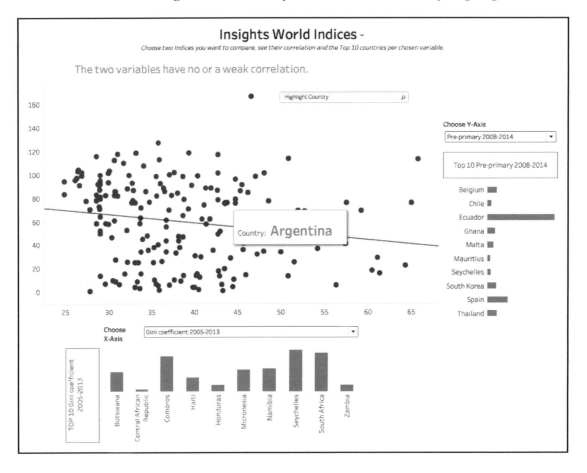

Here are some more ideas, I had during the process:

- Add an explanation on each index (depending on the audience).
- Add an explanation on the correlation.
- Add the p-value or other coefficients to the analysis and change the text accordingly.
- Use symbols for the selection per axis instead of parameters.
- Create a second dashboard with all possible combinations and color code the type of correlation (strong, weak).

Take a look at the following screenshot:

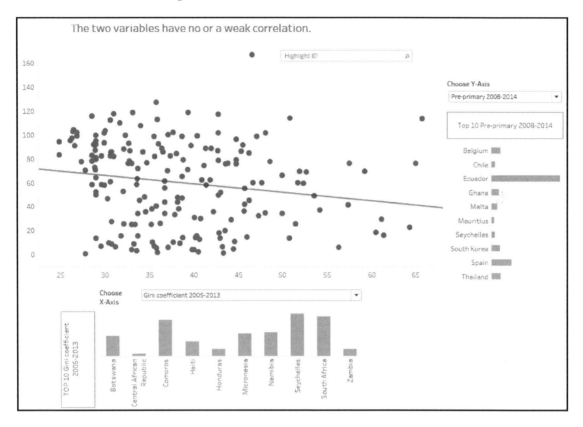

Let the user decide whether they want to combine indices them self or look at an overview.

Use case – Geo-spatial Analytics

It's Wednesday morning; your manager comes into your office and says that they want to check the red-light violations of the last year in Chicago. They are very busy and ask you to build a dashboard for them. In particular, they want to know where the most violations happen and whether we see trends over the last year. They give you two datasets: one with the camera locations and one with the violations and leaves. They come back and add, I need this within the next hour. What do you do?

First, make a quick plan on how to approach this problem. Take five minutes, think about the steps you would take, and sketch a dashboard design.

Here is an overview on how I would do it:

Tableau Prep > descriptive analysis and join, maybe clean the data > send output to Tableau > use map to visualize the location of cameras if possible > add the amount of violations per camera per time unit

Here is a step by step description of what I would do:

1. After loading both files into Tableau Prep, I see that a Join on the **LONGITUDE** and **LATITUDE** doesn't bring me anywhere:

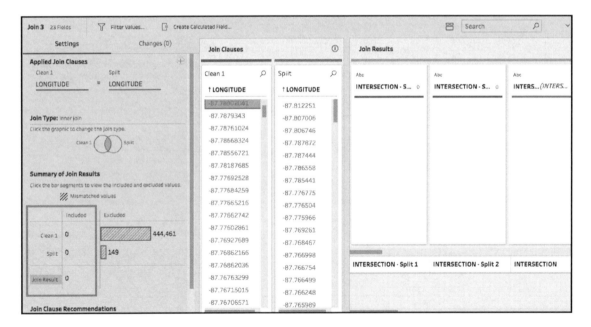

2. Considering the short amount of time I have, I try a different approach: a join on the intersections. This results in 0 joined rows as well, but this time I see why. In one dataset, the Intersection are marked with a - in the other dataset it's **AND**, also one uses capital letters, one isn't:

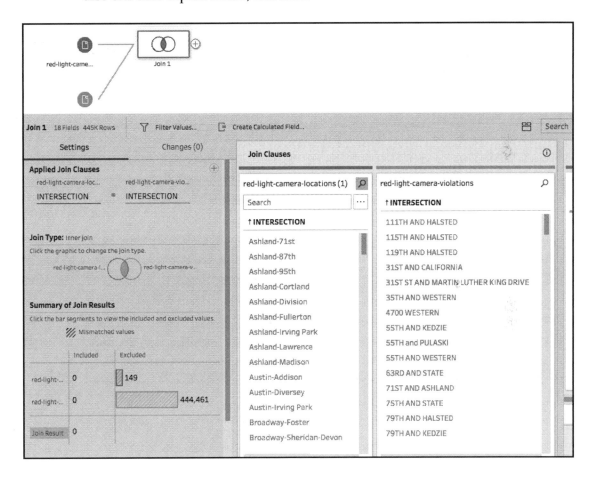

3. I add a cleaning step to make all the letters uppercase, and split the Intersections into two parts. I execute a **Custom Split** on - as well as on AND:

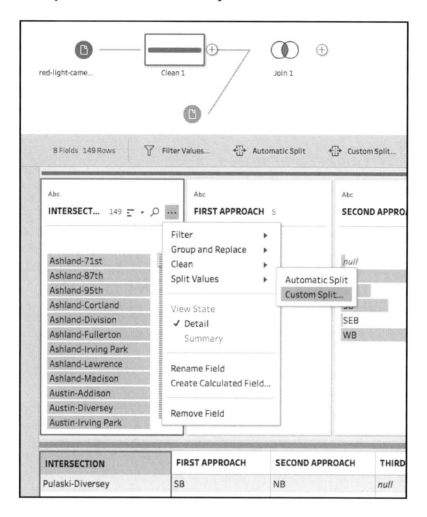

4. I also noticed that sometimes the intersection is mixed up, for example, instead of **Ashland - 71th**, its **71ST AND ASHLAND**. I am thinking about restructuring the datasets and creating a loop that will put the two streets in alphabetical order in the two splits, but I don't have time for this now. Therefore, my solution is to first join split 1 and split 1 as well as split 2 and split 2. In a second join, I use split 1 and split 2 and split 2 and split 1. Afterward, I union the two joins and create an output file (or directly load the prepped dataset in to Tableau Desktop):

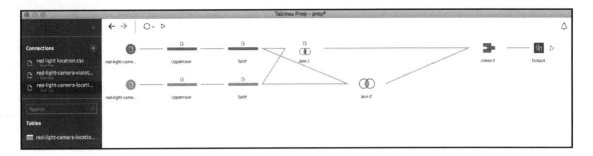

With this approach, I still don't include all the data but I have 380,000 rows out of 444,000. This should be enough to get a rough idea of patterns. If I have any time left, I will continue mapping the remaining mismatches.

5. Now I load everything in Tableau and visualize the red-light locations:

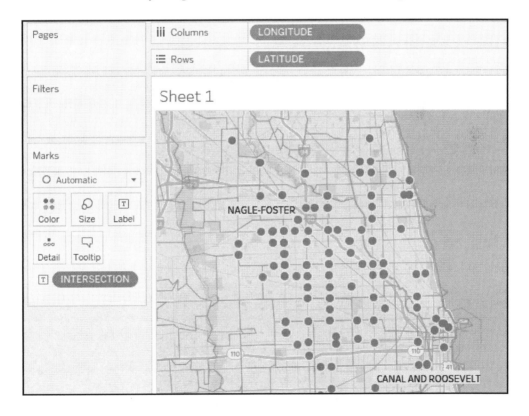

6. I like the map better when it shows a few more details, so I use the **Map Layers** to select all **Options**:

Select all the layers you want to see in the map:

7. Another nice functionality of Tableau is that you can add **Data Layer** to your view. I use the **Population** per block, as I hope it will give me some details on whether more or fewer violations happen in densely-populated areas:

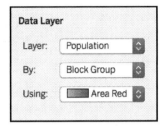

In the following screenshot you can see the population of Chicago:

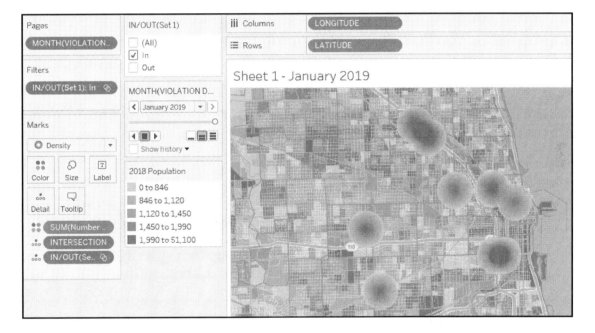

8. I added the **Month(Violation Date)** to Pages, in order for my boss to play through the months, this way, they can see where and when the amount of violations changes:

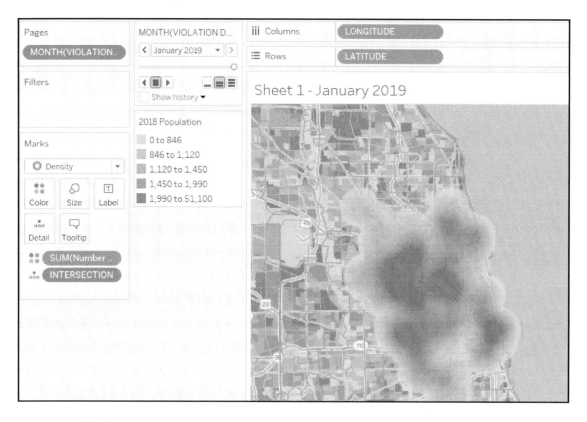

9. While playing it, I notice a pattern in some months. I want to take closer look, so I put all violations per intersection per month in a **Heatmap**:

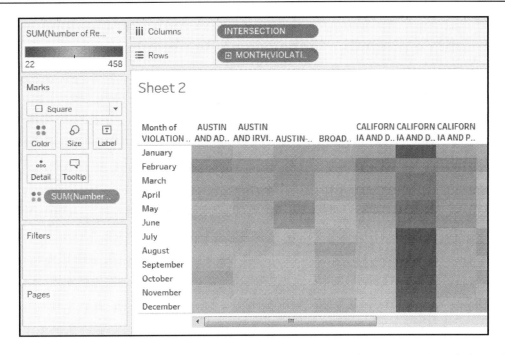

There are definitely more red-light violations from July to January and also still visible when plotting all intersections in one view. Some intersections pop out due to more violations overall (dark red lines) or fewer (dark blue lines):

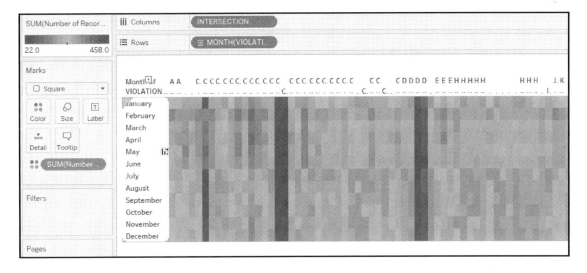

10. Interesting, this wasn't planned, but I will add this to my dashboard too, I think. For the case that my boss is interested in – the top 20 violation intersections – I create a set. He can decide whether he wants to see all red-light cameras, only the top 20, or only the bottom n. Also, I remove the population data and some layers as it distracts me:

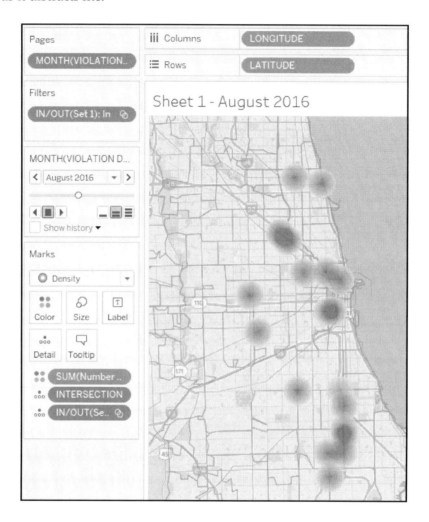

11. Time is almost up, the cleaning took too long, I am stressing. I wonder whether the mismatches during the cleaning, which I excluded so far, are from February to June and if that's why I see a pattern. I don't want my boss to draw the wrong conclusions, so I do a last quick check. I select only the mismatches in Tableau Prep and create a calculated field, **MONTH([Violation Date])** and I also that also here to pattern remains:

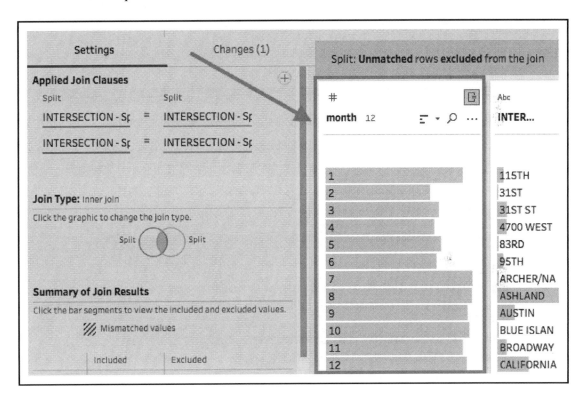

12. My boss is not back yet. I add a last graph that shows the total violations over the years, including a forecast. I make the background transparent and put it in the upper-right corner.

In one hour, I was able to produce the following dashboard:

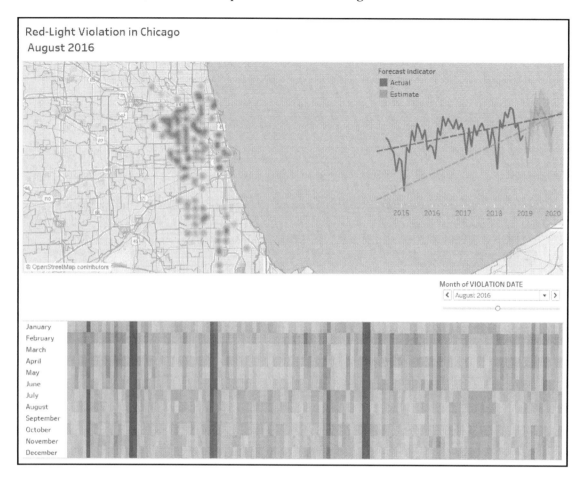

Could it be improved - yes, it always can. But, after this first iteration my boss can let me know if he needs something to be adjusted and I can do so. I am sure that I could spend many more hours improving it, but most times dashboarding is more about delivering. And a full production model is a different story of course. Especially if you work agile, split your work into deliverable, get feedback and continue working on it.

Summary

In this chapter, we looked into two use cases of self-service analytics. One is about world indices with a straightforward dataset, and one is about traffic-light violations, for which we had to join two datasets. Our main takeaway was, that you should always start by planning your work. Next, get to know the data, use descriptive statistics, and adjust your plan according to your intermediate results.

A dashboard is never really finished; you can always change things; your audience might change; stakeholder wishes might differ. Deliver a working visualization with basic functionality and continue to develop after you get feedback. Depending on your backlog or other circumstances, the basics might be enough.

The next chapter will be all about improving performance. With more and more data, performance is key, and could make the difference between success and failure.

13
Improving Performance

Recently, while teaching a Tableau Desktop class, a gentleman approached me regarding a dashboard he had built that was performing inadequately. He stated that his dashboard probably flouted several best practices for performance. He was correct! The dashboard had close to a dozen filters, most of which were set to show only relevant values. Also the dashboard was full of worksheets, some of which included thousands of marks. Although we did not look at the underlying data sources, based on our conversation, some of those data sources likely included complex joins. I was amazed that the dashboard performed as well as it did! This underscores a truth that many Tableau authors have experienced: Tableau can perform abysmally if best practices are not followed.

This chapter will address various aspects of performance with the intent of empowering you with techniques to create workbooks that load quickly and respond snappily to end user interaction.

In this chapter, we will discuss the following topics:

- Understanding the performance-recording dashboard
- Hardware considerations
- When it's necessary or advantageous to blend
- Efficiently working with data sources
- Tuning data sources
- Working efficiently with large data sources
- Intelligent extracts
- Optimizing extracts
- Using filters wisely
- Extract filter performance
- Data source filter performance
- Context filters
- Dimension and measure filters
- Table calculation filters

- Efficient calculations
- Avoiding overcrowding a dashboard
- Fixing dashboard sizing

Understanding the performance-recording dashboard

Beginning with version 8.0, Tableau included the performance-recording dashboard as a part of the installation package. Named `PerformanceRecording.twb`, the dashboard gives the Tableau author an easy way to understand and troubleshoot performance problems. Previous to 8.0, the Tableau author was relegated to deciphering raw log files, which can be challenging. The following exercises and associated discussion points will review various aspects of the Performance Recording dashboard, including how to generate it, how to use it to improve performance, and how it's constructed.

Exercise: exploring performance recording in Tableau desktop

Follow along the exercise steps:

1. Navigate to `https://public.tableau.com/profile/marleen.meier` to locate and download the workbook associated with this chapter.
2. Navigate to the Types of Events worksheet.
3. Select **Help > Settings and Performance > Start Performance Recording**.
4. Press *F5* on Windows or *command + R* on macOS to refresh the view.
5. Select **Help>Settings and Performance > Stop Performance Recording**.
6. In the resulting `PerformanceRecording.twb`, drag the Events timeline slider to the far left:

7. Note the **Timeline**. By referencing the **Events** legend, it can be easily understood even though the axis may be confusing. The axis in the following screenshot communicates that the recorded events took place in the $11{,}653^{th}$ second; that is, the **workbook** had been open over three hours when the recorded events took place:

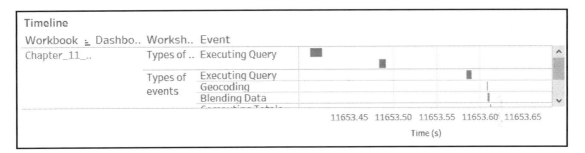

8. Within Events Sorted by Time, click on any green bar entitled **Executing Query**. Note that the Query section now populates. The **Query** is in TQL since the Types of Events worksheet is pointing to an extract:

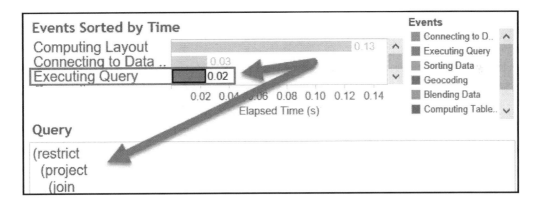

9. Navigate to the Events worksheet and right-click on the Event group located in the **Data** pane. Select Edit Group. Note the complete list of events that can be measured in Tableau. The most common events are listed and discussed later in this chapter.

10. To see the query in its entirety, navigate to the Query worksheet and set the fit to Entire View. Note that an especially long query may not be recorded in its entirety. In order to see every line of such a query, reference the log files located in My Tableau Repository.

Performance-recording dashboard events

In the *Exploring performance recording in Tableau Desktop* exercise of this chapter, the Events worksheet from the Performance Recording dashboard was accessed and the Event group was considered. The list of possible events is substantial. This section will not consider every event possibility, but will instead focus on the most common events that impact performance. And briefly consider how to address performance concerns.

See the following list regarding performance considerations:

Event type	Performance considerations
Connecting to Data Source	Poor performance when connecting to the data source could indicate network latency or database issues.
Generating Extract	See sections in this chapter for information regarding extract performance.
Compiling Query	Compile Query performance problems could indicate database issues.
Executing Query	See sections in this chapter on filtering and calculations.
Sorting Data	Performance issues related to sorting issues may indicate too many marks in the view.
Geocoding	Geocoding performance issues may indicate too many marks in the view or internet latency issues.
Blending Data	Blending Data performance may be improved by reducing the amount of underlying data or by filtering.
Computing Table Calculations	Since table calculations are typically performed locally, complex calculations may tax the end user's computer.
Computing Totals	The Computing Totals performance may be improved by reducing the amount of underlying data or by filtering.
Computing Layout	Computing Layout performance issues may be indicative of a dashboard with too many worksheets.

Behind the scenes of the performance-recording dashboard

This section explores what happens when performance recording is activated. Note that the following assumes the author is working on Tableau Desktop not Tableau Server. As covered in `Chapter 14`, *Interacting with Tableau Server* the Performance Recording Dashboard is also available on Tableau Server.

When recording performance, Tableau initially creates a file in `My Tableau Repository\Logs,` named `performance.[timestamp].tab.` Upon completion of the recording, Tableau copies the resulting TAB file to the `TableauTemp` directory, for example, `C:\Users\Marleen Meier\AppData\Local\Temp\TableauTemp\0nqsj2c0w2er7e194rx500aj9178.` The TAB file is renamed `perf_gantt.tab.` Additionally, there is a file named `PerformanceRecording_new.twb` located in the Tableau program directory, for example, `C:\Program Files\Tableau\Tableau 10.0\Performance.` That file is copied to the same temp directory where `perf_gantt.tab` is located and renamed `PerformanceRecording.twb.` That file is automatically opened once the recording stops, thus allowing the author to peruse the results.

Hardware and on-the-fly techniques

The number-one performance inhibitor for Tableau Desktop that I have observed while training in many different companies is underpowered machines. Developers almost invariably have excellent computers. Analysts and other business users, regrettably, often do not. In many cases, a few modest upgrades can make a significant improvement. Unfortunately, upgrading a computer may be impossible at many organizations due to a variety of factors, and procuring a new machine may also be quite difficult. Therefore, in this section, we will consider both optimal computer specifications and techniques for working with Tableau on underpowered machines.

Hardware considerations

The published minimum requirements for Tableau Desktop are as follows:

Windows	Mac
• Microsoft Windows 7 or newer (64-bit)	• iMac/MacBook computers 2009 or newer
• Microsoft Server 2008 R2 or newer	• OS X 10.11 or newer
• Intel or AMD 64-bit processor or newer	• 1.5 GB minimum free disk space
• 2 GB memory	
• 1.5 GB minimum free disk space	

The specifications listed for macOS are adequate assuming sufficient RAM (a minimum of 8 GB). Those for Windows, however, are insufficient for many use cases.

Instead, consider the following recommendations:

Recommended Specifications for Windows Computers	Notes
Microsoft Windows 7 or newer	Note that most Windows performance reviews report, at best, modest gains when upgrading. Therefore don't expect Tableau to run noticeably faster if upgrading beyond Windows 7. *Performance improvement expected by upgrading: Moderate.*
64-bit OS	32-bit OS only supports up to 4 GB of memory; 8 GB of memory or more is recommended. *Performance improvement expected by upgrading: High (provided the upgrade is accompanied by additional RAM).*
Intel i7 processor	The i5 processor works fine with Tableau, but the larger cache and faster processing of the i7 processor enables better multitasking and improves performance overall. *Performance improvement expected by upgrading: Moderate.*
8 GB memory or more	RAM is a major performance factor. In short, the more the better. 8 GB will suffice for most purposes, but 4 GB is often unsatisfactory, especially if running multiple instances of Tableau. Note that a 64-bit version of Tableau is required to take advantage of RAM in excess of 4 GB. More RAM is particularly important when using a TDE file as a data source, since a TDE file is typically loaded in RAM. *Performance improvement expected by upgrading: High.*

SSD (Solid-state drive)	An SSD outperforms an HDD by a wide margin. Part of the reason is simply better I/O (input/output) performance. Also, over time, an HDD will fragment, that is, data is scattered throughout the drive and performance consequently suffers. Fragmentation is irrelevant for an SSD. *Performance improvement expected by upgrading: High.*
NVIDIA graphics card	As of Tableau 8.0, rendering performance can be improved via OpenGL. OpenGL enables the Accelerated Graphics option within Tableau. This, in turn, allows Tableau to utilize a GPU (graphic processing unit) instead of a CPU (central processing unit) for some rendering operations. Accelerated Graphics requires a graphics card. NVIDIA is recommended here because, according to Dan Cory, a Technical Advisor to the Tableau Development leadership team, Tableau Software (the company) predominately uses NVIDIA graphics cards. Other graphics cards include ATI and Intel HD Graphics 2000, 4000, and 5000. Note that the Intel HD Graphics 4000 card requires updated video drivers for Tableau 9.0 and later. You can update video drivers via the device manager located in the Windows Control Panel. Accelerated Graphics is activated in Tableau via Help > Settings and Performance > Enable Accelerated Graphics. *Performance improvement expected by upgrading: Moderate.*

You may have noticed that the preceding table mostly does not address specific brands. For instance, there is no mention of Dell, Lenovo, or HP. Nor are there considerations of different brands of RAM or hard drives. Despite the proliferation of computer and component types (or perhaps as a result of this proliferation), computers and components have become commodities. In short, any name-brand equipment should work fine. In fact, off-brand equipment will often perform just as well, although the relatively small price savings may not justify additional risks. A little research combined with common sense should lead to satisfactory results when considering which brand of computer or component to purchase.

On-the-fly-techniques

Perhaps as a result of the above section you have ordered a new, more optimal computer. Or, more likely, you may keep it in mind should you have the opportunity to obtain a new machine in the near future, but for now, you have to make do with what you have. This section discusses tips that will help the Tableau author work more efficiently irrespective of the equipment used.

Exercise: pause/resume auto-updates

Auto-updates can be accessed either via the icon located on the toolbar, via **Worksheet > Auto Updates**, or by use of the shortcut key *F10* on Windows or *option + command + 0* on Mac. Auto-updates give the author the option of pausing/resuming auto-updates for the worksheet and/or for filters.

The following exercise demonstrates how this works:

1. Open the workbook associated with this chapter and navigate to the Auto Updates worksheet.
2. In the **Data** pane, select the Superstore dataset.
3. Place State on the **Rows** shelf.
4. Deselect **Auto update worksheet** via the toolbar:

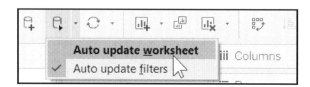

5. Place **City** on the **Rows** shelf to the right of State. Note that the view does not update.
6. Enable Auto update worksheet via the toolbar. The view now updates.
7. Right-click on State on the **Rows** shelf and select Show Filter.
8. Right-click on **City** on the **Rows** shelf and select Show Filter.

9. On the **City** quick-filter, click the drop-down menu and select **Multiple values (list)** and **Only relevant values**:

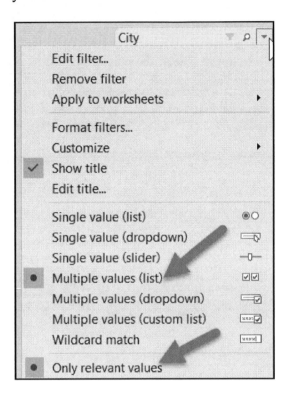

10. Deselect Auto Update Filters via the toolbar.
11. In the State quick filter, select only Alabama. Note that the City quick-filter does not update.
12. Enable Auto update filters via the toolbar. The City quick-filter now updates.

In practice, Auto update worksheet can be very helpful. The author may pause auto-updates, make multiple changes, and then resume auto-updates, thereby saving time.

In practice, Auto update filters is less useful. However, when using high-cardinality filters (that is, filters with many members), Auto update filters can be helpful.

Exercise: run update

The **Run Update** icon to the right of the Pause/Resume auto updates can be confusing.

The following brief example should help clarify this option:

1. Duplicate the previous worksheet, Auto Updates, and name the duplicate Run Update.
2. Pause all updates by clicking on the Pause Auto Updates icon.
3. Select several states at random in the State quick-filter.

4. Click on the Run update icon. As shown in the following screenshot, note that the shortcut key for Run update is *F9* on Windows. The shortcut on macOS is *shift + command + 0*:

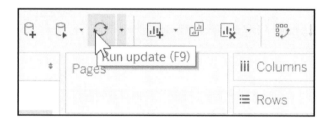

5. Select several more states at random in the State quick-filter. Note that auto-updating is still paused.

In short, Run update allows the Tableau author to intermittently refresh the view while still keeping Auto updates paused.

Exercise: small extracts

Although extracts will be discussed in more detail below, it seems fitting to mention extracts in the context of performance considerations while authoring. Even under optimal conditions, working with large data sources can be slow. If constant access to the entire dataset while authoring is not necessary, consider creating a small, local extract. Author as much of the workbook as possible and then when all the underlying data is truly needed, point to the original data source.

The following steps show a brief example of this technique in action:

1. In the workbook associated with this chapter, navigate to the Small Local Ext worksheet.
2. Select **Data | New Data Source** to choose a desired data source. This exercise assumes Sample - Superstore.xls, which installs with Tableau.

3. Drag **Number of Records** to the **Text** shelf. Note the resulting count.

4. Right-click on Sample - `Superstore.xls` and select Extract Data.

5. At the bottom of the **Extract Data** dialog box, select **Top** and choose **1000**:

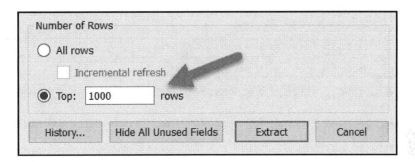

6. Click the **Extract** button and note that Number of Records now displays **1000** rows.

7. In the **Data** pane, right-click on Superstore and deselect **Use Extract**. Note that the Number of Records has reverted to the original value.

 By creating a small, local extract, the Tableau author alleviates two performance inhibitors: Network latency and dataset size.

Single Data Source > Joining > Blending

One of the beauties of Tableau is the ease with which one can connect to many different data sources in various ways. As mentioned earlier in this book, there are 70 connectors defined in Tableau 2018.3 for interfacing with a variety of data sources. Furthermore, this flexibility extends beyond simply connecting to single tables or files. Previous versions of Tableau accommodated joining within data sources and data blending disparate data sources. Since Tableau 10, it can even accommodate cross-joining data sources, and with Tableau 2019.1 you will be able to join published datasources on Tableau Server.

Although Tableau makes it easy to connect to various data sources, it should be stressed that Tableau is not an Extract, Transform, and Load tool. If complex joins and complex data blending are required to generate useful results, it may be advisable to perform ETL work outside of Tableau, for example in Tableau Prep. Such ETL work will ideally lead to better data modeling and thus easier authoring and quicker performance in Tableau.

Three ways Tableau connects to data

Consider the following three ways that Tableau connects to datasets:

- Tableau may connect to a single table. This is ideal as it allows the most functionality and easiest troubleshooting, while enabling Tableau to send the simplest queries and thus perform optimally. However, it is not always possible to connect to a single table and, although ideal, it is not reasonable to have such a strict limitation. The relationship between data sources and reporting tools is constantly changing. A reporting tool that is inflexible in the way it can connect to data will likely not be successful, no matter how elegant and beautiful the end results.

- The second way Tableau may connect to data is via joining. One table may not supply all the necessary data, but by joining two or more tables, all the needed data may be accessible. As the joins become more and more complex, performance may be impacted and troubleshooting may become difficult. Fortunately, Tableau can assume referential integrity and thus work quite efficiently with even complex joins.

- Finally, Tableau may utilize data blending.

 Data blending often performs admirably provided no more than one of the blended data sources is large and dimensions that are used for blending have relatively few members.

When blending multiple, large data sources, performance can be seriously impacted. The problem is further compounded when blending on high-cardinality dimensions. Also, data blending limits some functionality, such as the ability to use dimensions, row-level calculations, or LOD expressions, from a secondary data source. For these reasons, consider as a guideline that data blending should normally be avoided if a joining option exists.

Chapter 4, *All About Data – Joins, Blends, and Data Structures*, provides detailed information about joining and blending. For the purposes of this chapter, joining and blending discussions will be limited to performance considerations.

Using referential integrity when joining

Referential integrity is set via **Data > [Data Source] >Assume Referential Integrity**. When selected, Tableau only includes a joined table if it is specifically referenced by fields in the view. As a result, queries to the data source are simplified and performance improves.

> Referential Integrity assumes every key value in one table exists in a corresponding key in another table.

Ideally, referential integrity should be set at the database level as this will improve database performance as well as performance in Tableau. When referential integrity is set at the database level, Tableau will not include any reference to the joined table (unless that table is specifically referenced by fields in the view) even if **Data > [Data Source] > Assume Referential Integrity** is not selected.

The following example will explore how a query is altered when referential integrity is selected.

Exercise: referential integrity

Follow along the exercise steps:

1. Consider the following two tables. Note that C key does not exist in the Catalog table. Also observe that the total sales amount in the Music Sales table is $19,500:

Catalog		Music Sales		
Key	Instrument	Key	Sales	Date
A	Selmer Trumpet	A	$3500	8/15/2016
B	Conn French Horn	B	$4500	8/15/2016
D	Miraphone Tuba	C	$2500	8/16/2016
		D	$9000	8/17/2016

2. In the workbook associated with this chapter, navigate to the WO_Ref_Int worksheet.
3. Download the `RefIntegrity.xlsx` spreadsheet that is referenced in the caption of the worksheet.

4. Create an inner join between **Music_Sales** and **Cat** using the 'Key' field:

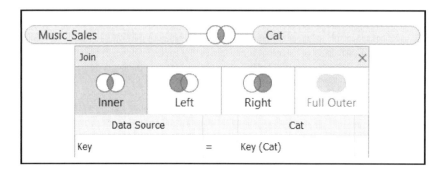

5. Rename the dataset WO_Ref_Int.
6. Within the WO_Ref_Int worksheet, right-click on the WO_Ref_Int dataset and ensure that Assume Referential Integrity is not selected.
7. Place Sales on the **Text** shelf and note the value of $17,000.
8. Select **Help > Settings and performance > Start/Stop Performance Recording** to observe the following query Tableau sent to the underlying data source. Note the inner join:

```
SELECT SUM([Music_Sales$].[Sale Amount]) AS [sum:Sale Amount:ok]
FROM [Music_Sales$]
INNER JOIN [Cat$] ON [Music_Sales$].[Key] = [Cat$].[Key]
HAVING (COUNT(1) > 0)
```

9. The value of $17,000 reflects the inner join. Since the C key was not included in the Catalog table, the associated $2,500 was not included in the total. (Recall that the total sales amount in the Music Sales table is $19,500.)
10. Navigate to the W_Ref_Int worksheet.
11. Right-click on the WO_Ref_Int data source to duplicate it.
12. Rename the duplicate data source W_Ref_Int.
13. Right-click on the W_Ref_Int dataset and ensure that Assume Referential Integrity *is* selected.
14. Place Sales on the **Text** shelf and note the value of $19,500. (If the view does not display $19,500, refresh the view by pressing *F5* on Windows or *command + R* on Mac.)

15. Observe the query Tableau sent to the underlying data source. Note that an inner join is not included:

```
SELECT SUM([Music_Sales$].[Sale Amount]) AS [sum:Sale Amount:ok]
FROM [Music_Sales$]
HAVING (COUNT(1) > 0)
```

The value of $19,500 demonstrates that the Catalog table was not referenced. Tableau assumed referential integrity and simply reported SUM(Sale Amount) from the Music_Sales table.

Advantages of blending

Joining should be chosen instead of blending whenever possible. However, there are exceptions, two of which are discussed here. First, data blending is advantageous (and usually necessary) when there is no common key shared between two tables. The following example demonstrates an occasion when cross-joining will not work and a data blend is required.

Exercise: necessary blending

This example uses a small secondary dataset with quota information and no unique row-level keys. It illustrates a use case in which it's easier to create and maintain a local spreadsheet than to properly model the same information in a database:

1. In the workbook associated with this chapter, navigate to the Necessary Blending worksheet.
2. In the **Data** pane, select the Superstore dataset.
3. Place Region on the **Rows** shelf and Sales on the **Text** shelf.
4. In the **Data** pane, select the Quota dataset and make sure that Region has an orange chain icon next to it to ensure that Region is used as a linking field. Note that the Quota dataset contains no row-level keys and thus is not eligible for joining.
5. Double-click on the Quota measure to place it on the view.
6. At this point, the blend is working well. The correct numbers are displaying, the secondary dataset is quite small, and there is only one linking field.
7. In the **Data** pane, select the Superstore dataset.
8. Drag Order Date on the **Rows** shelf to the left of Region. Note that the correct numbers are not displaying for Quota.

9. In the **Data** pane, right-click on Order Date and select **Create > Custom Date**.

10. In the resulting dialog box, set **Name** to **Year**, **Detail** to **Years**, and choose **Date Part**. Click **OK**:

11. In the **Data** pane, select the Quota dataset.
12. Set Year as a linking field.

Quota now displays correctly. Note that both Year and Region are used as linking fields. Though necessary for the second half of this exercise, linking on both fields is not ideal for performance because it requires Tableau to generate two additional queries. Follow the steps discussed above to turn on performance recording in order to review the queries Tableau generates.

In the above exercise, is it possible to cross join the 'Superstore' and 'Quota' data sources by joining on both the Region and the Year fields? Yes it is, however the different granularity of each dataset will cause Quota to be populated for each matching row, hence SUM(Quota) will show an incorrect value.

Use data blending when you work with two datasets that have different granularities, when a cross database join is not possible (for example, to cubes or extract only connections), when you have big datasets for which a blend will improve the performance. More info can be found here: https://onlinehelp.tableau.com/current/pro/desktop/en-us/multiple_connections.htm

Efficiently working with data sources

This section will cover some basics of database tuning and ways to work efficiently with large data sources. Since the topic is more focused on data sources than on Tableau, no exercises are included.

Tuning data sources

If you are connecting to large data sources and are experiencing performance problems, a conversation with a **database administrator (DBA)** may be beneficial. Clear communication coupled with a small amount of database work could dramatically improve performance. The conversation should include database-tuning points, such as explicitly defining primary and foreign keys, defining columns as NOT NULL, and indexing. Each point will be discussed here.

Primary and foreign keys

Primary and foreign keys are essential for joining tables. A primary key is composed of one or more columns in a table. The primary key should be unique for every row. Joining on a non-unique, row-level key may lead to erroneous results, as explored in the *A data blend vs a left join* section in `Chapter 4`, *All About Data – Joins, Blends, and Data Structures*. Explicitly defining primary keys in the database helps ensure that each key value is unique.

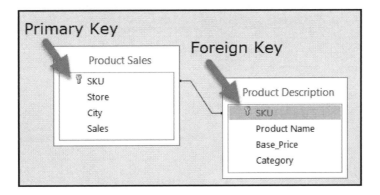

A foreign key is composed of one or more columns in a table that uniquely identify rows in another table. This unique identification occurs as a result of the foreign key in one table referencing the primary key in another table. Explicitly defining foreign keys in the database enables Tableau to bypass many integrity checks, thus improving performance.

NOT NULL

Tableau has published a PDF entitled Basic Performance Tips (`https://community.`
`tableau.com/docs/DOC-1041`) which states that Programmers and Tableau Desktop do not
like `NULL` data. Define each column in your tables with an explicit `NOT NULL` if possible. In
practice, DBAs debate when it is and is not appropriate to define columns as `NOT NULL`;
however, two things are clear. A primary or foreign key should be defined as `NOT NULL`.
This is self-evident since primary and foreign keys must be unique by definition. Also, any
column that is to be indexed should be defined as `NOT NULL` since otherwise an index may
be unusable. Indexing is discussed more fully in the next section.

Introduction to Index

Let's consider the following two questions regarding indexing:

- What is an index?
- What should be indexed?

The first of our two questions may be easily answered by a DBA, but is likely uncharted
waters for the Tableau author.

 An index is a copy of selected columns in a database table that has been
optimized for efficient searching.

Since these copied columns include pointers to the original columns, they can be accessed
to quickly find given rows and return the required data. A small example may prove
helpful.

According to The Boeing Company, the 787 Dreamliner has about 2.3 million parts.
Imagine a table that lists all of these parts in the Part_Name column. Your task is to search
this column for every part, starting with the 'fuse' string. On a non-indexed column, this
would require the examination of every row of data in the database. Such a search could be
quite slow. Fortunately, indexes can be used to reduce the number of rows searched, thus
making the process much faster. One type of structured data used for indexing is B-tree. A
B-tree data structure is sorted. Thus, when accessing an index using a B-tree data structure
to search for all parts starting with fuse, not every row has to be considered. Instead, the
database can skip straight to the fs and quickly return the desired rows.

Indexing

Now let's move on to the second question on indexing. What should be indexed? As shown in the following information box, the question of what can be indexed can be answered fairly succinctly.

Ideally, all columns used for joining or filtering should be indexed in the data source.

Later in this chapter, methods for efficiently using filters in Tableau regardless of indexing will be discussed. Although there are some basic performance considerations for creating more efficient joins in Tableau (for example, avoid an outer join when a left join will suffice), join performance is largely determined outside of Tableau. Therefore, it is typically more important to index columns used in joins than those used for filtering.

###ADD modern dw

Working efficiently with large data sources

A colleague of mine recently consulted with a relatively small mobile phone service provider. Even though the company was small, the volume could be in excess of 1,000,000 calls per day. The management at the company insisted on the ability to interface with detailed visualizations of individual calls in Tableau workbooks. The performance of the workbooks was, understandably, a problem. Was such low-level detail necessary? Might less detail and snappier workbooks have led to better business decisions?

In order to balance business needs with practical performance requirements, businesses often need to ascertain what level of detail is genuinely helpful for reporting. Often, detailed granularity is not necessary. When such is the case, a summary table may provide sufficient business insight while enabling quick performance. In the case of the mobile phone service provider, a daily snapshot of call volumes may have sufficed. Even an hourly snapshot would have greatly reduce the table size and improved Tableau's performance. As will be discussed in the next section, Tableau can be used to create summarized datasets through extracting.

Intelligent extracts

This section will discuss what a Tableau Data Extract is as well as how to efficiently construct an extract.

Understanding the Tableau data extract

An extract is a proprietary compressed data source created by Tableau Desktop. Since the 10.5 release, the file extension for an extract changed from the .tde to the .hyper format. Thus the new format makes use of the hyper engine, which was discussed in `Chapter 1,` *Getting Up to Speed – A Review of the Basics*. An extract can be stored locally and accessed by Tableau to render visualizations.

Consider the following points that make an extract file an excellent choice for improved performance:

- Extracts can be quickly generated at an aggregate level.
- See the walkthrough of the Extract Data dialog box below.
- Extracts are a columnar store.
- Relational databases typically store data using a Row Store methodology. A columnar store records as sequences of columns.
- In the following example, note that Row Store is excellent for returning individual rows, whereas Column Store is much better for returning aggregated data:

	Table		
	Instrument	Store	Price
Row 1	Selmer Trumpet	North	$3500
Row 2	Conn French Horn	East	$4500
Row 3	Getzen Trombone	South	$2500
Row 4	Miraphone Tuba	West	$9000

Column Store table:

Row Store		Column Store	
Row 1	Selmer Trumpet	Instrument	Selmer Trumpet
	North		Conn French Horn
	$3,500		Getzen Trombone
Row 2	Conn French Horn		Miraphone Tuba
	East	Store	North
	$4,500		East
Row 3	Getzen Trombone		South
	South		West
	$2,500	Price	$3,500
Row 4	Miraphone Tuba		$4,500
	West		$2,500
	$9,000		$9,000

To sum up:

- Extracts use compression techniques to reduce file size while maintaining performance.
- Extracts are architect-aware.
- An extract tries to utilize both RAM and hard drive space for optimal performance.

Constructing an extract for optimal performance

This section will discuss extracts from a performance aspect. Other aspects of extracts, such as scheduling and incremental refreshes, will not be considered here:

An extract is created via **Data > [Data Source] > Extract Data**:

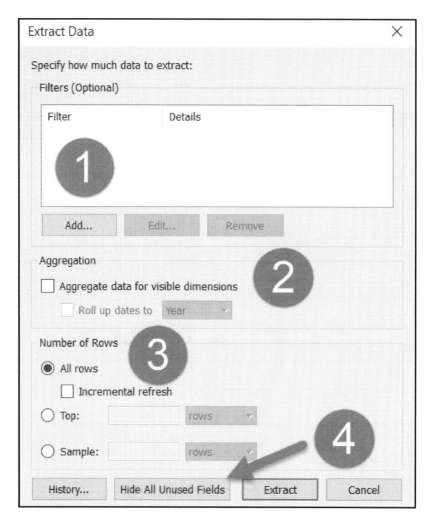

- **Filter the extract as needed**: Sometimes an extract that exactly reflects a data source is warranted, but often filtering various fields will still populate the extract with the required data while shrinking the size and improving performance. To add a filter, simply click **Add...** to access a dialog box identical to the filter dialog box used within a worksheet.

- **Aggregate to the level of the granularity represented in the view**: Aggregation not only reduces the file size but can also be helpful from a security standpoint. Without aggregation, an extract is constructed using row-level data. Therefore the Tableau author should note that if the extract is built without choosing to aggregate, any sensitive row-level data is accessible.

- **Reduce the number of rows**: As shown in the *On-the-Fly Techniques* section, reducing the number of rows can allow the author to create a small, local extract for quick workbook building after which the original data source can be accessed for complete analysis.

- **Hide all unused fields**: This option excludes all columns that are not used in the workbook from the extract. This can significantly reduce the extract size and increase performance.

Exercise: summary aggregates for improved performance

The following exercise will use two aggregates from a single data source, one at the State level and the other at the City level. These aggregated data sources will be used to create two worksheets. Each of these worksheets will be placed on a dashboard along with a third worksheet with row-level information. Finally, filter actions will be created to tie the three worksheets together. The purpose of the exercise is to demonstrate how small extracts might be used in conjunction with a larger dataset to create a more performant dashboard.

1. Open the workbook associated with this chapter and navigate to the State Agg worksheet.
2. In the **Data** pane, select the SS - State Agg data source.
3. Create a filled map using state by placing State on the **Detail** shelf and selecting Filled Map from the **Marks View** card.
4. Right click on the SS - State Agg data source and select 'Extract Data'.
5. Note that Tableau displays an error stating that it cannot find the referenced file. You can either point to the instance of Sample - Superstore that ships with Tableau or you can use the instance provided via the link in the worksheet's caption.

6. After connecting to the data source, Tableau will display the **Extract Data** dialog box. Within the resulting dialog box, select Aggregate data for visible dimensions and All Rows.

7. Click the Hide All Unused Fields button and then click on Extract. Note that the resulting extract only contains State. Also note that the data has been aggregated so that no underlying data is available:

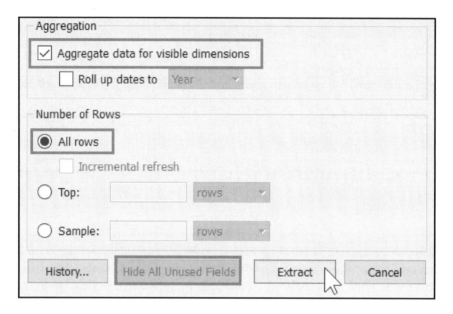

8. Navigate to the City Agg worksheet.

9. In the **Data** pane, select the SS - City Agg data source. Note that this data source has already been extracted and thus only contains State, City, and Sales. Also note that the data has been aggregated so that no underlying data is available.

10. Place City on the **Rows** shelf, Sales on the **Text** shelf, and State on the **Detail** shelf. Don't forget to include State even though it does not display on the view. It must be used so that the dashboard created at the end of the exercise works correctly.

11. Navigate to the Row Detail worksheet and select the Superstore dataset.

12. Create a crosstab view that displays Customer Name, Order ID, Row ID, Profit, and Sales.

One quick way to create this view is to double-click on each field.

13. Navigate to the Agg Dash dashboard and place each of the three worksheets on the dashboard.

14. Create the following actions via **Dashboard > Actions > Add Action > Filter**:

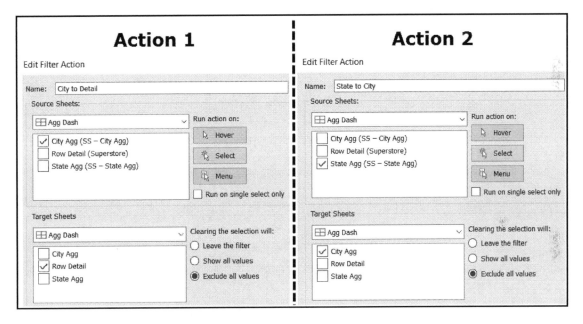

15. After creating these two actions, in the dashboard click on a state.

16. Click on a city.

17. Click in a blank portion of the City Agg worksheet to exclude all values on Row Detail.

18. Click on a blank portion of the State Agg worksheet to exclude all values on City Agg.

19. Format the dashboard as desired:

State Agg	City Agg		Row Detail				
	City		Customer ..	Order ID	Row ID	Profit	Sales
	Abilene	$1	Shirley Da..	CA-2012-1421..	6124	6.8	$21
	Allen	$290	Sylvia	CA-2014-1393..	4026	10.0	$30
	Amarillo	$3,773	Foulston		4027	2.9	$9
	Arlington	$5,848			4028	13.4	$154
	Austin	$6,058			4029	-22.5	$13
	Baytown	$10					
	Beaumont	$472					
	Bedford	**$226**					
	Brownsville	$1,292					
	Bryan	$617					
	Carrollton	$2,231					
	Cedar Hill	$123					

Having completed the exercise, note that the resulting dashboard is quite performant.

- When the user first opens the dashboard, only State Agg displays. This is performant for two reasons. First, displaying a single worksheet as opposed to every worksheet when opening the dashboard causes fewer initial queries and less rendering. Second, accessing a small extract is quicker than accessing a larger data source.
- Since the City Agg worksheet is also accessing a small extract, when the user clicks on a state, the City Agg worksheet will appear quickly.
- When the user clicks on a city, a call is made to the data source that only includes the information for that particular city. A relatively small amount of data is pulled and performance should be good for even larger datasets.

Another aspect of good performance practice, apart from using aggregate extracts should be considered for this exercise. The dashboard contains no quick filters. Often, using quick filters on a dashboard is unnecessary. If the worksheets on the dashboard can be used to filter, those worksheets can essentially do double duty. That is to say, worksheets can provide valuable analysis while simultaneously acting as filters for other worksheets on the dashboard. This represents a performance improvement over using quick filters, since adding quick filters would cause additional queries to be sent to the underlying data source.

In the preceding dashboard, each worksheet references a different data source. Therefore, one might ask, How are the action filters able to function across the different data sources? The answer can be found in the Filter Action dialog box. As shown in the following screenshot, 'All Fields' are considered Target Filters. Tableau simply matches any fields of the same name across each data source.

See the following screenshot:

Optimizing extracts

Extracts can be optimized for even better performance results. To optimize an extract, simply right-click on a data source and select **Data > Extract > Optimize**, as seen in the following screenshot:

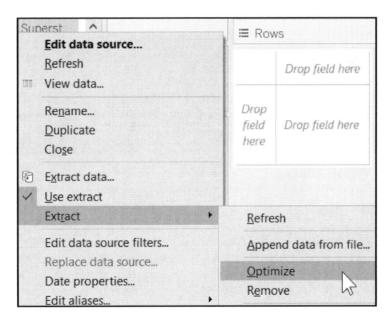

Optimization accelerates performance by materializing calculated fields when possible. This means that Tableau actually generates values for calculated fields in the extract so that those values can be looked up instead of calculated. Note that not all calculated fields are materialized. Fields that are not materialized include table calculations, changeable or unstable functions, such as NOW() and TODAY(), and calculated fields using parameters.

When an extract is first created, it is automatically optimized. In other words, calculated fields are automatically materialized when possible. However, over the course of time, calculated fields may be altered that will cause the extract to drop materialized fields. At such times, **Extract > Compute Calculations Now** must be selected in order to regenerate the materialized fields:

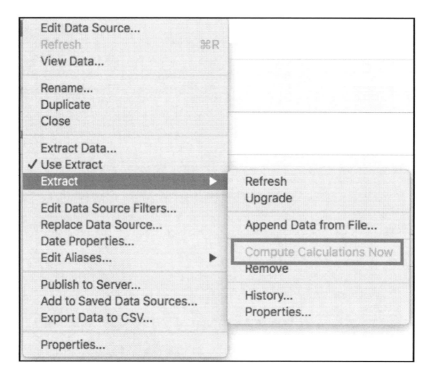

If an extract is set to refresh on Tableau Server, the extract is automatically optimized for each refresh.

The following example demonstrates calculated fields that are materialized and those that are not.

Exercise: materialized calculations

Follow along the exercise steps:

1. In Tableau, select **New > New** to create a new workbook.
2. In the new workbook, select **Data > New Data Source** and connect to the Sample Superstore dataset located in `My Tableau Repository/Datasources`.
3. Connect to the Orders worksheet.
4. Create the following parameters:

Parameter	
Name	Select Sufficient Profit Ratio
Data Type	Float
Allowable Values	Range
Min/Max	0.25 - 0.5
Step Size	0.01

5. Create the following calculated fields:

Name	Calculation
Profit Ratio	SUM([Profit])/SUM([Sales])
This Year's Profit	IF [Profit Ratio] > [Select Sufficient Profit Ratio] THEN "Sufficient Profit" END
Window Sum	WINDOW_SUM(SUM([Sales]))
Profitable?	[Profit] > 0

6. Right-click on the data source and select **Extract data**.
7. Click the Extract button.
8. When prompted, save the resulting extract to a location of you're choosing.
9. Open a new Tableau workbook, select **File > Open**, and select the extract created in the preceding step.
10. Note the following in the data source:
    - Profit Ratio, an aggregate calculation, was materialized.
    - This Year's Profit, which references a parameter, has the value of null and was not materialized.
    - Window Sum, a table calculation, has the 'undefined' value and was not materialized.
    - Profitable?, a row-level calculation, was materialized.

Parameters

If you make use of parameters in your dashboard, check whether you can eliminate those and use calculations instead. Also, split calculations if they can't be materialized as a whole. If parts of the calculation can be calculated within the extract creation, you will gain performance.

Using filters wisely

Filters generally improve performance in Tableau. For example, when using a dimension filter to view only the West region, a query is passed to the underlying data source, resulting in returned information for only that region. By reducing the amount of data returned, performance improves. This is because less data means reduced network bandwidth load, reduced database processing requirements, and reduced processing requirements for the local computer.

Filters can also negatively impact Tableau performance. For example, using Only relevant values causes additional queries to be sent to the underlying data source, thus slowing down the response time. Create a context filter and select All Values in Context. Also, creating quick filters from high-cardinality dimensions can slow performance.

The next section will focus on navigating filter usage to maximize efficient usage and minimize inefficient usage.

Extract filter performance

Extract filters remove data from the extracted data source. Simply put, the data isn't there. Thus, performance is enhanced by reducing the overall amount of data. Performance may also be improved since extracted data uses Tableau's proprietary, columnar dataset. Furthermore, extracts are always flattened, which will have performance advantages over connecting to datasets using joins.

To create an extract filter, begin by selecting **Data > [Data Source] > Extract Data**. In the resulting dialog box, choose to add a filter.

Data source filter performance

Data source filters are applied throughout the workbook. For example, if you create a data source filter that removes all members of the Country dimension except the USA, the 'Country' dimension will only include the USA for all worksheets in the workbook.

Data source filters improve performance in the same way as dimension and measure filters; that is, data source filters cause Tableau to generate a query to the underlying data source, which will limit the data that is returned. Less returned data generally results in quicker processing and rendering. A further advantage data source filters offer is ease of authoring. For example, if the Tableau author knows in advance that an entire workbook is going to be USA-centric, creating a data source filter saves you the trouble of applying a dimension filter to every worksheet in the workbook using that data source.

Also note that data source filters occur quite early in the process flow. All calculations (including calculations using Fixed LOD expressions that are rendered before dimension and measure filters are triggered) respect data source filters.

To create a data source filter, click the Data Source tab located in the bottom-left corner of Tableau. Then click on the **Add...** link located on the top-right corner of the page:

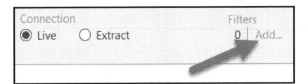

Context filters

A context filter is created simply by right-clicking on a field in the **Filter** shelf and selecting Add to Context.

Dimension and measure filters are independent. Each filter queries the data source independently and returns results. A context filter, on the other hand, will force dimension and measure filters to depend on it. This behavior can be helpful (and necessary) for getting the right answer in some circumstances. For instance, if a Tableau author accesses the Superstore dataset and uses a filter on Product Names to return the top-10-selling Product Names in a single Category, it will be necessary that Category be defined as a context filter. Otherwise, the Product Names filter will return the top 10 overall.

Will a context filter improve performance any more than a dimension or measure filter? The answer to that question changed with the release of Tableau 9.0. Consider the following SQL generated from Tableau 8.3 and 9.0. Note that in each case the Superstore dataset is used and 'Product Name' is constrained to the top 10 by Sales, and 'Category' is cast as a context filter displaying only 'Furniture'.

See a comparison:

SQL Generated by 8.3	SQL Generated by 9.0
SELECT [#Tableau_Context].[Product Name] AS [none:Product Name:nk] FROM [#Tableau_Context] INNER JOIN (SELECT TOP 10 [#Tableau_Context].[Product Name] AS [none:Product Name:nk] ...	SELECT [Orders$].[Product Name] AS [Product Name] FROM [dbo].[Orders$] [Orders$] INNER JOIN (SELECT TOP 10 [Orders$].[Product Name] AS [Product Name] ... WHERE ([Orders$].[Category] = 'Furniture'

The 8.3 query references [#Tableau_Context] and does not reference [Category]. This is because [#Tableau_Context] is a temp table that has been created in the data source (in this case SQL Server). Since the temp table only contains data for 'Furniture', a WHERE clause is not needed.

The 9.0 query references [Orders$] and does contain a reference to 'Category'. This is because [Orders$] is not a temp table and therefore a WHERE clause is required to constrain the results.

The preceding illustrates that when using Tableau 8.3 and earlier, if a context filter can be used that will produce a significantly smaller table than exists in the source database, performance might improve. However, since no temp table is created after 8.3, there may be no corresponding performance improvement in Tableau 9.0 or later; including Tableau 10.0.

At this point, you may wonder, Are there still some scenarios for which a temp table may be created for a context filter? Tableau documentation states the following:

> As of Tableau 9.0, context filters no longer create temporary tables, except for generic ODBC data sources and customized data sources.

The end result is that context filters are still necessary for some visualizations to get the right answer (see the *Understanding Order of Filtering* section in `Chapter 7`, *Level of Detail Calculation*), but performance enhancements beyond what is normally expected for dimension and measure filters may be unlikely. Of course, individual circumstances may differ and it's worth trying a context filter to improve performance.

Another question may be raised at this point: why did the Tableau development team change the way context filters are realized? Consider these answers. First, in some environments granting Tableau permission to create temp tables may require additional rights and thus make Tableau more difficult to deploy. Also, if a context filter creates a temp table that is not significantly smaller than the source table, performance may actually degrade.

Dimension and measure filters

Dimension and measure filters can improve performance. Since either a dimension filter or a measure filter will cause Tableau to generate a query to the underlying data source, which will limit the data that is returned, performance is improved. Simply put, the smaller the returned dataset, the better the performance.

Dimension and measure filters can degrade performance. Since Tableau not only generates queries to the underlying data source in order to display visualizations, but also generates queries to display filters, more displayed filters will slow performance. Furthermore, displayed filters on high-cardinality dimensions can inhibit performance. (A dimension with many members is referred to as having high cardinality.) Consider the example of a filter that displays every customer in a dataset. Performance for such a filter might be slow because every customer in the underlying dataset must be located and returned, and then Tableau has to render and display each of these customers in the filter.

When using two or more dimension or measure filters on a view, a relevant filter may be used to limit the choices that display. For example, if a view includes a filter for City and Postal Code, the latter might be set to show Only relevant values. This is advantageous to the end user in that it adjusts the number of Postal Codes that display to reflect only those pertinent to the cities selected in the first filter. However, using relative filters will cause additional queries to be sent to the data source and thus may degrade performance.

See screenshot:

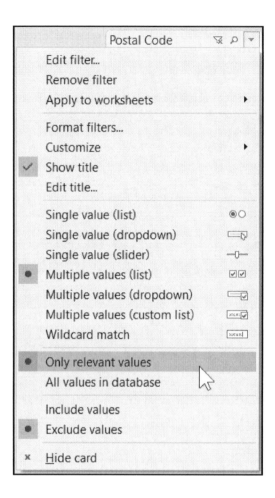

Table-calculation filters

Using table calculations as filters do not have the same corresponding performance enhancements as dimension or measure filters. As discussed above, dimension and measure filters reduce the returned dataset. Table calculation filters do not. In the Tableau process flow, table calculations are not rendered until **after** the data is returned from the data source. This means that table calculations cannot be used to generate queries to limit returned data. Or, to put it another way, table-calculation filters cause all data related to a given dimension or measure to be returned, after which Tableau executes the filter on the returned dataset.

Exercise: late filter

Follow along the exercise steps:

1. Open the workbook associated with this chapter and navigate to the Late Filter worksheet.
2. In the **Data** pane, select the Superstore data source.
3. Create a calculated field named Cust Name Tbl Calc with the following code:

```
LOOKUP ( MAX ( [Customer Name] ),0 )
```

4. Place Customer Name on the **Rows** shelf.
5. Place Cust Name Tbl Calc on the **Filters** shelf and constrain to show only Aaron Bergman.
6. Place Sales on the **Text** shelf.
7. Right-click on Sales and select **Quick table calculation > Rank**.

In this exercise, the entire list of customers is returned to Tableau, after which Tableau deploys the filter. Essentially, using Cust Name Tbl Calc as a filter merely hides the underlying data. This is useful because the rank returned for 'Aaron Bergman' is correct. Merely filtering on 'Customer Name' would return a rank of '1' for 'Aaron Bergman'. Unfortunately, the correct results come with a performance hit. Running the performance recorder on this exercise will show that the table calculation negatively impacts performance.

Fortunately, with the advent of LOD calculations in Tableau 9.0, using table calculations as filters is often not necessary. See the *Practical fixed* section in Chapter 7, *Level of Detail Calculations*, for more information.

Using actions instead of filters

Another way to improve performance might be to use Actions instead of Filters. You can develop a dashboard that shows a high-level overview first, and goes into detail only once the user selects something. By selecting a mark in the high-level overview, an action will be triggered. The user can dive deeper into details, but the level of detail will only be increased step by step. Hence, less data has to be loaded at once. A very nice presentation from TC 2018 regarding this topic can be found at https://www.youtube.com/watch?v=veLlZ1btoms&amp;amp;t=1s.

Efficient calculations

Calculations may be constructed differently and yet accomplish the same thing. Look for instance at the following example which shows that a **If** statement can be replaced but simpler code:

Scenario I	Scenario II
• Create a calculated field with the following code: ``` IF SUM (Profit) > 0 THEN'Profitable' ELSE'Unprofitable' END ``` • Place the calculated field on the **Color** shelf.	• Create a calculated field with the following code: ``` SUM (Profit) > 0 ``` • Place the calculated field on the **Color** shelf. • Right-click on 'True' and 'False' in the resulting legend and rename to 'Profitable' and 'Unprofitable'.

Since either of these scenarios will return the desired results, which should be used? The deciding factor is performance. This section will explore what to do and what to avoid when creating calculated fields in order to maximize performance.

Boolean/Numbers > Date > String

As the header suggests, calculations that use Boolean values or numbers are more performant than those that use dates. Calculations that use dates, in turn, are more performant than those using strings. This is not only true of Tableau but also in computer science as a whole.

Based on this information, Scenario II listed in the table above is more performant than Scenario I. Scenario I causes Tableau to create a query that requires the data source engine to handle strings for reporting profitability, whereas Scenario II sends only 1s and 0s to determine profitability. The third step for Scenario II (that is, aliasing 'True' and 'False' to 'Profitable' and 'Unprofitable') is merely a labelling change that happens after the aggregate dataset is returned from the data source. Labelling is quick and easy for Tableau.

Exercise: an efficient and an inefficient way to determine N figure salary

The following exercise uses two calculations to determine the number of integers in individual annual income. The first method, while perhaps using more easily-readable code, uses an STR function and is thus slower. The second method avoids the STR function and is thus quicker:

1. Open the workbook associated with this chapter and navigate to the Salary worksheet.
2. In the **Data** pane, select the data source named Salary.
3. Place Tax Payer on the **Rows** shelf and Salary on the **Text** shelf.
4. Create the following calculated fields:

Name	Calculation
X Figure Salary 1	LEN(STR([Salary]))
X Figure Salary 2	INT(LOG([Salary]) + 1)

5. Complete the view with both newly-created calculated fields:

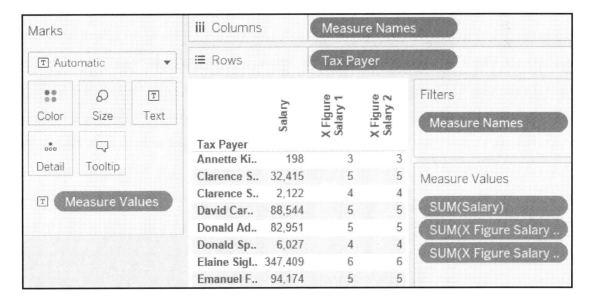

Exercise: date vs integer

The following exercise uses two calculations and two parameters to determine sales in the Superstore dataset. One parameter is set to Date and the other is set to Integer. The calculations associated with the parameters handle each data type accordingly. Even though the resulting query that is sent to the data source is similar in each case, a potential performance boost is realized when Tableau uses integers as opposed to dates.

Follow along the exercise steps:

1. Open the workbook associated with this chapter and navigate to the Chosen Year - Date worksheet.
2. In the **Data** pane, select the Superstore data source.
3. Create the following parameters:

Parameter 1		Parameter 2	
Name	Select Year - Date	Name	Select Year - Int
Date Type	Date & Time	Date Type	Integer
Display Format	Select Custom and inout yyyy	Display Format	Select Custom and input 0;-0
Allowable Values	Range	Allowbale Values	List
Min/Max	Set from field Order Date	Min/Max	2011 2012 2013 2014
Step Size	1 Year		

Note that the display format 0;-0 in `Select Year - Int` is needed so that a comma does not display; for example, 2,013.

4. Create the following calculated fields:

Name	Calculation
Chosen Year - Date	IF YEAR([Order Date]) = YEAR([Select Year - Date]) THEN [Sales] END
Chosen Year - Int	IF YEAR([Order Date]) = [Select Year - Int] THEN [Sales] END

5. Place State on the **Detail** shelf and *Chosen Year - Date* on both the **Color** shelf and **Text/Label** shelf.

6. Right-click on the Select Year - Date parameter and choose to show the parameter control.
7. Set the parameter as desired.
8. Navigate to the Chosen Year - Int worksheet.
9. Place State on the **Detail** shelf and *Chosen Year - Int* on both the **Color** shelf and **Text/Label** shelf.
10. Right-click on the `Select Year - Int` parameter and choose to show the parameter control.
11. Set the `Select Year - Int` parameter the same as the Select Year - Date parameter.

The displayed results of both the Chosen Year - Date and Chosen Year - Int worksheets is the same; however, Chosen Year - Int performs better.

Level-of-detail calculation or table calculations

In some instances, a LOD calculation might be faster than a Table Calculation and vice versa. Try both to see which one performs better. Also, if they're not really needed, use neither one.

Additional performance considerations

To conclude this chapter, let's consider a few other possibilities for improving performance.

Avoid overcrowding a dashboard

Often end users want to see everything at once on a dashboard. Although this may be perceived as beneficial, it often is not. Consider the inclusion of a large crosstab on a dashboard. Does scrolling through pages of details add to the analytical value of the dashboard? Perhaps the answer is 'no'. Furthermore, an excess of information on a dashboard may obscure important insight. Diplomatically arguing for leaner dashboards may lead to better decision-making as well as better performance.

Fixing dashboard sizing

Dashboards can be set to an exact size or to Range or Automatic. Exact size results in quicker performance because once Tableau Server has rendered a view for one end user that render stays in cache and can be reused for the next end user that accesses that dashboard. 'Automatic' and 'Range', on the other hand, cause Tableau Server to attempt to determine the resolution size used by each end user and render the dashboard accordingly. This means that Tableau Server does not use the instance of the dashboard stored in cache for the next end user; this, in turn, impacts performance.

Setting expectations

If an end user is expecting near-instantaneous performance then, of course, anything less is disappointing. Explaining in advance that a complicated, detailed-oriented dashboard may not be performant can help in at least two ways. First, upon explaining the likely performance problems, a compromise may be reached that results in the creation of a less complicated dashboard that still delivers valuable information. Second, if it is absolutely necessary for the dashboard to be complicated and detailed-oriented, at least the end user has been warned that patience may be needed when interfacing it.

Summary

We began this chapter with a discussion of the Performance Recording dashboard. This was important because many of the subsequent exercises utilized the Performance Recording dashboard to examine underlying queries. Next, we discussed Hardware and On-the-Fly Techniques where the intent was to communicate hardware considerations for good Tableau performance and, in the absence of optimal hardware, techniques for squeezing the best-possible performance out of any computer.

Then we covered working with data sources, including joining, blending, and efficiently working with Data Sources. This was followed by a discussion on generating and using extracts as efficiently as possible. By focusing on data sources for these three sections, we learned best practices and what to avoid when working with either remote datasets or extracts.

The next sections explored performance implications for various types of filters and calculations. Lastly, we looked at additional performance considerations, where we explored a few more thoughts about dashboard performance as well as setting expectations.

In the next chapter, we will turn our attention to Tableau Server. Tableau Server is a dense topic worthy of a book. Thus, our exploration will be truncated to focus on Tableau Server from the desktop author's perspective.

3

Section 3: Connecting Tableau to R, Python, and Matlab

Part 3 of this book will cover connecting Tableau to R, Python, and Matlab.

The following chapters are in this section:

Interacting with Tableau Server

14

Tableau Server is an online solution for sharing, distributing, and collaborating on content created in Tableau Desktop. Benefits include providing an environment where end users can securely view and explore data visualizations that are constantly updated from underlying data sources so that content is always fresh.

This chapter assumes the reader has access to Tableau Server with sufficient privileges to publishing data sources and editing in the web-authoring environment. If you do not have access to Tableau Server but would like to work through the exercises in this chapter, consider downloading a trial version which, as of this writing, is fully functional for two weeks. If you would like a longer trial, consider joining the Tableau beta program at `http://www.tableau.com/getbeta`, which will give you access to each beta release in which you participate.

The scope of this chapter is limited to the Tableau Desktop author's interaction with Tableau Server. Topics such as installation and upgrades, authentication and access, security configuration, and command-line utilities are not directly related to the Tableau Desktop author's interaction with Tableau Server and are thus are not included in this chapter. However, the help documentation is quite good. Also consider watching some videos from TC 2018 about Tableau Server (for example, `https://www.youtube.com/watch?v=zAWgg_KbSS8`). If you have questions related to any of the topics listed here or other Tableau Server topics, be sure to visit the online help site at `https://www.tableau.com/support/help`.

This chapter will explore the following topics:

- Tableau file types
- Tableau data source
- Tableau packaged data source
- Tableau workbook
- Tableau packaged Workbook
- Other file types
- Tableau Server architecture
- Tableau Server architecture approaches to avoid
- Tableau Server architecture approaches to adopt
- Tableau Server revision history
- Tableau Server web authoring environment
- Basic web-authoring instructions
- Exploring the capabilities and limitations of the Tableau Server web-authoring environment
- Comparing and contrasting Tableau Desktop with the Tableau Server-web authoring environment
- User filters
- Performance-recording dashboard
- Exploring performance-recording on Tableau Server
- More Tableau Server settings

Tableau file types

We will begin our discussion of Tableau Server by considering the various Tableau file types. This may seem a surprising place to begin, but as you read, you will discover that a clear understanding of file types provides the Tableau Desktop author with foundational knowledge for efficiently and effectively interacting with Tableau Server.

The file types discussed previously that are relevant for understanding how to interact with Tableau Server are considered in some depth. The file types that are not relevant for understanding Tableau Server are considered only briefly. Some file types (for example, those associated with license activation) are not considered.

Tableau data source

Let's now look at the various data sources available in Tableau. Take a look at the following Tableau data file:

- **File format type**: XML.
- **What it contains**: Metadata.
- **Why it's useful**: The `.tds` file is important because it allows the Tableau author to define default formatting and aggregation, calculated fields, data types, field types, and more. Furthermore, the `.tds` file can be published to Tableau Server and thus accessed by other authors in the environment. This effectively makes a `.tds` file a playbook, which ensures consistency across the organization. This important feature will be explored more fully in the *Tableau Server architecture* section.
- **How it's generated**: A `.tds` file can be generated by right-clicking on a data source in the **Data** pane and selecting **Add to Saved Data Sources...**, followed by selecting **Tableau Data Source** in the resulting dialog box. A `.tds` file can also be generated when publishing to Tableau Server via **Server** | **Publish Data Source** | **[data source]**. The exercise section is included that demonstrates how to publish a `.tds` file and also a `.tdsx` file.

- **How to access it**: The `.tds` file type is usually accessed in one of two places. First, it can be stored in **My Tableau Repository** | **Datasources**. When stored in this directory, a `.tds` file will display in the left portion of **Start Page** under the **Saved Data Sources** section. The second place a `.tds` file is often stored is on Tableau Server. Navigating to **Data** | **New Data Source** and choosing **Tableau Server** allows the Tableau author to point to the `.tds` and `.tdsx` files that have been published to Tableau Server.

Tableau packaged data source

Take a look at the following Tableau data file details:

- **File format type**: Compressed.
- **What it contains**: Metadata and a data extract.

- **Why it's useful**: The .tdsx file is useful because it can be accessed for both metadata and data. Tableau authors can access a .tdsx file located on Tableau Server as a data source, thus eliminating the need for a workbook to connect directly to an external data source. A published .tdsx file can be placed on a schedule so that it is regularly updated from the underlying data source.
- **How it's generated**: A .tdsx file can be generated by right-clicking on a data source in the **Data** pane and selecting **Add to Saved Data Sources...**, followed by selecting **Tableau Packaged Data Source** in the resulting dialog box. Like the .tds file, the .tdsx file can also be generated when publishing to Tableau server via **Server | Publish Data Source | [data source]**. See the next exercise section for more details.

- **How to access it**: A .tdsx file is accessed the same way a .tds file is. First, it can be stored in **My Tableau Repository | Datasources**. When stored in this directory, a .tdsx file will display in the left portion of **Start Page** under the **Saved Data Sources** section. The second place a .tdsx file is often stored is on Tableau Server. Selecting **Data | New Data Source** and choosing **Tableau Server** allows the Tableau author to point to the .tds and .tdsx files that have been published to a given instance of Tableau Server.

Exercise: publishing a data source to Tableau Server

Lets take a look at the following steps to see how we can publish a data source to Tableau Server:

1. Navigate to `https://public.tableau.com/profile/marleen.meier` to locate and download the workbook associated with this chapter.
2. Navigate to the **Publish** worksheet.
3. Reference the **Caption** in the worksheet to download the content necessary to complete the exercise.
4. Select **Data | New Data Source** and connect to `My Superstore.xls`, which was downloaded in the previous step.
5. Connect to the **Orders** table.
6. Name the data source `My Superstore`.
7. Return to the **Publish** worksheet.
8. If you have not already done so, log into an instance of Tableau Server.
9. In the **Data** pane, select the **My Superstore** data source.

10. Select **Server | Publish Data Source | My Superstore**.
11. In the resulting dialog box, choose desired settings.

In the bottom of the dialog box, you will see an option entitled **Include external files**. Selecting this box will cause Tableau to create and upload a package data source, that is, a `.tdsx` file. Deselecting this box will cause Tableau to generate and upload a `.tds` file. Of course, in this case, since the data source is an Excel file, deselecting **Include external files** would cause Tableau to create a data source that would only be accessible via your local machine.

See the following screenshot:

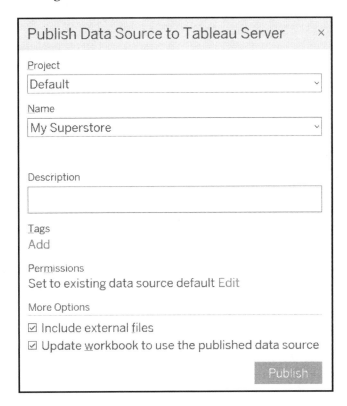

Tableau workbook

Take a look at the following Tableau data file details:

- **File format type**: XML.
- **What it contains**: Metadata and schema. The schema defines the visualizations in the workbook. Note that schema, in this context, refers to the XML that defines the visual components of the workbook, including the visualizations displayed on worksheets as well as the layout of dashboards and stories.
- **Why it's useful**: The .twb file type is the file type most often used by the Tableau author. It is necessary for creating visualizations that point to a live dataset. Thus, real-time solutions will utilize this file type.
- **How it's generated**: A .twb file is created via **File | Save As**, then select the .twb file type in the resulting dialog box.
- **How to access it**: A .twb file can be opened via Tableau Desktop or accessed via a browser that points to an instance of Tableau Server. Since a .twb file is XML, it can be opened, viewed, and updated via a text editor.

Tableau packaged workbook

Take a look at the following Tableau data file details:

- **File format type**: Compressed.
- **What it contains**: Metadata, schema, and optionally, one or more data extracts.
- **Why it's useful**: The .twbx file type is required for use with Tableau Reader. It can also be effectively used with Tableau Server when accessing data sources to which Tableau Server does not directly connect, such as flat files, Microsoft Excel, and Microsoft Access. Drawbacks to the .twbx files will be discussed next.
- **How it's generated**: A .twbx file is created via **File | Save As**, then select the .twbx file type in the resulting dialog box.
- **How to access it**: A .twbx file can be opened via Tableau Desktop or accessed via a browser that points to an instance of Tableau Server. Since a .twbx file is a compressed file, it can also be unzipped via a compression utility, such as WinZip or 7-Zip.

Other file types

The remaining file types you should be familiar with are not particularly relevant for Tableau Server and will thus only be briefly discussed here. There might be some issue with the compatibility of Tableau Desktop Extracts and Tableau Server Versions. A full list of compatibility scenarios can be found at `https://www.tableau.com/support/hyper-resources`. Let's take a look at the following other file types:

- **Hyper**: To know more about hyper, you may refer to the following website `https://www.tableau.com/support/hyper-resources`.
- **Tableau Data Extract**: The `.tde` file can be generated via the following: if a `.twb` file is opened in Tableau Desktop, a `.tde` file can be created by right-clicking on a data source in the **Data** pane and selecting **Extract Data**. After selecting the desired options, Tableau will provide a dialog box for the author to save the `.tde` file in a given location. The extract file can be used to create a local snapshot of a data source for a quicker authoring experience. That same local snapshot is also portable and can thus be used offline. Often the data extracts compressed inside the `.twbx` and `.tdsx` files are in the `.tde`/`.hyper` format. An important clarification should be made here: often Tableau authors will refer to publishing an extract to Tableau Server. The extract that is published is not a `.tde` or `.hyper` file. Rather, it is a `.tdsx` file. Refer to Chapter 13, *Improving Performance* for additional information about the extract file format.
- **Tableau Bookmark**: The `.tbm` file can be generated via **Window | Bookmark | Create Bookmark**. It can be useful for duplicating worksheets across multiple workbooks and also for sharing formatting across multiple workbooks.
- **Tableau Map Source**: The `.tms` file is discussed in detail in Chapter 9, *Mapping*.
- **Tableau Preferences Source**: The `.tps` file can be used to create custom color palettes. This can be helpful when an organization wishes to use its color scheme within Tableau workbooks. The `.tps` file that Tableau utilizes is called `Preferences.tps` and is located in the **My Tableau Repository**. Since it's an XML format, it can be altered via a text editor. Matt Francis has posted a helpful blog at `wannabedatarockstar.blogspot.com` that clearly communicates how to adjust this file. Also reference the Tableau help page.

Tableau Server architecture

Now that we have reviewed the various Tableau file types, we can use that information to understand different ways to architect a Tableau Server environment. Since this is not a book dedicated to Tableau Server, this architecture discussion is presented a high level. The intent is to help the Tableau Desktop author understand how to interact with Tableau Server so that the workbooks best serve the end user. Take a look at the following diagram:

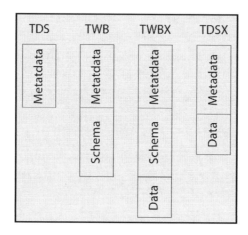

The preceding diagram visually represents the contents of the four file types that are most relevant when considering how the Tableau Desktop author should interface with Tableau Server. To be clear, the previous sections of this chapter provided descriptions of the various file types. Each of these descriptions included the line *What it contains*, which is visually represented in the preceding diagram.

Each of the four file types listed in the graphic includes metadata; two include data and two include schema.

Let's consider four approaches to the Tableau Server architecture and how each presents advantages and disadvantages the Tableau Desktop author should be aware of. The first two approaches presented should generally be avoided. The second two approaches should generally be adopted. Of course, these four approaches do not encompass every possible approach. They do, however, provide a basic framework.

Tableau Server architecture approaches to avoid

If the following Tableau Server architecture approaches should be avoided, why mention them at all? Because they are often utilized! An administrator who hasn't had the opportunity to go to Tableau Server training may default to these approaches and may even build out a large infrastructure before realizing that it's difficult to maintain and scale.

Tableau Server architecture: TWB-centric

Take a look at the following diagram depicting the Tableau Server architecture:

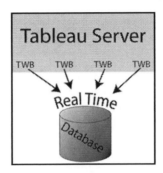

The preceding diagram shows the `.twb` files that have been published to Tableau Server. The diagram also communicates that, since the `.twb` files do not include any data, each workbook must access an external data source in order to display a visualization. Furthermore, this access will cause Tableau to return data in real time, that is, the latest data available in the external data source.

The TWB-centric approach to the Tableau Server architecture results in the following advantages and disadvantages:

- The following are the TWB-centric advantages:
  - **Small footprint**: The small-footprint advantage stems from the small file size; the `.twb` files are rarely larger than a few MB. Small file sizes leads to fewer issues for revision history.

- **Easy revision history**: This is in contrast to the `.twbx` files, which can become quite large and thus unexpectedly overload a hard drive when storing many copies via revision history.
- **Real time**: The real-time advantage is as a result of `.twb` files always pointing to an external data source. As the data source updates, the workbook that is based on a `.twb` file updates. Of course, real time in this case should not be mistaken for stock ticker; that is, updated results do not display in a worksheet unless the end user performs a manual refresh. Even when manually refreshed, a worksheet may be regenerated from the cache as opposed to making a call to the data source. This will depend on the settings in Tableau Server.
- The following are the TWB-centric disadvantages:
  - **Difficult to maintain**: From one perspective, maintenance is fairly easy; that is, a `.twb` file can be quickly downloaded, edited, and then re-uploaded. From another perspective, the TWB-centric approach can be quite a chore. Consider a change to a single foreign key in a data source that breaks every workbook in production. Editing dozens of workbooks (or more) to rectify the issue would not be trivial.
  - **Potentially poor performance**: Another disadvantage of the TWB-centric architecture is potentially poor performance. This is because it requires the `.twb` files to point to external data sources. Network latency and slow database servers will negatively impact workbook performance. It should be noted, however, that some data source engines (such as the **massively parallel processing** (**MPP**) systems discussed in `Chapter 5`, *All About Data – Data Densification, Cubes, and Big Data*) can potentially outperform the following architecture options.

To sum up, avoid the TWB-centric architecture. A TDS-centric architecture maintains all the advantages of a TWB-centric architecture and mitigates the maintenance difficulties we just discussed.

Tableau Server architecture: TWBX-centric

Let's take a look at the following diagram, which depicts the TWBX-centric architecture:

The preceding diagram shows .twbx files that have been published to Tableau Server. Assuming that the .twbx files contain extracts for each required data source, no call is necessary to external data to display a visualization.

The TWBX-centric approach to the Tableau Server architecture has a strong advantage and various disadvantages:

- The following are the TWBX-centric advantages:
  - **Typically performant**: The TWBX-centric approach has at least one advantage: performance. Since a .twbx file can include data extracts, no calls to external data sources are required. This circumvents problems with network latency and slow database servers, thus enabling quick performance. Note that a .twbx file can be scheduled for refreshes thus ensuring that the data is never stale.

- The following are the TWBX-centric disadvantages:
  - **Large footprint**: Unfortunately, the TWBX-centric approach has major drawbacks. The large-footprint disadvantage can occur as a result of large `.twbx` files.
  - **Very difficult to maintain**: These files can be as large as several GB. Such large files are very difficult to maintain and can lead to potential problems with revision history. Large `.twbx` files can be difficult and time-consuming to download, update, and re-upload.
  - **Potential problems with revision history**: Also, as mentioned previously, revision history on large `.twbx` files may unexpectedly overload a hard drive.
  - **Not real time**: Furthermore, the TWBX-centric solution is not real time.

For most Tableau Server implementations, the TWBX-centric solution should be avoided. The Tableau Server administrator who observes a `.twbx` file in excess of 500 MB should likely contact the author who uploaded the file in order to seek a better solution. This is not to say that the `.twbx` files should never be used on Tableau Server. If a Tableau author uses a local spreadsheet as a data source, a `.twbx` file will almost certainly be used in order for the workbook to function on Tableau Server. However, this will typically not lead to large `.twbx` files. Thus the disadvantages we just listed would not apply.

To sum up, avoid the TWBX-centric architecture. A TDSX-centric architecture maintains all the advantages of a TWBX-centric architecture and mitigates most of the difficulties we just discussed.

Tableau Server architecture approaches to adopt

Previously, we considered two approaches to Tableau Server architecture to avoid. Now let's consider two approaches to adopt.

Tableau Server architecture: TDS-centric

Let's take a look at the following diagram, which depicts the TDS-centric architecture:

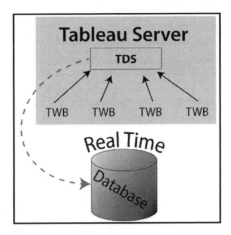

The preceding diagram shows the .twb files that have been published to Tableau Server. The .twb files point to a .tds file as a data source. The .tds file points to the database.

The TDS-centric approach to Tableau Server architecture results in various advantages and at least one disadvantage:

- The following are the TWB-centric advantages:
  - **Small footprint**: Like the TWB-centric approach, the TDS-centric approach has the advantage of a small footprint, which stems from the small size of the .tds and .twb files.
  - **Easy revision history**: These small file sizes result in fewer issues for the revision history.

- **Easy to maintain**: By using .twb files with their corresponding small footprints, maintenance is relatively easy since .twb files can be quickly downloaded, updated, and then re-uploaded. Furthermore, pointing to a .tds file has an additional maintenance advantage. If changes are made to the metadata in the .tds file (for example, a calculated field is updated), those changes will trickle down to every .twb file that points to the .tds file, thus allowing for an update in a single location to impact multiple workbooks. Above we considered a scenario in which a change to a single foreign key broke every workbook in production. By utilizing the TDS-centric approach, updating the metadata in a .tds file to account for the change to the foreign key could instantly fix the problem for every .twb file that points to the .tds file.
  - **Real time**: As with the TWB-centric approach, the TDS-centric approach provides a real-time advantage.
- The following is the TWB-centric disadvantage:
  - **Potentially poor performance**: Lastly, the TDS-centric architecture has a disadvantage: potentially poor performance. This is because a .tds file must point to external data sources which could, in turn, introduce network latency and slow database engines that negatively impact workbook performance.

To sum up, consider adopting the TDS-centric approach, especially when a real-time solution is required. The TDS-centric architecture maintains all the advantages of a TWB-centric architecture while providing easier maintenance.

Tableau Server architecture: TDSX-centric

Let's take a look at the following diagram, which depicts the TDSX-centric architecture:

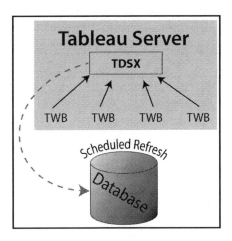

The preceding diagram shows the .twb files that have been published to Tableau Server. The .twb files point to a .tdsx file as a data source. The .tdsx file can be scheduled to refresh regularly so that the data does not become stale.

The TDSX-centric approach to the Tableau Server architecture results in various advantages and at least one disadvantage:

- The following are the TDSX Centric advantages:
  - **Typically quick performance**: The TDSX-centric approach allows for typically quick performance. Since then .twb files point to a .tdsx file that resides on Tableau Server, problems with network latency and slow database servers are circumvented.
  - **Smallish footprint**: By using the .twb files with their corresponding small footprints, maintenance is relatively easy since the .twb files can be quickly downloaded, updated, and then re-uploaded.

- **Easy to maintain**: Furthermore, pointing to a .tdsx file has an additional maintenance advantage. If changes are made to the metadata in the .tdsx file (for example, a calculated field is updated), those changes will trickle down to every .twb file that points to the .tdsx file, thus allowing for an update in a single location to impact multiple workbooks.
  - **Revision-history-friendly**: This is revision history friendly.
- The following is the TDSX-centric disadvantage:
  - **Not real-time**: Not real-time, can be mitigated with frequent updates.

The term smallish footprint has been used in the preceding list since the .tdsx files can become quite large even though the .twb files remain small.

To sum up, in most environments, a TDSX-centric architecture should be the approach you use. Even the one disadvantage, not real-time, can be mitigated with frequent updates. That said, a TDS-centric approach should be used when a real-time solution is required or when accessing a data source engine that outperforms Tableau extracts.

As previously stated, this discussion of Tableau Server architecture is at a high level. Different environments require different approaches. Thus, some combination of these two approaches may often be appropriate. Also, there may be specialty cases that utilize one of the approaches to be avoided. For example, it may be advantageous in some environments to programmatically generate a .twbx file for different end users, thus allowing those end users to download the .twbx files that contain only their data.

Tableau Server revision history

In Tableau 9.3, revision history was introduced for workbooks, including the .twb and .twbx files. In Tableau 10.0, revision history was extended to data sources, including the .tds and .tdsx files. By default, Tableau Server's revision history is set to 25. In other words, the past 25 versions of each workbook and data source are retrievable.

In Tableau Desktop, if you attempt to upload a workbook or data source with the same name as a previously uploaded file, Tableau Desktop will display a warning such as **Data source is already in use. Publishing will overwrite the existing data source**. If you proceed with the upload, revision control will be activated and the previous version of the file will remain accessible as a revision.

To access the revision history for individual workbooks and data sources in Tableau Server, simply select **Content | Data Sources** or **Content | Workbooks**, and click on the dropdown for the desired data source/workbook. In the dropdown, select **Revision History...** to open a dialog box in order to choose which previous version to restore:

The Tableau Server browser interface provides easy access to adjust revision history settings and also to access revisions of individual workbooks and data sources. To adjust revision history settings, simply click on **Settings** and scroll to **Revision History**:

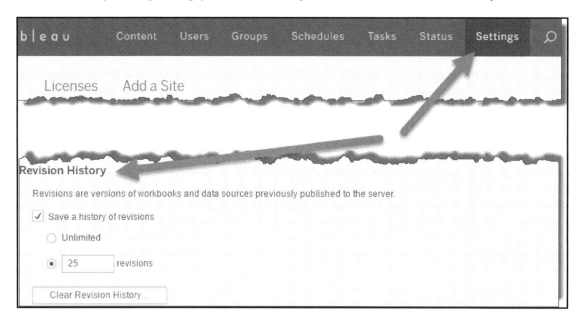

If you'd like to peek beneath the hood of Tableau Server to begin to understand how revision history works, do the following: on a computer with Tableau Server installed, go to the directory for revision history. By default, this is located at
`C:\ProgramData\Tableau\Tableau Server\data\tabsvc\dataengine\revision`.
In the revision directory, there are files with alphanumeric names. Simply rename one of those files with the appropriate extension (for example, `.twbx`) to open the file in Tableau Desktop.

Tableau Server web-authoring environment

Web authoring is a Tableau Server feature introduced in 8.0 that provides an interface for authoring that is similar to Tableau Desktop. Originally, the web-authoring interface was pretty limited, but more features are introduced with each version. Thus, the capability gap between the Tableau Server web-authoring environment and Tableau Desktop have shrunk. In Tableau 10, the web-authoring environment provides robust capabilities for creating and applying table calculations and also provides capabilities for creating dashboards, though the dashboard functionality is still fairly rudimentary.

As of this writing, some features are still missing altogether in the Tableau Server web-authoring environment. For instance, there is no interface for creating parameters or for connecting to data sources that have not already been published to Tableau Server. A fairly detailed comparison of the Tableau Desktop and web-authoring environment capabilities is included later in this chapter.

The question of what one can and cannot do in the Tableau Server web-authoring environment is quite important. After all, why pay for additional copies of Tableau Desktop when the web-authoring environment will suffice? The following exercises provide an opportunity to explore some of the limitations and workarounds of the web-authoring environment.

Basic web-authoring instructions

The following two very brief exercises demonstrate how to access the authoring environment within Tableau Server.

Exercise: editing an existing workbook on Tableau Server

Let's perform the following steps to edit an existing workbook on Tableau Server:

1. Log into an instance of Tableau Server.
2. Open an existing workbook within Tableau Server through **Content** | **Workbooks**.

3. Click on the **Edit** icon:

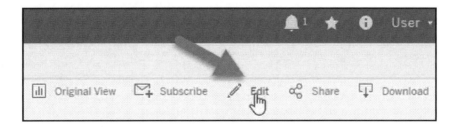

Exercise: creating a new workbook on Tableau Server

Let's perform the following steps to create a new workbook on Tableau Server:

1. Log into an instance of Tableau Server.
2. Navigate to an existing data source via **Content | Data Sources**.
3. Click on the dropdown for the desired data source and choose to create a new workbook:

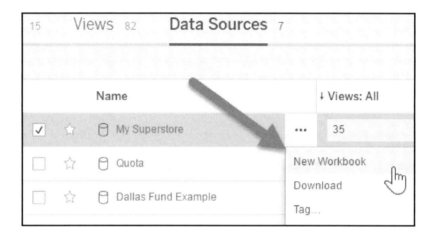

Capabilities and limitations of web-authoring

Although a comparison list is provided below, a good understanding of the capabilities and limitations of the Tableau Server web-authoring environment is most effectively explored by creating worksheets and dashboards in that environment. In that spirit, consider accessing the workbook associated with this chapter and referencing the **Sales & Quota** worksheet in order to build out your own variation in Tableau Server. As you attempt to build the worksheet, you will discover the web-authoring environment's exciting possibilities and sometimes frustrating limitations. Once you complete the build, compare your solution with the one included below. This should help you understand which shortcomings can be overcome and which cannot.

If you do not have access to the Tableau Server web-authoring environment, the following step-by-step instructions and the subsequent commentary should be helpful. Reading through the exercise carefully should help you to understand what can and cannot be accomplished in the web-authoring environment.

Exercise: the Tableau Server web-authoring environment

Let's perform the following steps to understand the Tableau Server web-authoring environment:

1. Access the workbook associated with this chapter and note the **Sales & Quota** worksheet:

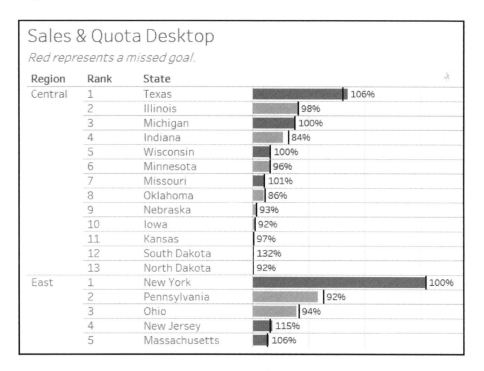

2. In the caption of the worksheet, you will see a dropbox link with the Microsoft Excel spreadsheets for **My Superstore** and **Quota**. Download and then publish both to an instance of Tableau Server. See the *Exercise – publishing a data source to Tableau Server* section for instructions.

3. Log into Tableau Server and create a new workbook based on **My Superstore**. See the *Exercise – creating a new Workbook on Tableau Server* section for instructions.

4. Click on the **Sheet 1** tab and rename the sheet **Sales & Quota**.

5. Add a new data source with the **New Data Source** icon:

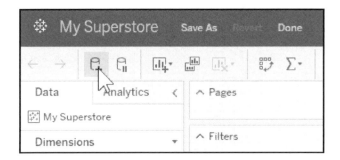

6. In the resulting window, choose the Quota data source.

7. Within the **My Superstore** dataset, create the following calculated fields. Calculated fields can be created in the web-authoring interface by clicking on the dropdown next to the word **Dimensions** in the **Data** pane:

Quota	% Achieved	Quota Met?	Rank
SUM([Quota].[Quota])	STR(ROUND((SUM([Sales]) / [Quota]*100))) + '%'	IF SUM([Sales]) >= [Quota] THEN '✔' ELSE '✘' END	RANK(SUM(Sales))

8. From the **Data** pane, perform the following:
    1. Place **Measure Values** on the **Columns** shelf.
    2. Place **Region** on the **Rows** shelf.
    3. Place **Rank** on the **Detail** shelf.
    4. Click on the dropdown on **Rank** and select **Discrete**.
    5. Move **Rank** from the **Detail** shelf to the **Rows** shelf after **Region**.
    6. Place **State** and **Quota Met** on the **Rows** shelf after **Rank**.
    7. Place **% Achieved** on the **Label** shelf.
    8. Place **Measure Names** as the last dimension on the **Rows** shelf and also on the **Color** shelf.

9. On the **Filters** shelf, click the dropdown associated with **Measure Names** and select **Show Filter**:

10. In the **Measure Names** filter, check only **Quota** and **Sales**.
11. Click on the dropdown for **Rank** on the **Rows** shelf and select **Edit Table Calculation...**.
12. In the resulting dialog box, select **Specific Dimensions** and check only **State**.
13. Click on the **Color** shelf to adjust the colors as desired:

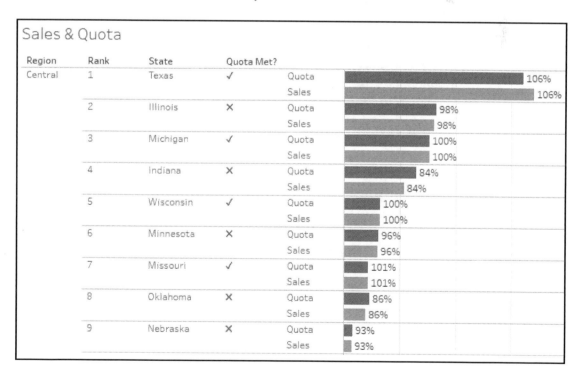

The preceding worksheet looks different from the Tableau Desktop version. Let's consider some of the differences and similarities between the two environments that we discovered as a result of working through the exercise:

- While Tableau Desktop provides connectivity to many data sources, the web-authoring environment only provides access to data sources that have already been published to Tableau Server.
- The web authoring environment provides very limited formatting capabilities.
  - Consider the **% Achieved** calculated field. The String (STR) function was included because the interface does not allow the number format to be changed.
  - Also note that label formatting is limited to show/hide.
- The table-calculation functionality in the web-authoring environment is quite robust.
- Data blending is functional.
- The shortcut for deploying **Measure Names** and **Measure Values** on a view utilizing an axis is not available.
  - To clarify, the Tableau Desktop shortcut is as follows: an author can place a measure on the **Columns** or **Rows** shelf and then place a second measure on the resulting axis in the view to deploy **Measure Names** and **Measure Values** and thus view multiple measures on the same view type.
  - Note that in a new worksheet in the web authoring environment, placing a measure on the **Text** shelf and then double-clicking on a second measure will deploy **Measure Names** and **Measure Values**.
- Building a dual axis chart is not possible.
  - In the Tableau Desktop instance of the **Sales & Quota** worksheet, a dual axis is utilized.
- Reference lines are very limited.
  - Reference lines in Tableau Desktop are very flexible. Reference lines in the web-authoring environment do not allow for the modified bullet chart that was built in the Tableau Desktop worksheet example. Thus, the preceding exercise took a compromise approach.

- The **Color** shelf functionality is different and more limited.
  - As you completed the last step in part II of the exercise, you probably noticed that the **Edit Color** dialog box is different and somewhat more limited than in Tableau Desktop. There is no functionality for choosing specific colors for each dimension member, adding borders and halos, or defining individual RGB colors:

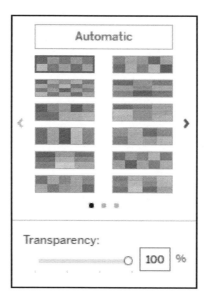

- Titles and captions can be hidden or displayed but not edited.
  - In Tableau Desktop, the title has been edited to display Red represents a missed goal. Also the caption displays a dropbox link. This is not possible in the web-authoring environment.

Comparing Tableau Desktop and web-authoring

Sometimes it's unclear which individuals in an organization require a Tableau Desktop license and which only need a Tableau Server user license. For example, a technologically-oriented executive with limited time to learn new software could go either way. On the one hand, they may want to delve into the details of the data, but on the other, they may not be able to invest the time necessary to learn enough about Tableau Desktop to warrant the price of an additional license. When the web-authoring environment was released in Tableau Server 8.0, the features were fairly rudimentary. The busy executive may have been best served with a Tableau Desktop license. Since that time, more and more capabilities have been introduced. Today, that same executive may be reasonably content with using the web-authoring environment.

The following compare-and-contrast list should provide a quick way to decide who should receive which license type. Note that the list is primarily intended to communicate the major capabilities and limitations of Tableau Server's web-authoring environment when compared to Tableau Desktop. Basic functionality capabilities, such as the ability to place a field on a shelf, are assumed and thus are not included:

Tableau Desktop feature	Available in Tableau Server web authoring environment?
The **Analytics** pane • Constant Line • Average Line • Median with Quartiles • Box Plot • Totals • Average/Median with 95% CL • Trend Line • Custom Reference Line, Reference Band, Distribution Band, Box Plot	✓
• Forecast • Cluster	✗
The **Data** pane	

• Duplicate, Show/Hide, Rename Fields • Replace Data Source • Connect/configure data sources outside of Tableau Server • Convert to Measure/Dimension • Convert to Continuous/Discrete • Change Data Type • Change Geographic Role • Edit Aliases • Create Group • Create Set • Create Bin • Create calculated fields including table calculations and LOD calculations • Group by Folder/Data Source Table • Create Hierarchy	✔
• Create Extract • Create Folders • Find a Field • Create Parameter	✘
The **View** • Adjust Measure Aggregation • Create Basic Visualization Types such as Bar, Line, Area, Crosstab, Map, Treemap, Pie • Create New Worksheet • Enable/Disable Sheet and Dashboard Highlighting • Fit Options (Standard, Fit Width, Fit Height, Entire View) • Show Mark Labels • Show/Hide Caption/Title • Utilize Measure Names/Measure Values • Create Intermediate to Advanced Chart Types, such as Dual Axis, Bullet, Bar-In-Bar • Edit Axis • Map Options • Turn on/off Stack Marks	✔
• Adjust Color, Shape, and Size via Marks View Card • Sorting	✔ with limited functionality.
• Formatting	✔ with very limited functionality.
• Hide Legends • Map Layers and Format Windows	✘

The **Filters** • Deploy Measure and Dimension Filters • Range – At least and At most • Only Relevant Values • All Values in Database • Display/Hide Filter • Include/Exclude • Choose filter type (Single Value, Multiple Values, List, Dropdown, Slider, and so on) • Search a filter for specific values • Apply to All Using Related Data Sources • Apply to All Using This Data Source • Apply to Only This Worksheet • Customize (Show All Value, Show Search Button, Show Apply Button)	✓
• Extract filter • Context filter • Special (Null, non-null values) • Row level filter • Data source filter • Wildcard filter • Conditional filter • Top/Bottom filter	✗
The **Dashboard** • Create New Dashboard • Add Horizontal, Vertical and Blank Objects • Add Objects as Tiled or Floating • Adjust Position of Floating Objects • Adjust Dashboard Size • Use a Worksheet as a Filter • Deploy Highlighters • Hide/Show Legend • Hide/Show Filter • Download crosstab, data, image, pdf, workbook • Save/Save As... • Fit Options (Standard, Fit Width, Fit Height, Entire View) • Add Web Page and Text Objects • Adjust Size of Floating Objects	✓
• Add Image • Create Custom Actions • Device Preview	✗
Story	✓

The rights regarding if you are allowed to use web authoring and to which extend are often related to your licensing model. For more information please read the following Tableau help article: https://onlinehelp.tableau.com/current/pro/desktop/en-us/server_desktop_web_edit_differences.htm.

User filters

Students often ask me the following question, I have sales managers over various territories. It's important that the sales managers see only their metrics; that is, not the metrics of the other sales managers. In order to accomplish this, do I have to create separate workbooks for each sales manager?

Fortunately, the answer is no. Tableau provides user filters that allow the Tableau author to make sure that each of those sales managers sees only the information for which they have clearance.

Exercise: deploying a view-level user filter

This exercise assumes the reader has a new, default install of Tableau Server. By default, Tableau installs with a JaneDoe and a JohnSmith user. Both are used in this exercise:

1. Access the workbook associated with this chapter and navigate to the **View Level User Filter** worksheet.
2. Note that the view is a field map of the USA with State on the **Detail** shelf, **Region** on the **Color** shelf, and **Sales** on the **Label** shelf.
3. Log into an instance of Tableau Server via **Server | Sign In**.
4. Select **Server | Create User Filter | Region**.
5. In the resulting **User Filter** dialog box, select **JaneDoe** and check the **Central** region. Also select **JohnSmith** and check the **East** region.
6. Name the user filter **Sales Manager** and click on **OK**.

 Note that **Sales Manager** is actually added to the **Sets** portion of the **Data** pane.

7. Click on the **Data Source** tab to access the **Data Source** page:

8. In the upper-right corner of the **Data Source** page, click on **Add** to add a data source filter:

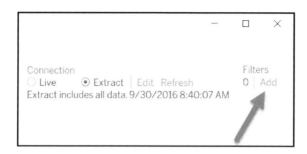

9. In the resulting dialog box, click the **Add** button to add a filter on **Sales Manager**.

10. Return to the worksheet. In the right portion of the status bar, click on the dropdown to access **Filter as User**:

11. Choose **JohnSmith** and note that the results display only the **East** region:

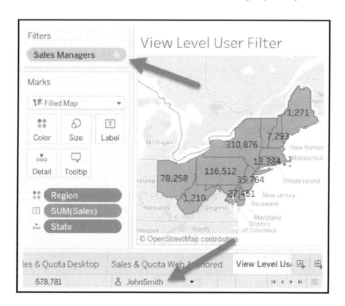

Once the workbook is published to Tableau Server, users who access the workbook will only see the information the filter allows.

You may have noticed that a data source filter was added, as opposed to simply adding a dimension filter to the **Filters** shelf. This is important because any user with web-authoring permission can simply remove a filter from the **Filters** shelf. In the case of this exercise, the user would then be able to see metrics for every region. Data source filters, however, cannot be removed via the web-authoring environment and are thus more secure. Furthermore, a data source filter is workbook-wide, which further secures the data.

Also note that user and group filters can be published as part of the data source. In other words, the .tdsx and .tds files discussed here can include data source filters based on users and groups. This allows for centrally-maintained security that is transparent even to those users with editing privileges.

Performance-recording dashboard

In Chapter 13, *Improving Performance*, we explored the Performance Recording dashboard. Sometimes a workbook may perform satisfactorily on Tableau Desktop but, mysteriously, may perform poorly when published to Tableau Server. In such cases, accessing the Performance Recording dashboard on Tableau Server can be very helpful.

Exercise: exploring Performance Recording on Tableau Server

The following exercise provides step-by-step instructions for doing so:

1. Navigate to an instance of Tableau Server.
2. On the toolbar, click on **Settings**:

3. In the resulting page, locate the **Workbook Performance Metrics** section and select **Record workbook performance metrics**.
4. Click on **Save**.

5. Navigate to a workbook of your choosing and open a view. Note that the ending portion of the URL is :iid=<n>.

6. Type :record_performance=yes& immediately before :iid=<n>. For example,
   http://localhost:8000/#/views/Finance/Taleof100Start-ups?:recor d_performance=yes&:iid=5. Note that the toolbar now includes a **Performance** link:

7. Click the **Refresh** icon on the toolbar. It is located to the left of **Pause**. Click on the **Performance** link and observe the resulting performance-recording dashboard that displays.

More Tableau Server settings

Once a dashboard has been published, users can use set alerts, certified datasources, subscribe, add comments to a dashboard, and more, depending on their permission.

Alerting

As of this writing, an alert can be set on a continuous numerical axis only. However, there are ideas in the Tableau forum that will increase the flexibility on setting alerts.

 In the Tableau ideas forum, users can write down what ideas they have for future releases and the community can vote for them. Ideas with high votes are likely to be picked up soon. You can find the forum here: https://community.tableau.com/community/ideas.

On Tableau Server, in the upper-right corner, you will find the Alert button. Click on it and another window will pop up:

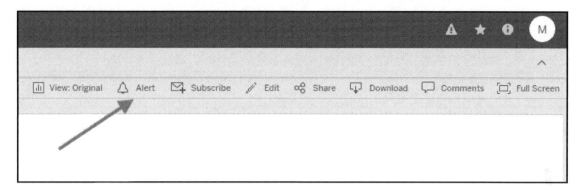

In the new popup, a condition and a threshold can be entered. Also, the frequency of dashboard refresh and thus the check if the threshold has been breached or not, can be specified too:

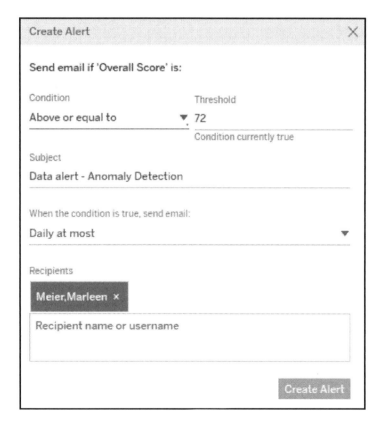

If an alert is set, all people or groups specified in that alert will receive an email once the threshold has been breached. The email will contain a static image and a link to the interactive version on the Server.

Subscribing

Subscriptions can be found on Tableau server in the upper-right corner:

They work in a similar way to alerts: people or groups can be subscribed and will receive an email with an overview of the regarding dashboard at a set time. The scheduling can be predefined by the administrator, for example, every morning at 7:

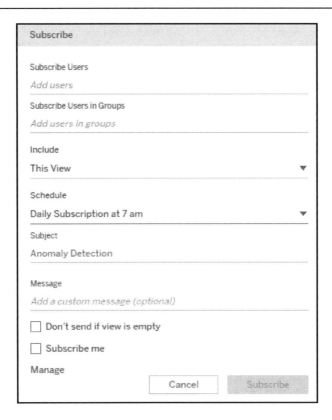

Creating custom views

It might happen that users filter a dashboard thats been uploaded to Tableau Server or click on some values that will lead to a change of the view. The user can save those views by clicking on the **View** button (again in the upper-right corner of Tableau Server):

The following window will open up; name the view and save it! You can easily go back to the original view by clicking on the **View** button:

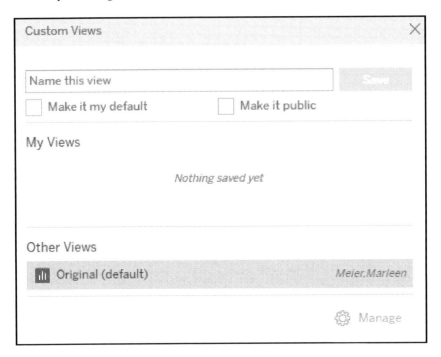

Commenting

Last but not least, you can comment on views – original or edited, both are possible. To do so, click on the **Comments** button in the upper-right corner:

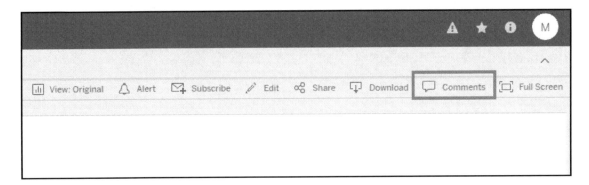

You can mention a colleague in the comment with **@colleaguesname**, and they will receive an email with your comment in it. It is also possible to add screenshots to your comment.

For more details on commenting, check out `https://onlinehelp.tableau.com/current/pro/desktop/en-us/comment.htm`.

Certified Data Source

When a company starts to work with Tableau and Tableau Server, there will be a point where questions about governance, best practices, and data quality will be raised. One built-in feature of Tableau Server is especially helpful regarding data quality: the certified data source badge. This badge can be given to a published data source by administrators or project leaders. Obviously, this badge can be defined in multiple ways, but let's assume that it verifies the data's correctness, completeness, timeliness, and so on. Employees can trust this data and don't have to worry about quality checks when analyzing.

Other options are recommended data sources and recommended data tables.

To read more about this topic, check out the following blog from Tableau Online Help: `https://onlinehelp.tableau.com/current/pro/desktop/en-us/datasource_recommended.htm`.

Tableau Service Manager

As mentioned before, this chapter was not supposed to go into the detail with command-line utilities, however I want to take the chance and mention that with the Tableau 2018.2 release tabadmin is gone, and a new command-line interface has been introduced: Tableau Services Manager, or tsm. If you want to learn more about this Administrators' favorite, check out this blog post from The Information Lab: `https://www.theinformationlab.co.uk/2018/07/31/3-reasons-tableau-services-manager-tsm-is-exciting/`.

Summary

We began this chapter by considering the various Tableau file types – in particular, the `.tds`, `.tdsx`, `.twb`, and `.twbx` file types. This provided us with a foundation to understand different ways to architect a Tableau Server deployment. We considered four basic architecture scenarios and the advantages and disadvantages of each.

Next, we looked at Tableau Server Revision History, where we learned that version-control features beginning in Tableau 9.3 can provide a safety-net against inadvertently overwriting files. This was followed by a section on the Tableau Server web-authoring environment, which compared and contrasted that environment with Tableau Desktop. The primary purpose of this section was to establish a knowledge base for determining which personnel should have Tableau Desktop licenses and for whom the web-authoring capabilities of Tableau Server should suffice.

Then we discussed user filters and the Performance Recording dashboard. User filters enable Tableau author to ensure that users are only able to access data for which they have clearance. Although the Performance Recording dashboard was covered in `Chapter 13`, *Improving Performance*, in this chapter we learned how to access it with Tableau Server. And finally, we looked at some handy features, such as alerts, subscriptions, commenting, and certified data sources.

In the next and final chapter, we will branch out from the Tableau world, and will consider how to integrate with R, Python, and MATLAB. Knowledge of the programming integration will help the Tableau author accomplish analytics tasks that are beyond the capabilities of Tableau, while still using Tableau to visualize the results.

15
Programming Tool Integration

For the seventh year in a row, Tableau has been identified as a leader in Gartners Magic Quadrant for Analytics and Business Intelligence. The latest Quadrant from 2019 can be seen in the following screenshot:

Based on the Gartner press release in February 2018, Tableau is said to score highly, due to its consistent and spontaneous approach. It allows people from various fields to prepare, evaluate, and perform data without technical skills. However, for those who want to go beyond Tableau's built-in functionality, one can make use of the R (release 8.1), Python (release 10.1), or MATLAB (release 10.4) integration. How does the integration empower Tableau? It happens through calculated fields. Tableau dynamically interfaces with Rserve, TabPy, or MATLAB to pass values and receive results. And, as announced at Tableau Conference 2018, Tableau Prep also has the R and Python Integration on the radar!

In this chapter, we will cover the following topics:

- The architecture
- R installation and integration
- Installation
- Using R functions
- Introduction to correlations
- Introduction to regression analysis
- Introduction to clustering
- Introduction to quantiles
- Troubleshooting in Tableau and R
- Examples of troubleshooting in Tableau and R
- R scripts and Tableau table calculations
- Python installation and integration
- Using Python functions
- Introduction to sentiment analysis
- MATLAB installation and integration

The architecture

The basic Tableau-to-R, -Python, and -MATLAB architecture is quite simple: Tableau pushes data to RServe, TabPy, or MATLAB, respectively, and then retrieves the results. Naturally, whether you are viewing a workbook on Tableau Desktop or via Tableau Server, if you wish to run R, Python, and MATLAB calculations, then Rserve, TabPy, or MATLAB, must be accessible.

See details in the following screenshot:

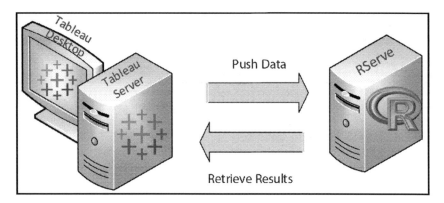

For a proper understanding of the architecture, let's also look at the Tableau/R workflow. Terms used in the following screenshot, which you may be unfamiliar with, will be discussed in this chapter:

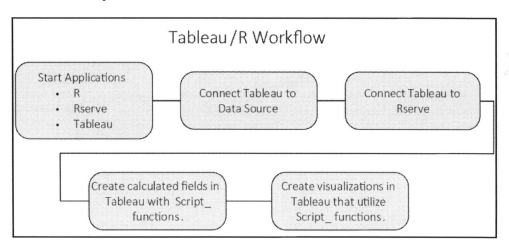

This preceding screenshot can be used in the same way for Python and MATLAB.

R installation and integration

In order to adequately understand how Tableau and R work together, it's important to grasp the big picture. To facilitate that understanding, we'll cover high-level concepts and information in this section before delving into calculated fields and R scripting details.

Installation

Installing R is typically not difficult, but it does involve more than simply double-clicking on an executable. In order to successfully connect Tableau with R, you will need to make sure that permissions are correctly set and that various components – some required and some just nice to have – are correctly implemented. We will cover the basics, review a couple of the typical challenges faced during installation, and provide troubleshooting guidance.

Installing R

Perform the following steps to install R:

1. Download R by visiting `http://www.r-project.org/` and choosing a CRAN mirror. Note that R works best in a Linux or UNIX environment; however, in order to learn R and to begin working with Tableau/R functionality to complete the exercises in this chapter, installing the Windows version is adequate.
2. Install R by double-clicking on the download executable.
3. Open R.

Various issues may arise when installing R. For example, you may experience problems due to insufficient permissions for the R working directory. This issue may first become evident when attempting to install R packages. To rectify the problem, determine the working directory in R with the `getwd()` function. Next, either change the working directory via `setwd()` or, at the operating-system level, set the appropriate read and execute permissions for the working directory.

Issues can also arise due to firewall and port-configuration problems. By default, Tableau will connect to Rserve via port 6311 so make sure that port is open and available. Alternatively, within Tableau you can specify a different port when connecting to R.

 The documentation at `http://www.r-project.org/` provides detailed information regarding overcoming a variety of installation challenges.

Integration: starting Rserve, connecting to Tableau, and installing RStudio

To start R within a Windows environment, navigate to **Start** > **Programs** > **R x64 3.2.0**. (Of course, your version of R may differ from mine.)

This will open the RGui, which can be seen in the following screenshot:

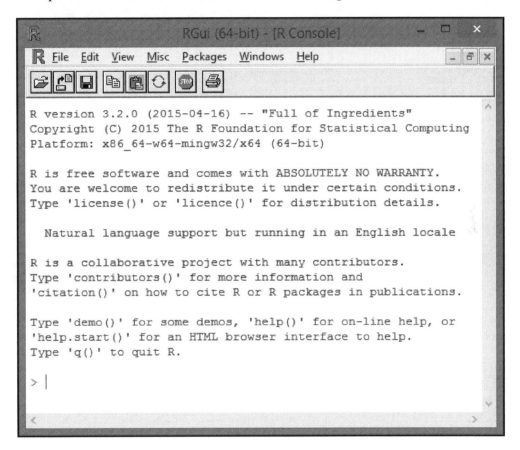

In order to establish a connection with Tableau, you will need to start Rserve. Technically, Rserve is a separate package; however, by default, it is installed with R:

- In order to make sure that the Rserve package is installed, within R enter `rownames(installed.packages())`.
- Several packages should be listed including RServe.

- If for some reason the `Rserve` package did not install with your instance of R, you can do so via `install.packages("Rserve")`.
- To start Rserve, enter `library(Rserve); Rserve()`.

 The semicolon (;) represents a new line of code in R.

Now that you have successfully installed R and started Rserve, you are ready to connect Tableau to R. Within Tableau, select **Help** > **Settings and Performance** > **Manage External Service Connection**.

The default settings in the following screenshot will work for most local installations:

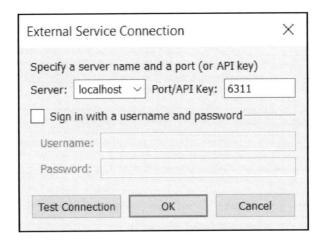

Although not required, RStudio Desktop provides a better user interface than the default RGui that installs with R. RStudio includes a console that features Intelligent Code Completion (that is, IntelliSense), a workspace browser that provides easy access to files, packages and help, a data viewer, and much more all within a single, unified environment. The Open Source Edition of RStudio is sufficient for many uses. You can download the application via `www.rstudio.com`.

After you have done so, see here an example of an RStudio screen:

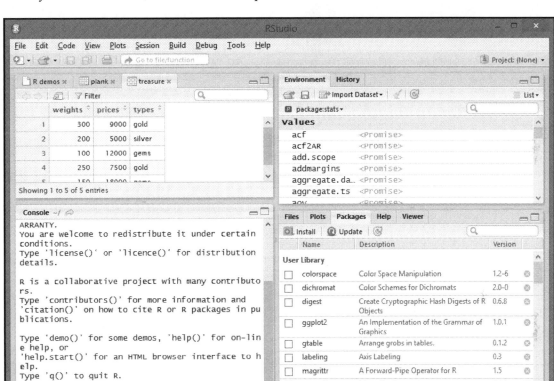

While integrating Tableau with R doesn't require any interaction with an R interface, you will probably want to try out your R code in a GUI, such as RGui or RStudio, before embedding the code in Tableau. This will allow you to take advantage of useful accompanying features relevant to the R language, such as help, examples, and sample datasets tailored to R. Note that the Calculated Field Editor in Tableau simply acts as a pass-through for R code and does not provide any support.

Using R functions

Now that we have successfully connected Tableau with R, let's write some code in Tableau to invoke R. Within Tableau, open the Calculated Field Editor.

Notice within the Functions panel those entries beginning with SCRIPT_ ,as shown in the following screenshot:

The SCRIPT functions are used by Tableau to invoke R. The function names communicate the data type of the returned results; SCRIPT_REAL returns float values, SCRIPT_BOOL returns T|F values, and so forth.

The syntax of a SCRIPT function is represented in the following diagram:

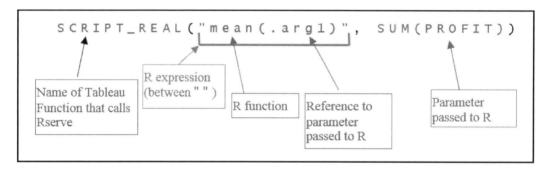

Exercise: reproducing native Tableau functionality in R

For our first exercise, we will use the AVG, MEDIAN, and STDEV functions in Tableau and compare the results with the mean, median, and sd R functions. This will allow you to practice the SCRIPT functions, begin to understand R syntax, and compare results generated by Tableau with those generated by R.

Perform the following steps:

1. Navigate to `https://public.tableau.com/profile/marleen.meier#!/` to locate and download the workbook associated with this chapter.

2. Navigate to the **median | mean | sd** worksheet.

3. Select the **Superstore** data source.

4. Create the following Tableau-centric calculations:
   - **Tab Avg**: `WINDOW_AVG(SUM(Sales))`
   - **Tab Median**: `WINDOW_MEDIAN(SUM(Sales))`
   - **Tab Stdev**: `WINDOW_STDEV(SUM(Sales))`

5. Place the **Region** dimension on the **Rows** shelf and the **Sales** measure on the **Text** shelf.

6. Place each resulting calculated field onto the view. Be sure that **Compute Using** is set to **Table (down)**:

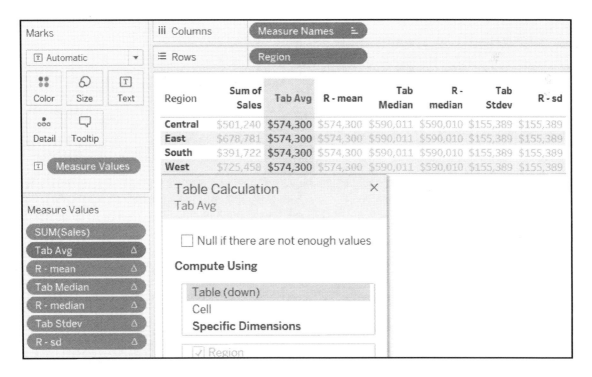

7. Create the following R-centric calculations. Note that R functions (such as `"mean"`) are case-sensitive.
   - **R - mean**: `SCRIPT_INT("mean(.arg1)", SUM(Sales))`
   - **R - median**: `SCRIPT_INT("median(.arg1)", SUM(Sales))`
   - **R - sd**: `SCRIPT_INT("sd(.arg1)", SUM(Sales))`

8. Place each of the R calculated fields onto the view. Since `SCRIPT` functions are categorized as table calculations (more on that later), be sure that each instance of the R calculated fields has **Compute Using** set to **Table (down)**.

9. Observe that, other than a slight rounding difference between **Tab Median** and **R - median**, the results of the Tableau and R functions are identical.

10. To address the rounding difference adjust the code for **R - Median** as follows:

```
SCRIPT_REAL("median(.arg1)", SUM( [Sales] ))
```

Note that `INT` has now been replaced with `REAL`, demonstrating that, as the names suggest, `SCRIPT_REAL` works with float values and `SCRIPT_INT` works with integers.

Introduction to correlations

The preceding exercise, *Reproducing native Tableau functionality in R*, was designed to get you started using R in Tableau. But of course there's no reason in a real-world scenario to access the R engine to reproduce functionality that is native to Tableau. As shown in the architecture screenshot represented in the *The Architecture* section, calling the R engine adds an extra process which could potentially slow performance.

The next exercise demonstrates a correlation functionality that is not natively available in Tableau. As of this writing, correlation is currently available in the 10.1 beta but this does not necessarily mean that the official 10.1 release will include such functionality.

A correlation is a number that represents the degree of relationship between two variables. There are many approaches used to determine the degree of correlation, but the most common is the **Pearson correlation coefficient** (**PCC**), which considers only the linear relationship between two variables. PCC is measured from -1 to +1 where -1 is complete negative correlation, 0 is no correlation, and 1 is complete positive correlation. In R, the `cor` function defaults to PCC and is what we will use.

Exercise: correlations

Our goal in this exercise is to determine the correlation between **SUM(Profit)** and **SUM(Sales)**:

1. Navigate to the **Correlation** worksheet.
2. Select the **Superstore** data source.
3. Build the initial view by placing the **Category** and **Sales** fields on the **Columns** shelf, **State** and **Profit** on the **Rows** shelf, and filtering to **Top 5** by **Sum of Sales** on **State**.
4. Drag **Customer Name** to the **Detail** shelf:

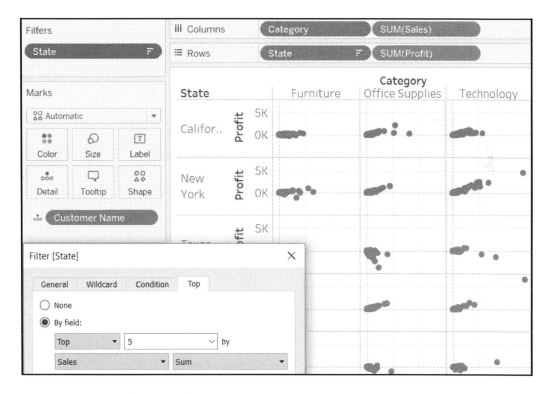

5. Create a calculated field named `P_S_Correlation` with the following code:

```
SCRIPT_REAL("cor(.arg1, .arg2)", SUM(Sales), SUM(Profit))
```

6. Create a calculated field named `Negative P_S_Correlation` with the following code.

```
WINDOW_MAX( [P_S_Correlation] ) < 0
```

7. Place `P_S_Correlation` on the **Label** shelf.

8. Place **Negative P_S_Correlation** on the **Shape** shelf.

9. After adjusting the worksheet for visual appeal, your results should look similar to the following screenshot. The takeaway, as a fictional **Superstore** business analyst, is that you've identified that by customer, some departments in some states actually have a negative ratio of **Sales** to **Profit**. In other words, the more a customer buys, the lower the profit.

You should see the following plots now:

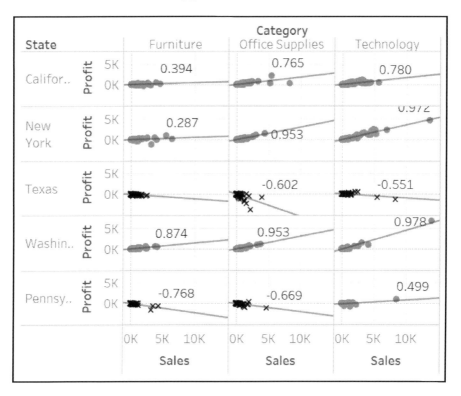

Introduction to regression analysis

Succinctly stated, regression analysis is a technique for estimating variable relationships. There are various types of regression analyses, the most popular of which is linear regression. As demonstrated in the following screenshot, linear regression estimates a line that best fits the data:

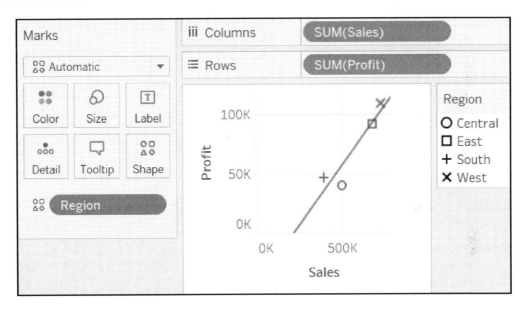

Notice that this screenshot is from Tableau. It's a simple scatter plot with trend lines turned on. Trend lines, in Tableau, default to linear but also include logarithmic, exponential, and polynomial, which are all examples of regression analysis. By accessing **Worksheet** > **Export** > **Data** on a visualization utilizing a trend line, you can generate an Access database with predictions and residuals for marks on the view. But this is a tedious process and does not give a robust, dynamic solution for implementing more vigorous uses of linear regression. Using R provides much more flexibility.

Linear regression may use single or multiple variables. Single-variable equations are great for learning, but multiple-variable equations are typically necessary for real-world application. The following exercise includes multiple-variable equations.

Exercise: regression analysis

Our goal for this exercise is to determine how closely a linear regression model of Profit fits `COUNT(Quantity)`, `SUM(Sales)`, and `AVG(Discount)`:

1. Navigate to the **Regression** worksheet.
2. Select the **Superstore** data source.
3. Build the basic layout by placing **Profit** on the **Columns** shelf, **State** on the **Rows** shelf, and filtering to **Top 10** by **Sum of Profit** on State.
4. Create a calculated field entitled `Profit_Expected` utilizing the following code:

   ```
   SCRIPT_REAL("
   x <- lm(.arg1 ~ .arg2 + .arg3 + .arg4)
   x$fitted",
   SUM(Profit), COUNT(Quantity), SUM(Sales) , AVG(Discount)
   )
   ```

5. Create a calculated field entitled **% Diff** that calculates the percent difference between `Sum(Profit)` and `Profit_Expected`:

   ```
   SUM(Profit)/Profit_Expected - 1
   ```

6. Create a calculated field entitled `Profit_Expected (residuals)` to return the difference between `Sum(Profit)` and `Profit_Expected` in terms of dollars:

```
SCRIPT_REAL(" x <- lm(.arg1 ~ .arg2 + .arg3 + .arg4) x$residuals",
SUM(Profit),COUNT(Quantity), SUM(Sales), AVG(Discount))
```

7. Place `Profit_Expected` on the **Profit** axis.
8. Move the instance of **Measure Names** from the **Rows** shelf and place it on the **Color** shelf. Also, take an instance of **Measure Names** from the **Data** pane and place it on the **Size** shelf.
9. From the menu, select **Analysis > Stack Marks > Off.**
10. Drag the calculated fields **% Diff** and **Profit_Expected** to the **Label** shelf:

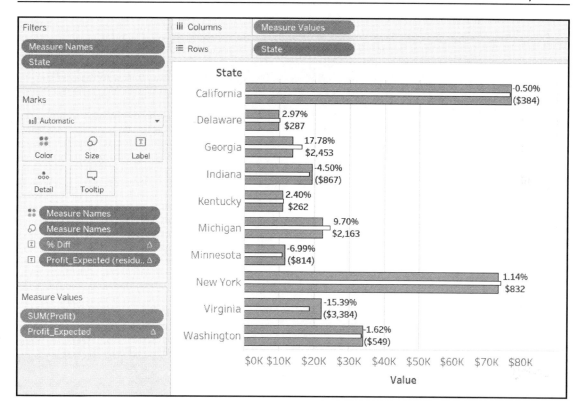

Now that we've completed the exercise, let's take a moment to consider the code.

We'll focus on the code in *step 3* since that will provide the necessary insight to understand the code represented in the other steps:

`SCRIPT_REAL`	This Tableau function calls the R engine and returns a float value.
`"x <- lm(.arg1 ~ .arg2 + .arg3 + .arg4);x$residuals"`	This is the R expression that houses a variable, a function, and an argument, and then returns predicted values.
`x <-`	This is the variable to be populated by the subsequent R function.

`lm`
`(.arg1 ~ .arg2 + .arg3 +`
`.arg4)`
	This R function is used to fit linear models. It can be used to return regression based on variables provided by the argument.
	The information within the parentheses is referred to as an argument and is used to fit the model. Specifically, the response is to the left of the tilde (~), and the model is to the right. Thus, this is a multi-variable linear regression where `.arg1 = SUM(Profit)`, `.arg2 = COUNT(Quantity)`, `.arg3 = SUM(Sales)`, and `.arg4 = AVG(Discount)`. In English, the argument could be read as `SUM(Profit)` is modeled as the combined terms of `COUNT(Quantity)`, `SUM(Sales)`, and `AVG(Discount)`.

`x$fitted`	The `lm` function returns many values as part of its model object, including coefficients, residuals, rank, and fitted values. `x$fitted` is referencing the fitted values generated as a result of passing data to the model.

`", SUM(Profit),`
`COUNT(Quantity),`
`SUM(Sales) ,`
`AVG(Discount))`
	These are the parameters used to populate the `.arg#` variables.
	Note that the double-quote (") designates the end of the code passed to R, and the comma (,) designates the second half of the Tableau function, that is, the expression.

Introduction to clustering

Clustering is used to select smaller subsets of data with members sharing similar characteristics from a larger dataset. As an example, consider a marketing scenario. You have a large customer base to which you plan to send advertising material; however, cost prohibits you from sending material to every customer. Performing clustering on the dataset will return groupings of customers with similar characteristics. You can then survey the results and choose a target group.

Major methods for clustering include hierarchical and K-means. Hierarchical clustering is more thorough and thus more time-consuming. It generates a series of models that range from *1*, which includes all data points, to *n*, where each data point is an individual model. K-means clustering is a quicker method in which the user or another function defines the number of clusters. For example, a user may choose to create four clusters from a dataset of a thousand members.

Clustering capabilities were included with Tableau 10. According to Bora Beran, the Tableau development team had a few non-negotiable goals for a clustering implementation in Tableau: solid methodology, repeatable results, quick processing time, and ease of use. By utilizing the Howard-Harris Method and the Calinski-Harabasz Index within a K-means framework, the team succeeded on all accounts. Be sure to check out Bora Beran's blog (`https://boraberan.wordpress.com/2016/07/19/understanding-clustering-in-tableau-10/`) to learn the details.

There are numerous ways the Tableau development team could have approached clustering. R, for instance, provides many different clustering packages that use different approaches. A Tableau author may have good reason to choose one of these different approaches. For example, clustering results are always identical when using the native Tableau clustering capabilities. But they do not have to be. By using R for clustering, the underlying data and the view may remain unchanged, yet clustering could differ with each refresh. This could be advantageous to you, looking for edge cases where marks may switch between clusters. The following example explores such a case.

Exercise: clustering

Our goal in this exercise is to create four clusters out of the countries of the world based on birth rate and infant mortality rate:

1. Navigate to the **Cluster** worksheet.
2. Select the **World Indicators** data source.
3. Build the initial view by placing **Infant Mortality Rate** on the **Columns** shelf, **Birth Rate** on the **Rows** shelf, and **Country** on the **Details** shelf.
4. Right-click on each axis and select **Logarithmic** and deselect **Include Zero**. This will spread the data points more uniformly and will help make the visualization more aesthetically pleasing and easier to read.

5. Note the null indicator in the lower-right corner of the view:

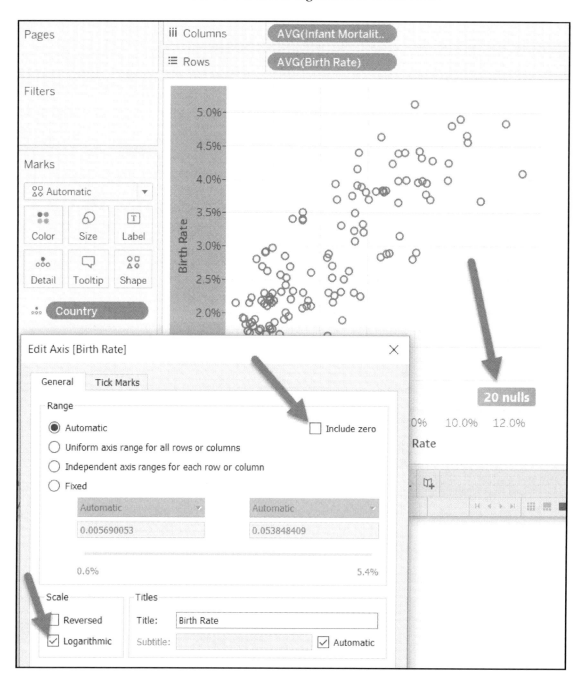

6. Create a calculated field named `cluster` with the following code:

```
SCRIPT_INT("
m <- cbind(.arg1, .arg2);
kmeans(m,4,nstart=5)$cluster",
AVG( [Life Expectancy Female] ), AVG([Life Expectancy Male]))
```

7. Drag the `cluster` calculated field you just created to the **Shape** and **Color** shelves. Note that the Rserve engine throws an error. This is because nulls exist in the underlying data set. For example, the data does not include an **Infant Mortality Rate** for **Puerto Rico**.

 If nulls exist in the dataset, Tableau displays a warning in the lower-right corner of the view. R, however, throws an error.

8. To rectify the error, drag instances of both the **Infant Mortality Rate** and the **Birth Rate** fields onto the **Filters** shelf. Within the **Filter** dialog box, select **Special > Non-null Values**.

9. Note that R still throws an error.

10. The error states **...cannot take a sample larger than the population....** R is expecting to cluster all countries but the **Cluster** calculated field is set to **Compute Using > Table (across)**.

11. Set **Cluster** to **Compute Using > Country**.

12. The resulting view should look similar to the following screenshot:

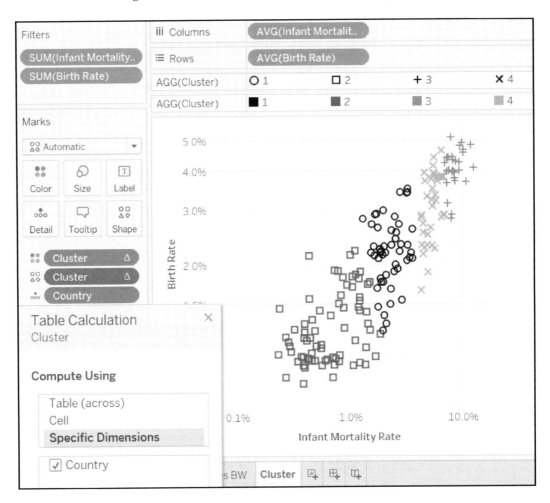

13. Press *F5* and observe that the clustering changes with each refresh.

Now that we've completed the exercise, let's take a moment to consider the code we saw:

`SCRIPT_REAL`	This Tableau functions calls the R engine and returns a float value.
`"m <- cbind(.arg1, .arg2);` `kmeans(m,4,nstart=1)$cluster"`	This is the R expression that houses a variable, a function, and an argument, and then returns clusters.
`m <-`	This is the variable to be populated by the subsequent R function.
`cbind`	This R function combines the following `.arg#` variables into columns.
`(.arg1, .arg2)`	The variables within the parentheses are referred to as an argument. Each variable contains vector information. Specifically, `.arg1 = AVG( [Infant Mortality Rate] )` and `.arg2 = AVG([Birth Rate])`.
`kmeans(m,4,nstart=1)$cluster"`	`kmeans` declares the method of clustering. `m` contains the vector created by the `cbind` argument. The `4` integer declares the number of clusters. `nstart` declares the number of random sets.
`", AVG( [Infant Mortality Rate] ),` `AVG([Birth Rate]))`	These are the parameters used to populate the `.arg#` variables. Note that the double-quote (`"`) designates the end of the code passed to R. and the comma (`,`) designates the second half of the Tableau function, that is, the expression.

Introduction to quantiles

Quantiles are often considered to be synonymous with quartiles. They are not. Quantiles are the sets that make up an evenly-divided population of values. A quartile is a type of quantile—as is a quintile, a tercile, a decile, and so forth.

To understand how quantiles evenly divide a population of values, consider the following example from Tableau:

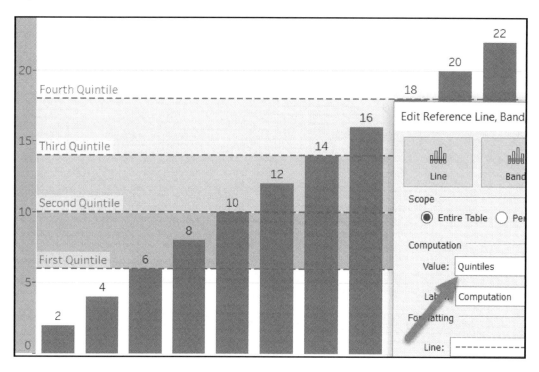

In the preceding example, our data points are 2 - 22 by even numbers. Quantiles are set to **Quintiles**. The **Fourth Quintile** is calculated thus: *22 * (4/5) = 17.6*. The closest value in the population when rounding up is 18. Therefore, 18 is set as the rank that accounts for approximately four-fifths of the values of the total sorted population.

As evidenced in the preceding screenshot, Tableau allows you to view quantiles via right-clicking on an axis and choosing **Add Reference Line** > **Distribution** > **Computation** > **Quantiles**. The functionality of quantiles thus accessed, however, is quite limited. Primarily this is because reference lines do not generate measures that can be placed on shelves. This limits visualization options. Generating quantiles via R greatly expands those options.

Our goal for this exercise is to create *n* quantiles through R in order to view customer distribution by sales. We will further expand the exercise by creating parameters that restrict the number of members in the total dataset to a given percentile range. Finally, we will fine-tune the visualization by adding jittering.

Exercise: quantiles

Let's have a look at the following steps:

1. Navigate to the **Quantiles** worksheet.
2. Select the **Superstore** data source.
3. Change the view type to **Shape** on the **Marks** view card.
4. Drag **Sales** to the **Rows** shelf, **Customer ID** to **Details** shelf, and copies of **Region** to the **Color** shelf and the **Shape** shelf:

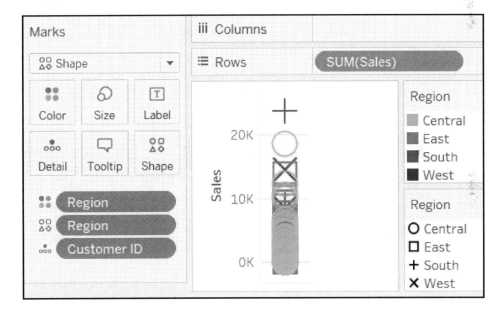

5. Create and display a parameter entitled **Number of Quantiles** with the following settings:
   - **Data Type**: Integer
   - **Allowable Values**: All

6. Create a calculated field entitled **Quantiles** with the following code:

```
SCRIPT_REAL("
x <- .arg1;
y <- .arg2[1];
m <- c(1:y)/y;
n <- length(x);
z <- c(1:n); for (i in c(1:n)) z[i] <- 0;
for (j in c(1:y)) for (i in c(1:n)) z[i] <- if (x[i] <=
quantile(x,m)[j] && z[i] == 0 ) j else z[i];
z;"
, SUM(Sales), [Number of Quantiles])
```

7. Right-click on the newly-created calculated field **Quantiles** and select **Convert to Discrete**.

8. Create and display two parameters, Select `Percentile Bottom Range` and Select `Percentile Top Range`. Use the following settings:
    - **Data Type**: Float
    - **Allowable Value**: Range
    - **Minimum**: .01
    - **Maximum**: 1
    - **Step size**: 0.01

9. Create a calculated field entitled Percentile with the following code:

```
RANK_PERCENTILE(SUM([Sales])) < [Select Percentile Top Range]
AND
RANK_PERCENTILE(SUM([Sales])) < [Select Percentile Bottom Range]
```

10. Drag **Quantiles** to the **Columns** shelf and set **Compute Using** to **Customer ID**.

11. Drag **Percentile** to the **Filters** shelf and set **Compute Using** to **Customer ID**. For the filter value, select **True**.

12. Adjust size, color, and fit, and then set the parameter values as desired.

13. You may wish to add these additional steps to further enhance the visualization. To utilize jittering, create an **Index** calculated field via `Index()` and place that field on the **Columns** shelf. Set **Compute Using** to **Customer ID**. Be sure to deselect **Show Header** so Index does not display in the view.

14. Right-click on each axis and select **Logarithmic** and deselect **Include Zero**.

You should see the following on your screen:

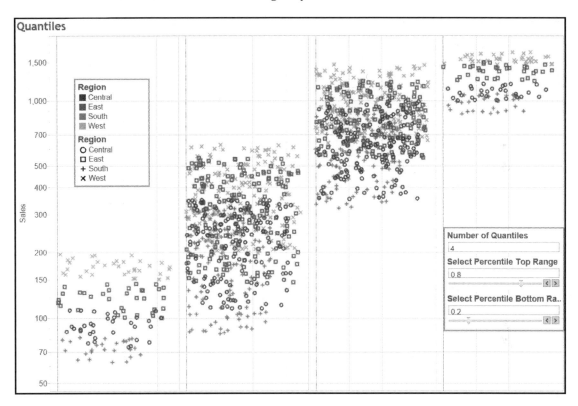

Now that we've completed the exercise, let's take a moment to consider the code. We'll focus on the code in *step 5* since that will provide the necessary insight to understand the other steps:

`SCRIPT_REAL`	This Tableau functions calls the R engine and returns a float value.
`x <- .arg1;`	x is the variable on which we'll create quantiles. The variable, in this case, is [Sales].
`y <- .arg2[1];`	This variable sets the quantile count. [1] forces a single number to be set and not a vector.
`m <- c(1:y)/y;`	m distributes probabilities evenly from 1:y.
`n <- length(x);`	This sets the size of the loops. The loops are discussed below.

`z <- c(1:n); for (i in c(1:n))` `z[i] = 0;`	z sets the initial response vector by setting everything to 0.

`for (j in c(1:y))  for (i in`
`c(1:n)) z[i] = if (x[i] <=`
`quantile(x,m)[j] && z[i] == 0 )`
`j else   z[i];`
	For each `quantile` we go through the z vector, and for each entry we test whether the value of x is less than the upper limit of that `quantile`. If x has previously been set, we leave it. Otherwise, `z[i] = ` `that quantile (j)`.

Troubleshooting in Tableau and R

The interaction between Tableau and R can be challenging to negotiate. You may experience numerous problems that at first seem difficult to understand. These problems, however, usually stem from a few underlying causes. This section will address some of those underlying causes.

Examples of troubleshooting in Tableau and R

It's important to make sure that the variables you pass to an R argument line up with what R is expecting. Consider the following example based on code from the *Exercise – Correlations* section:

`SCRIPT_REAL("cor(.arg1, .arg2)",   SUM([Sales]),` `SUM([Profit]))`	Initial code from exercise 2.
`script_real("cor(.arg1)",   SUM([Sales]),` `SUM([Profit]))`	Adjusted code from exercise 2. Note that `cor` now only receives one variable.
`Error in cor(.arg1): supply both 'x'   and 'y' or a` `matrix-like 'x'`	Adjusted code throws this error.

It's certainly no surprise that R would throw an error in this case. The `cor` function requires two variables, but the adjusted code only provides one. As stated in the returned error message, a second variable is required.

Be sure that the number of variables you pass to R matches the number of expected variables. Otherwise, you may receive an error or unexpected results.

R scripts and Tableau table calculations

R scripts are table calculations. Like all table calculations, this means that you can only utilize fields that are on your view. Also, it's important that you set partitioning and addressing correctly otherwise you may receive unexpected results. Let's adjust the partitioning and addressing from the *Exercise – Correlations* section and observe the results.

Note in this screenshot that **Compute Using** is set to **Customer ID**. This is necessary to correctly calculate the correlation between **Sales** and **Profit**:

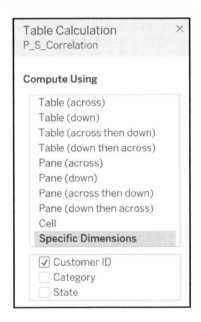

Adjusting **Compute Using** to **State** will result in very different and fairly meaningless results:

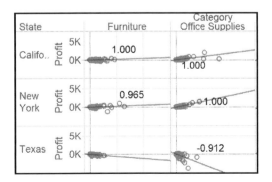

Performance challenges

In the *Exercise – Quantiles* section, you may have noticed that the greater the number of quantiles set with the **Number of Quantiles** parameter, the longer it takes the results to display. This is because R runs the loops in the **Quantile** calculated field one iteration for each quantile. For example, if the **Number of Quantiles** parameter is set to **1**, the loop is instigated only once. If it is set to **2**, it runs twice, and so forth.

 The rule of thumb is that R code is executed once for every partition. The more partitions, the slower the performance. Therefore, when using R code, reduce the number of partitions whenever possible.

Python installation and integration

Python is an interpreted programming language and very well known for its readability. The first release was in 1991, so quite some time ago (longer than most people would guess), and it has been developed by Guido van Rossum.

Installation

Installing Python is typically not difficult, but it does involve more than simply double-clicking on an executable. In order to successfully connect Tableau with Python, you might have to install some libraries and execute comments on the command line. The following paragraphs will guide you through this process.

Installing Python

The easiest way to install Python is by performing the following steps:

1. Download Anaconda with the Python 2.7 version: `https://www.anaconda.com`.
2. Open Anaconda and click on **Environments**:

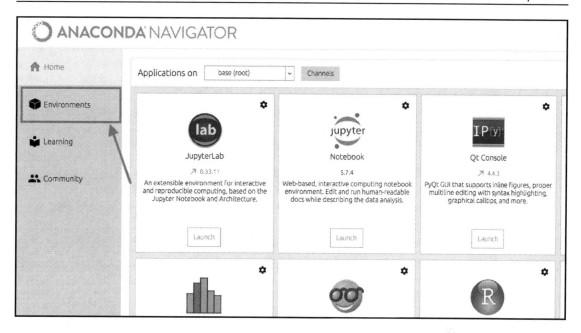

3. Make sure that **tabpy-client** and **tabpy-server** are installed:

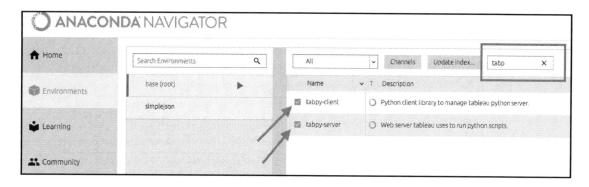

You can now make use of Python via the Anaconda included with Jupyter Notebook or the Spyder IDE.

Integrating Python

In order to integrate Python and Tableau, some additional steps are needed:

1. Go to Tableau's GitHub Page, clone **TabPy** (`https://github.com/tableau/TabPy`), and save it to a location on your computer:

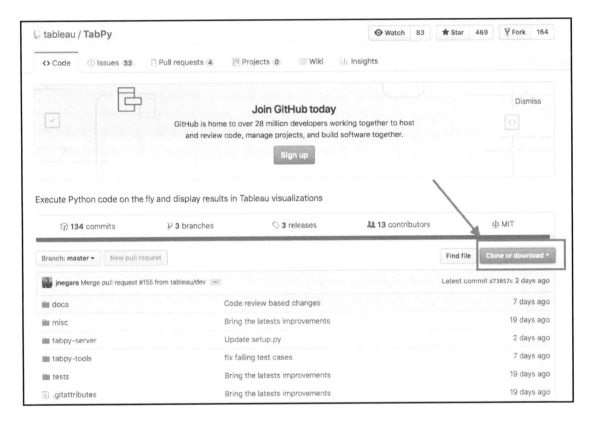

2. Unzip the file and save it locally.
3. Open your command line and move to the location where you just stored the **TabPy-master**.
4. Execute the following command for macOS or Windows:

   ```
   ./startup.sh
   ```

5. Execute the following command for Windows:

   ```
   startup.cmd
   ```

6. You should now see that **TabPy** has been initialized:

```
[(base) marleens-air:TabPy-master meiermarleen$ ./startup.sh
Setting TABPY_ROOT to current working directory.
Installing TabPy-server requirements.
Read the logs at /Users/meiermarleen/Downloads/TabPy-master/tabpy-server/install
.log
Parsing command line parameters...

Starting TabPy server...
Using default parameters.
2019-01-30 20:44:05,287 - __main__ - INFO - {"INFO": "Loading state from state f
ile /Users/meiermarleen/Downloads/TabPy-master/tabpy-server/tabpy_server/state.i
ni"}
INFO:__main__:{"INFO": "Loading state from state file /Users/meiermarleen/Downlo
ads/TabPy-master/tabpy-server/tabpy_server/state.ini"}
Initializing TabPy...
Done initializing TabPy.
Web service listening on 127.0.0.1 port 9004
```

7. Open Tableau, select **Help > Settings and Performance > Manage External Service Connections**, and select **localhost** for **Server** and enter 9004 for **Port**:

8. Click on **Test Connection** and you should see the following popup:

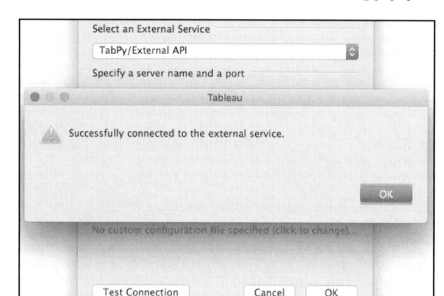

The full documentation on how to get TabPy up and running can be found at `https://github.com/tableau/TabPy`. If you don't want to or can't install TabPy on your machine, Tableau also offers a docker container that will install the latest version of TabPy. You can find more information here: `https://hub.docker.com/r/emhemh/tabpy/`.

Using Python functions

Just like R, TabPy makes use of the script functions in Tableau. I want to mention a few use cases from the Tableau community that are suitable to reproduce at home.

Random and random normal

Many calculations are easily accessible via the calculated fields, others via the table calculations – and if there aren't, many smart people within the Tableau community come up with a workaround. One of those examples is a random number. Zen Master Joshua Milligan came up with the following: `https://vizpainter.com/random-numbers-even-with-extracts/`.

But, it is also possible to do so with the Python integration. We will look at two exercises.

Exercise: random number

Perform the following steps:

1. Create an Excel sheet with only one **Index** column and rows with the numbers 1 - 1,000:

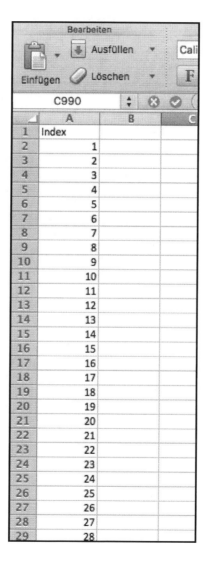

2. Connect Tableau to this Excel sheet.
3. Connect Tableau to Python.
4. Create a `Random` calculated field. The **Random** field should look as follows:

```
SCRIPT_REAL("

from numpy import random as rd

return rd.random(_arg1[0]).tolist()

",
SIZE()

)
```

Does this remind you of something? Indeed: the `Window_Max` function.

Instead of `SIZE()`, you can also use `WINDOW_MAX(INDEX())`.

5. Drag **Index** to **Rows** and **Random** to Columns.
6. Disable **Aggregate Measures** on the **Analysis** tab.
7. Change the **Mark** type to **Density**:

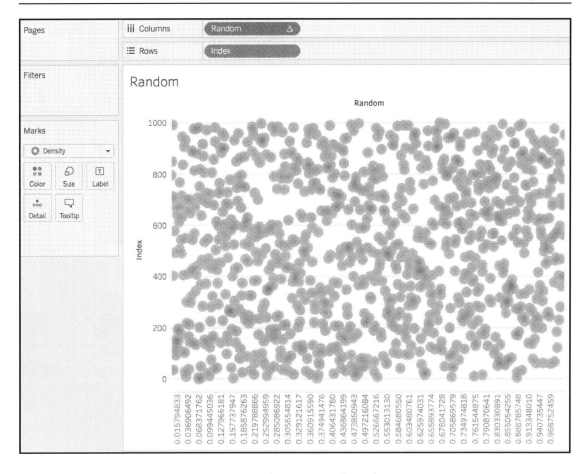

In the preceding screenshot, you can see the **1000** random data points.

Exercise: random normal

Now, let's reproduce a random variable with a normal distribution:

1. Reuse the workbook from the previous exercise.
2. Create a `Random Normal` calculated field:

```
SCRIPT_REAL("

from numpy import random as rd
mu, sigma = 0, 1

return (rd.normal(mu, sigma, _arg1[0])).tolist()
```

```
",

SIZE()
)
```

3. Place **Random Normal** on **Columns** and **Index** on **Rows**.
4. Disable **Aggregate Measures** on the **Analysis** tab.
5. Change the **Mark** type to **Density**.

You can now see a plot with the **1000** data points normally distributed:

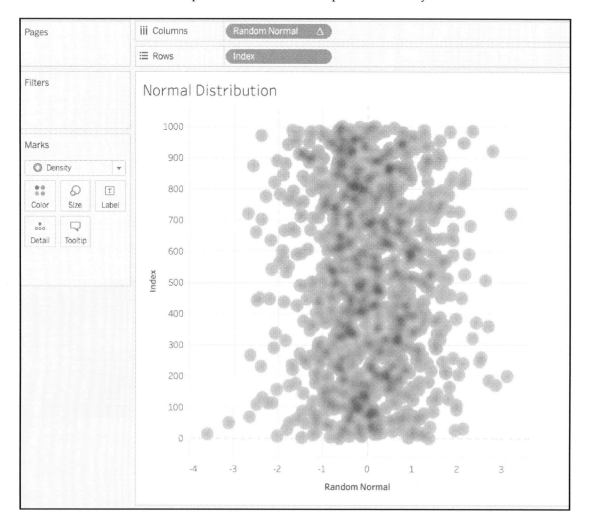

To give your users more flexibility, you can also add parameters to your view that interact with the Python integration. For example, create the following two parameters. Here is the first:

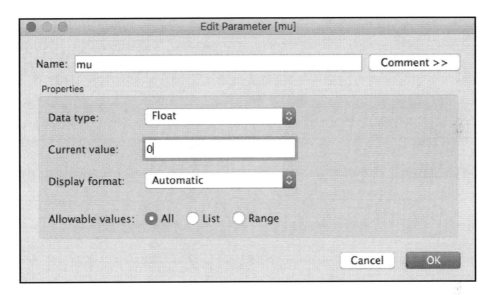

And here is the second:

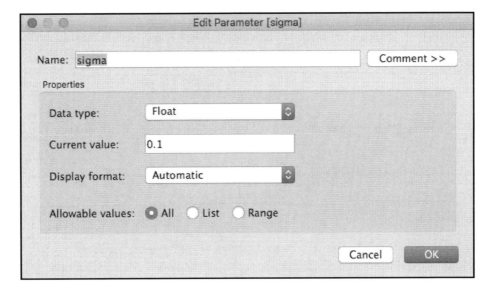

Then change the calculated field accordingly:

Add the parameter control to your view and your users can decide which variables they want to pass to Python:

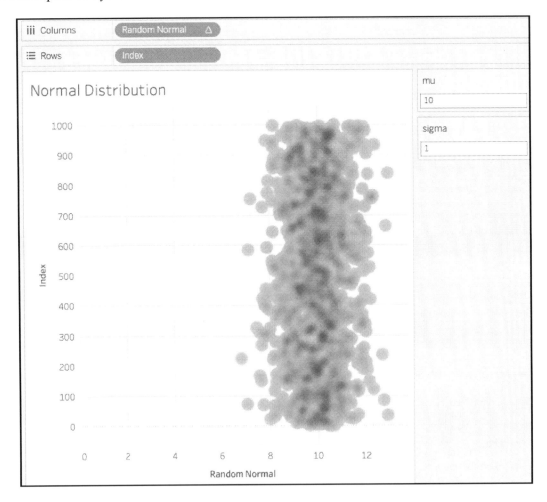

With the random number being available in Tableau you can, for example, visualize a Monte Carlo simulation.

 More information on how to do it can be found here: `https://` `jacksontwo.com/exploring-python-tableau`.

Introduction to sentiment analysis

Next to machine learning and artificial intelligence, another term is being used more and more: **natural language processing (NLP)**. This is the process of machines understanding words and their meaning. Sentiment Analysis falls into this category; the technique has different flavors but one of them is to measure polarity, that is, whether the speaker has a positive or negative opinion. Use cases are for example: Data sets of Reviews, Tweets, Comments, Plots, Lyrics, and so on. Let's have a look!

Exercise: sentiment analysis

This exercise is based on the idea of Brit Cava, who used the Makeover Monday data from the top 100 song lyrics in order to try out the Tableau-Python integration. You can find the blog post here: `https://www.tableau.com/about/blog/2016/12/using-python-sentiment-analysis-tableau-63606`. Let's reproduce it with another dataset:

1. Navigate to the **Sentiment** tab in the workbook associated with the chapter.
2. Connect to the **Lord of the Rings** data source.
3. Connect Tableau to Python.
4. Create a **Sentiment Scores** calculated field:

```
SCRIPT_REAL("from nltk.sentiment import SentimentIntensityAnalyzer
text = _arg1
scores = []
sid = SentimentIntensityAnalyzer()
for word in text:
 ss = sid.polarity_scores(word)
 scores.append(ss['compound'])
return scores
"
,ATTR(dialog))
```

5. Create a `Colour Coding` calculated field:

```
IIF ([Sentiment Scores] > 0, 'Positivity', 'Negativity')
```

6. Because the data isn't perfect, I created a group of same character names from char field. Put **char (group)** on the filter shelf and filter the top **20** characters by count of dialog:

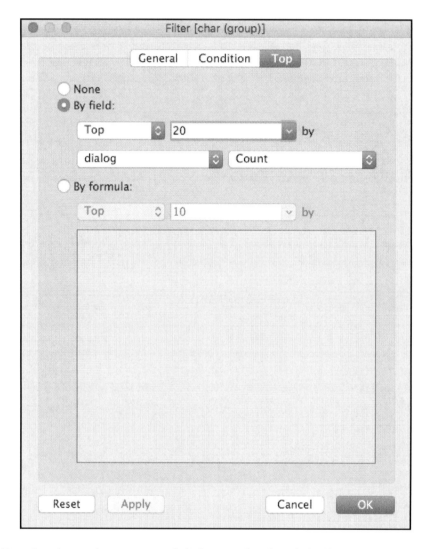

8. Put char (group) on rows and dialog on the detail shelf. Change the chart type to bar.

9. Add **Sentiment Scores** to columns and **Colour Coding** on to the **Color** shelf:

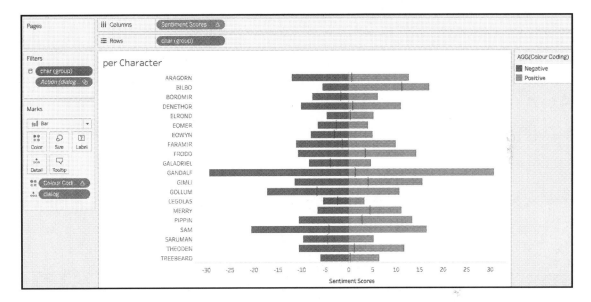

10. Make this filter applicable to all sheets that use this datasource:

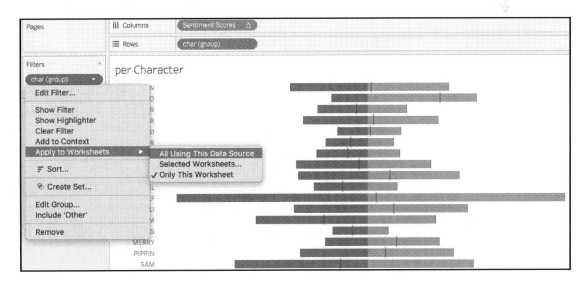

11. Create a second sheet and replace **char (group)** with **movie**:

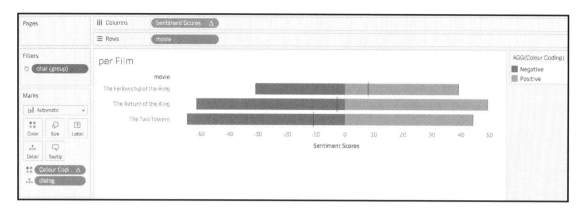

12. From the **Analytics** pane, drag the **Median with 95% CI** onto both sheets:

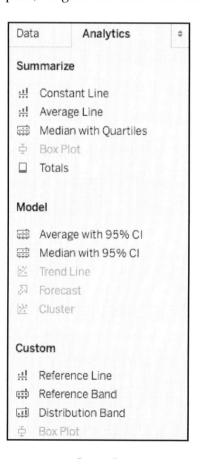

13. Create a dashboard with the movies on top and the character at the bottom, then activate the filter function of the two sheets:

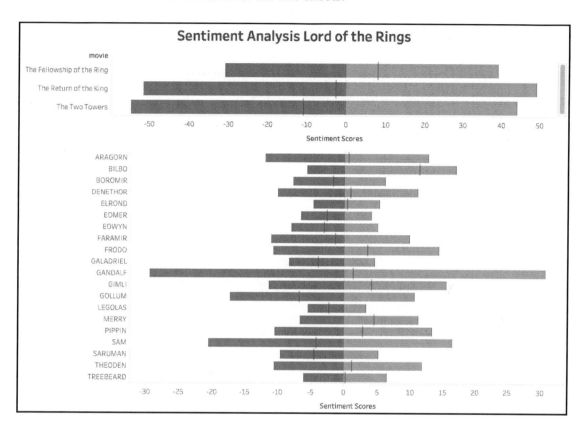

Et voilà, you created a **Sentiment Analysis** of the three **Lord of the Rings** films based on their tendency of using a greater number of positive or negative words:

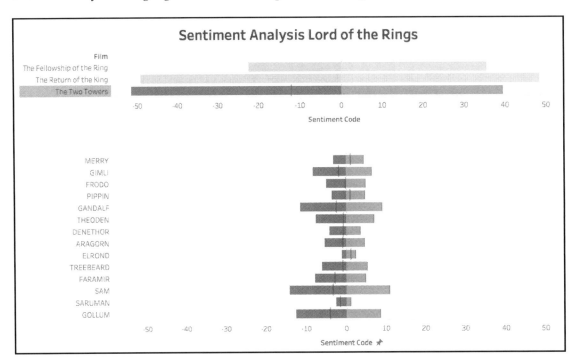

The raw data needed some preparation, I will walk you through it in the following steps:

1. The `.csv` I used had an **Index** field, the movie title, the character name, and then the dialog divided word by word over x columns. So we need to create a pivot in order to get a fourth column with all words underneath each other:

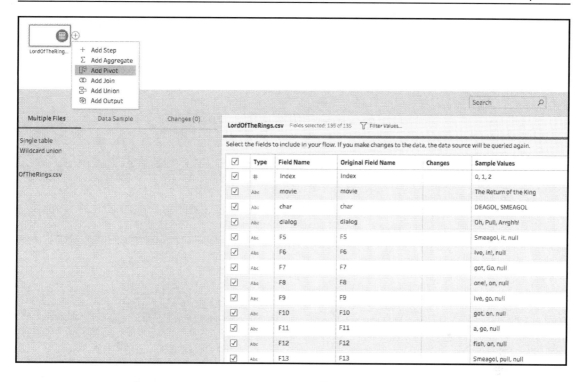

2. I renamed some fields:

3. I performed some cleaning steps, such as removing numbers and removing extra spaces:

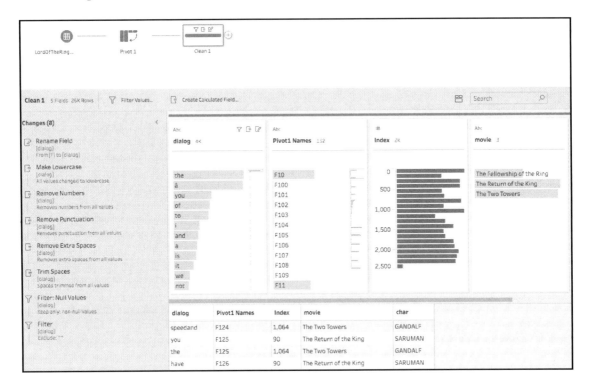

4. I used the cleaned data as input for our sentiment dashboard.

MATLAB installation and integration

Last but not least, we are going to have a look at MATLAB, which enables users to perform computationally-intensive tasks in an authoring environment built for engineers and data scientists. MATLAB has a variety of built-in functions and applications, such as image processing, control design, financial modeling, or computational natural sciences.

Installing MATLAB

MATLAB is, unlike Python and R, a paid computing environment. Students often get licenses from their universities.

> A free trial of 30 days or the licensed version can be downloaded from `https://www.mathworks.com/`.

Integrating MATLAB

Once you have MATLAB installed on your machine, one option is to integrate with Tableau by using the external service connection.

Define the **Server** and **Port**:

Or you can connect to MATLAB with a web data connector. The advantage here is that Tableau connects to an API, the API sends `.json` script back, which will then be transformed into an extract and fed into Tableau on a row level. This increases the performance of the dashboard compared to the External Service Connection.

> A helpful presentation from TC 2018 in New Orleans can be viewed at `https://www.youtube.com/watch?v=i3zU7ufn1-8t=2286s`.

Functions of MATLAB

MATLAB is a little bit different compared to R and Python, as the code will be written first on the MATLAB interface and only then you pull the data in a `Script_` function. One example of a MATLAB use case from the Tableau Online Help is the visualization of the shortest route (you can find it here: `https://www.tableau.com/about/blog/2017/8/put-your-matlab-models-and-algorithms-work-tableau-74016`). The following calculated field will call a script on the MATLAB server and only the fields from the Tableau Dashboard will be added as input variables, with `TSP/GetLatLongVector` being the script on the MATLAB server and `AVG([Longitude])`, `AVG([Latitude])` being the fields from Tableau:

```
SCRIPT_INT('TSP/GetLatLongVector', AVG([Longitude]), AVG([Latitude]))
```

Another example in the area of optimization problems is one about the optimal portfolio.

More details about the two use cases can be found here: `https://www.tableau.com/about/blog/2017/8/put-your-matlab-models-and-algorithms-work-tableau-74016`.

What are your personal goals with a programming integration? If you have a great idea, feel free to share it with the Tableau community.

Summary

This chapter just scratched the surface regarding the options of working with R, Python, and MATLAB. Although we covered architecture, workflow, installation, as well as some of the more popular functions and use cases, there is much more to explore. In fact, the possibilities of Tableau's Programming integration remains largely uncharted territory in the BI community. The intrepid in data visualization are pushing the envelope, but there's much to be done. For those readers looking to enhance their career options, expertise in both packages could offer great advantages.

I want to thank you all for participating in this learning process, being motivated and engaged! Whenever you have more questions, remarks or feedback, feel free to reach out to me or to the Tableau community. I wish you a lot of success with your personal Tableau career and I hope to be in touch soon.

Other Books You May Enjoy

If you enjoyed this book, you may be interested in these other books by Packt:

Tableau 2019.x Cookbook

Dmitry Anoshin, Teodora Matic, Slaven Bogdanovic, Tania Lincoln, Dmitrii Shirokov

ISBN: 9781789533385

- Understand the basic and advanced skills of Tableau Desktop
- Implement best practices of visualization, dashboard, and storytelling
- Learn advanced analytics with the use of build in statistics
- Deploy the multi-node server on Linux and Windows
- Use Tableau with big data sources such as Hadoop, Athena, and Spectrum
- Cover Tableau built-in functions for forecasting using R packages
- Combine, shape, and clean data for analysis using Tableau Prep
- Extend Tableau's functionalities with REST API and R/Python

Getting Started with Tableau 2018.x
Tristan Guillevin

ISBN: 9781788838689

- Discover new functionalities such as density, extensions, and transparency introduced in Tableau 2018.x
- Connect tables and make transformations such as pivoting the field and splitting columns
- Build an efficient data source for your analysis
- Design insightful data visualization using different mark types and properties
- Build powerful dashboards and stories
- Share your work and interact with Tableau Server
- Use Tableau to explore your data and find new insights
- Explore Tableau's advanced features and gear up for upcoming challenges

Leave a review - let other readers know what you think

Please share your thoughts on this book with others by leaving a review on the site that you bought it from. If you purchased the book from Amazon, please leave us an honest review on this book's Amazon page. This is vital so that other potential readers can see and use your unbiased opinion to make purchasing decisions, we can understand what our customers think about our products, and our authors can see your feedback on the title that they have worked with Packt to create. It will only take a few minutes of your time, but is valuable to other potential customers, our authors, and Packt. Thank you!

Index